Southampton

Post-Qualifying
Social Work Practice

Post-Qualifying
Social Work Practice

Patricia Higham

Los Angeles • London • New Delhi • Singapore • Washington DC

First published 2009

SAGE Publications Ltd
1 Oliver's Yard
55 City Road
London EC1Y 1SP

SAGE Publications Inc.
2455 Teller Road
Thousand Oaks, California 91320

SAGE Publications India Pvt Ltd
B 1/I 1 Mohan Cooperative Industrial Area
Mathura Road
New Delhi 110 044

SAGE Publications Asia-Pacific Pte Ltd
33 Pekin Street #02-01
Far East Square
Singapore 048763

Library of Congress Control Number: 2008922904

British Library Cataloguing in Publication data

A catalogue record for this book is available from the British Library

ISBN 978-1-4129-4643-8
ISBN 978-1-4129-4644-5 (pbk)

Typeset by C&M Digitals (P) Ltd, Chennai, India
Printed in Great Britain by TJ International Ltd, Padstow, Cornwall
Printed on paper from sustainable resources

Mixed Sources
Product group from well-managed forests and other controlled sources
www.fsc.org Cert no. SGS-COC-2482
© 1996 Forest Stewardship Council
FSC

Contents

Acknowledgements   vii
Preface (Stuart Brook)   viii
List of contributors   ix

Introduction: What is post-qualifying social work practice?   1
   (Patricia Higham)

Part One: Essential elements for PQ practice   5
   (Patricia Higham)

1 Continuing professional development and PQ social work frameworks:
    flagships for social work reform or sinking ships?   7
    (Patricia Higham)

2 Consolidating values in PQ practice   22
    (Kish Bhatti-Sinclair)

3 Partnerships with people who use services and carers   34
    (Patricia Higham and Claire Torkington)

Part Two: Specialist practice   47
   (Patricia Higham)

4 Children, young people, their families and carers   49
    (Celia Doyle and Susan Kennedy)

5 PQ social work practice in mental health   63
    (Ric Bowl)

6 Social work and older people: a view from over Offa's Dyke   76
    (Aled Wyn Griffiths, Joanna Griffiths and Averil Jarrett)

7 Engaging with the social model of disability   89
    (Bob Sapey)

8   Learning disability   103
        (Kathy Boxall and Speakup Self-Advocacy and Eastwood Action Group)

9   European skills and models: the relevance of the social pedagogue   122
        (Jacob Kornbeck and Eunice Lumsden)

Part Three: PQ functions   **133**
        (Patricia Higham)

10 Inter-professional learning and multi-professional practice for PQ   135
        (Roger Smith)

11 Research and reflective practice   148
        (Eithne Darragh and Brian Taylor)

12 Practice education   161
        (Patricia Higham and Mavis Sharp)

13 Leadership and management   173
        (Victoria Stewart, Laurence Taylor Clarke and Joyce Lishman)

Part Four   Learning organisations and criticality   **187**
        (Patricia Higham)

14 Employment perspectives and learning organisations   189
        (Nicholas Blinston and Patricia Higham)

15 PQ issues, career development and criticality   203
        (Patricia Higham)

Glossary   212
References   216
Index   239

Acknowledgements

Thanks are given to the chapter authors, including colleagues at the University of Northampton who contributed chapters, and to those who contributed ideas and support, including Lesley Best (from the University of Northampton), Mavis Sharp, Claire Torkington, and Jack Higham; and Zoe Elliott-Fawcett and Susannah Trefgarne at Sage. Whilst preparing the book, I visited the Nottinghamshire-based Carers' Council (Allies in Adult Mental Health) and the University of Northampton School of Health's Service Users' and Carers' Group to consult about the book's proposed content. I thank both groups for their comments, which have been incorporated in the book.

Preface

Social workers practise in complex changing organisational contexts. A growing emphasis on devolved local service delivery and user-centred approaches leads to more individual control over scarce resources. Alongside these changes, social workers experience a performance culture characterised by business plans, objectives and targets at organisational, team and individual levels.

The chapter authors convey enthusiasm for social work's professional contribution in specialisms across the public, private and voluntary sectors. Social work will make a positive impact through engaging with service users, carers, communities and disadvantaged groups. If social workers wish to bring added value through their practice, one wonders how this might be achieved without engaging with vibrant, informative and supportive PQ frameworks.

Stuart Brook

Stuart Brook was formerly Director of Social Services for Nottinghamshire County Council. Following retirement from this role, he now works in the voluntary sector with a children's charity, is a non-executive Board Member of the Nottinghamshire Primary Care Trust, and works with colleagues as a magistrate on the Nottingham bench.

List of contributors

The views expressed by the chapter authors are based on their individual reflections of personal and professional experiences, but do not represent the views or policies of their employers.

Kish Bhatti-Sinclair is a lecturer in the division of Social Work Studies, University of Southampton.

Nicholas Blinston is head of the Workforce Development Unit, Adult Services, Housing and Health, Nottingham City Council.

Ric Bowl is director of community mental health programmes, University of Birmingham.

Kathy Boxall is a lecturer in social work in the Department of Sociological Studies, University of Sheffield.

Eithne Darragh is a principal social worker in mental health services in the Northern Health and Social Care Trust, Northern Ireland.

Celia Doyle is a senior lecturer in the Early Years Division of the School of Education at the University of Northampton.

Aled Wyn Griffiths is senior lecturer in social administration, School of Social Sciences, College of Business, Social Sciences and Law, Bangor University.

Joanna Griffiths is Statutory Head of Social Services – Adult Commissioning, Conwy.

Patricia Higham is an independent consultant who is a visiting professor of social work at the University of Northampton. She is a non-executive director of an NHS Primary Care Trust and emeritus professor at Nottingham Trent University.

Averil Jarrett is manager of the Post Qualifying Consortium for Wales and a freelance trainer/ practice assessor.

Susan Kennedy is a senior lecturer in the Social Work Division of the School of Health at the University of Northampton.

Jacob Kornbeck is an administrator (action coordinator) in the European Commission (Sport Unit), a book review editor of the *European Journal of Social Work*, Board Member of Dansk Forening for Socialpædagogik, and a part-time lecturer at the Danish School of Education in Copenhagen and Solvay Business School (Brussels, Belgium).

Joyce Lishman is professor of social work and Head of the School of Applied Social Studies at The Robert Gordon University, Aberdeen.

Eunice Lumsden is a senior lecturer in the Early Years Division of the School of Education at the University of Northampton.

Bob Sapey is a senior lecturer in applied social science at Lancaster University.

Mavis Sharp is a practice educator who currently is a Regional Development Officer for Skills for Care East Midlands.

Roger Smith is professor of social work research at DeMontfort University.

Speakup Self Advocacy and Eastwood Action Group are self-advocacy groups in Rotherham: Bryan Adams, Mariane Alexander, Chris Andrews, Joe Atkinson, Katie Beck, Trevor Cheetham, Janice Chicken, Carole Clarke, Richard Davis, Trev Duxbury, Roy Farnsworth, Vicky Farnsworth, Rob Flute, Annette Flynn, Christine Gervis, Shelley Leigh Hadfield, Laura Hitchin, Barry Hoden, Susan Lister, Kathy Masterman, David McCormick, Fayaz Mohammed, Alan Padfield, Shaida Parveen, Naheeda Razaq, Rabeena Sadiq, David Storey, Ernest Waring, Kerry Widdison and Naila Yousef all contributed to Chapter 8.

Victoria Stewart is a senior lecturer in the Aberdeen Business School and course leader for the Postgraduate Certificate Social Services Leadership at The Robert Gordon University, Aberdeen.

Brian Taylor is a senior lecturer in social work at the University of Ulster.

Laurence Clarke is managing director of the Tayslor Clarke Partnership in Glasgow, a leadership and organisational development consultancy for the private and public sectors.

Claire Torkington is a practice teacher/tutor and Project Manager for East Midlands Skills for Care

Introduction: What is post-qualifying social work practice?

Patricia Higham

This book explores post qualifying social work practice (PQ) – the practice that takes place after qualifying as a social worker, starting in most instances (except for independently employed practitioners) with a newly qualified social worker's induction as an employee, and then consolidation of qualifying level competences. PQ social work experience, supported by continuing professional development (CPD), leads to enhanced knowledge and skills within specialist practice areas. Over time, PQ social work may demonstrate practice expertise, denoted by leadership within the profession.

This vision of moving from competence to expertise within PQ social work practice is important for social workers. Social work is now a registered profession and a protected title in the United Kingdom. All UK social workers have to register with their Care Council in order to practise, and as a consequence of registration, have to undertake CPD. Registration requires social workers to complete PRTL (post registration training and learning) of specified days over three years.

PQ social work practice is not just about acquiring experience – there are clear expectations that social workers will continue to develop their practice through professional development.

'CPD' and 'PQ' are interrelated terms with somewhat different meanings.

- *Continuing professional development (CPD)* denotes flexible learning and development undertaken after successful completion of a professional qualification. Although CPD learning does not always have to be assessed or result in an award, CPD activity should always result in personal and professional development. CPD, a broader concept than PQ, is the over-arching concept within which specific PQ awards and activities are located.
- *Post-qualifying education and training (PQ)* is designed normally as specific assessed modules or awards whose content and assessment are prescribed by a social work regulatory body, and whose aims are to develop social workers' practice in accordance with employers' requirements. The principle of demonstrating practice achievement underpins PQ.

Assumptions

The chapters make assumptions – that social workers will work in diverse organisational structures, that they should be aware of European social work models, and that values and relationships are essential.

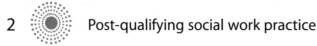

Values and relationships

PQ practice promotes professional relationships that consult, engage with, and support the choices of people who use services and carers rather than wield hierarchical power. Social workers are expected to pursue goals of social justice through advocacy (Bateman, 2000; Brandon and Brandon, 2000) and emancipatory practice (Pease and Fook, 1999). They are required to take responsibility for their own practice and contribute to the practice of others by becoming a mentor, enabler, or assessor of students' and colleagues' work-based learning.

Diverse organisational structures

The main multi-professional groupings for social workers are *health and social care* (social workers in NHS Trusts alongside health professionals, social workers engaging with adults with mental health problems, learning disabilities, physical disabilities and older people) and *children and young people's services aligned with education* (social workers alongside children's centre workers, early years workers, education welfare officers, teachers, personal advisers, and learning mentors).

Social workers work for third-sector organisations (both private and charitable), employment agencies, social inclusion initiatives, as well as for local authorities. Some social workers may be self-employed. In England, adult social care and children's services are structurally separate, and in England and Wales, criminal justice work is organisationally separate.

European social work models

Social workers will benefit from exploring European social work models that are becoming known in the UK, and incorporating aspects, where appropriate, into new forms of practice. As well, UK social workers engage with refugees, migrants, and asylum-seeking families and individuals.

Consultation with service users and carers

Whilst preparing the book, the editor attended a service-user group and a carers group, and asked what they thought was important for PQ candidates to learn. They made three requests: first, that social workers should be knowledgeable of current events that affect decisions about service provision; second, that social workers should monitor new research, treatments and trends; and third, that social workers must recognise the importance of values for practice. The chapters attempt to address these concerns.

Who is the book for?

The book is written for UK-based social workers, and is relevant for trainers and managers as well as practitioners from other professions (health, children's workforce, housing, education, justice, youth work, careers guidance, community workers, and social care workers). Experienced social workers and newly qualified social workers will benefit from reflecting on practice issues discussed in the book. Managers will find chapters helpful for understanding PQ and CPD choices in the context of workforce strategies. Educators and trainers can draw on the book's overview of PQ issues.

Aims and objectives

The overall aim is to enhance (and hopefully inspire) social workers' continuing professional development of knowledge, skills and values within specialist areas of practice. Specific objectives are to:

- Increase knowledge for practice;
- Explore values dilemmas;
- Encourage social workers to reflect on their practice, and through critical self-appraisal, construct different ways of thinking about and doing social work that build confidence in their professional identity;
- Promote PQ learning and career development.

Structure

The book draws on contributions of social work academics and practitioners in the UK and Europe. Contributors reflect critically on a range of relevant PQ concerns: ethics and values; evidence from research; National Occupational Standards, knowledge, skill and service frameworks; Care Councils' requirements for CPD/PQ and post-registration training and learning (PRTL); and relevant policies. Anonymised examples from practice, research, and teaching encourage self-analysis. Each chapter suggests further reading to stimulate thinking beyond that provided within the book's limited length. A glossary explains acronyms and technical terms. Users, carers, and social workers acted as 'critical friends', commenting on the book's emergent content for its relevance to 'real world' issues.

Following the Introduction, four Parts are each introduced by a bridging statement:

- **Part One: Essential elements for PQ practice** – includes frameworks, values, and working with service users and carers (Chapters 1–3).
- **Part Two: Specialist practice** – covers children and families, mental health, older people, the social model of disability, learning disability, and European skills and models (Chapters 4–9).
- **Part Three: PQ functions** – concerns multi-professional practice, research and reflective practice, practice education, and leadership and management (Chapters 10–13).
- **Part Four: Learning organisations and criticality** – covers recruitment, retention, career development, and critical reflective practice (Chapters 14–15).

Part One

Essential elements for PQ practice

Patricia Higham

The starting point of social workers' continuing professional development is to understand PQ education and training's structures (Chapter 1), then to consolidate qualifying level practice by emphasising values and ethics (Chapter 2), and forming partnerships with people who use services and their carers (Chapter 3). All three chapters in Part One convey messages that apply across all the specialisms.

Chapter 1 *Continuing professional development and post-qualifying social work frameworks: flagships for social work reform or sinking ships?* by Patricia Higham, compares the four country-specific PQ frameworks and argues that PQ practice must differ from that at qualifying level – instead of being preoccupied with 'competence', it should promote critical reflective practice and innovative thinking that move social workers towards capability and expertise.

Chapter 2 *Consolidating values in PQ practice* by Kish Bhatti-Sinclair discusses values as a continuous thread running through practice, beginning with the qualifying degree, registration on the social care register, and the start of PQ practice. Consolidation of practice, as a first PQ step, helps social workers consider the values dilemmas they will confront in practice.

Chapter 3 *Partnerships with people who use services and carers*, by Patricia Higham and Claire Torkington, explores critical views of user involvement, and argues that social workers must relinquish some of their power (echoing Chapter 2) and form different kinds of relationships with users and carers.

Chapter 1

Continuing professional development and PQ social work frameworks: flagships for social work reform or sinking ships?

Patricia Higham

Introduction

Chapter 1 draws on the international definition of social work (Topss UK Partnership, 2002) to consider the impact of social work reviews on social work roles (and by implication, on how social workers' opportunities for CPD are determined). The chapter compares the four country-specific social work PQ frameworks for England, Northern Ireland, Scotland and Wales that replaced a UK-wide framework, and discusses possible impediments to establishing PQ frameworks as flagships. The last part of the chapter considers whether PQ frameworks can be fit for purpose, citing a lack of agreement on the purpose of PQ, preoccupation with 'competence', and insufficient understanding of why teaching, learning and assessment for PQ must differ from that at qualifying level. To avoid the 'sinking ship' scenario, the chapter suggests that the PQ frameworks should ensure that the practice of a social worker in possession of a PQ award – at any level – will be different from a social worker without PQ.

A workshop (Blinston et al., 2006) for the Cambridge 2006 UK Joint Social Work Education Conference introduced some of these ideas. Opinions expressed are the author's own and do not represent organisational strategies.

Definition of social work

An agreed definition of 'social work' – specifying the skills and knowledge that should inform contemporary practice – might help social workers establish their identities in multi-professional teams (now the preferred model for delivering services). The international definition of social work (agreed at the July 2000 Annual Meeting in Montreal of the International Association of Schools of Social Work and later adopted by the European Association of Schools of Social Work) typifies social work's 'new look'. Despite the Quality Assurance Agency Social Work Benchmark Group arguing in 2000 that 'the precise nature and scope of [social work] is itself a matter for legitimate study and critical debate' (QAA, 2000: 2.2), in 2002 the Topss UK Partnership adopted the international definition of social work as the Key Purpose of Social Work within the Social Work National Occupational Standards. This contemporary international definition has achieved wide acceptance in the United Kingdom:

> Social work is a profession that promotes social change, problem-solving in human relationships and the empowerment and liberation of people to enhance well-being. Utilising theories of human behaviour and social systems, social work intervenes at the points where people interact with their environments. Principles of human rights and social justice are fundamental to social work. (Topss UK Partnership, 2002)

The definition suggests that social workers may practise a range of theoretical approaches with different people in different contexts, adopting social work roles characterised by partnerships with people who use services, carers and other professionals, assessing individual need within social contexts, and empowering and emancipating rather than institutionalising individuals. By implication, the definition suggests that experienced social workers must move beyond 'competence' towards capability and expertise that require partnerships and power-sharing.

What kinds of knowledge, skills and values support this definition?

Lymbery (2001) argues that to achieve the aims of social work, the profession draws on knowledge of structural oppression, power, service user rights, and inclusion; codes of ethics and practice that promote service users' citizenship, rights, and responsibilities; and practice expertise that embraces strategies for social inclusion and inter-agency, multi-professional structures. A scrutiny of the country-specific PQ frameworks' regulatory standards suggests that the frameworks provide opportunities for building these areas of knowledge, skills, values, and practice expertise.

Social work reviews' impact on roles

Reviews of social workers' roles and tasks in Scotland and England argue that social workers should carry out particular roles, whilst other roles might be shared with other professionals. Governmental reviews of social work roles have affirmed the importance of social work, but identify changed emphases for practice.

- In Scotland, the Twenty-first Century Review of Social Work (Scottish Executive, 2006c; see also Asquith, Clark and Waterhouse, 2005) recommended changed social work roles (to include social control, assisting with 'navigation across boundaries', and safeguarding well-being) within a proposed four-tier approach to practice. The Scottish Executive Report *Changing Lives* (2006c) led to training for performance improvement, service redesign, practice governance, leadership and workforce development.
- In Wales, the Garthwaite Report (2005) considered workforce issues and recommended relaunching social work as a profession, improving pay and career structures, and improving supervision policies. Garthwaite was followed by *Fulfilled Lives: Supportive Communities,* the Welsh Assembly Government's ten-year strategy for social services (WAG, 2007).
- Northern Ireland conducted a review of public administration that resulted in changed organisational structures, with the PSS Development and Training Strategy 2006–2016, a key document for PQ. A social work review will take place in 2008.
- In England, the Department of Health and the Department for Education and Skills published *Options for Excellence* in October 2006, which led to a GSCC review (2007c) of social workers' roles and tasks. Options for Excellence considered 'social care' (including social work) as a single entity rather than within wider contexts of health care, education, young people, and supported social housing – therefore its recommendations were less likely to resolve service fragmentation (Preston-Shoot, 2006). The subsequent literature review (Beresford, 2007; Blewett et al., 2007) on social workers' roles and tasks emphasised social work's ability, at its best, to work with ambiguous, complex, and uncertain situations, with Beresford (2007) offering an analysis of social work from users' perspectives.

From a UK-wide framework to country-specific PQ frameworks

A consideration of the strengths and weaknesses of the predecessor UK-wide PQ framework helps to explain why different PQ frameworks were considered necessary. The previous framework, established in 1991 and regulated by the General Social Care Council (GSCC), offered two award levels, each built around six requirements. Regional Post-Qualifying Consortia managed the framework by accrediting programmes of learning for 'professional credits'. Although PQ Consortia were successful in setting up collaborative partnerships between universities and employers and establishing PQ education and training's importance, attention was diverted from the key task of strategic workforce planning by having to function like a mini-university – accrediting programmes, assessing portfolios, and organising assessment boards (GSCC website, 2006b). 'Professional credit' lacked credibility outside the world of social work and never gained wide acceptance, in contrast to nursing, whose professional development framework led to relevant academic awards.

Over time, the numbers of enrolled PQ candidates decreased (GSCC, 2006a: 40). The most successful PQ programme was PQ1 (consolidation of qualifying level competences) – a single requirement usually delivered as a separately certificated module within an award (GSCC website, 2006b). Most social workers did not progress beyond PQ1 to complete a full award. The success of PQ Consortia was more evident in Scotland, Wales and Northern Ireland, where a singleton Consortium in each country was able to exert influence and arguably establish more consistent practice standards. In England, standardisation was more difficult to achieve (Higham, 2001) because the 17 regionally based Consortia worked independent of each other. Phasing out 'professional credit' (except in Northern Ireland) and replacing it with academic credits and quality assurance in the new frameworks addresses one of the 1991 framework's flaws. However, separate frameworks will create future difficulties for social workers wishing to transfer PQ achievements across the four UK country-specific frameworks.

Overview of the country-specific PQ frameworks

PQ Consortia announced their closure dates and the UK-wide PQ social work awards began to be phased out from 2007, a process to be completed in 2009. England's new framework began in autumn 2007, and other countries' frameworks from 2008. Unlike the 1991 framework, the country-specific PQ frameworks are designed to promote strategic workforce planning and human resources strategies (new roles, recruitment, retention, and career progression) by developing the social work workforce.

PQ frameworks' choices of curricula are influenced by employers' human resources strategies, which seek to sustain the workforce's motivation and commitment and develop new roles and skills. Each framework potentially will provide social workers with opportunities to develop the appropriate knowledge, skills and confidence for practice within multi-professional teams that are characteristic of contemporary organisational structures, and for acquiring new roles that assist career progression. Almost as soon as they were introduced, it became evident that the four country-specific PQ frameworks (GSCC, 2007a) might have to be revised because of governmental reviews of social work.

England

The General Social Care Council, which regulates English social work education, designed a PQ framework with awards at three levels: Post-Qualifying Award in Specialist Social Work, Post-Qualifying Award in Higher Specialist Social Work, and Post-Qualifying Award in Advanced Social Work. Five specialisms are offered, most at each award level: mental health; adult social services; practice education; leadership and management; and children and young people, their families and carers. Skills for Care England, in collaboration with the Children's Workforce Development Council (CWDC, 2007), assumed responsibility for organising employers' planning networks to commission awards from GSCC-accredited provider universities (GSCC, 2005a). Standards and content for awards are based, *inter alia*, on GSCC requirements (including Codes of Practice), National Occupational Standards, and Skills for Care/GSCC guidance on assessment of practice in the workplace (GSCC, 2002b).

Wales

Unlike England's award-based system, the Wales Modular Framework for Post-Qualifying Learning and Development in Social Work (CCW, 2005) is based on credit-rated academic modules rather than on awards (although awards will be developed). The Care Council for Wales approved a revised

PQ framework in March 2005, whose purpose (CCW, 2005; PQ Consortium for Wales, 2005) is to provide flexible life-long learning in continuing professional development as well as increase social workers' expertise, address their learning needs in a range of settings, link the learning of workers in related professions and other social care workers, and allow social care organisations to develop as learning organisations.

The Care Council for Wales collaborates with employers to develop an all-Wales CPD portfolio, which enables employers to link attainment of particular modules to specified posts or career progression. The framework encourages learners to accumulate modules to achieve a higher education award. Awards and credits for the awards are cumulative, with social workers being able to progress through different levels. Three priorities for awards cover induction of new social workers, mental health, and children (childcare) (CCW, 2006).

Like the social work degree in Wales, the framework requires learning and assessment to recognise the Welsh context of the awards; reflect and promote research-minded and evidence-based practice, anti-discriminatory practice and the Code of Practice for social workers; and be relevant to social work practice. Employers in Wales can be commended for extending the principle of cultural identity by developing successfully the PQ skills and qualifications of social workers employed in Wales who originate from countries outside the United Kingdom (Higham, 2005).

Scotland

Scotland (SSSC, 2004) seeks to develop the entire social service workforce, including social workers, within a systematic CPD framework. The Scottish Social Services Council report recognised employers' need to 'support their staff to enable them to develop and maintain their competence' (SSSC, 2004: 3). Scotland acknowledged the value of extending the PQ Consortium's positive achievements to the whole of the workforce. Learning networks and centres of excellence help to promote continuing professional development. The report intended that specialist awards would assist career development and take into account employers' expectations and policy priorities (SSSC, 2004: 6), including the development of integrated services (2004: 15).

The PQ Consortium in Scotland expressed concern that its demise and planned replacement by employers' and training providers' regional learning networks would mean a lack of consistency and the resulting fragmentation of PQ provision (Community Care, 2006). The SSSC (2005) published rules and requirements for specialist training of social service workers in Scotland, including social workers. (Training for social services workers may well share topics and concerns with programmes specifically designed for social workers, but roles and responsibilities differ across the workforce, and the programmes' approaches will reflect this differentiation.)

Northern Ireland

The Northern Ireland Social Service Council (NISSC) announced that it would establish rules and requirements, maintain standards, and manage the funding for a new PQ social work framework (NISCC, 2005a). The already established Northern Ireland PQ Partnership (the PQ Consortium) continues to play a central role, and is responsible for developing the successor framework, its accreditation, and assessment (NIPQETP, 2005). Northern Ireland's revised PQ framework aims for more flexibility, accessible seamless learning opportunities that respond to occupational needs across all sectors, alignment to career structures and opportunities, comprehensive provision (including relevant developments and in-service training) and academic and professional pathways. Three types of award are: Specific award (60 credits); Specialist award (180 credits); and Leadership and Strategic Work award (180 credits). Not all programmes will carry academic credits although their level is postgraduate.

From 2003, unlike other countries of the United Kingdom, Northern Ireland graduates of the social work degree began the first part of their PQ training during their first assessed year in employment (AYE). Also unlike other UK countries, Northern Ireland proposed that its PQ awards should be postgraduate, designed explicitly (but not exclusively) for social work graduates.

Comparison across countries

Although PQ frameworks are country-specific, they share some aims:

- To develop practitioners beyond beginning levels of competence in specialist areas of practice;
- To promote inter-professional learning and multi-professional practice;
- To develop leadership and management skills.

The frameworks display similarities in their structures and requirements. Most importantly, as discussed above, the countries have reviewed social work, thus influencing the kinds of learning prescribed for PQ. All four countries have introduced regulated frameworks governed by statutory rules and legislation with clear written regulations. Each country has specified its framework standards – the expected outcomes that determine the content and shape of learning and assessment for modules and awards. In each country, PQ standards draw on National Occupational Standards, as well as Codes of Practice and specialist practice standards. All four countries require providers of learning to offer opportunities for Accreditation of Prior Certificated Learning (APCL) and Accreditation of Prior Experiential Learning (APEL), so that social workers with credits from the previous UK-wide framework might be able to gain credit for these within the new frameworks. (Working out the details of APCL/APEL credit is left to university and employer partnerships.)

Each framework made arrangements for assessing practice, including a practice education qualification. All countries require universities to issue transcripts of learning to candidates, and to appoint external examiners with appropriate qualifications. In principle, there is provision for recognising and accepting internationally qualified social workers into each framework. Each country 'commissions' programmes of learning from established employer partnerships that engage with universities and other stakeholders. All countries involve people who use services as stakeholders to ensure that PQ learning is relevant.

To sum up, all four countries have set expectations of relevance and quality through specifying standards, regulating processes, and involving employers and the people who use services. Access to learning is encouraged through requirements for APCL/APEL, and there is some provision for internationally qualified social workers. The requirement for work-based learning and assessment in every country affirms its.

Majority trends

Majority trends are evident across three countries, with Northern Ireland taking different decisions that can be attributed in part to its social work qualification being offered entirely at undergraduate level.

- Three of the four countries (England, Scotland and Wales) do not plan as yet a direct link between the requirements for post-registration training and learning (PRTL) and PQ. Northern Ireland proposes a link between PRTL and PQ by 2010, when established career structures linked to agreed training and qualifications and to continuing registration will be in place (NISCC, 2006).
- The Post-Qualifying Consortia will close in England, Wales and Scotland, but the Northern Ireland Consortium will assume the role of managing the successor Northern Ireland PQ framework.
- Other social services/carer and professional groups can access the frameworks in England, Scotland and Wales by taking modules but are not eligible for social work professional awards. In Northern Ireland, social workers attending a multi-disciplinary programme are able to obtain an award.
- In England, Scotland and Wales, PQ frameworks stop at masters degree level, ignoring the rapid growth in the United Kingdom of part-time, practice-based Professional Doctorates (ESRC, 2005), although Northern Ireland recognises the potential appeal of a professional doctorate (Prof D) (see Chapter 15).

Different orientations towards CPD and PQ

Different orientations towards promoting CPD or PQ awards can be identified. The English framework is based on achievement of awards, whilst in contrast the Wales framework is essentially a CPD framework based on individual modules. It is not clear how individual CPD modules will fit within the proposed English PQ framework. Since CPD activity of 15 days over three years (PRTL – post-registration training and learning) is the only requirement for social workers' re-registration, an emphasis on CPD might have been a wiser choice for England.

The English PQ framework represents an uneasy compromise of academic levels; the Wales PQ framework also fudges this issue. The GSCC is concerned that the many social workers who lack a degree should have opportunities to undertake PQ study at undergraduate level 6 (England and Wales level 6, Scotland level 10) and thus attain an honours degree. However, over time, as social work becomes a graduate profession, candidates' preferences will lead to all postgraduate awards.

The Scottish framework emphasises CPD rather than awards. Scotland chose to develop the entire social service workforce with CPD programmes and centres of excellence, e-learning, and a learning exchange (SIESWE, 2006a), providing a support infrastructure that is likely to improve CPD attainment. Scotland replaced the Practice Teaching Award with a four-stage modular framework based on the Scottish Credit and Qualifications Framework (SCQF, 2006). These practice-learning qualifications (SIESWE, 2005) contain very detailed requirements and guidelines, which leave little discretion to providers, thus apparently addressing the PQ Consortium's concerns. If all

PQ awards in Scotland are as prescriptive, they may not be flexible enough to meet individual CPD needs for personal development.

First year in practice

The four countries take different approaches to requirements for the newly qualified social workers' first year in practice: England introduced a requirement for a 'consolidation of qualifying level competences' module in its Specialist awards, but Scotland has not chosen to institute 'consolidation'. Although the other three countries at the time of writing are producing guidance on the first year in practice, Northern Ireland is the only UK country to require an assessed year in employment (AYE) following the degree.

Will the PQ frameworks be successful?

To improve their chances for success, the PQ frameworks must address potential impediments – complex organisational contexts, underdeveloped workforce planning, PQ's cost, and insufficient fitness for purpose.

Complex organisational contexts

The country-specific PQ frameworks can be criticised for being overly complex and over-regulated, thus lacking flexibility to respond to new practice challenges. Regulatory bodies' lengthy PQ requirements may overload the content of awards. University PQ providers operate differing credit frameworks, thus potentially hindering flexible access by future candidates. A diverse scattered workforce employed by many statutory, private and third-sector organisations is responsible for delivering social work, and this characteristic, together with organisational changes, creates additional complexities that potentially limit PQ access.

Underdeveloped workforce planning

A shortage of qualified social workers continues to impact on service delivery nationally, regionally, and locally (CCW, 2003, 2007; Scottish Executive, 2002b; SfC, 2005; NISSC, 2002). Employers compete for scarce social work staff, but do not always succeed in retaining social workers in their workforce. Social work employers are not yet accustomed to workforce planning or assuming a planning role for education and training – therefore they may fail to recognise the benefits of PQ for addressing recruitment and retention issues. Because of difficulties in covering day-to-day work, line managers may feel unable to release social workers for PQ activities, thus exacerbating some social workers' low morale (Aldridge, 2006; PQ Consortium for Wales, 2005; Rowland, 2003, 2006) (see Chapter 14).

Potential lack of portability across UK countries

An important issue is whether social workers undertaking PQ in one UK country will gain recognition in another. The country-specific frameworks do not mention portability, and differ in their approach to awards and other aspects. Awards developed in separate UK countries may not be transferable, thus impeding staff mobility and social workers' wider career development. The frameworks' silence on this issue is worrying, particularly since they are likely to make some provision for internationally qualified social workers now working in the UK.

PQ's cost

Full awards are expensive to fund; stand-alone, academically credit-rated modules will be expensive because the universities cannot obtain a Higher Education Funding Council subsidy for less than full awards. Part-time candidates balancing study with busy workloads will take a long time to complete an award. Unless employers collaborate on sponsorships for sufficient numbers, programmes may not run. Informal intelligence from employers indicates that relatively small numbers of social workers will be released for PQ, thus threatening programme viability and making it difficult to negotiate economies of scale and drive down tuition costs. Only inter-professional award frameworks may be able to attract sufficiently large numbers that could reduce costs, but although modules may be open to other professionals, each country has established a framework that is specific to social work (in Scotland, to social care), rather than an inter-professional one.

Insufficient 'fitness for purpose'

Because of PQ's ill-defined purpose, a continuing preoccupation with 'competence', insufficient differentiation between qualifying-level and PQ-level teaching, learning and the assessment, and the resulting neglect of the pedagogical features of PQ-level practice, the PQ frameworks' 'fitness for purpose' is open to debate.

No agreement on PQ's purpose

Lack of agreement on the overall purpose of PQ learning, or even on defining its purpose, triggers additional concern about PQ's fitness for purpose. Employers in the four UK countries define the purpose of social work PQ differently, some stating anecdotally that PQ's purpose is to 'make social workers competent – a kind of remedial programme following qualification', whilst other employers suggest that PQ should develop more complex specialist skills and equip social workers for advanced senior roles.

Doel, Flynn and Nelson (2006) identified the main purpose of PQ as professional development: enhancing and updating existing skills and knowledge, opportunities for reflective and analytical thinking, with commitment to broad CPD rather than training. These findings replicate those of Rowland (2003, 2006), based on data from 130 PQ candidates.

In 2006, Skills for Care East Midlands (2006) convened a group of practitioners to debate and agree a PQ definition, prompted by a lack of precision in different interpretations of its purpose. Their statement echoed Doel et al.'s and Rowland's findings, but expanded into new territory by emphasising the personalisation of practice, contributing to the learning of others, multi-professionalism, and linking PQ attainment to new roles, responsibilities and self-esteem. This statement, subsequently endorsed by regional employers, represents the views of a small group of practitioners in one region of England. PQ frameworks across the UK would benefit from embarking on similar attempts to define the PQ's purpose, and then comparing the results. It is likely that similar threads, as well as different understandings, would run through different statements of purpose.

Preoccupation with competence

A potentially damaging aspect of the PQ frameworks is an apparent preoccupation with evidencing 'competence', an attribute linked to practice at the point of qualification, rather than thinking about how practice can be developed beyond competence. When Torkington (personal communication, 2007) led work-based learning and assessment workshops in the East Midlands, she discovered that employers wanted to retain direct observation to provide evidence of competence. They exhibited a tension between feeling that many newly qualified social workers are not yet competent and wanting social workers to become autonomous practitioners. The preoccupation with a narrow concept of 'competence' does not allow development of practice expertise, and arguably might limit social workers' career development opportunities.

Regulatory bodies in three UK countries disappointingly continue to focus on 'competence' rather than on seeking to develop social workers as expert 'consultants' in line with skills escalator (NHSMA, 2004a) principles (see Chapter 15). In England, the GSCC's revised PQ framework 'aims to be: focused on the assessment of competence in practice' (GSCC, 2005a: 4, 2). The GSCC considers that the purpose of PQ's specialist level is to enable practitioners to consolidate, extend and deepen initial professional competence in specialised contexts (GSCC 2005a: 19) but does not clarify how this deeper level differs from 'competence' at qualifying level.

One of Scotland's revised PQ teaching, learning and assessment requirements (SSSC, 2005: 30, P) is to 'make sure that … there is direct and verifiable evidence of practice competence'.

Northern Ireland identifies the aims of its proposed new PQ framework (NIPQETP, 2005: 4, 14c) as 'offering a broad range of opportunities for … developing breadth of competence'.

PQ/CPD and competence: the view from Wales

Wales has adopted a different interpretation of practice to be developed by PQ. Instead of 'deeper competence', Wales's key principles of its revised PQ framework (CCW, 2006: Appendix 1) are to develop 'a model which promotes enhanced practice' and 'a shift in assessment from behavioural competences to enhanced skills and knowledge'. Its PQ framework therefore might align more easily with a career ladder that promotes practice expertise.

Beyond competence

Is competence a suitable concept for defining PQ study? The Department of Health (2002: 16) explained 'competence' for the qualifying degree level as a product of knowledge, skills and values. Eraut (1994: 159) comments thoughtfully that 'competence', initially a rationale for justifying professional examinations or assessments, has became a tool of governmental regulatory control over the professions. Viewing a competent practitioner as 'tolerably good but less than expert' (1994: 160) places competence at the level of newly qualified practitioners when professional learning is just beginning. Eraut (2006) explains 'competence' as an ability to undertake required roles and tasks to an expected standard, but argues that deciding the scope of professional competence is open to debate. Competence, therefore, is not a fixed entity but a shifting concept, and this effectively demolishes the binary view of social workers being either 'competent' or 'not competent'.

Eraut prefers to use the term 'capability', explained as 'everything that a person can think or do' (2006: 5; 1994: 208–10). This recognises that practitioners have reserves of capability beyond the limits of narrowly defined competence. The Higher Education for Capability (HEC) Submission to the Dearing Review of Higher Education presented a rationale for capability in its manifesto (HEC, 1994), explaining it as a broader, richer notion than 'competence' – concerned with growth and potential as well as with a current performance. 'Capability' integrates knowledge, skills, understanding and personal qualities, intertwined with a capacity for autonomous learning (Stephenson, 1994). Thus, capability addresses knowledge, skills, values and esteem.

Benner (1984), who adapted the Dreyfus and Dreyfus (1986) model of skills acquisition for nurses, placed 'competence' on a staged ladder that begins with a 'novice' practitioner, progresses to 'advanced beginner', 'competence', 'proficiency', and then reaches 'expertise'. The Benner stage of 'competence' is reached at the end of the social work degree, but 'proficiency' and 'expertise' develop over time through practice, supervision, and formal PQ study.

Model of skills acquisition (adapted from Benner, 1984)

Novice

Novices cannot use discretionary judgement. They stick to taught rules or plans, with little perception of how individual situations may differ.

Advanced beginner

Advanced beginners' perceptions of situations are limited, treating attributes and aspects separately and with equal importance. Decision-making is less laboured. Analytical approaches are used only in new situations or when problems occur.

Competent

Competent practitioners no longer rely entirely on rules and guidelines, but can use maxims for guidance, according to the meaning of different situations, undertake deliberate planning, and perceive deviations from 'normal' patterns.

(Continued)

(Continued)

Proficient

Proficient practitioners use guidelines based on attributes or aspects and, after prior experience, recognise the global characteristics of situations. They begin to see their actions in relation to longer-term goals, to recognise what is most important in a situation, and to cope with the crowdedness of pressurised contexts where many separate factors vie for attention.

Expert

Expert practitioners grasp situations intuitively based on deep tacit understanding, see situations holistically rather than in terms of aspects, and envision what is possible.

The Dreyfus/Benner model portrays stages of proficiency and expertise as a growing ability to internalise rules, demonstrate intuitive understanding, and think through situations more rapidly. Eraut (2006) criticises the Dreyfus/Benner model for being too individualistic and therefore inappropriate for practitioners who typically work in multi-professional teams where ethical concerns require a sharing of knowledge with other team members. Instead, he advocates 'situated' practice that acknowledges social, economic, political, and psychological contexts, and the conditions and situations in which practitioners function. Although supporting the Dreyfus/Benner stage of 'proficiency' as a logical progression from 'competence', Eraut (2006: 8) considers that progressing to 'expertise' requires different kinds of learning to attain deliberative skills of critical analysis, develop different interpretations of complex situations, and practise effectively with other professionals and service users. These capabilities differ from the intuitive, rapid, internalised actions that Dreyfus/Benner propose.

Reflective practice and critical analysis

Eraut, Dreyfus, and Benner made significant contributions to social workers' understanding of how professionals learn and develop their practice. Schön's model of reflective practice (1983, 1987, 1991b) is particularly important. Schön theorised two kinds of reflection: 'reflection-in-action', requiring practitioners to think on their feet and test ideas within practice situations, and 'reflection-on-action' (1983: ix), considering actions of the past. Over time, as part of their practice repertoire, practitioners build thoughts and memories of remembered actions and relative formative events.

Reflective practice must not be regarded as a magic formula for improving practice, but it can help PQ practitioners become more aware of significant aspects of practice situations, decisions, and actions. However, growing awareness is not sufficient – critical analysis is a necessary next step towards developing practice capability. Eraut (1994) and Usher, Briant and Johnson (1997) expressed some dislike of Schön's portrayal of reflective practice, doubting whether reflection-in-action can take place in rapidly occurring practice situations. Eraut's most cogent criticism of

Schön's concept of 'reflection' is that it is a process not situated within a context, and therefore, without critical analysis, it could result in seemingly instinctive but unethical decisions.

Kolb's model of experiential learning (Kolb and Fry, 1975; see Chapters 2 and 11) is indebted to Dewey's process of logical thinking for effective enquiry (1933, 1938, 1997). The Kolb model comprises a cycle that moves from concrete experience to observation and reflection on the experience, then to forming abstract concepts following reflection, and finally, to testing the concepts in new situations. Kolb encourages practitioners to use reflection for finding new meanings in their practice. Practitioners should avoid perceiving 'concrete experience' as something that 'just happens'. The hallmark of a PQ-level practitioner is to regard 'concrete experience' as emerging from planned interventions that the practitioner subjects to critical analysis (Furlong, 2003) after the events take place. Kolb's process, used in this way, can help practitioners develop capability in practice (Torkington, personal communication, 2007).

Two aspects for PQ to address are the nature of knowledge and its relationship to critical practice, and the use of reflexive approaches that encourage development of critical reflective practice. A review (SCIE, 2003b) of the sources and purpose of knowledge in social care/social work identified five non-hierarchical sources of knowledge: the policy community, organisations, researchers, users and carers, and practitioners. The notion that practitioners can be sources of knowledge, creating frameworks for understanding from their practice experiences and theorising from practice, may be difficult for practitioners to accept. But PQ provides opportunities for practitioners to expand their knowledge base from external sources and also, through appropriate learning and teaching strategies, to recognise and present for analysis their own emerging practice frameworks. This is more than so-called 'practice wisdom' – practitioner knowledge is one side of a prism that contains (in equal value rather than as a hierarchy) practitioner knowledge, academic and research knowledge and service user knowledge. For example, PQ can become a vehicle for promoting integration of knowledge sources through critical and reflexive approaches. PQ at its best could stimulate practitioner research (Best, 2007).

Learning organisations

Kolb, Schön, Dreyfus and Dreyfus, Benner and Eraut are interested in how professionals learn from, and within, their practice. Their pedagogical theories extend the concept of practice to levels beyond competence. But individual practice takes place in organisational contexts – as Eraut (2006) argues, practice is 'situated'. Without supportive environments within organisations, formal PQ study and individual reflection may not be enough to help practitioners develop beyond competence.

Schön was interested in organisational learning, in collaboration with Argyris (Argyris and Schön, 1978, 1996). One of Schön's 'givens' is that rapid societal change compels organisations to respond and adapt. He supported the goal of a 'learning society' that promotes continuous organisational learning (Etzioni, 1968) for helping organisations to deal with change (Schön, 1973: 57). This links to the concept of the 'learning organisation' (Senge, 1990: Senge et al., 1994; see Chapter 14), characterised by networks, experimentation, and devolved structures. A learning organisation is a necessary corollary of PQ frameworks that should enable individual practice to develop and thrive despite organisational turbulence.

Discussion

These theories suggest approaches for teaching, learning, and assessing PQ. Instead of relying on didactic instruction, PQ must win practitioners' trust by encouraging them to share their knowledge and experiences in blame-free environments. Teaching and learning strategies for PQ can enable practitioners to learn from their own practice experiences. Parton and O'Byrne's (2000) constructive social work is useful for PQ because it promotes different discourses and uses narrative processes that make evident the inner resources of individuals. Telling the story of a practice experience in an action learning set can open up different possibilities for future practice. The constructive social work model listens, acknowledges the likelihood of uncertainty, and promotes the art of social work (England, 1986), echoing Keith-Lucas's classic (1972) account of the 'art and science' of helping. Fook and her colleagues (Fook, 2002; Fook et al., 2000; Napier and Fook, 2000) have studied how practitioners theorise and create knowledge, viewing critical reflection as a way of 'self-researching' experience.

It follows that assessment of PQ practice must differ from that at qualifying level. Instead of relying on snapshot observations of unrelated episodes of practice, PQ assessment ideally should create a picture of how practitioners develop their capability, over time, towards proficiency and expertise. Holistic assessments that make use of critical reflective analyses in practice-based projects, backed by the verification statements of line managers, colleagues and service users as well as carefully chosen linked observations, may come closer to capturing the desired levels of PQ development than replicating assessment methods of the qualifying degree.

Appropriate PQ teaching, learning and assessment, supported by a learning organisation environment for practice, will enable practitioners to develop higher-level skills. The key question to be addressed by the book as a whole is: 'how will a social worker in possession of a post-qualifying award – at any level – be expected to be different from a social worker without?' An analogy could be drawn with higher education's level descriptors at bachelor's and master's degree levels (QAA, 2001; SCQF, 2007). The higher the academic level, the greater the expectation of autonomous learning and original thinking. Therefore, PQ practice should demonstrate autonomy, original thinking, creativity, responsibility, problem-solving in unfamiliar contexts, critical understanding of practice issues, and an appropriate exercise of professional judgement.

Disappointingly, Blewett, Lewis and Tunstill's (2007) literature review on social work roles and tasks in England and the GSCC (2008) Report on social workers roles and tasks did not distinguish between the initial stage of qualification and more experienced levels of experience. The Scotland Twenty-first Century review (2006c) suggested four tiers of practice. More attention is being paid to the status of the 'newly qualified social worker'. Although (as previously noted) Northern Ireland is the only UK country with an assessed year in practice following completion of the degree, the other UK countries are placing more importance on induction and the first year in practice, suggesting that this may be a first step to differentiating different levels of practice, and ultimately establishing clearer outcomes for PQ.

Conclusion: flagships or sinking ships?

The PQ frameworks are ambitious. Despite their flaws, they merit support because their success will help social work to establish itself fully as a profession whose social workers are skilled at working in partnership with people who use services and carers – experts by experience (CSCI, 2007) – to create better outcomes. Employers, universities, practitioners, service users and carers can avert the 'sinking ships' scenario for PQ by addressing the issues appropriately, thus helping the country-specific PQ frameworks to become flagships for the social work profession.

Questions for reflection

1. Do you consider the PQ frameworks fit for purpose? What is missing?
2. Is 'capability' a more suitable concept for assessing PQ than 'competence'?
3. How will critical reflection help social workers develop their practice?

Further reading

Eraut, M. (1994) *Developing Professional Knowledge and Competence*. London: Routledge.

This is a classic approach for understanding how to develop knowledge within a competence framework.

Fook, J., Ryan, M. and Hawkins, L. (2000) *Professional Expertise: Practice, Theory and Education for Working in Uncertainty*. London: Whiting & Birch.

The authors studied professional practitioners who developed over five years from beginning practice to effectiveness, and propose a theory of professional practice expertise in conditions of uncertainty, together with educational strategies that promote this expertise.

Taylor, C. and White, S. (2000) *Practicing Reflexivity in Health and Welfare*. Buckingham: Open University Press.

This book counters the evidence-based practice approaches that have become so dominant in discourses about the relationship of knowledge to practice. It promotes reflexivity as a technique for analysing practice, narrative approaches and argues that practitioners must not only apply knowledge but also *create* new knowledge from their practice experiences.

Chapter 2

Consolidating values in PQ practice

Kish Bhatti-Sinclair

Introduction

Chapter 2 examines values dilemmas that arise for newly qualified social workers as they attempt to establish a unique individual professional identity, and for experienced social workers as they develop new skills and knowledge at PQ levels. Consideration of power and practice examples will illustrate these values dilemmas.

Care standards legislation across the UK

On 1 October 2001 the Care Standards Act 2000 in England and Wales, the Health and Personal Social Services Act 2001 in Northern Ireland, and the Regulation of Care (Scotland) Act 2001 in Scotland established four separate care councils for each UK country to regulate the social care profession. Banks (2004) argues that care standards legislation put into motion a policy goal that required minimum, consistent, country-wide qualifying and PQ standards on fitness to practice, staff development and the professional values contained in the Codes of Practice for employees and employers regulated by the Care Councils (GSCC, 2005a). The legislation thereby instituted greater centralised and individualised control over practice. For example, the employers' Code of Practice sets out employers' responsibilities to plan and provide for their workforce and oversee the conduct and behaviour of individual employees, whilst the employees' Code lists employees' responsibilities towards employers, colleagues, service users, carers and the public. The increase in governmental control over practice is a contested issue for some social work academics (Cowden and Singh, 2007; Jones et al., 2004; Leadbetter, 2004), who criticise the state's authoritarian stance towards social work that, in their view, threatens social workers' freedom to challenge injustice.

Care standards legislation established registration as an important constituent of professional social work identity (and some would say, control), and incorporated ethics and values within national occupational standards and practice requirements. Although its declared primary aim was to safeguard and protect vulnerable adults and children, the legislation also provides a basis for benchmarking excellence and quality through developing and reviewing practice and service user knowledge (SCIE, 2006b). On the positive side, despite governmental control of social work, greater openness and clarity are now recognised as constituents of 'best practice' that inform policy developments on information-sharing, confidentiality, and social workers' accountability to employers, service users and carers for their actions. Contested issues, however, include the suspicion that increased levels of state control over social work will diminish social workers' independent professional judgements that serve to curb oppressive power over vulnerable individuals.

Nevertheless, regulation of social work is a reality. Qualified practitioners' understanding of their practice responsibilities according to care standards requirements is supported by a continuous thread that links the qualifying social work degree, registration requirements, CPD, and PQ. PQ in the UK is meant to develop a confident, well-rounded workforce that is able to self-manage processes (such as supervision) as tools that help improve public services 'across organisational, sectoral and professional boundaries' (GSCC, 2005a: 17). CPD, including PQ education and training, should provide 'a ladder of progression' (Higham, 2006: 199) for newly qualified as well as for more experienced staff.

PQ frameworks establish expectations that both new and experienced social workers will progress in career pathways that extend knowledge, improve skills, and embed values in practice with children and families, vulnerable adults or in mental health, including, *inter alia*, developing appropriate skills for leadership, management, supervision, practice education, and mentoring. The Codes of Practice imply that employers will support educational opportunities to help social workers attain their personal and professional goals, but much depends on the level of employers' commitment (see Chapter 14).

PQ and consolidation of practice

Newly qualified social workers are signed off as 'competent' at the point of qualification, in line with National Occupational Standards in Social Work (NOS SW) and the Codes of Practice (GSCC, 2005a). Then they are expected to consolidate their practice at PQ level, and, thereafter, develop practice specialisms. Consolidation extends the standard of practice attained at the conclusion of a qualifying social work award. At the consolidation stage newly qualified social workers require well-supported, structured opportunities to improve their practice. Experienced social workers, immersed in daily practice concerns, initially may appear less keen to engage with additional training and educational demands, but will increasingly find themselves facing new specialist practice requirements that require them to consolidate experiences from familiar practice settings and transfer learning into new practice areas.

In England, consolidation constitutes the first module of the Specialist Social Work Award level. Northern Ireland includes consolidation in the assessed year in employment (AYE) undertaken before beginning the Northern Ireland (NI) PQ Framework. In Scotland, consolidation is less defined. Wales will produce guidance on requirements for the first year in employment, and entry requirements for programmes, including mental health. All PQ programmes must ensure that candidates can contribute to the learning and development of others and actively promote and value diversity.

Registration of social workers indicates a rise in public and political influences on the nature of social work services and, consequently, on the education and training required to translate new policies into action (Higham, 2006). Enhancing knowledge and skills at PQ levels can support responses to new policies, as well as help social workers build their career trajectories. Depending on whether PQ enables them to question their assumptions and recognise the contested nature of policies and practice, social workers actively engaging with PQ are likely to increase their capacity to meet daily demands whilst continuing to hold to wider social, ethical and organisational goals.

Social workers' values will be tested whilst they develop their PQ practice. Fook (2007: 34) argues that:

> it is vital in social work to retain a value position, and there are increasing calls to maintain the integrity of professional work by doing this. … Professional expertise must, therefore, include the ability to maintain a higher order of values … the ability not only to respond to daily conflicts in particular situations but also to continue to work, at another level, in terms of broader goals. … This broader vision … gives meaning and allows a sense of continuity despite uncertainty.

Fook's argument links to Chapter 1's discussion of social workers reflecting critically on their practice (Schön, 1983), constructing and reconstructing the meaning and intent of what they do (Parton and O'Byrne, 2000).

The challenge for social workers lies in finding appropriate strategies for sustaining their values in difficult situations – e.g. to remain true to their profession. The sources of energy and vitality required to sustain social work values throughout a professional career deserve some consideration.

Values and ethics for PQ practice

The PQ frameworks require ethical practice with people affected by unemployment, homelessness, racism, poor health, illness and disability. Social workers practising in close proximity to a major seaport or airport are likely to be asked to support any unaccompanied or asylum-seeking minor in an emergency situation. The practice study below illustrates a situation that challenges values in practice.

Practice example: Yousef

A local school refers Yousef, a 13 year-old boy, to children's services because he appears to be excessively tired, constantly falling asleep at his desk and unable to concentrate. The town in which the school is located is situated in a mainly rural area 15 miles from a port city. The school is unable to engage with any adult carers responsible for Yousef. Susan, a newly qualified social worker at the local area office, is asked to explore this practice situation by her supervisor, who is acting as Susan's mentor during her period of consolidation of practice.

On further investigation, Yousef is found to be of Afghanistani origin and living with a small group of men in an extremely poor, overcrowded flat over a take-away in the local high street. His English language is limited. Susan has to meet with Yousef a number of times to gain his trust and find a means of communication that is appropriate and helpful. After some time and with the help of an interpreter, Susan discovers that Yousef was sent abroad by worried parents as an unaccompanied minor 18 months ago and is being looked after by a distantly related uncle and his friends. Yousef works at night in the take-away to earn money for his upkeep, thus explaining his tiredness at school.

After initial assessment, Susan and her mentor discuss Yousef's situation during supervision. The information on Yousef is hazy but he appears to be an asylum seeker with little means of financial, family and emotional support. This requires both Susan and her mentor, at different stages of their careers, to examine their own knowledge and skills, drawing on critical reflection to confront and address the ethics dilemma, so that Susan's future actions in respect of Yousef are consonant with social work values.

Supervision and mentoring

Kohli (2007) suggests that professionals who work with young people should possess a bank of knowledge and skills that enable the young people to bring order to their surrounding world and make active and positive links between past and present experiences in a coherent manner. The process of supervision enables social workers to evaluate the professional and personal resources required for meeting a particular service user's cultural, religious, financial and housing needs, and to reflect on the complexities of implementing law, policy and procedures and applying social work values to practice. Within supervision, a newly qualified social worker gains from a mentor's expertise, and a mentor benefits from the newly qualified social worker's fresh perspectives.

Most newly qualified social workers will not have gained sufficient opportunities to develop such capability, no matter how challenging they found their student placements. Regretfully, the usual situation has been that, once qualified, prospects of newly qualified social workers receiving regular supervision diminish, along with the time to consolidate their experiences as newly qualified social workers. As well as PQ education and training providing ongoing, structured opportunities for consolidation, supervision in the workplace also should play an essential part in consolidating practice.

Complexities and conflicts in practice

The example of Yousef suggests that individual service users experience complex situations. Sensitive responses to these will prompt appropriate interventions. Assessments of need require procedural duties that exacerbate the prevalence of computer-based form-filling, often in a small interview room where the technology of the computer screen takes centre stage. Rafferty and Stayaert's evaluation (2007) of digital technology confirms the view that, although efficient internal and external communication is an organisation's desired and necessary aim, much work remains to be done on how to use efficient methods in ways that are consonant with social work values: 'Social workers have found working with computerised information systems raises technical and ethical complexities and feel it detracts from face-to-face work' (Rafferty and Stayaert, 2007: 173).

Modern technological approaches to communication may limit social workers' ability to relate directly, respectfully and comfortably with, for example, a young service user like Yousef, who is affected by experiences of abuse or neglect. Banks (2004: 154) argues against allowing constraints of systems and procedures to override an individual's needs: 'Agency values, translated into detailed procedures, are dominating professional activity at the expense of professional values relating to respect for service users, confidentiality and so on; and the scope for professional judgement based on expertise and professional values seems to be seriously constrained by the new accountability requirements.' For these reasons, regulation and administrative requirements become contested issues.

A way forward is to use critical reflection (Sage and Allan, 2004; Schön, 1987; Chapter 1) to explore how far requirements for accountable, accurate records dominate assessment procedures, and then evaluate and improve recording processes. The following practice example is a reflective evaluation by Janette, an experienced social worker, which illustrates how reviewing professional practice can address emergent values conflicts.

Practice example: Janette's reflection on her supervision of Robert, a newly qualified social worker

I noticed that when I discussed the practice example with Robert and asked him questions, I would continue to type whilst he answered, which must have been quite off-putting, and I wondered if his opinions were devalued by this. As a practitioner, I am very aware that if a person is to feel listened to, and if I am to convey understanding, empathy and a sense of being genuine, then attention must be given to communication (including non-verbal communication such as body language, eye contact and facial expressions). Retrospectively, our discussions sounded very disjointed and punctuated with the sounds of my word-processing at the computer discouraging a free-flowing dialogue. Another concern is that my use of the computer seemed to exacerbate the power dynamics in the supervisory relationship as I was in control of what information was recorded and the equipment itself.

This example suggests that simple rules may enable better communication for supervision, but also for service users. With some attention to how it might be used, social workers can deploy technology as a practice tool to address service users' needs effectively. Critical reflection may result in:

- Ongoing discussions with colleagues on the ethics of using computerised systems;
- Timetabling and agenda-setting that allows the recording of key action points; and
- Shared responsibility for record keeping.

Good practice can be shared within an organisation so that an ethical dimension is applied to policy guidance on using information technology.

Experienced social workers

Experienced social workers are likely to express somewhat different ethical concerns from those of newly qualified social workers. Over time, day-to-day practice demands accumulate and can lead to disillusionment. Social workers may find themselves responding to organisational demands at the cost of challenging situations that threaten service users' safety and well-being. One way to address disillusionment is to provide PQ learning opportunities that encourage critical reflection, evaluation and questioning, along with some relief from immediate pressures. This approach is likely to result in a fresher, more optimistic approach – a reconstruction of practice (Jordan and Parkinson, 2001; Parton and O'Byrne, 2000) that asserts social work values more confidently.

Using critical reflective practice throughout their careers will help practitioners maintain an *ethical* identity. A self-generated PQ portfolio for experienced practitioners will help them acquire more capability for values-based practice. By drawing together reflective accounts of experience (including diary narratives), a portfolio consolidates their practice experiences. Harrison and Ruch (2007: 42) argue that a PQ portfolio can link creative examination of the self, as a thinking/feeling practitioner, to development of a *professional* identity. Conceptualised in this way, a PQ portfolio can track the CPD of social workers motivated to attain 'best practice' as well as to gain promotion. The portfolio provides a place for developing personal, reflective accounts of practice that focus on the use of self (Doel and Shardlow, 2005; Sage and Allen, 2004) as an effective resource, and ability to practise in stressful, complex situations whilst grounded in social work values of respect, equality and self-determination (Clark, 2000).

Consolidation of practice includes a critical examination of contexts and their impact on learning. Fook (2007: 37) suggests that experience located in time and place plays an important part in developing understanding and the application of knowledge: 'Learning is, therefore, holistic, involving a range of features, including emotions, activities, social expectations and hidden impulses. In this approach the culture and context of learning become much more integral to aspects of the learning

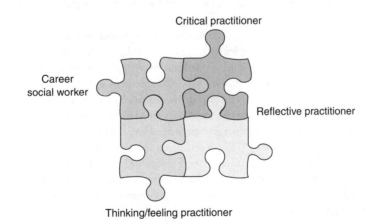

Figure 2.1 Adaptation of Kolb and Fry's cycle of experiential learning (1975) in relation to PQ (Source: Bhatti-Sinclair)

process'. An adaptation of Kolb's cycle of experiential learning (discussed in Chapter 1) fits social workers' different roles together like the pieces of a jigsaw to create a whole that characterises a critical, reflective and thinking/feeling practitioner. The practitioner ideally should be able to balance and combine appropriately the roles of being a career social worker, a critical practitioner, a reflective practitioner, and a thinking and feeling practitioner.

Practice example: Miki's portfolio

Miki qualified with a MA in social work three years ago. She kept evidence of learning in a portfolio that includes practical details such as certificates, lists of qualifications/training, criminal records information, verification and references from service users, employers and others, and evidence of Care Council requirements to maintain registration. Although Miki has added material when necessary in recent years, this has largely comprised training and other information to support the minimum CPD requirements of the Codes of Practice and her employer.

Most professionals like Miki maintain documentation that meets minimum requirements, but PQ portfolios may be used more reflectively to include evaluative commentary on significant daily incidents that are critically reflected upon and evidenced by supervision records, daily narratives or diaries, photographs or other significant visual material. Seen in this way, the PQ portfolio is more than a collection of documents. It becomes a CPD tool to be compiled and maintained throughout a career. Sometimes learning from experience may be easily absorbed or (more likely) forgotten in the daily pressures of busy working environments, but the techniques of consolidation enable practitioners to examine their practice and evaluate their personal and professional development.

Both newly qualified and experienced practitioners can document in their consolidation portfolios the probable clash of personal principles with organisational demands, and ponder ideas on how to respond to these pressures. For example, a portfolio may provide a vehicle for newly qualified social workers to understand the contradictory mix of excitement and frustration they face when realising that social workers often work directly to the agendas of others who are more powerful (such as local politicians) and with whom the social worker may have little shared understanding or commitment. The PQ portfolio can encourage experienced social workers to consider probable conflicts between their dual commitments – as professionals to ethical principles and as employees to their employer's legal and procedural requirements. Fook (2007: 37) argues that: 'reframing understandings of practice provides more opportunities for the development of new practices. In this process, participants also experience "liberation" or empowerment, as if freed from ways of constructing situations that restrict options and ways of doing and being'.

Techniques such as this, framed broadly within PQ education and training, are likely to help experienced social workers rekindle creative ideas. A portfolio's contents are in the control of the individual practitioner, who can add or delete content according to the audience. Motivation for undertaking PQ should be based on this creativity, and supported by employers who recognise the link between providing educational opportunities and the recruitment and retention of staff.

Power

Social workers may find it difficult to grasp the extent of social worker power (Ferguson and Lavalette, 2004; Sheppard, 2006) within everyday roles and tasks, even at the basic level of applying legislation to service provision. Experienced social workers will be more aware of the power accompanying professional roles, but may find power relations more complex within and across individual relationships and organisations. An important aspect of social work practice is to understand how power affects social workers' self-image, as illustrated by the example below.

Practice example: Emma

Emma is a social worker nearing retirement, whose practice is located in a professional social work team in a large hospital. Although Emma accepts that she has an important role in the care management process within her small team, she feels isolated, overwhelmed and constrained by situations and contexts within the broader health and social care arena.

Aware of the power enshrined in laws that protect adults, Emma seeks actively to advocate for and promote the individual needs of older adults, but is concerned that financial and other resources do not take into account the life-changing decisions and exposure to risk faced by vulnerable adults. The local primary care trust is underperforming, NHS funds are limited, and the local authority's lack of resources has led it to raise its eligibility levels for community care. Emma is further constrained by the short-term nature of her practice. Turnover is rapid, and relationships and sustained contact with service users are limited because the models of care management focus mainly on assessment.

Emma thinks that PQ opportunities are not relevant to social workers who, like her, work in a small team that can ill afford to release staff on a regular basis for CPD. Emma feels out of touch with CPD demands, and plans to meet the Care Council's re-registration requirements through attendance at internal meetings and in-service training events. Her reluctance to engage with PQ and the possibility of taking early retirement mean that Emma has not sought any guidance on the PQ opportunities that might be available to her and other colleagues. She thinks that there is nothing more to do except stay put and wait to retire.

Organisations may promote universal principles such as respect for the individual and self-determination (Banks, 2004) but experience difficulties in supporting social workers like Emma. Emma places a higher value on providing services than on her own learning and development needs, but she fails to recognise that her professional learning could enhance the quality of services that she provides.

Consolidation of practice for experienced social workers like Emma should focus on rediscovering professional identity (McMichael, 2000) and regaining the confidence to make ethical challenges with and on behalf of service users as well as with the wider organisation.

Organisational power dynamics in relation to practitioners' ethnicity, cultural and religious differences are rarely considered within processes for managing performance. Prejudice, stereotyping and labelling (Higham, 2006) influence all relationships, and impact on the workplace, as illustrated by the example below.

Practice example: Rebecca

Kemal manages a large multi-agency mental health team that recently recruited a newly qualified social worker, Rebecca, who has strong fundamentalist Christian beliefs that she affirms early in supervision. Rebecca reveals that her particular evangelical denomination does not accept gay and lesbian relationships but she is willing to discuss this further in relation to contact with service users, colleagues and the wider team/organisation. Aware of laws such as the 1998 Human Rights Act and the 2000 Sexual Offences Act, Kemal's position as a representative of the employing organisation requires him to respond sensitively, fairly and with balance. He must ensure that the wider team does not judge Rebecca adversely but also that Rebecca does not engage in discriminatory behaviour to service users, carers and colleagues. Kemal is concerned about the basis on which Rebecca is likely to make decisions and how her adherence to a particular fundamentalist Christian denomination will impact on others.

Kemal wants to provide opportunities that will enable Rebecca to explore how her personal beliefs relate to differences in general, and whether her beliefs will result in intolerance and wider prejudice towards others. But Kemal, as a non-Christian, has to be aware of his own values and principles. He must ensure that he does not misuse his power as a representative of Rebecca's employer and as someone with expert knowledge and experience that could overly subdue and suppress Rebecca, who has little organisational knowledge or alliances from which to seek support or advocacy. Kemal must recognise that Rebecca has successfully attained her social work qualification and therefore previously demonstrated a commitment to social work values.

Clark (2000) argues that social workers generally adopt an enthusiastic, even strident approach to promoting core professional values such as social justice and the uniqueness of the individual. An over-righteous approach to disseminating a stance on values sometimes may result in soft answers to hard questions about discrimination and oppression. Social workers rarely explore their personal attitudes and behaviour on an everyday basis. Beckett and Maynard (2005) suggest that, as a result, they may miss opportunities to recognise dilemmas posed by uses and abuses of personal, structural and institutional power, because they rarely explore them.

The requirement that professional social workers acquire a sound knowledge base and skills to intervene appropriately compels them to examine their values in relation to how they exercise power.

According to Clark (2000: 54): 'professionals are, therefore, expected to be knowledgeable on a range of subjects defined by the scope of their work; ethical social work must be properly informed and expertly practised'. Becoming knowledgeable as expert practitioners requires an understanding of societal influences on social work as it developed over decades, and how UK social work emerged from its charitable and religious roots into a profession with substantial legal powers (Healy, 2005; Payne, 2005).

The step beyond PQ consolidation is capability, when social workers acquire deeper, more specialised knowledge and skills, and learn to use these skilfully and confidently in their practice (Chapter 1). At these further stages of PQ, social workers should display an ability to challenge injustice in a judiciously critical manner – in Rebecca's example, to separate her inner personal religious beliefs from her active responses to particular individuals and/or groups in society. Social workers undertaking PQ will learn to separate ideology (overarching values and principles) from actuality (how values and principles may manifest themselves in practice).

PQ, whether at consolidation or further stages, requires social workers to take their own personal ethical standpoints into account, consider how their personal values and principles impact on their practice, and reflect on whether their personal views prevent them from achieving as high a practice standard as they might wish. The process of critical reflection can be painful, but ethical and values-driven practice can emerge from greater self-knowledge. These values will be approaches that are grounded in 'real-world' contexts and situations, as illustrated by the practice example of Rebecca.

Negotiating social work values

The context of most social work organisations is increasingly secular and 'liberal', and so it is not always easy for individual social workers to apply the social work values articulated by the NOS (DH, 2002), Codes of Practice (GSCC, 2002a), and BASW Code of Ethics (BASW, 2002). Sheppard (2006) comments that knowledge of self and others (particularly of service users) is a goal most professionals strive for in their working lives. However, professionals rarely evaluate how motivating factors might affect service users' choices and self-determination. Social workers are voluble in support of social work values and principles, but Sheppard (2006: 122) warns of the dangers of conformity: 'when promoting social functioning ... social workers are getting dangerously close to forcing, or at least encouraging, social conformity ... it tends toward social policing of the morals and behaviours of people rather than promoting them as valuable persons in their own right'.

Examining the use of values and ethics in practice begins with gaining a rounded understanding of how the 'personal' self relates to the 'professional' self. Attitudes and experiences gained from family and other influences are the foundation stones on which most practitioners build their professional identities. If the motivation to become and remain a social worker is based on religious or cultural beliefs, then most individuals will draw on these beliefs to form their professional identities but also combine beliefs and experiences from all available sources. Most social workers separate personal attitudes from actions. However, individuals communicate within complex webs of human relationships, continuing to develop ideas, attitudes and behaviours in response to everyday problems. These concerns can be transformed into good practice when a social worker becomes aware of how he or she conceptualises and uses power in relationships with colleagues, managers, service users, and carers.

> ## Exercise: power in social work organisations
>
> Examine the relevant features, activities and expectations of your employing organisation (or if self-employed, the organisations that you undertake work for) and consider the following questions:
>
> 1 Where does power lie and in what form?
> 2 How is the power being used?
> 3 How does this affect your practice?

Codes of Practice

The content of the UK Codes of Practice is broadly consistent with the long-standing British Association of Social Workers (BASW) Code of Ethics, which BASW members are required to uphold throughout their careers. There are, however, some differences. The Codes of Practice relate to professional rights as well as responsibilities, but do not include concepts of individual freedom and choice. The Code of Ethics and Codes of Practice differ in their views of religious practices because faith is often seen as an individual choice and therefore beyond the public domain. The surfacing of misconceptions over this issue in organisational situations requires action, but the basis for challenging individuals to change the philosophical basis of individual professional identities is unclear. The answer lies in whether personal attitudes affect behaviour in ways that contradict the country's and employer's legal and policy framework – for example, if a social worker's beliefs result in discriminatory practice with service users or colleagues.

Most social workers learn to abide by both Codes and balance their personal views with their professional ones. Social workers who are responsible for supporting vulnerable individuals' development, well-being, and safety are required to practise in an ethical, critically reflective manner within fair, equitable environments. Developing a theoretical knowledge base on which to make decisions will improve skills, self-confidence, and self-esteem, and reduce stress levels. Essentially, ethical PQ practice requires an ability to understand and explain universal principles expressed within nationally agreed values and ethics, and interpret them in everyday practice.

Involving service users and carers

People who use services appreciate a range of practitioner skills: reliability, good record keeping, language and communication (Doel and Shardlow, 2005). Values like 'trustworthiness' may be seen as crucial. PQ developments actively seek and listen to service users' views (SCIE, 2004b). Regretfully, the notion of active participation often falls short of a clear understanding of process, knowledge, different perspectives, ethnicity, and experience of models of involvement. A newly qualified social worker is likely to have had limited, short-term professional experience with service users. Service user involvement is therefore important (Chapter 3).

Conclusion

Recently established infrastructures in each UK country promote PQ's overall goal to raise and maintain national standards of social work practice. The challenge for social workers is to sustain their commitment to social work values within challenging situations. Consolidation of experience is offered as a way by which social workers can begin to evaluate their practice and strengthen their commitment to social work values and ethics.

Questions for reflection

1. How will critical reflection help you increase awareness of ethical issues in PQ practice?
2. Can you identify a power issue that affects your practice?
3. How might the Code of Practice help you to maintain your commitment to values in practice?

Further reading

Banks, S. (2004) *Ethics, Accountability and the Social Professions*. Basingstoke: Palgrave Macmillan.

This book provides a wide exploration of professional ethics, including a chapter on the form and function of Codes of Ethics in relation to professional aspirations, educational tools and mechanisms for regulation, and a chapter that balances arguments of autonomy and accountability.

Beckett, C. and Maynard, A. (2005) *Values and Ethics in Social Work: An Introduction*. London: Sage.

This book contains an overview of values and moral philosophy both within ideology and everyday practice, with a particularly good chapter on values and religion that focuses on the dilemmas and challenges posed by faith and belief in a professional context.

Higham, P. (2006) *Social Work: Introducing Professional Practice*. London: Sage.

The focus on practice is extremely valuable, particularly in relation to roles, responsibilities, knowledge and skills. The chapter on values for practice is particularly useful as it defines values and relates them to the key ethical principles and possible obstacles. The chapter on skills for practice and continuous professional development is particularly good.

Chapter 3

Partnerships with people who use services and carers

Patricia Higham and Claire Torkington

Introduction

Chapter 3 portrays how PQ practice is changing (and will change further) to reflect service users' and carers' participation. PQ frameworks across the UK share a belief that service users' and carers' involvement is essential to PQ's relevance.

- In England, user and carer involvement is integral to regional planning networks and programme design and delivery, including teaching, assessment and programme planning (GSCC, 2005a; 2005b).
- The Northern Ireland PQ Rules include a broad statement on user and carer involvement. The Northern Ireland Social Care Council's (NISCC) accreditation requirements stipulate that PQ programmes include all stakeholders appropriately (NIPQETP, 2005).
- In Scotland, all relevant stakeholders, including people who use services and carers, are involved in the design, delivery and evaluation of programme provision (SSSC, 2004, 2005). Service users' roles are considered particularly important – evidenced by practice learning qualifications (PLQ) (SIESWE, 2005) that are structured to enable access and achievement by people who use services and carers.
- In Wales, the PQ Rules (CCW, 2005, 2006) require users' and carers' involvement.

Service user and carer engagement with PQ is consistent with their increasing participation in planning and providing services. This chapter discusses their involvement in PQ frameworks, and whether the concept of user involvement is problematic. The chapter argues that social workers need to form different kinds of relationship with service users and carers, relinquish some of their social work power, recognise the strengths and expertise of services users, and engage with them in ways that reflect these changes.

Planning and delivering services

An important principle is that professionals and people who use services and their carers should plan services together, and that service users and carers should contribute knowledge and expertise to practice. This requires the social worker to demonstrate:

- A culture of listening – encouraging service users to influence decisions about the services they receive, as well as how those services are planned and delivered to all service users;
- An ongoing process for empowering and supporting service users to influence change, either within an organisation or by directly leading policy and service development (REU and SCIE, 2006: 3).

This view of participation suggests that social workers have to define their own values and beliefs by critically reflecting on their self-perceptions, attitudes, cultures, and methods of communication (Chapter 2), and then make fundamental changes in their practice, whilst recognising that under certain circumstances the scope of participation may be limited:

- Social workers often work in situations where individuals behave in ways that limit and damage the rights, development, potential and freedoms of others.
- Social workers have a body of expertise that leads them to examine service user and carer situations from wide perspectives of evidence-informed knowledge, whilst the service users' expertise may consider situations from perspectives based on their own personal experiences – 'experts by experience' (CSCI, 2008; GSCC, 2005b: 7, s 20).

Professionals and service users ideally should both recognise each other's expertise and also accept each other's rights and responsibilities. Heyes (1993) claims that a lack of clear guidelines on user involvement has permitted professional views of participation to dominate. However, power (Chapter 2) can be negotiated and is likely to shift according to each situation. Critical reflection on practice (Chapters 1 and 2) will help the social worker to find appropriate ways of working with users and carers.

Partnership and participation issues

Social workers historically have neglected service users' and carers' voices. One of the first studies of service users' views, *The Client Speaks* (Mayer and Timms, 1970), revealed that users wanted practical help from social workers, but instead were offered psychosocial casework. Service users expressed negative reactions to the portrayal of people with disabilities in *A Life Apart* (Miller and

Gwynne, 1972). Currently, the growing influence of service user movements (Shaping Our Lives, 2007) and their emphasis on rights, responsibilities, and individual choice may clash with 'traditional' social work practice. PQ candidates are required either to have users contribute to the assessment of their practice and/or incorporate user views and perspectives in other ways. However, it is unlikely that candidates will draw on the views of involuntary service users because of legal issues.

Cowden and Singh (2007) argue that the voice of service users can become a 'fetish' – upheld as authentic and truthful but exerting little real influence. Welfare reform in the late 1970s and early 1980s sought to modernise the welfare state, thereby seeming to promise much to service user groups that were part of the New Social Movements (Oliver and Barnes, 1998) clamouring for change. The other purpose of reform was to spend less on welfare, thus threatening the viability of service user participation. Cowden and Singh are equally critical of 'professional' users who become trainers and consultants rather than striving for political change, and of the objectification of 'service users' as an entity distinct from 'service providers', when often the two categories overlap. Considered from these perspectives, service user and carer participation may be problematic because of tokenism.

Building participation and partnerships calls for learning what service users and carers want from a partnership with social workers. The General Social Care Council (GSCC), the Commission for Social Care Inspection (CSCI), Skills for Care (SfC), and the Social Care Institute for Excellence (SCIE) jointly published eight principles (GSCC/CSCI/Skills for Care/SCIE, 2006) that outline what users and carers can expect when social workers engage with them. Although specific to England, the philosophy for engaging with service users and carers is shared across the other three UK countries and states that we will:

1. Be clear about the purpose of involving service users or carers in aspects of our work.
2. Work with people who use social care and health services to agree the way they are involved.
3. Let service users and carers choose the way they become involved.
4. Exchange feedback about the outcome of service users' and carers' involvement in appropriate ways.
5. Try to recognise and overcome barriers to involvement.
6. Make every effort to include the widest possible range of people in our work.
7. Value the contribution, expertise and time of service users and carers.
8. Use what we have learned from working with service users and carers to influence changes in our ways of working, and to achieve better outcomes.

Different levels of engagement with service users and carers

PQ candidates' engagement with service users and carers also will differ according to the candidate's role, previous experience, the PQ award level, and the country's PQ framework. The three practice examples below are drawn from adult services; however, expectations for practice with children, young people, families and carers (CYPFC), and with mental health are similarly exacting. The first example focuses on engaging with a service user whilst consolidating, extending and deepening practice in a specialist context.

Practice example: consolidation

Lew Davies, a social worker in an adult services team in a northern city, sought to provide Mr Patel, a frail older man with considerable health support needs, with appropriate advice about his future care and support – whether to move into a residential care home, supported housing with extra care, or remain in his present home with community care support. Lew was aware that as a white male of Welsh origin, he might not fully understand all the issues arising from Mr Patel's cultural and family circumstances. He also recognised that because of his own lack of knowledge of Mr Patel's first language, and Mr Patel's lack of fluency in the English language, he might not be able to gather all the relevant information. He therefore asked Mr Patel if it would be helpful to meet with a worker from a local advocacy organisation, who spoke Mr Patel's language and understood some of the cultural issues. Mr Patel appreciated this offer, but debated whether to accept additional help, saying that he did not want to reveal his private matters to someone from within his own community because confidentiality would not be observed. Consequently, Lew found a translator who had no direct knowledge of, or contact with, Mr Patel's community.

The next example illustrates the level of capability (see Chapter 1) where the social worker makes complex judgements and discharges high levels of responsibility for coordinating social support and the management of risk. At this level, Lew must demonstrate his engagement with policy and practice issues.

Practice example: capability

As well as responding to Mr Patel's expressed wishes, Lew investigated feedback from service users about their particular advocacy service, and was troubled to discover that most of the feedback was negative. Mr Patel's comments were typical of others' statements about that advocacy organisation. Subsequently, Lew suggested during supervision with his line manager that his social work agency should develop a formal contract with an organisation which could offer advocacy to older people from a range of cultures. On the basis of his knowledge of Mr Patel's and other service users' feedback, Lew recommended that this should not be the organisation previously used, due to a range of evidence that it had failed to offer a quality service.

The PQ level of 'expertise' typically develops knowledge and skills for professional leadership and improvement of services. Taking the practice example a stage further, Lew will engage in direct practice with Mr Patel, suggest a different policy approach for advocacy service to his line manager, and demonstrate leadership.

Practice example: expertise

Lew was convinced that older people should have culturally appropriate and better quality advocacy services. Subsequently, he offered to lead a development group that would explore criteria for commissioning a new advocacy service. As the group's leader, Lew ensured that it consulted with a range of service users and carers on what they wanted from an advocacy service. Lew then reached the conclusion that an advocacy organisation should be user-led to reflect the authentic voices of people who use services and carers. Lew discovered that there were no user-led organisations in the area. He knew that developing a user-led organisation would take time and resources. He also wanted the development group to have user representation and, ideally, user leadership. The development group coopted members from users' and carers' groups. The outcomes of Lew's efforts were to hand over leadership to service users, with some agreed criteria for developing a culturally appropriate advocacy service with clear quality standards that included confidentiality and respect for persons, and an agreement from his employers to resource the development of a user-led organisation.

PQ standards for social workers' participation with service users and carers

PQ candidates are required to meet a range of standards and expectations which require user and carer involvement, including generic level standards, specialist standards, underpinning values, the National Occupational Standards (NOS) for social work or, in Scotland, the Scottish Standards in Social Work Education (SiSWE), Codes of Practice for employees, and guidance on assessment of PQ practice.

The National Occupational Standards for Social Work (NOS SW) (Topss/Skills for Care, 2002), which are part of the underpinning standards for PQ frameworks in all four UK countries (as well as for the social work qualifying degree) affirm the contributions of service users and carers. The NOS approaches to user and carer involvement impart an overall sense of being based on a professional model of consultation in which sharing information, rather than an attempt to redistribute power, is the key process – an approach that some service user organisations think does not go far enough.

- All social work NOS Key Roles and Units refer to assessing, planning and reviewing with users and carers.
- NOS Social Work Unit 2 includes 'work with individuals, families, carers, groups and communities to help them make informed decisions', implying a partnership approach (Topss/Skills for Care, 2002: 2.4, 18).
- Key Role 3 provides the strongest requirement for partnership working: 'support individuals to represent their needs, views and circumstances' and focuses on advocacy and decision-making.

One of the less positive aspects of the new PQ frameworks is the large number of standards and requirements that PQ candidates are expected to attain for successful completion of the modules and awards. Universities should be able to mitigate the effect of overly long and complex assessment requirements by combining and integrating the many standards and requirements.

Impact of legislation, policy and social work reviews

Legislation, policy developments and social work reviews strengthened requirements for public and private bodies to involve users and carers in service planning and delivery. In Scotland, a discussion document (Scottish Executive, 2007) sought the views of the public, users and carers to inform its Action Plan for Health and Well-being. The *National Training for Care Management: Practitioners Guide* (Scottish Executive, 2006b: 10, 5) explains the rationale for refocusing care management to enable users and carers to exercise the same power as other consumers of services.

Wales published a ten-year strategy for social services, *A Strategy for Social Services in Wales over the Next Decade: Fulfilled Lives, Supportive Communities* (Welsh Assembly Government, 2007). Although this strategy mainly addresses local authorities, it calls for active engagement with more people, including service users, carers and families. The 2002–03 annual report (SSIW, 2004) of the Chief Inspector for the Social Services Inspectorate for Wales (SSIW) viewed empowering users and carers as key to improvements for social services in Wales. *Designed for Life* (Welsh Assembly Government, 2005) proposed a ten-year vision of transforming health and social care services in Wales through shaping services around service users and rebalancing services towards the community. The Assembly Government's 'Carers' Champion' (Carers UK, 2006), working in partnership with others, is developing a refocused carers' strategy.

A Northern Ireland service user and carers reference group (Carers Northern Ireland, 2007) supports the Northern Ireland Social Services Council's responsibilities for registration and regulation, the promotion of education and training, and the professionalism of the social care workforce by developing a user-centred approach. The NISCC also works with Carers NI to consult with carers across Northern Ireland.

In England, *Options for Excellence* (DH/DfES, 2006) proposed a workforce development strategy with four stands: perception, partnership, professionalism and participation. The participation strand calls for users and carers to contribute to decisions about services and quality reviews. People who use services will be asked to help with developing new workforce skills for 'learning organisations' (Senge, 1990; Chapters 1 and 14), and will be encouraged to take paid jobs in social care. In England and Wales, for adult services, *Our Health, Our Care, Our Say* (DH, 2006c) makes it clear that organisations providing health and social care services will be expected to seek the views and wishes of patients and service users, and act on these views by involving local people in decision-making.

Across the UK, children's services recognise that listening to children's and young people's views is likely to result in service improvements. The appointment from 2001 of Children's Commissioners in each of the four UK countries (Children Act 2004: s 2), to act as independent champions, is a significant step towards valuing the contributions of children and young people. In 2007, the Children's Commissioners responded to Home Office proposals for unaccompanied asylum-seeking children (Home Office IND (2007)) calling for challenges to the UK's approach to these children, which allegedly treats young people as suspect immigrants rather than as children entitled to protection under the UN Convention of the Rights of the Child.

Theoretical perspectives on user and carer participation

Theoretical perspectives can help social workers reflect critically on issues of participation, and subsequently change how they engage with users and carers. Arnstein's (1969) ladder of participation, devised during a period of civil rights movements and social changes in the USA, resonates appropriately with contemporary issues in the way it identifies service users' different levels of participation in organisations and the organisational features that might impede user and carer participation. The ladder suggests a hierarchy whose apex is full citizen control, but Arnstein admits that some organisations may be unable or unwilling to rise to the top of the ladder. Current UK organisational structures for health, social care and children's services encourage partnership and delegated services, but stop short of citizen control, thus strengthening Cowden and Singh's (2007) argument that user involvement is a fetish rather than a reality.

A ladder of citizen participation (adapted from original source, Arnstein, 1969)

Degrees of citizen power:	Citizen control
	Delegated power
Degrees of tokenism:	Placation
	Consultation
	Informing
Non-participation:	Therapy
	Manipulation

The social model of disability (Campbell and Oliver, 1996; see Chapter 7) advocates a shift in power between the professional and the service user towards more service-user involvement and decision-making, and is a useful theoretical tool for analysing organisational power in relation to service users and carers. This chapter supports the adoption of the social model, but social workers should be aware of criticisms of its approach to gender (Morris, 1991, 1998) and its reluctance to admit the impact of physical impairments (Shakespeare and Watson, 2002).

Cowden and Singh (2007) question the 'ontological primacy' that designates users as 'consumers' who, in market terms, know best. Because some service users have experienced oppression, impoverishment and marginalisation to the extent that they fail to recognise their own oppression or how to challenge it, Cowden and Singh suggest that 'consumer views' are limited. Freire's (1970) pedagogy of the oppressed recognised that different kinds of learning are needed to help oppressed people confront how they are denied power. Practitioners committed to user involvement recognise the importance of enabling users and carers to develop knowledge and skills that previously were denied them.

Attitudinal change through critical dialogue

Beresford et al. (2007: 217) claim that service users 'have been routinely and institutionally devalued, discriminated against, pauperised and denied their human and civil rights'. The following example illustrates this point.

Practice example: Joanne

Joanne Hackett, a middle-aged woman with learning disabilities, described how she was told by her social worker that she would be moving to independent living, without being given any say in the decision or any choice in where she would live. Later, Joanne was assigned a different social worker who took time to talk to Joanne and find out what she wanted. The outcome was that Joanne moved to live as part of a family and this living arrangement helped to fulfil her needs and wishes.

Cowden and Singh (2007: 5) argue for an approach to user involvement where front-line staff 'reclaim the agenda of critical practice' and 'user perspectives are neither privileged nor subjugated, but are situated in a process of creative critical dialogue with professionals, linked to the development of a concept of welfare driven by emancipatory rather than regulatory imperatives'.

To make service users' and carers' participation more effective, social workers must challenge their customary thinking. Sometimes a moment in social workers' experience may cause a complete rethinking of their perspective on an issue and reconstruction of their practice (Parton and O'Byrne, 2000; Chapter 1).

Rethinking a perspective (Torkington, personal communication, 2007)

A social work trainer attended a meeting whose purpose was to encourage voluntary organisations to provide practice-learning opportunities for intending social workers. She explained that these had to be organisations with a care function for people who are vulnerable. One woman, who was a facilitator for a self-advocacy group for people with learning disabilities, said firmly, but not unkindly: 'The people in our group would run a mile if you tried to offer them "care".' Her comment had a profound effect. What the woman was expressing was an approach to service provision where the user of services is not 'cared for' but is the coordinator of their own services that 'enable' rather than 'disable'.

Individual budgets and direct payments

Scourfield (2007) argues that relationships between the state and the citizen have been reconstructed: public responsibilities have been transferred to the individual, but with two dissimilar characteristics: on the one hand, schemes such as individual budgets (Glendinning et al., 2007) reflect growing individualisation; and on the other hand, partnership is recognised as important. Claiming that direct payments and individual budgets enable service users to be 'modern citizens' who are clients, consumers, service users, managers, and entrepreneurs of social care, rather than just care recipients, Scourfield (2007) advocates person-centred approaches to reconcile these different characteristics.

Direct payments and individual budgets provide examples of service users becoming autonomous citizens. Lord and Hutchison (2003: 72) assert that 'individual funding is consistent with the world wide trend towards increased democracy, self-determination, and community development'. Contemporary service user groups challenge the traditions of a collectivised welfare state by drawing attention to the resulting inequality of relationships between users and professionals who assume powerful service provider roles. Scourfield argues that using independence and choice as an organising principle ignores the reasons why the welfare state was first created – to ensure that those who are necessarily dependent are treated with respect and dignity and to provide a collectivised approach to risk by making available reliable forms of support outside the market or family.

Participation in planning and delivery of PQ programmes

Service users' involvement in the social work qualifying degree provides some lessons for engaging them in PQ programmes. Shaping Our Lives, a user-led organisation, identified barriers to involvement (Branfield and Beresford, 2006). Some were practical (access issues, lack of capacity on the part of user-led organisations, incompatibility between user involvement and benefits policies, and lack of training for users and their organisations); other barriers were attitudinal (university culture, and academics attaching a low value to service users' knowledge).

Barriers can be overcome by providing adequately resourced practical support – paying for user expertise, taking broadly defined issues of access seriously, supporting a committed and experienced 'champion' for user involvement, and having a service user co-chair relevant committees. Attitudinal support (users treated with equal value, explicit work to address issues of equality and inclusion in processes and objectives, and learning to respect each other and treat each other accordingly) is important. Shaping Our Lives' efforts to achieve participation took place over time, thus enabling stakeholders to acquire skills, gain trust and confidence, negotiate and reach agreement, learn about each other's perspectives, and express their views within a safe forum.

Torkington and her colleagues (SfC, 2007a) invited service user groups and individuals to participate in a project that gathered their views about PQ work-based assessment processes. As part of this project, a group of SureStart parents devised and used a questionnaire that developed their skills in conducting community consultations. The project's perspective on involvement was that the quality and effectiveness of services were matters of concern for the whole community.

Torkington's group thought that PQ learning and assessment should not interfere with receiving a service or actively participating in planning that service. Users and carers expressed genuine concern for, and interest in, social workers' training and education, and wished to support the learning process, but did not want their participation in direct observations of social workers' practice and giving feedback taken for granted. A group of mental health users expressed concern about power issues, including perceived risks of declining to participate in work-based assessment. To address these concerns, users and carers must be able to exercise informed choice through a confidentiality agreement.

A finding supported by all was the view that line managers should be actively involved in observing and assessing their staff's performance, beginning with newly qualified social workers through to PQ and beyond.

Suggestions for building partnerships

Agreeing a contract

Beresford et al. (2007: 223) suggest that partnerships in individual relationships between social workers, users and carers can be modelled on the lines of a business contract, in which negotiation of rules and shared values precedes business. The contract would require social workers to understand and be committed to opportunities for redress, and to take account of users' unequal positions, the barriers that exclude them from participating fully, and the lack of power and control they commonly experience. A contract would:

- Share and promote the idea of user independence, choice and equality – a social model perspective (Beresford et al., 2007: 223);
- Make working together easier and avoid misunderstandings by having planned processes and written agreements;
- Provide a framework for negotiating arrangements for individual users.

Role clarity

Partnerships require service users to be made fully aware of the social worker's role, its extent, limitations, and boundaries. This point was affirmed when Skills for Care England undertook consultation about the PQ framework, during which some service users stated that social workers did not explain their roles at the outset of a working relationship, thus increasing the likelihood of misunderstandings and conflicts (SfC, 2007a).

Networking

Social workers could promote opportunities for networking between individual users, users and user-led organisations, and organisations. Branfield and Beresford (2006) argue that networking has a positive impact both on individuals and on user-led organisations, by helping them establish successful partnerships with formal organisations. User-led organisations' fragility, the efforts required for active involvement, and a lack of mobility in rural areas were difficulties that impeded networking on an individual basis.

Issues are similar for organisational networking: inadequate and insecure funding (with risks of competition between organisations because of insufficient resources); the unequal positions of small user-led organisations competing with large charitable organisations; dependence on a small core of activists without the resources to expand membership; and the limited profiles and ranges of most user-led and controlled groups, leading to particular user profiles not being catered for (young disabled people, black and ethnic minority involvement).

Building strong communities

Postle and Beresford (2007) state that, first, practitioners should not assume that people in user groups are an homogeneous whole, although it is likely that they all will experience marginalisation and social exclusion; and, second, that although practitioners should not assume that people in marginalised groups will necessarily receive social work support, social workers generally engage with people from groups that encounter marginalisation.

To reach more individuals in need, contemporary social policies aim to build strong communities that avoid stigmatising particular individuals and groups, thus reducing the prevalence of acute needs. Policies have shifted from targeting needs to broad-brush preventive approaches. Consultation about which new services should be provided takes place with communities rather than with specific recipients of services. For example, the NHS Patient and Public Involvement Programme (PPIP) (DH, 2007d) recognised that patients supply certain kinds of expertise based on their own experiences, but the public is a wider constituency of interested citizens. Both need to be consulted for their views, consonant with new community-based LINks perspectives for broader Patient and Public Involvement Programme (PPIP) in the NHS (DH, 2007d).

User-led organisations

Historically, social work practice has taken some steps to practise in ways that encourage active citizenship. However, Postle and Beresford (2007) argue that these changes would not have been possible without the impact of user-led movements, which were initially characterised by self-help and mutual support but then became involved in direct service provision, campaigning and action for change (Barnes, 1997; Carter and Beresford, 2000). A key feature of this development is building capacity – developing confidence and enabling group members to embark confidently on more activities (Postle and Beresford, 2007), an echo of the concept of PQ 'capability' (Eraut, 2006: 5; 1994: 208–10; Chapter 1.)

Capacity building

Postle and Beresford (2007) maintain that, whilst a decline in traditional political activity has occurred, people in marginalised groups increasingly have made their voices heard through self-help initiatives and campaigning. They suggest that social workers' support of user voices is consistent with the definition of social work (Topss UK Partnership, 2002; Chapter 1). The definition makes a cogent claim for a 'liberation' approach (Freire, 1970) towards working with users and carers, but although Topss/Skills for Care used this definition for developing the National Occupational Standards for Social Work (Topps/Skills for Care, 2002), the published Standards do not single out a 'liberation' approach.

The shift from being a passive recipient of services to taking part in campaigning for change was summed up by a woman member of a an adult mental health carers group: 'I think the primary aim at the beginning was to provide relatives' support groups so that relatives could come and discuss the problems they were having in either getting the level of care or whatever and it's blossomed out a lot since the early days and we're quite a pressure group now, aren't we?' (Postle and Beresford, 2007: 146).

A potential for change lies in forming alliances with service users and carers. 'Capacity building' could include development of users' skills, which accords with the principle of empowerment (Postle and Beresford, 2007: 152) rather than emphasising narrow activities of 'training' that incorporate people into existing systems and structures. The capacity-building approach is different from traditional individualised practice associated with social work. It is important to note that building the capacity of carers groups will share some concerns with user groups, but perspectives and agendas will differ.

Professionals can support advocacy – either as advocates themselves (although this approach has been criticised by some groups), or by putting people who use services in touch with user-led advocacy services. Beresford (1994) argues that, where conflicts of interest arise, social workers must try to protect users' interests. Social workers' roles are not straightforward in these situations: 'Nonetheless, exploring creative ways to work with groups of people which challenge tokenistic notions of consultation, ensuring the sharing of knowledge and information, has far greater potential for empowerment' (1994: 154). A key issue (see Chapter 2) is how far social workers are prepared to go in sharing power, empowering service users and carers, supporting the social model (Campell and Oliver, 1996; Morris, 1991), and promoting emancipatory practice (Pease and Fook, 1999).

Conclusion

What differentiates the PQ approach to service users' participation and partnership from that at qualifying level? As Chapter 2 argued, PQ practice requires social workers to share power with, consult, and support users and carers, rather than assume a distant professionalism. At the same time social workers should recognise the problematic aspects of engagement that might result in a tokenistic 'fetish' (Cowden and Singh, 2007) rather than true participation. At PQ levels, social workers must consider, critically analyse, and select different strategies for engaging with users and carers, and make their own reasoned judgements about the outcomes that will likely follow particular choices.

PQ social work practice has to face the dilemma of balancing individual practice with collective actions – can a social worker empower through individual interventions, or it is necessary to undertake community development/community social work (Popple, 1995), and engage with user and carer-led groups? This dilemma calls into question social workers' future roles. Current policy directions imply that social workers should deploy different skills, for example, by supporting user-led organisations. The social work definition (Topss UK Partnership 2002; Chapter 1) claims that 'principles of human rights and social justice are fundamental to social work'. Social workers' practice, therefore, should pursue the goals of social justice through new kinds of partnerships with people who use services and carers.

Questions for reflection

1. What are the barriers to user and carer involvement in your specialist practice?

2. As a PQ candidate, how will you try to overcome those barriers?

3. How might service users and carers describe the difference between the practice of social workers with PQ and those without? What would they look for?

Further reading

Doel, M. and Best, L. (2007) *Experiencing Social Work: Learning from Service Users*. London: Sage.

In this book, service users tell their stories of positive social work practice assuming that social workers learn more from what goes right than what goes wrong. The authors suggest that reflecting on the lessons learned will enable practitioners to feel uplifted by social work's potential for positive change, support and social justice.

SCIE (2004a) *Has Service User Participation Made a Difference to Social Care Services?* Position Paper No. 3. March. London: SCIE.

Drawing on six literature reviews, the paper argues that whilst the participation of service users is widely accepted, little analysis of the impact of that participation has taken place. They conclude with messages for practice – the importance of measuring outcomes as well as processes, ensuring whole-organisation commitment and giving greater attention to the diversity of participants.

Advocacy in Action (2007) 'Why Bother? The Truth about Service User Involvement', in M. Lymbery and K. Postle (eds), *Social Work: A Companion to Learning*. London: Sage. pp. 51–62.

This chapter puts to rest some of the 'excuses' used to justify the lack of user involvement in social work training although the messages are transferable to partnership in practice. Drawing on their years of experience in social work education, the authors conclude that there are no valid reasons for lack of involvement. Users are essential partners in all aspects of social work and the answer to the question in the chapter title is 'immeasurably so!'.

Part Two

Specialist practice

Patricia Higham

Part Two is about specialist areas of social work practice. The chapters consider PQ's role for dealing with the uncertainties of contemporary practice. Chapters 4–9 address one of the book's specific aims – to encourage social workers to reflect on their practice and, through critical self-appraisal, to construct different ways of thinking about and doing social work.

Although limited space precludes separate chapters on issues such as drugs, HIV/AIDS, asylum and immigration, youth offending, etc., some of these are illustrated through practice examples. Chapter 4 portrays the impact of asylum and immigration on children and young people. Chapters 4–8 address themes of diverse organisational structures and values and relationships in specialist contexts, whilst Chapter 9 addresses globalisation and European social work models.

Chapter 4, *Children, young people, their families and carers*, by Celia Doyle and Susan Kennedy, explores whether PQ can help social workers to develop a critical appraisal of what is 'out there' in order to re-examine their roles and practice within changing demands. The discussion helps to build confidence by offering different ways of thinking about and practising social work with children, young people, families and carers.

Chapter 5 *PQ social work practice in mental health*, by Ric Bowl, asserts that mental health social work is undergoing turbulent times, particularly in England and Wales. The chapter argues that over-emphasising individual skills and competence may obscure the values promoted by mental health social work and the contested nature of mental health knowledge, but finds some reasons for optimism in new policy frameworks for mental health.

Chapter 6 *Social work and older people: a view from over Offa's Dyke*, by Aled Wyn Griffiths, Joanna Griffiths and Averil Jarrett, critically analyses social work with older people in Wales, arguing that distinctive legal issues and policies for Wales are not sufficiently recognised in the PQ literature.

The service users and carers who were consulted on the book's content were particularly concerned that 'disability' should be portrayed within the context of the social model of disability. Chapter 7 *Engaging with the social model of disability*, by Bob Sapey, relates social workers' understandings of 'disability' to social work's claim to be a profession, and considers whether social work can promote empowerment, intervene appropriately and, subsequently, meet PQ requirements. Sapey criticises social workers' compartmentalisation of their work – a criticism of practice, but perhaps also, on a different level, a criticism of social workers who might decide to read only those chapters relating to their specialism, and who therefore will miss the relevant discussions of values (inherent in the social model of disability) that appear in Chapter 7 and also Chapter 8.

Chapter 8 *Learning disability*, by Kathy Boxall and the Speakup Self-Advocacy and Eastwood Action Group, examines definitions of learning disability, historical developments of learning disability services, specialist learning disability social work, user involvement, and advocacy. People from Speakup Self-Advocacy and Eastwood Action Group discuss their experiences of social work and offer suggestions for PQ linked to recent policy and practice. The chapter argues that if PQ social workers are to defend learning disability social work, they should draw on relevant research and literature, although not necessarily that with a social work focus.

Chapter 9 *European skills and models: the relevance of the social pedagogue*, by Jacob Kornbeck and Eunice Lumsden, considers the 'social pedagogue' (a European social work practitioner model) in Belgium, Denmark and Germany, and its implications for PQ social work practice in the UK. The chapter's key concern is whether PQ can offer UK social workers opportunities to adopt a social pedagogue role. This chapter is particularly relevant for social workers practising within the changing organisational structures of children's services, particularly in England, where there is an interest in exploring social pedagogy.

Chapter 4

Children, young people their families and carers

Celia Doyle and Susan Kennedy

Introduction

Chapter 4 explores how PQ candidates can develop a critical appraisal of what is 'out there' and re-examine their roles and practice within changing organisational boundaries and demands. The chapter offers alternative ways of thinking that will build confidence for practice with children, young people and families. Its content draws on relevant literature, policy documents and research, and also on dialogue with PQ candidates. Anonymised practice examples illustrate key issues.

Do academics have a role in bringing about a social work revolution? Can they make a positive impact on practice? The academic world of social work has often been charged with being out of step with the 'real world' of practice. PQ candidates have stated that they struggle to see the point of theory when all that is needed is 'common sense'. For those social workers embarking on PQ, these views are sometimes, but not always, entrenched and are usually accompanied by weariness, cynicism and suspicion. Candidates may view PQ awards as yet more 'hurdles' imposed upon them at a time when they feel disempowered and disillusioned. Their most voiced question is: will this PQ training really help me 'out there' in my day-to-day practice?

In response, it is suggested that PQ most certainly does help. In a challenging time for the social work profession, social workers who are academics have an opportunity to engage PQ candidates in debates about 'their' profession and 'their' practice, inspiring them to think and practise in confident skilled ways.

'Out there'

Now that social work has achieved professional status, social workers must demonstrate through training and education that they can raise the standards of professional practice and ultimately deliver better services. Fook (2002: 153) suggests that the social work educator's role in this process is 'connected teaching' – to establish a learning environment that centres on practitioners and their practice, that encourages growth through interaction and dialogue, and is explicit about connections inside and outside the classroom.

The years between 1997 and 2004 'saw the creation of a plethora of new agencies, either quangos or statutorily enforced partnerships, in almost every aspect of social care' (Philpot, 2006: 1). Managers and practitioners have had to keep abreast of innumerable policy and legislative documents. Social workers employed in children's and young people's services continue to deliver day-to-day services in which significant changes and new recommendations have arisen, often as a consequence of inquiries into the deaths of children such as Victoria Climbié, who died of multiple injuries inflicted by her carers and was the subject of a public inquiry (Laming, 2003). Shortly afterwards, a much-publicised murder of two 10 year-old girls by a paedophile took place, into which there was also an inquiry (Bichard, 2004). The UK government was prompted to publish the Green Paper *Every Child Matters* (DfES, 2004) that recommended changes that would transform children's services and ensure every child had the support he or she needed to:

- Be healthy;
- Stay safe;
- Enjoy and achieve;
- Make a positive contribution;
- Achieve economic well-being.

The subsequent Children Act 2004 gave effect to the Green Paper's proposals. Part 1 established Children's Commissioners to promote children's views and interests throughout the UK. Other parts related to the better integration of planning and delivery of children's services throughout England and Wales. In Northern Ireland, the Children (Northern Ireland) Order 1995 was supplemented by amendments and the Protection of Children and Vulnerable Adults (Northern Ireland) Order 2003. Scotland has seen a number of policy developments such as *It's Everyone's Job to Make Sure I'm Alright* (Scottish Executive, 2002a) and the Protection of Children Act (Scotland) 2003, as a result of Laming (2003), Bichard (2004) and other child death inquiries (Dumfries and Galloway Child Protection Committee, 2000).

These legislative and organisational changes have impacted on practice. The introduction of processes aimed at 'reforming' public services is designed to quantify and justify service outcomes, which has meant that 'the policing function dominates practice objectives at the expense of other priorities' (Stepney, 2006: 1295). Social workers in children's and young people's services are so busy 'getting the job done' that they may have lost sight of what and who they are, and with it, their professional uniqueness and style of intervention.

This illustrates that modernising developments have resulted in social workers having to navigate their way through a labyrinth of new rules and procedures whilst meeting deadlines and targets in new regulatory landscapes (Stepney, 2006) to achieve organisational performance indicators. MacDonald (2006: 4) argues that social workers have become marginal to policy-making, and as a result are less able to influence the directions of practice, whilst PQ may produce social workers who practise within a 'new institutional order' that ignores social injustice.

However, the social work profession and social work education have a long history of leading the way in tackling social injustice: 'social justice, in particular, has been stressed in social work' (Banks, 2006: 39). PQ opens up a range of possibilities for assisting practitioners to develop strategies for bringing about changes that make a difference to service users' lives. The practice challenge is to get beyond the regulatory rhetoric of modernising agendas and raise social workers' consciousness so that they can truly see and understand their positions within policy and practice contexts (Stanley and Wise, 1993: 121).

PQ candidate perspectives

For several years, the University of Northampton and the employer partnership responsible for the previous PQ programme for children and families gathered data from PQ candidates about issues they faced and practice changes they wanted to make. The programme offered candidates the opportunity to make sense of the world in which they were practising and how it was constructed. The candidate group comprised practising social workers and health professionals who produced powerful arguments from their practice experiences that exposed gaps, discrimination, oppression and inequality in service delivery. The findings provided a lynchpin for developing effective practice.

Three major areas of concern were: (1) lack of clarity about purpose and role; (2) finite resources and eligibility criteria; and (3) inter-professional and multi-professional practice.

1 Lack of clarity about purpose and role

Social workers and health professionals thought that practice landscapes under modernising agendas had served to undo good practice and effectively erase the roles specific to both professions, leading to a sense of uncertainty and lack of clarity about 'who does what'. Rather than looking back at some lost halcyon days of practice, they remembered different times when both professions were easier to access and each understood what locality and community meant. Rabia, a health visitor studying alongside the PQ candidates, commented: 'Changes in health visiting (by employers possibly outside of the Health Service) to emphasise a public health role will mean that M. and her family will lose my support in the future – so much for working in partnership and in the community.'

Discussing links between theory and practice, Coulshed and Orme (2006: 9) argue that 'social workers, to be truly effective, should be constantly asking "why?" It is in this quest for understanding ... that theory informs practice'. Academic study can encourage this questioning in relation to purpose and role, although it might be uncomfortable to confront every question about social workers' or health visitors' functions and tasks. Also fundamental for skilled practice is an increased understanding of practice contexts of law, social policy, agency policies and procedures, regulatory processes and theoretical approaches.

2 Finite resources and eligibility criteria

Social workers and other professionals on PQ programmes did not understand, disagreed with, or felt powerless to change agencies' gate-keeping procedures that restrict eligibility for services. Trevor, a PQ candidate and social worker, commented: 'Family support is a resource restricted by service structures, the imposition of cost–benefit analysis and eligibility criteria that undermines the human rights of the child.'

Banks (2006) argues the importance of social workers (including those working in large relatively mechanistic bureaucracies) engaging in critical reflection. PQ education and training can help practitioners to examine and reflect upon eligibility criteria and resource constraints with which they work.

3 Inter-professional and multi-professional practice

Contemporary social work recognises the importance of multi-professional practice, with different professions having their own particular philosophy, knowledge base and focus. Ever since the landmark Maria Colwell case (DHSS, 1974), problems with professionals communicating and cooperating to safeguard and enhance the welfare of children has been a constant theme (Reder et al., 1993).

Inter-professional learning plays a part in developing this new form of practice (Chapter 10), and can result in positive regard (Rogers, 1961/1967) for each profession and professional. Importantly, knowledge exchange can support practice. The PQ students discovered a general consensus about determining 'risk' and/or 'need' for children and young people's development, health, education and parenting. Social workers and other professionals enjoyed working together. They identified that conflict between agencies occurred when trying to access services via whatever eligibility criteria were being used at the time.

Sam, a health visitor on a PQ programme, commented that: 'working together with social workers has been great. We have more in common than not. Being able to share concerns about how services are currently delivered has been helpful and clarified that none of us want to do the other's job but that we can support each other in providing services to children and young people only if there are enough of us around.'

The next sections look at specific areas of practice with children, young people, families and carers, and how PQ can help to address these issues, remembering that the social work task in relation to children and young people is so vast that not all aspects can be addressed in this chapter. The three concerns – lack of clarity of role and purpose, interdisciplinary working, and finite resources – are themes throughout the following sections.

Preventive and supportive practice

Government initiatives have encouraged supportive and preventive work from the earliest years to early adulthood. One of the largest initiatives for the earliest years is SureStart, a government initiative 'which aims to achieve better outcomes for children, parents and communities' (SureStart, 2007) through a holistic approach to delivering services. The introduction of SureStart was followed by the Childcare Act 2006, designed to help transform children's and early years services and take forward some of the key commitments from the 2004 Ten Year Childcare Strategy.

At the other end of the spectrum are new initiatives for young people such as the Green Paper *Youth Matters* (DfES, 2005: 23) with the aim of providing coherent, integrated systems of support with 'children's trusts at the heart of these developments, orchestrating a mixed economy of services and opportunities for young people'.

Since the 1989 Children Act local authorities have a general duty to support children in need. Section 17 (1) states that it shall be the duty of every local authority to 'safeguard and promote the welfare of children within their area who are in need'. However, deciding which children are 'in need' can be controversial, because although Section 17 (10) gives definitions of 'in need', these are very broad. Even when a child is unequivocally in need, such as a young person with a profoundly restricting disability, the hurdles that have to be overcome to obtain support for a family can be immense, as Merrick, a social worker and PQ student, explained:

> Within our team a 'four hour rule' applies. Team managers or principal social workers can agree up to four hours provision of domiciliary or similar care to a family on completion of an Initial Assessment. Anything over four hours requires completion of a Core Assessment. After completing an Initial Assessment I'd concluded that the family needed eight hours per week domiciliary care. Based on my professional judgement, the time-cost of undertaking a further assessment is not justified in this case where the child is dying of cancer.

A PQ candidate gave the following example to illustrate some of the issues facing qualified practitioners trying to support a young person. The candidate was particularly concerned about the young person's ability to be defined as a 'child' when it was difficult for him to produce proof of his birth date.

Practice example: Abeko

Abeko is a young man from Somalia who witnessed his parents and grandparents being killed during fighting in his country. With the help of his uncle he managed to escape, and eventually arrived in the UK as an unaccompanied minor. In the troubles he lost all identifying documents. He states that he is 15 years old, had been attending school and fled from Somalia to escape the violence, but also in hope that he could continue his education. He is very tall and appears physically mature.

Questions for reflection

1. From his physical attributes, Abeko could well be over 18 years old, in which case he is not a 'child in need' under the Children Act 1989. Should judgements about eligibility as a child be based purely on a person's birth date or, in its absence, the physical appearance of being over 18 years?

2. Abeko is clearly vulnerable, suffering from post-traumatic stress, developmentally immature and eager to continue his education. What interventions would be suitable, whether or not he is a child or adult, to help him cope with overcoming trauma and with starting a new life in a substantially new context?

Providing support for refugees and asylum seekers has had a long history in the UK. Recently, the number of traumatised children from a wide variety of cultures, often without certain documentary proof of age, is one of the new challenges faced by health, social work and education. The social work role is ambiguous. Abeko's case reveals a young man with social, mental health and educational issues such instances demand that professions work together to help these disadvantaged young people. Clearly, eligibility criteria when a young person cannot prove his or her age becomes central to the intervention. PQ education and training helped Abeko's social worker understand that 'child' and 'childhood' are socially constructed concepts (James and Prout, 1990). There is no sudden acquisition of competence as soon as a young person celebrates his or her 18th birthday.

During the Northampton PQ programme, a study of legislation demonstrated that challenges to the rigidity of defining 'child' as someone below age 18 has been successful in terms of care leavers. Under the Children Act 1948 most help for care leavers was limited to advice and befriending up to the age of 18 (Leeding, 1976). However, from the late 1980s a different perspective recognised that the reality of childhood and the need for parental support continues beyond the 18th birthday. The Children Act 1989, amended by the Children (Leaving Care) Act 2000 and the Children (Leaving Care) Act (Northern Ireland) 2002, requires local authorities to provide various forms of assistance to care leavers until the young person reaches the age of 21 and in some instances education or training expenses to the age of 24.

Whilst looking at legal issues during the PQ programme, candidates also recognised precedents for a discourse of 'competence' rather than rigid age limits. A key precedent was set by the case of Gillick v. West Norfolk & Wisbech Area Health Authority and Department of Health & Social Security [1985] 3 All ER 402. Mrs Gillick mounted a legal challenge to a 1980 DHSS circular allowing doctors to give contraceptive advice or treatment to a girl under age 16 without her parents' knowledge. Ultimately, the House of Lords decided that as long as a child had sufficient understanding, he or she can consent to treatment even if under 16 years old. These two aspects of law, revisited during PQ, can arm social workers with arguments to challenge a purely rigid age assessment and instead advocate for a developmental competence approach to assessment.

Another outcome of the reflections on this practice example was that the candidate appreciated that whatever his age Adeko was traumatised, and if he was to benefit from any educational and social opportunities, he needed intervention to help him cope with the trauma he had experienced. The PQ candidates learned about possible strategies such as the Six Part Story and BASIC Ph method of assessing and helping people who had suffered from repeated distress (Dent-Brown, 1999; Lahad, 1992). Briefly, this intervention developed from work with people traumatised by war and can be used with adults and children. The traumatised person is asked to tell a story in response to six questions:

- 'Who is your main character/hero?'
- 'What is your hero's task?'
- 'What hinders this?'
- 'What or who can help?'
- 'What do they do, or what happens?'
- 'What happens in the end?'

The way that the person tells the story can demonstrate his or her most prominent coping strategies:

- (B) Using beliefs;
- (A) Affect ie using emotions;
- (S) Social interaction;
- (I) Using imagination;
- (C) Cognitive understanding; and
- (Ph) Physical activity.

Therefore, a person who uses imagination (I) will feel safer working through trauma by using imaginary situations, but someone who uses cognitive strategies (C) will benefit from direct 'talking therapy'.

Safeguarding and child protection

Gough and Stanley (2007: 205) note that a developing 'political vision over the last forty years has produced a plethora of policies and procedures in child protection across the world'. PQ candidates questioned how far these had improved services to vulnerable children. Mary, a social worker in a local authority children's services team, summed up the issues for current practitioners: 'the political language is ambiguous and unclear. Where have the words "child protection" gone? Safeguarding and support are all very well but what do they actually mean in terms of services for children?' The theme of finite resources, with decisions profoundly influenced by resource constraints, is illustrated by Collette, a local authority social worker and PQ candidate, who said:

> Services for disabled children will continue to be marginalised. Organisational structures and target-driven approaches alongside societal views about disabled children mean that protection issues are 'lost'. Everyone is so busy trying to work with finite resources that we are in a position that there are now eligibility criteria within eligibility criteria. I spent three hours at a child protection conference where a disabled child was clearly at risk. It took so long because child protection numbers needed to be kept down and the children's services team could not take another case. Eventually agreement was reached about the risks and the child was placed on the Child Protection Register. I think what swung this was the fact that I had done my research and felt confident from being on the PQ programme. But it felt like a fight with no winners, just casualties.

The practice example below shows how, despite government policy, procedures and guidance, profound difficulties and dilemmas remain for child protection workers.

Practice example: Aleesha and Kiran

Aleesha escaped from Afghanistan with her parents and two brothers when she was aged 14. She became pregnant by her boyfriend (who was unknown to her parents) but did not dare tell her family. She ran away from home and was taken into care. Her foster carers also fostered her baby, Kiran, thereby enabling Aleesha to keep him. As soon

(Continued)

(Continued)

as she was 17 she was given a small flat. Her boyfriend disappeared, leaving Aleesha to bring up Kiran on her own. A woman called Madge helped Aleesha, and she eventually moved into Madge's house as her partner.

The two women are very protective of Kiran, now aged 8. They escort him to school and insist that he stays with them at playtime. They will not let him take part in any sport in case he hurts himself or let him eat or drink in school in case he chokes. Even in the hottest weather he is heavily clothed and refuses to take any clothes off 'in case he catches cold'. He is unable to use the toilet by himself because his mother and Madge always wipe his bottom and hold his penis. Kiran is quiet and withdrawn but has occasional severe tantrums in school. The school staff think that he is intelligent but underachieving. He is also overweight because his carers not only feed him well but also do not allow him to exercise.

Questions for reflection

1. Is overprotection is a form of emotional abuse?

2. Kiran is always dressed in ways that would hide any injuries, but during his tantrums is he acting out violence perpetrated against him?

3. Is the intrusive 'assistance' with toileting a form of sexual abuse?

4. Is Kiran's development being impaired and would any intervention improve matters for him?

5. Although Aleesha in many respects is a diligent and devoted mother, is any assessment of child abuse being influenced by discriminatory attitudes to her because of her ethnicity or because she lives in a partnership with another woman?

Here again are key themes that illustrate the social worker's dilemmas. What is the social worker role in situations where intervention might cause more harm than good? The emotional damage to Kiran if he is taken into care could be as profound as the damage caused by him remaining at home. However, if social workers fail to act by the time Kiran reaches secondary school, he is likely to be deeply underachieving, unable to socialise, and grossly obese. It is the infamous 'damned if you do, damned if you don't' situation so often faced by social workers. Interdisciplinary working is required to assess the educational underachievement and obesity and to intervene effectively. Finally, time and energy are likely to be expended trying to determine Kiran's eligibility to access different funding resources. Is Kiran an abused child? The service implications depending on whether a child is 'in need' or 'at risk' are substantial, as articulated by Velma, a PQ candidate who is a senior social worker in a referral team:

Social work interest in a child and their family only happened when issues of child protection 'came to light'. Until then the whole family had been referred to a variety of voluntary organisations that found the issues too complex to deal with or lacked the professional knowledge. When a Schedule 1 offender was known to be visiting the family, the mother was firmly told about protecting 'her children'. Then there was an interest in the family, but only because Children's Services were now firmly within a 'legally' binding process to intervene that took precedence over financial constraints and in-house structures. The risks were considered too high to ignore.

There are no easy answers to the dilemmas in practice situations such as that of Kiran. However, Kiran's social worker, helped by discussion with other PQ candidates, realised that she was not alone in having to resolve the various difficulties. The situation of Kiran and his mother, Aleesha, also prompted a debate about evidence-based practice (see Chapter 11; see also Smith, 2004). Candidates were able to look at arguments for practice built upon a sound research base and measurable outcomes, balanced against concerns that this approach negates flexibility and reflexivity (Gibbs and Gambrill, 2002). Greater consensus was reached for the concept of evidence-*informed* practice. Evidence provided by education and medical staff, as well as research findings into the emotional development and psychological abuse of children (Doyle, 1997, 2001; Harris, 1989), could demonstrate how far Kiran's health and attainment were being significantly harmed. Such evidence would be an essential ingredient in informing practice.

In addition, debates about power (Chapter 2) in relation to decision-making within an anti-discriminatory and anti-oppressive practice framework enabled the social worker to recognise that power 'needs to be understood as potentially liberating as well as oppressive' (Payne, 1997: 268) and that abuse occurs when parent figures fail to use power properly or misuse it (Doyle, 2006). This provided the social worker with a framework for exploring how far Aleesha and Madge were misusing their power over Kiran, and how social workers' power could be used to obtain appropriate services for Kiran.

Children in substitute care

Here a plethora of policies and government proposals has led to legislation – e.g. *Care Matters* (DCSF, 2006) and the Children and Adoption Acts 2002 and 2006 – but these still leave social workers with problems of day-to-day decision-making, as illustrated below.

Practice example: Krystyna

Social workers believed that Krystyna's mother had been trafficked from Eastern Europe into the UK and forced into prostitution. Her father is unknown but assumed to have been a 'customer'. Krystyna was severely neglected by her mother, who developed a drug dependency. Krystyna was eventually taken into care just before her third birthday. In appearance, she is an attractive, blond, blue-eyed child. After a period with short-term foster carers, Krystyna was placed for adoption. However, the adoptive parents found their 'angelic' child had behavioural problems, and the adoption broke down in less than six months. This became a repeated pattern. Krystyna is now aged six, and has experienced nine different changes of carer. Contact was re-established between Krystyna and her mother shortly before the mother died from a drugs overdose. The fact that Krystyna is no longer able to see her mother has left her feeling bewildered.

Questions for reflection

1. How should the social worker explain the mother's death to Krystyna?
2. Would life-story work be beneficial?
3. Would direct therapeutic work be of any value?
4. If so, what type of therapy?
5. Could therapy be justified in terms of cost?

To help address these dilemmas, during their PQ programme, candidates revisited child development theories. Krystyna's social worker was reminded that, according to Piagetian theory (1983), at the age of six, Krystyna would need concrete explanations of abstract concepts such as death. The work of Vygotsky (1978) emphasises the importance of caring adults helping children to expand their cognitive understanding. Candidates shared their knowledge of ways of explaining death to young children, such as drawing an analogy with a balloon that is full of life when filled or, for children with a belief in an afterlife, the life cycle of a butterfly or a mayfly.

The use of narrative

Storytelling or narrative is a useful way of explaining difficult issues (Sunderland, 2000). Life-story work (Rose and Philpot, 2005), woven into play therapy, and BASIC Ph (described above) would be useful interventions. Theraplay (Gower, 2004; Jernberg, 1999), a form of therapy for children and their carers, can be particularly helpful in enhancing attachment between children and their foster carers or adoptive parents. Ann Jernberg and Phyllis Booth pioneered theraplay in 1967. Its goal is to enhance attachment, self-esteem, trust in others and joyful engagement through four key aspects: (structure, nature, engagement and challenge), with an emphasis on positive interaction between children and their parents.

Although being mindful of cost implications, exploring issues of identity would also be helpful – these are significant for all children, not just children from ethnic minorities, a factor that was affirmed during the PQ programme when the candidates revisited and re-evaluated Erikson's (1965) developmental theory.

Partnership and the involvement of service users

'The difference that service users can make to social services planning and development is now recognised in government policy' (SCIE, 2004a: 1). Chapter 3 acknowledged that working in partnership and directly involving service users, including children and their parents, are essential components of anti-discriminatory and generally ethical practice. (For a discussion of values, see

Chapter 2.) As the practice example below shows, this is often a far more complex task than policy-makers anticipate.

Practice example: Sian and Siobhan

Sian and Siobhan are sisters aged 13 and 9. They have a younger brother Seamus, aged 4. Their mother died of cancer two years ago and subsequently their father experienced bouts of deep depression. When their father becomes severely depressed, the girls have to undertake all the household tasks. Sian is sight-impaired so has difficulty with some of the tasks, leaving Siobhan to assist her father, sister and brother, do the shopping and deal with all correspondence and documents. Both girls' schools have expressed concern about their academic underachievement, the girls' tiredness and their difficulty in making friends. They have no local extended family to help them.

Questions for reflection

1. Should the children be taken into care?

2. How can the father best be involved in partnership with social services?

3. How can the true wishes and feelings of the girls and Seamus be determined, and how can they be involved as service users?

The two daughters are service users both as children in need and as young carers. The plight of young carers was barely recognised until the mid-1990s through the work of Dearden and Becker (1995) and Frank (1995). Since then, websites, resources and ongoing research (www.loughborough) alert social workers to young carers' needs. Similarly, children whose parents have mental health problems were largely ignored until the later 1990s, but now substantial resources (www.youngminds.org.uk; Wilson, 2000a,b) have been designed to help them. Meanwhile, there has been an increased focus on enabling children, including those as young as Seamus, to voice their views and opinions (Doyle and Lumsden, 2005; Hutton and Partridge, 2006).

Sharing practice experiences

It can be difficult for busy practitioners to keep abreast of new research and resource provision. However, PQ candidates found that sharing their information needs with academic staff and fellow candidates helped them navigate purposefully through the potentially beneficial sources of

information. Whilst expressing concerns about intolerable situations, social workers and health professionals also acknowledged that sharing experiences and knowledge (within the bounds of confidentiality) led to changed perceptions and built confidence. Yasmin, a GP who took two modules of the PQ programme, wrote: 'Sharing experiences has enabled me again to recognise the need for continuous learning and critical reflection on the professional task.' Mehrunisha, a principal social worker in a fostering and adoption team, observed: 'My strengths and skills have been affirmed and having the opportunity to critically examine research and practice has meant that I am more conscious of the issues.'

Healy (2005) affirms the importance of context. By exploring practice issues with other candidates within their particular contexts, practitioners begin to perceive some of the driving forces that influence intervention approaches in children's and young people's lives.

The practice examples illustrate how practitioners can use narrative accounts for analysis of their everyday practice. Hockey and James (2003) highlight the importance of narrative as a medium for expressing inner thoughts and feelings, and encouraging practitioners to cultivate *analysis* and *reflection* by looking closely at their practice accounts, what they have said and the language used.

Social workers have been criticised for apparently being unable to 'analyse' information that they have gathered. By highlighting analysis in their contextual narratives, practitioners can 'unpick' their practice and its context and explore issues. Below is an opportunity to analyse a practice example. You may wish to explore your own answers to the questions posed by the situation.

Practice example: Kyle and Mia

Kyle and Mia are half-sisters, aged 6 and 4 respectively. Kyle is white and was conceived after her mother, Lisa, who is also white, had a brief encounter with a relative stranger. Mia's father, Joe, who is black British, lives with his parents, who moved to the UK from Jamaica before his birth. The girls see little of their maternal grandparents who are both in poor health. Lisa is now in the later stages of a terminal illness and arrangements have to be made for the girls' future. None of Lisa's family can offer them a home. However, Mr and Mrs Johnson, Joe's parents, want to care for both girls.

Questions for reflection

1. The Johnsons are Mia's grandparents but have no 'blood-tie' with Kyle. How far might the Johnsons favour their 'own' granddaughter over a step-granddaughter? If they did favour Mia, would this matter?

2. The Johnsons and Mia are black but Kyle is white; there are concerns about the issues facing black children placed with white carers. How far are these concerns also present when a white child is placed with black carers?

3. Should the fact that potential adopters are a different ethnicity and/or race from the prospective adoptive child preclude adoption?

4. Thinking of contemporary attachment theories (Chisolm, 1996) and those focusing on sibling attachments (Dunn and Kendrick, 1982), how far does the opportunity for siblings to be adopted together outweigh other disadvantages?

PQ gives social workers the time and space to challenge apparently beneficial policies that ultimately can have adverse effects on children's welfare. As Chapter 2 argued, an unthinking or over-zealous approach to social work values such as anti-discriminatory practice can do more harm than good. Lau (1991) describes how social workers adhered rigidly to the concept of placing 'black' children with 'black' substitute carers when they labelled a child with a dual Chinese and white British heritage as 'black' (being not entirely white). They placed her with black (African-Caribbean) foster carers. In the social workers' view, this satisfied the child's cultural and identity needs. In Kyle's situation, a placement with carers who, while not being 'blood' relatives, are familiar and understand her cultural and identity needs might outweigh any disadvantages related to not sharing her skin colour.

Critical reflection provides opportunities for students to deconstruct practice actions, theories, discourse and outcomes and investigate practice alternatives. By exploring, through narrative, her role as a social worker in adoption, Mia and Kyle's social worker was able to understand how the overriding issue of placement stability framed her understanding of same-race placements and her intervention. The practice example highlights the social worker's role in adoption and how, by analysing events, the social worker was able to identify and clarify roles and responsibilities.

Conclusion

Returning to the opening issues, is PQ relevant and is the academic world of social work out of step with the 'real world' of practice? One may argue that PQ programmes can encourage practitioners to turn the question around to one of whether practice itself is out of step with the real world. An example is the situation of Adeko, where the social worker was so focused on whether or not Adeko had lived for more or less than 18 years, that he missed the essential question of how both society and social workers construct the concepts of 'child' and 'childhood'.

PQ can offer much to social workers intervening in the lives of children and their families. Sharing the difficulties of the role with academic and training staff as well as with fellow candidates can help practitioners to feel that their dilemmas are recognised by people who understand the issues that social workers face. However, PQ goes beyond simple sharing to the acquisition of new tools for intervention, including a greater appreciation of the context and interpretation of relevant laws and policies. Examples include service user participation (Warren, 2007) in the situation of Sian, Siobhan and their family, and the introduction of relatively new interventions such as theraplay (Gower, 2004) with Krystyna's situation.

Time and encouragement should be given for PQ candidates to revisit well-known theories and research (Piaget, 1983; Vygotsky, 1978), or become acquainted with newer contributors (Dunn, 1988, 1993; Harris, 1989). Sharing practice situations can enhance social workers' ability to apply theory to practice, as seen in Krystyna's situation, when she needed help to understand the death of her mother.

PQ aims to raise consciousness; it helps social workers analyse research critically and become more knowledgeable. Evidence from previous PQ candidates has demonstrated that despite initial cynicism and weariness, candidates conclude that undertaking PQ benefits their practice. Thus they affirm Laming's argument (2003: 367) that 'it is now generally recognised that training is not confined to the beginning of professional life, but must be a life-long process'.

Finally, to return to the opening question, 'do academics have a role in bringing about a social work revolution?', academics can help introduce practitioners to innovative research and writing, assist them in applying theory to practice and so help them review their practice and reflect on the context in which they work. This in turn helps practitioners to gain confidence to question and challenge when appropriate. Laetitia, a health visitor who was a student on the programme, stated: 'Health services will not like it. But I care enough to speak out – it feels exciting.' And the final word is from Jenny, a social worker in a leaving care team, who, on completing her PQ programme, stated: 'I feel more confident about my role and responsibilities. I also feel more confident about challenging for and on behalf of service users and myself.'

Further reading

Coulton, M., Sanders, R. and Williams, M. (2001) *An Introduction to Working with Children*. Basingstoke: Palgrave.

This book covers a wide range of topics, including the origins of child welfare, child development, family support, protecting and looking after children, anti-discriminatory practice, and children's rights. Despite its breadth, the book also has sufficient depth of analysis and challenge to engage students and practitioners at PQ level.

Doyle, C. (2006) *Working with Abused Children* (3rd edition). Basingstoke: Palgrave Macmillan.

This book opens with a valuable chapter on the nature of theory and the links between theory and practice. It draws on research to examine the personal and environmental factors contributing to maltreatment. Ways of intervening at individual, family, group and societal levels are explored, and many of the chapters have relevance for anyone working with children in distress and their families.

Green, S. and Hogan, D. (eds) (2005) *Researching Children's Experience*. London: Sage.

Whilst of evident use to those researching with children, it also has an appeal for practitioners needing to understand children's perspectives for assessment purposes or to represent children's wishes and opinions. There are chapters on ethical considerations, naturalistic observations and exploring children's views through focus groups.

Chapter 5

PQ social work practice in mental health

Ric Bowl

Introduction

Chapter 5 begins by considering recent legislative and policy changes that impact upon mental health social workers. It examines the nature of PQ social work in the context of mental health services, providing an example of multi-professional training to illustrate the particular contribution of PQ social work. The final section considers both the potential impact of the PQ frameworks and how PQ mental health social work should develop.

Tensions in organisational and policy contexts

Mental health social work is going through turbulent times, especially in England and Wales. Whilst all community-based mental health staff have been shown to experience high levels of stress and some dissatisfaction with their jobs, social workers are less satisfied than other professionals (Carpenter et al., 2003; Coyle et al., 2005). Like others within the social care workforce, mental health social workers derive considerable intrinsic job satisfaction. This comes particularly from contacts with service users, from making a difference in people's lives, and from the support they receive from co-workers and through supervision (Huxley et al., 2005a). Nonetheless, over half the respondents in a recent enquiry into mental health social workers' views were ambivalent about or dissatisfied with their jobs. A fifth had specific plans to find another (Huxley et al., 2005a). These findings are reflected in an increasing national concern about the difficulties of recruiting social workers to work in mental health (NIMHE, 2005b) and, in particular, difficulties in recruiting and retaining Approved Social Workers (ASWs) (Huxley et al., 2005b).

One source of the disquiet of mental health social workers is the impact of integration with Health Trusts in England. Although its exact form varies from authority to authority, the break-up of social services departments is almost complete. Mental health social workers are increasingly

employed by or seconded to NHS Mental Health Trusts or Health and Social Care Trusts, as has long been the case in Northern Ireland. Beforehand, many mental health social workers in England worried that integration would lead to an erosion of respect for and understanding of social perspectives – that these would be undermined within organisations dominated by medical models of intervention (Peck and Norman, 1999). Others saw integration as an opportunity to champion the value of social interventions and be involved more directly in shaping policy and interventions.

Mental health social workers have particularly highlighted the absence of appropriate professional supervision within many NHS Trusts. Commitment to developing and sustaining practice through regular professional supervision is one of social work's strengths (Hawkins and Shohet, 2006). Skilled supervision is seen as essential to maintaining abilities to think through the complex situations faced when working with people in acute mental distress and facilitating difficult decisions, particularly about risk. Supervision is also seen as an important forum for learning and developing skills.

Other professionals, who may not understand the role supervision has played within social work practice or who may feel unskilled to provide appropriate support, now manage many mental health social workers. Approved Social Workers (ASWs), known as Mental Health Officers (MHO) in Scotland, found this a particular concern. The ASW role involved the considerable responsibility of independent judgement about whether or not individuals' liberty should be taken away – a role often located within the legal system elsewhere in the world. That judgement was made within situations often characterised by anxiety, conflict and risk both to themselves and to others. Sometimes, difficulties occurred in arranging conveyance to hospital by ambulance or in securing police assistance because of pressure on those services. Perhaps most significantly, alternatives to hospital admission were slow to develop, and even where social workers would have liked to avoid the use of compulsion, resource constraints could make that impossible. It is no surprise that ASWs appreciated the value of appropriate debriefing within supervision. Yet research in this area highlights not just that ASWs experienced high levels of stress and emotional exhaustion but also that this was compounded by less support from supervision (Evans et al., 2005).

Social workers in the field also voice concern about the limited numbers of people with an understanding of social interventions and commitment to them in key decision-making positions. Many NHS Trusts have directors or leads for social care/social work but they are sometimes at the periphery of organisations or isolated, with few other social care professionals occupying senior positions. Perhaps as a corollary of this, social care workers have perceived that the value of services addressing a *social* rather than a '*clinical*' function is questioned – for example, day care services have been increasingly targeted for cutbacks, despite being consistently rated in service user feedback as being among the most useful resources.

New mental health roles

The second area of disquiet has centred on the creation of new roles within mental health services in England and Wales such as 'Primary Care Graduate Mental Health Workers' (PCGMHWs) and 'Support, Time and Recovery (STR) Workers'. Few mental health social workers would dispute the value of the roles that these new workers are expected to perform, but many of their tasks are not fundamentally different from those of mental health social workers or other social care workers. The 're-badging' of existing workers to meet STR targets is evidence of this. What is disquieting is that arguments that have been consistently made for new resources for existing social work and social care roles have fallen largely on stony ground. Yet money is made available to create apparently new types of roles in new posts. Some mental health social workers have taken this as a vote of no confidence – it is seen to devalue social interventions by implying that others without the same level of training and qualifications could perform these social intervention tasks. As such, it also can be perceived as part of a process of de-professionalisation – replacing trained and skilled professional workers by less well-trained and less skilled workers (Karban, 2003).

The role of the Graduate Primary Care Workers is a particularly illustrative case. Many aspects of their role seem similar to the tasks described by Firth et al. (2004) in their analysis of mental health social work practice within a primary care setting. Some of these tasks are the very elements of the mental health social work role – for example, preventive work; work with those experiencing common mental health problems; and relatively unstructured 'counselling' interventions aimed at building self-esteem or encouraging self-help that have been increasingly squeezed from mental health social work roles by an emphasis on case management and on risk avoidance (Karban, 2003; Ramon, 2006; Rapaport, 2005). Yet the role of the Graduate Primary Care Worker can be performed by someone whose only qualification, prior to the short PCGMHW training programme, is a degree, not by someone with at least two years professional training.

Another concern arises from the confusion between multi-disciplinary working and 'non-disciplinary' working. One of the potential gains for service users from integration would be to see patterns of effective multi-disciplinary working established within integrated community mental health teams (CMHTs) (Carpenter et al., 2003) spreading throughout mental health services as a whole. Multi-disciplinary working has been shown to be strongest where individuals have confidence in their own professional background – in the knowledge base, values and skills of their discipline (Onyett et al., 1995). Yet some have seen integration as a chance to erode distinctions between roles.

Research in London, for example, identified three broad views on a desirable future among senior mental health managers responsible for social work:

- 'Traditionalist' – an orthodox view of social work, advocating for the rights and empowerment of service users from a sociological stance, with strong links to the local authority and other branches of social work;
- 'Eclecticist' – enthusiastic about multi-disciplinary teamwork and reducing boundaries between roles, but keen to preserve professional diversity;
- 'Genericist' – a belief in reducing role demarcation and removing statutory differences where appropriate and working towards a generic mental health practitioner (McCrae et al., 2004: 313).

Most current practice could be described as eclecticist, with a useful blurring of boundaries between roles – for example, in community mental health teams between community psychiatric nurses and social workers. Professionals in those settings say they value learning about each other's roles and working in partnership but they do not want to become each other (Carpenter et al., 2003). Collaborations between doctors and Approved Social Workers in assessments under the Mental Health Act about whether compulsory powers should be applied or not provide good

examples of multi-professional practice. Despite early concerns about conflict and strife, and inevitably some difficult relationships, in most areas these assessments are prime examples of the strength gained by sharing different perspectives within assessment, characterised by respect for each other's different knowledge bases, skills and values (see Chapter 10 on inter-professional practice and education).

Nonetheless, despite evidence of the efficacy of integrated models of values, theory and practice that a clear professional identity brings to practice, mental health services have focused increasingly on individual tasks (Karban, 2003). This often ignores the contested nature of knowledge, the different values underpinning a range of professional approaches, and the benefits that can accrue from applying different perspectives within constructive multi-disciplinary working (Walton, 1999). The result is a lack of consensus about the specific roles of different professionals and which tasks can be shared, with a rising incidence, particularly within community mental health services, of role conflict and role confusion. This in turn is an important element in the growing dissatisfaction of the workforce, particularly mental health social workers (Carpenter et al., 2003; Coyle et al., 2005).

The mental health social worker and the Approved Mental Health Professional

Despite the stresses that accompany it, an important source of strength and confidence for social workers has been the ASW role and the recognition it brings (Walton, 2000). However, the Mental Health Act 2007 (DH, 2007b) replaced Approved Social Workers in England and Wales with Approved Mental Health Practitioners (AMHP). This has opened up the role to nurses, occupational therapists and psychologists, as well as social workers. Before they can take on the role, they will undertake AMHP training and their ability to perform the role will be assessed.

However, the ASWs' ability to provide a uniquely socially informed perspective, balancing those of the medically trained professionals involved in an assessment, did not derive from a 60-day ASW training programme alone. Critically, that programme was underpinned by (a minimum) two-year initial qualification programme plus a minimum of two years PQ experience. (Following the introduction of the social work degree, the initial qualification is three years at degree level.) In that context, social workers developed:

- Knowledge of how social structures and conditions affect the development of severe mental distress and recovery from it – for example, roles of family dynamics, stigma, abuse and discrimination;
- Knowledge and experience of reconciling individual service users' rights and needs and those of others through the application of a range of legislation;
- Values that have at their core a commitment to anti-discriminatory practice, to service users' rights to independence, and to service users' right to have a clear voice in decisions about intervention;
- Knowledge and practice skills in a range of social interventions with individuals, families and communities.

For many mental health social workers, the extension of the role performed by ASWs to health professionals who lack that underpinning training and experience represents a lack of respect for and belief in their knowledge and skills and for the role of social interventions (Walton, 2000).

Reasons to be cheerful

In the light of these developments, it is easy to understand the concerns of mental health social workers but it is important to recognise that the policy framework also contains signs of encouragement for social work. The first comes from the *National Service Framework for Mental Health* (NSF) (DH, 1999). Whilst the NSF is predominantly oriented towards changing provision by health professionals, it places considerable emphasis on the importance of social interventions.

The NSF contains implications for social work/social care in all its standards, including an emphasis on the need for all assessments to include social functioning and needs arising from service users' personal circumstances; on the complexity of individuals' needs, including need for support with education and training, housing, social skills and social networks; on the role of non-medical support during crises; and on carers' needs.

Standard One, however, contains the most important signals, stating that health and social services should promote mental health for all, work with individuals and communities, combat discrimination against individuals and groups with mental health problems and promote their social inclusion.

The NSF cites interventions shown to be successful, including work with communities in tackling local factors undermining mental health *and* also work with individuals to enhance their psychological well-being. The first model of intervention has always been part of the work of social workers – not just within the recommendations of the Barclay Committee (NISW, 1982) – and remains so, however much individual social workers may feel their time is squeezed by the pressures of what seems like limitless community care assessments. Early guidance on the role of ASWs also envisaged working to create and support alternatives to hospital admission as well as undertaking assessments!

Many of the specific forms of work with individuals that the NSF lists – including tackling feelings of a lack of control and exclusion from decision-making, supporting individuals through crises by promoting skills and decision-making, and providing support in challenging discrimination against people because of their mental distress – are important elements of social workers' roles. Whilst the range of service models and examples of good practice that are cited to support this standard may tend to focus on special projects rather than the work of mainstream social workers, the standard is a clear endorsement of what social workers do.

Similar affirmation of these core elements of the mental health social work role is found in the government report on *Mental Health and Social Exclusion* (Social Exclusion Unit, 2004), published for England, but in the expectation of its relevance to the other countries of the UK. This also is accompanied by an over-emphasis on what might be achieved by special projects and gives little recognition to what social workers already do – indicative of the need for mental health social workers to be more proactive in making the scope of their roles clear. The report focuses particularly on the need to provide people with genuine choices about what happens to them and the

support they receive; to support people's engagement in social activities and promote positive views of their potential; to challenge discrimination; to facilitate access to 'the basics' – housing, finance and transport; and to support people into employment.

Ten Essential Shared Capabilities

There are also the Ten Essential Shared Capabilities (ESC) (DH, 2004d) which it is intended should be attained by all workers in mental health services within England and which have been actively promoted in Scotland.

ESC: Ten Essential Shared Capabilities for Mental Health Practice (DH, 2004d)

1   Working in partnership.
2   Respecting diversity.
3   Practising ethically.
4   Challenging inequality.
5   Promoting recovery.
6   Identifying people's needs and strengths.
7   Providing service user-centred care.
8   Making a difference.
9   Promoting safety and positive risk-taking.
10   Personal development and learning.

The ESC might seem unexceptional to social workers because they are all encompassed by social work values. Yet, these are not values that are exclusive to social work, and they are not values that are always easy to sustain. Social workers have had to work hard to put these values into practice and understand something about the pitfalls. Social workers can play an important role in sharing their knowledge and experience. Other professionals seem genuinely concerned, for example, to respect diversity, to challenge discrimination and work with people's strengths, but do not always have much experience of what that means in practice.

Promoting recovery

Another important element within the ESC is 'promoting recovery', a concept that has emerged primarily from the service user movement. It is in danger of becoming clouded and can have different dimensions, usefully outlined in the National Institute for Mental Health in England's *Guiding Statement on Recovery* (NIMHE, 2005a).

'Promoting recovery' can be best explained in the sense that the primary goal for many service users is not becoming symptom-free (which is not to say that would not be welcome to many!) but to achieve 'recovery' – to transcend the degraded and stigmatised status of 'mental patient' and occupy a meaningful role within the community (Jacobson, 2004). What service users are looking for in recovery-oriented services are the very forms of support – facilitating their participation within social and occupational activity, focusing on their strengths and promoting autonomy – discussed within the National Service Framework and the work on social exclusion. It is encouraging that NIMHE regard these as goals that all mental health workers should be striving to incorporate within their practice, but given their other roles and responsibilities, it is difficult to see all mental health workers giving these the same priority for action as social workers.

Importance of the social work role in mental health

Finally, recognition of this congruence between the role of social workers and the emphasis of current mental health policy is recognised within the latest report from NIMHE's initiative on the development of the mental health workforce: 'Social work and social workers are important. Social work makes an important contribution to mental health services and is a crucial component in their development. Social work values, skills and knowledge already encompass the approach set out in current government policy documents' (DH, 2007c: 117).

What is mental health social work?

The discussion so far has identified both concerns about, and encouragement for, the roles of social workers within current mental health policy, as well as a concern to identify exactly what the social worker's role is within mental health services and how it differs from others' roles. The work that emanated in 2005 from NIMHE, in partnership with the Department of Health and others, provides only limited help, although it does give a broad view of the knowledge base and skills expected of mental health social workers.

The Scottish Executive's review of the future of social work (Scottish Executive, 2006a, c) provides a more detailed analysis. The social worker's task is identified as:

- Developing effective therapeutic relationships;
- Working alongside people to help them build resilience, maintain hope and optimism and develop their strengths and abilities;
- Meeting people on their own terms, in their own environment, whilst retaining the professional detachment needed to help people who use services to understand, come to terms with, or change their behaviour;
- Acting as agents of social control – confronting and challenging behaviour and managing situations of danger and uncertainty – managing risk and the distressing consequences of things going wrong in people's lives.

The review highlighted social workers' skills and experience in providing pragmatic but theoretically informed interventions when working with turbulence, complexity and uncertainty and outlined a range of circumstances when social workers are identified as particularly well equipped to be the lead professionals in collaborative work. It also identified some functions that only social workers can perform.

Reserved Functions of the Social Worker (Scottish Executive, 2006c: 30)

Social workers should assess, plan, manage the delivery of care and safeguard the well-being of the most vulnerable adults and children, in particular, those who:

- are in need of protection; and/or
- are in danger of exploitation or significant harm; and/or
- are at risk of causing significant harm to themselves or others; and/or
- are unable to provide informed consent.

To do this social workers must:

- carry out enquiries and make recommendations when necessary as to whether or not a person requires to be the subject of protection procedures; and
- be responsible for the development, monitoring and implementation of a plan to protect the person, in particular, identify and respond appropriately to any risks to the achievement of the plan and/or any need for the plan to be revised because of changing circumstances.

This certainly reflects what mental health social work has become. Despite their focus on enhancing social inclusion, promoting a recovery orientation and focusing on individuals' strengths, it is important to recognise the contexts in which this occurs. Developing packages of care to sustain someone experiencing mental distress within the community, conducting assessments concerning levels of risk and deciding whether or not to implement legislative powers are at the core of social work. Even within that restricted role, mental health social workers bring particular understandings and values that come from their training and professional development. Specifically, they bring training, assessed knowledge, skills and experience of:

- Analysing interpersonal dynamics and skills in working with them;
- Understanding the experience of oppression and discrimination and adopting strategies for challenging their impact;
- Making the empowerment of individuals a central goal of intervention;
- Developing empathetic relationships that enable all of these to become possibilities.

Hence the greatest challenge in extending the ASW role in England and Wales to other professionals is not ensuring that nurses, occupational therapists, or psychologists, for example, will be capable of exercising independence from doctors, because many will possess the appropriate individual qualities that can be enhanced and assessed in AMHP training. What they will not have at the outset of that training is the long experience, which social workers bring, of exercising judgement about the balance of needs between carers, service users and communities, and whether or not legislation should be applied. Nor, whatever their personal qualities, will their training and professional development have included an assessment of their knowledge and skills in, and experience of, the particular understandings and values inculcated within social work training and practice that have been so important in characterising the balancing nature of the ASW's assessment (Walton, 2000).

Nor is this contribution unique to ASW assessments. Tew and Anderson (2004) and Ramon (2006) argue that concern with holding on to ASW status has distracted mental health social workers from demonstrating the contributions that their knowledge, skills and values can make to both understanding and tackling mental distress. There can be no doubt that social work has an important contribution to make. Beresford (2005) is among those who have highlighted the limitations of the increased stress within mental health services on compliance with biochemical treatments – despite evidence of the limited impact of such treatments on recovery, for example, from schizophrenia (Tew, 2005a). Emphasis on compliance pathologises service users, saying there is something wrong with them that must be 'fixed'. Because of the illness model's resilience, time-limited, structured psychological interventions are often seen in the same way.

Both Tew (2005b) and Beresford (2005) provide alternative emphases that do more than recognise the role of social factors, and particularly the impact of power, on the development and progress of an individual's distress. An alternative emphasis argues that social factors should be at the centre of efforts to aid an individual's recovery. Intervention should focus on understanding the impact of trauma, of families' emotional lives, of limited opportunities and of stigma. Intervention should examine how responses to such experiences can lead to psychiatric labels and sometimes self-destructive survival strategies.

Supporting service users to engage with the roots of what they are experiencing can be valuable in itself but also should lead to a consideration of the strategies for supporting service users in reclaiming power. These might include providing practical support, challenging others whose influence impedes recovery, finding opportunities for service users to build their self-esteem, helping to build or repair relationships and might include more structured intervention like cognitive behavioural therapy. Critically, such work must take place in the context of user partnerships that recognise their knowledge and understanding and focus on their strengths and capabilities. Social workers are uniquely placed to practise in this way, which requires exactly the knowledge, skills and values that they possess.

Service user views

Service users also express support for the particular contributions of mental health social workers. A recent analysis of mental health service users' narratives reports familiar concerns about stigma, social exclusion, inconsistencies over diagnosis and the impact on their lives and their relationships of mental distress itself (Cree and Davis, 2007). The analysis also identifies some negative experiences of social work – for example, disquiet about a service user not being a priority for social workers until a crisis occurs. Some of the support received positively also came from more structured interventions,

such as cognitive behavioural approaches or the exercise of compulsory powers. Service users understood that sometimes detention was necessary, and they appreciated the social worker being prepared to assess risk and step in when intervention was needed.

Relationships

The idea of 'relationship' was seen as very important – service users experienced a consistency and depth in their relationships with social workers that they did not get with other professionals. Building a consistent relationship is necessary if people are to be facilitated in revealing the facts behind their distress, such as experience of sexual abuse. Listening and being person-centred, not illness-focused, were seen as being important because they showed that social workers were responding to their needs as a person. Equally important was facilitating service users to find a voice – often about abuse – and taking steps to take control of their own lives. So too was providing practical and emotional help and advocacy – 'giving help' is an idea that figures significantly in these accounts – which is not seen as being in contradiction with empowerment but sometimes as an important step towards it. (See Chapter 3 on service users and carers.)

Discussion

None of this is intended to devalue other workers' skills and understandings. A convincing argument can be made that, in multi-disciplinary contexts, whilst social workers need knowledge and understanding, they do not have to be as 'expert' as others in identifying symptoms, in making sophisticated judgements about stages of relapse and about medication. It may be a positive advantage that social workers come to assessments from a different viewpoint, understanding those areas but giving priority to issues of empowerment, anti-oppression, social inclusion and other elements of social contexts in which people's experiences of mental distress are shaped. Within the context of creative and positive inter-professional relationships, tensions between these concerns and a focus on the exact nature of someone's ill health and the need for appropriate treatments can then be played out.

The practice example below is intended to stimulate debate about the nature of the social work role within mental health services and its relationship to other roles.

Practice example: Sue Toussaint

Sue Toussaint is a 17 year-old British woman of African-Caribbean origin living in a market town. She has had no previous contact with mental health services. Her mother referred her to the crisis resolution service because of recent changes in Sue's behaviour. For the last three years, Sue experienced feelings of paranoia and low mood. She reports hearing voices telling her what to do. She has been resistant to any referral to services and her mother was reluctant to push it.

Sue lives with her mother and has no contact with her father, from whom Sue's mother is divorced. Sue's father was reported to be a violent man – Sue reports witnessing him assaulting her mother more than once – and when Sue was nine years old he was jailed following a violent incident. Recently, Sue ceased attending her local college and often stayed in her room all day. She reportedly has become increasingly aggressive and has broken windows in the house. She threatened suicide and recently admitted to her mother that she had smoked cannabis since she was 14. She says smoking cannabis makes her 'feel normal'. Sue's mother is becoming increasingly run down and unsure what to do next.

Questions for reflection

1. What is the potential social work role?

2. Can you identify theoretical or empirical research that would justify and inform social work intervention?

3. What aspects of that intervention should be carried out by a social worker?

4. Which other professionals would it be important to work with?

Developing PQ social work in mental health services

The previous sections sought to show what social work can bring to an understanding of mental distress and the strategies mental health services can employ in tackling distress. How can that contribution be deepened and developed?

Until now the pattern of continuing professional development (CPD) for mental health social workers has been limited, largely consisting of 'one-off' courses on legislative changes or the introduction of administrative procedures, such as local systems for recording risk assessments, supplemented by ASW/MHO training. Also, whilst respect for an evidence base is built into the National Occupational Standards for social work, the assumption persists that PQ social workers struggle to stay informed about developments within their evidence base. Despite exceptions to this assumption, social work does not have the same tradition, compared to health, of keeping informed about or contributing to the evidence base (McCrae et al., 2005).

The reasons for this unsystematic CPD approach comprise the lack of opportunity, unsuitability of traditional research approaches, and no resulting career reward or advancement (see Chapter 15). The impact of the PQ frameworks remains to be tested. In England, programmes in specialist mental health social work services began in September 2007, with the expectation that all mental health social workers would undertake PQ to deepen their understanding of mental health contexts. Other

UK countries would offer their own mental health programmes. Coupled with the requirement to evidence CPD to continue registration as a social worker, this could broaden the base of PQ training in mental health social work. If mental health social workers are going to succeed in developing their practice, employers need to support this learning, including providing study leave.

The practice focus of PQ programmes reinforces the desirability of mental health social workers becoming critically reflective practitioners within a learning organisation (see Chapter 1). So far, however, mental health programmes being commissioned by regional networks in England have been limited in scope, largely focusing on ASW/AMHP training. Other areas for PQ programme development can be identified – in forensic mental health work and in social work with children experiencing mental distress, for example – but there are pressing operational needs to prioritise AMHP training and doubts about where funding will be found for meeting other training needs.

Such developments may also encourage mental health social workers to become more involved in producing evidence about the social origins of distress and/or social interventions. Here other barriers must be overcome, not least the limited views of proponents of evidence-based practice within medicine about what is good evidence. They argue for a hierarchy of research with random controlled trials (RCTs) at the top and the expert testimony of those who receive the services at the bottom. This fails to recognise that RCTs are from a particular tradition of science, which has come into question even within the world of physical science. Social scientists are more inclined to embrace complexity and favour approaches that recognise the role played, in shaping a particular social world, by the perceptions of the actors within it (Fay, 2000), recognising that the views of those engaged in particular social activities, such as interactions between mental health practitioners and service users, may never be reconcilable into an agreed account. Nonetheless, these views are important to understanding those interactions and making services work better for people.

Both Pilgrim (1997) and Gould (2006), who focuses particularly on the failure of RCTs to recognise the influence of the individual (recipient or provider) on the outcome of interventions and their inadequacy in producing prescriptions for non-medical interventions, provide more detailed critiques of RCTs' limitations. That is not to say evidence from RCTs should be ignored, but the acceptance of a wider view of an appropriate evidence base is argued. (For an alternative view, see Chapter 11.)

Beresford (2005) makes a powerful argument for an evidence base to have knowledge at its centre – for example, about what should be priorities for intervention and what facilitates recovery – generated within the user movement by looking at and analysing shared experiences. As well as accepting that knowledge, social work can also learn from how it was generated.

Mental health social workers should not be deterred from undertaking larger-scale pieces of research but could achieve much by being more systematic in monitoring their activity and describing the impact of what they do (Firth et al., 2004 is a good example of what this approach can contribute). This in turn can be taken further by building practice models from critical reflection on experience (Plumb, 2005).

The 2007 Mental Health Act has produced another role in England and Wales that might go some way to meeting mental health social workers' aspirations for career development, extending the former role of Responsible Medical Officer to that of Responsible Clinician (see Chapter 15), a role that might be taken by mental health professionals other than doctors – including social workers. However, whether the role will be attractive to social workers has been controversial, with some feeling it has too narrow a focus and is set in the context of the medical model – contradicting social work's broader perspective. There is also concern about whether social workers can carry it out on an equal basis to other professionals, because Article 5 of the European Convention on Human Rights requires decisions about renewal of detention to be supported by 'objective medical expertise' (apparently now overcome by the need for responsible clinicians' decisions in this area to be supported by a report from a member of a different profession). What should be important in establishing individual practitioners' suitability for these posts is whether they can meet the required Department of Health knowledge and skills for the posts. Certainly the drafts in circulation would suggest them to be as attainable by experienced mental health social workers as by any senior practitioners.

Conclusion

This chapter explored the contributions PQ social work makes within changing organisational relationships that leave advocates of mental health social work concerned about its survival. The argument has been made that social workers in England and Wales should not be overly concerned about the loss of the ASW role. What is important is to demonstrate the distinctive role social workers can play not only as AMHPs – and certainly if this role and the knowledge and skills which accompany it are taken seriously, it will often remain a role best performed by social workers – but also within their other practice within multi-disciplinary teams. Furthermore, social workers should be more proactive in producing evidence about what they know and achieve. If they don't and the contribution brought by their knowledge, skills and understanding is lost, mental health services throughout the UK and those that use them will be much the poorer.

Further reading

Tew, J. (ed.) (2005) *Social Perspectives in Mental Health: Developing Models to Understand and Work with Mental Distress.* London: Jessica Kingsley.

All the chapters are of interest but Chapters 1, 4 and 12 by Jerry Tew consider the contribution of social perspectives, and particularly ideas about power, towards understanding the origins of distress and suggesting strategies to build recovery. Chapter 6 by Sally Plumb describes in detail the trauma model and its relevance to social work practice and recovery. In Chapter 2, Peter Beresford explores the contribution that service users have made to our understanding about distress and recovery and indeed to methods for understanding them.

Chapter 6

Social work and older people: a view from over Offa's Dyke

Aled Wyn Griffiths, Joanna Griffiths and Averil Jarrett

Introduction

> We are not old … old is always fifteen years older than I am. We are young to ourselves most of our lives, young to our elders as long as we have any. (Baruch, in Stott, 1981: 176)

The task of writing Chapter 6 poses two ambitious challenges – first, and not necessarily in order of difficulty, the chance of contributing to the debate and critical reflection about the likely role of social work with older people and, second, the opportunity to ground discussion where possible on Welsh evidence and experience. The justification for attempting the impossible, and borrowing material from other parts of the UK only in the absence of Welsh evidence or for the sake of comparison, is that we invite our Wales-based PQ candidates to adopt a similar methodology. This is not to suggest that we encourage xenophobia – clearly PQ assessors in Wales share the delight of reading submissions that make regional and cross-boundary comparisons together with references to international scholarship. The point at issue, however, is what stance to take when candidates refer to non-Wales-based material when such equivalents exist. For instance, in the context of adult protection, reference to the Department of Health's Guidance document *No Secrets* (DH, 2000) as opposed to the Welsh Guidance *In Safe Hands* (National Assembly of Wales, 2000). Needless to say, those candidates who reflect on both, but ground their observations on the local response, bring smiles to us all. To date in Wales, as illustrated below, failure to address what the Care Council for Wales (CCW) recently christened the 'Welsh context of Social Work' (CCW, 2007) has been one of the most frequently cited explanations for PQ referrals and resubmissions.

Despite difficulties, we are convinced that the time is ripe both to revisit the professional and academic discourse associated with social work and older people and also to flag up the not insignificant impact of devolution on social services delivery and practice in relation to older people. Similar claims can no doubt be made for Scotland and Northern Ireland. Interestingly, the Scottish Executive has taken a lead by commissioning the report *Effective Social Work With Older People* (Kerr et al., 2005). The fact that this chapter's primary focus is on Wales is, however, apposite. The UK's population is ageing (National Statistics Online, 2007), but the population of Wales is ageing at a greater rate than its UK counterparts (Phillips and Burholt, 2007). Wales has a slightly older population than the rest of the UK (20.2% and 18.2% of pensionable age, respectively). According to figures produced by Eurostat in 2003, Wales also had a higher proportion of older people than any of the then existing 15 European member states bar Italy (Dunkerley, 2007). Life expectancy for men and women in Wales has increased over the past 50 years, but the proportion of persons reporting longstanding, limiting ill health is higher in Wales than for other UK regions (Edwards, 2002). The largest concentrations of older people tend to be in rural parts of Wales. It is estimated that over 15 years the number of people of retirement age will increase to 28% of the population. Similarly, the number of older people aged 85+ will increase by over a third (Milsom, 2006).

One of the central beliefs of the Celtic tradition was that the well-being of the king reflected itself in the well-being of the land. True to our Druidic roots, we begin with the Welsh dimension of the challenge and admit at the outset that like John Toshack, Wales's soccer manager, and his sporting equivalents our claim to Welsh sources may be tenuous and thin – the distant 'grandmother' or 'grandfather' connection sometimes will be very evident. Our posturing on the issue has a serious aspect – to underline how difficult it is these days to decide on which material to demand from PQ candidates in their submissions, given the dearth of social work and legal texts that acknowledge, let alone discuss in any detail, the differences in policy and quasi-legal expectations that impinge on post-devolution UK practice. As Lord Justice Thomas (2007) commented when discussing the legal context: 'Although England *and* Wales is now commonly the jurisdictional title, it would be a delusion not to take into account the fact that many do not understand that Wales is now in several respects different; the ghost of "*for Wales, see England*" lives on'.

This chapter's first part outlines some hurdles and challenges facing Wales-based PQ candidates. Thereafter the chapter will outline briefly some major policies and developments that are likely to impact on social services for older people. Finally, the discussion focuses on academic deliberation and practice aspirations concerning the future potential role of social work with older people.

Hurdles and challenges in Wales – some snakes and ladders

Community Care and the Law (Clements and Thompson, 2007) undoubtedly is the major exception to a general rule that most social work and relevant legal texts largely disregard the fact of devolution. Even this book requires considerable diligence and index wizardry by a student with a Welsh agenda. The devil and magic are in the detail – perhaps the point is best made by reference to a few of the growing number of developments that illustrate how minute yet significant the differences actually are in relation to both provision and practice. First, in England, for instance, Community Care Assessment Directions (DH, 2004e: 4088369) now exist on how to carry out a community care assessment. No such Directions exist in Wales. Second, in England social services authorities can be fined for delayed discharges of care, whereas in Wales, the Welsh Assembly Government (WAG) has resisted the temptation of implementing Part 1 of the Community Care (Delayed Discharges) Act 2003. Third, parallel but different provisions exist for adult placement schemes in the two countries, but the Welsh provisions are essentially less generous and limit the numbers that can be placed in such schemes to two persons per scheme and not three, as in England. Fourth, the legal requirement to prepare community care plans under the NHS and Community Care Act (s. 46: 1), abandoned in England, continues in Wales, although the framework for making such plans has been recast to encompass more recent statutory developments, such as those contained in the Local Government Act 2000 (WAG Circular – NAFWC/36/00). Fifth, and probably the distinction most often acknowledged and referred to in relevant texts, is the Guidance pertaining to eligibility criteria and community care assessments referred to as Unified Assessment in Wales (UFSAMC, 2002) and as the Single Assessment Process in England. The choice of different terminology was apparently motivated by the desire to emphasise a coordinated and streamlined approach to the assessment and care management that was sought and deemed necessary for success (para 1.3). The difference is not confined to nomenclature. The Welsh Guidance document is broader, incorporating elements of the English Policy and Practice Guidance *Fair Access to Care Services* (*FACS*), together with that pertaining to the Single Assessment Process. Finally, it is also necessary to provide the equivalent of what might be termed loosely a 'government health warning' – that some documents which boast identical titles are subtly different. For instance, the Care Programme Approach guidance, which places obligations on health and social services authorities in respect to assessment for specialist psychiatric services for adults, is worded a little differently – the more inclusive and generous wording on this occasion being those in the Welsh documents.

The hurdle facing a PQ candidate attempting to learn about the differences is raised considerably by the lack of easily accessible government information about social services requirements. The Department of Health website provides an archive which generally ensures that accessing Guidance and Directions in an English context is usually straightforward. In contrast, accessing similar material issued by the WAG is a much more difficult exercise. As Clements and Thompson (2007: 19) properly and bravely conclude: 'the [WAG] website is lamentable'. They suggest that the Assembly's failing in this respect is so grave that it might well amount to maladministration and failure to comply with the Freedom of Information Act 2000 (2007: 19). The Scottish Parliament's website details, in contrast, are overwhelming – some information is available in no less than ten languages, including British Sign Language (BSL).

The importance of remedying the information deficiency cannot be overstated, particularly because the recently enacted Government of Wales Act 2006 has added considerably to the WAG's legislative competence. Until this recent legislation, the Assembly's powers were essentially limited to making subordinate legislation under powers provided for in Westminster. Under the latest Act, the Assembly has the power to pass 'Measures' which are similar in effect to Acts of Parliament (Rees, 2007). Among the number of fields of interest specified where such Measures are permissible are social welfare, health and health services, housing, transport, sport and recreation, education and training, all areas which are clearly relevant to a non-ageist socially inclusive agenda. It has been confirmed that powers will be sought to bring in legislation to address the current disparity in charges for domiciliary care across Wales (Announcement, Deputy Minister for Social Services, 17/11/2007). As things stand, charges vary enormously, with seven of the 22 social services authorities having a maximum charge of more than £100 per week. Another seven have not set a maximum charge. The maximum weekly rate in the lowest-charging authority is £16.20 compared to £185 in the highest. The highest charging, Powys, is also possibly the most rural social services authority in Wales.

Expectations of PQ learning in Wales are also much wider and more demanding than simply fine-tuning legal obligations. The opportunity for policy development in Wales has been grasped with both hands. The so-called 'modernisation' agenda is alive and well with no less than six strategic documents in the last four years, namely:

- *The Health and Well-being Strategy* (2003);
- *The Strategy for Older People in Wales* (2003);
- *Designed for Life: Creating World-class Health and Social Care for Wales in the 21st Century* (2005);
- *National Service Framework for Older People in Wales* (2006); and
- *A Strategy for Social Services in Wales over the next Decade* (2007);
- *Fulfilled Lives, Supportive Communities* (2007).

As some of the titles suggest, ambitions are grandiose and some of the official claims made are equally magniloquent. For instance, 'The publication of the *Strategy for Older People* is a landmark for Wales. For the first time, we have systematically analysed the aspirations and needs of older people in Wales and produced a Strategy and Implementation Action Plan to address priority issues over the next decade and beyond' (WAG, 2003: 3, para 1). Another bold claim is that the strategy embraces the United Nations' Principles for Older Persons (see below). The Strategy acknowledges a need to promote the Care Sector in Wales, but regrettably makes no specific mention of social work. It also draws attention to the fact that among adults, the highest proportion of Welsh speakers still tends to be older people and for older people whose first language is Welsh, there can be added difficulties of communicating in English. It refers specifically to a Welsh Consumer Council Report *Welsh in the Health Service* (Welsh Consumer Council, 2000), which concluded that Welsh language provision in the NHS in Wales was poor, and that Welsh-speaking older people are one of the key groups of Welsh speakers that may not be treated effectively because of communication problems (2000: 2, 35). It suggests that language, community and cultural issues also may be significant in defining the needs of older people among black and ethnic minority communities in Wales, but concedes that more research is needed to identify and develop services that can respond appropriately to these and other groups who require distinctive tailored support (2000: 2, 9).

It is still early days, so perhaps it is not surprising that the conclusion of one academic evaluation about whether differences in policy amount to a distinct macro social policy agenda was cautious, save only to suggest that in Wales there is perhaps less enthusiasm for marketisation (Means, 2007). Others posit a more significant shift, and accept that it is only since devolution that a concerted policy in relation to older people has been articulated in Wales – the emergence of a broader perspective on ageing, beyond traditional health and social care territories – an approach which funnels the focus on the social, economic, and cultural experiences of individuals and the diverse communities in which they live (Phillips and Burholt, 2007).

Beyond dispute is that policy in relation to older people is one of WAG 's priority areas. The establishment of a post of Deputy Health Minister with specific responsibility for coordinating services for

older people in the Assembly is hopefully indicative of genuine commitment. The Older People (Wales) Act 2006 breaks new ground, with the imminent appointment of a Commissioner for Wales – probably the first post of its kind in the world (Williams, 2007). The appointee will be required to promote awareness of the interests of older people in Wales and the need to safeguard those interests. Among the other general functions specified in the legislation are the elimination of discrimination and encouragement of best practice in regard to the treatment of older people in Wales (s. 2). In considering what constitutes the interests of older people in Wales, the Commissioner will be required to have regard to the United Nations' Principles for Older People (adopted by the General Assembly on 16 December 1991) namely their independence, participation, care, self-fulfilment, and dignity (9, s. 25).

The need to reflect critically on the Welsh dimension was recognised in Wales with the establishment, under the previous UK-wide PQ framework, of a single PQ Consortium for Wales, funded by the Care Council and member organisations, including all 22 unitary authorities, large independent and voluntary organisations and academic institutions across Wales. The Consortium's focus and greatest volume of delivery has been achieved through work-based learning via a portfolio route. Its formal arrangements also provided for accredited programmes or a combination of the two, but the portfolio route has been the main route to successful delivery. Ironically, it appears that the primary explanation for the emergence of what in Wales has clearly become the most popular route to a PQ qualification was the inability of the then social services authorities to adopt a more segmented and traditional form of delivery.

There were difficulties for agencies during local government reorganisation in supporting PQ candidates with appropriate supervision and contextual arrangements, with the immediate problem being not financial but one of organisational discontinuity. It was therefore agreed that the Consortium would take forward plans to establish a PQ portfolio route, recruit supervisors directly, and seek 'seed corn' funding from the regulatory body (PQ Consortium Wales management board minutes, 21 June 1995). The Consortium drew on expertise from Wales and beyond, and adopted a robust approach to the requirement to address the Welsh context. The *PQ Handbook* (PQSWCW: 5) specifies, *inter alia*:

- In Wales it is also important to demonstrate your understanding of working within the Welsh cultural context and to show your understanding of the need to develop language sensitive practice.
- Your understanding of the legal and policy context of your work and an understanding of appropriate research.

Given the information deficit outlined above, addressing the Welsh context certainly required a leap of faith, perseverance and acknowledgement of the need for a steep learning curve. Our review of PQ assessment activity reveals how indicative an appropriate reference to the Welsh context has been in respect to the success or failure of submissions. Some 38 candidates were invited to resubmit in the year 2006–7. Assessors' detailed feedback often highlighted a number of shortcomings. Accordingly, the rough evaluation of the data below needs to be treated with considerable caution. However, it appears that in 18 of the 38 portfolios referred, a lack of consideration of the Welsh language, culture, and policy was a primary, significant, or one factor among a number of factors specified. (Table 6.1)

The need to comply with provisions of the Welsh Language Act 1993 no doubt helps to pencil in cultural and legal issues in the context of assessment and service provision in Wales. It is

Table 6.1

Technical e.g. lack of witness statements	Quality of ethical statement	Quality of presentation	Lack of reference to policy and legislation	Too descriptive/lack of reflection	Lack or inadequate reference to Welsh culture, language, and policy developments
4	1	1	6	8	18

clearly good social work practice to extend the principle of language choice to those who speak other languages across the UK. Both assessment and service provision should be conducted in culturally sensitive ways. The following practice example, decided by the Commissioner for Local Administration in England (local government ombudsman), provides a salutary example.

Practice example: Mr B

Mr A complained of the delay in providing a culturally appropriate care package for his Vietnamese father-in-law, Mr B, and that the authority had acted unreasonably in refusing to reimburse costs incurred when a suitable care package was not provided. Mr B had suffered a severe stroke and, following a long hospital stay, returned home with a care package provided by the social services department. After about two years, the department felt that Mr B's needs would be better met within residential care. The family resisted, claiming that their culture required that Mr B should remain at home with his family and that Mr B's carers should be able to communicate with him in Vietnamese, his own language. An interim care arrangement provided by the authority broke down within a few days because of Mr B's aggressive behaviour towards carers who could not communicate in Vietnamese. A satisfactory care package was eventually arranged, but the Ombudsman considered that the time taken to do so had been unreasonable. At the Ombudsman's suggestion, the local authority agreed to pay Mr A compensation of £17,436 which was equivalent to the amount it would have cost to provide Mr A with care for an eight-month period (local settlement 01/B/17685).

Some key social service policy issues in Wales and beyond

As tentatively suggested above, there is probably less enthusiasm for marketisation in Wales than over Offa's dyke. A key aim of the community care changes introduced by the NHS and Community Care Act 1990 was the promotion of a flourishing independent sector alongside good quality public services. To this end, social services authorities in England were obliged to spend 85% of a government grant provided to help fund the changes (known as a Special Transitional Grant) on the purchase of non-local authority services. No such edict was made in Wales, with the result that many social services authorities in Wales have continued with strong in-house provider services. Whilst the scrutiny of Joint Reviews and WAG policy documents has increasingly advocated the promotion of a mixed economy of care, it is clear that there remains some ambivalence or reticence in Wales in relation to policies that undermine public provision. For instance, the Community Care (Direct Payments Act) 1996 provided for an extension of direct payments to persons of post-65 years of age in Wales and in England alike. However, the promotion and introduction of direct payments has been slow in Wales. Similarly, there is some uncertainty about whether individual budgets, a species of direct payments, will be introduced in Wales. Such schemes have been widely piloted in England, but only in Wrexham has there been any similar developments in Wales.

The Westminster government's White Paper suggests that the development of individual budgets potentially can change significantly the way that home care and support are provided (DH, 2006c). Under this system, users of adult social care services each hold an individual budget that brings together and places a financial value on the support they receive from different sources. Individuals can use their budget in a number of ways – for example, to purchase their own support, or to purchase services from a social services authority, or a mixture of the two. The claim is that this development will enable social care users to exercise choice and control as consumers without the difficulties of handling money or employing staff (Age Concern, England, 2007: 59). Others are more sceptical, pointing out that the proposals do not include any additional resources, and that there is a danger that implementation of the proposals may add to the existing considerable pressures on carers (Clements, 2007). The cautious Welsh approach in this context has been made transparent: 'We will review the opportunities for individual budgets in the light of pilot projects in England' (WAG, 2007: para 4, 5).

Carers

As the recent *Annual Report of the Chief Inspector for Wales 2005–6* (SSIW, 2006: para 4, 23) acknowledges that carer organisations continue to report the belief among many carers that little actual support is provided for them: 'Many carers believe there is very little point in accepting a carer's assessment because there is not likely to be any available service to meet their needs'. Numbers of carer assessments are lower in Wales than in England – 41% and 45% respectively (Seddon et al., 2006). Even when such assessments occur, they are invariably narrow in focus, with an emphasis on practical aspects of caring to the detriment of psychological and relational aspects (Seddon et al., 2006: 12). Among older people, as Seddon et al. point out, it is not uncommon to find a person with a cognitive impairment providing care for a partner with physical limitations, who, in turn, prompts the memory of their 'carer'. As the authors suggest, 'Increasingly there is a focus on the caring relationships and there is a danger that the quality and dynamics of these relationships may be lost somewhere between the separate assessments of the two parties involved' (2006: 16).

The inadequacy of services for carers is an important issue in the context of social work services for older people. Of the nearly 6 million people who provide unpaid care for relatives or friends in Wales and England, some 8,000 are in their nineties (Hopkins, 2006). In line with UK profiles, the majority of carers in Wales are older people themselves, either through spousal care (14% of service users over age 85 have carers who are over 75 years) or caring for a younger disabled member of the family (Phillips and Burholt, 2007). The highest proportion of caregiving tends to be in areas of higher than average levels of deprivation and long-term illness, with carers in such areas themselves tending to be in poor health. Among the local authorities in the UK with the highest proportions of the population providing intensive unpaid care were Neath, Port Talbot and Merthyr Tydfil (Young et al., 2005). Social services authorities perhaps serve older carers of adults with learning disabilities especially poorly. A study in an English local authority of older adult carers (70+) of adults with learning disabilities highlighted their sense of isolation, vulnerability, and scepticism about the lack of good faith that the participants claimed typified professional intervention. Some asserted that professionals did not understand their situation. Some actually refused any professional input due to attempts to move the service user to alternative housing (Bowey and McGlaughlin, 2007).

Eligibility criteria

In Wales, as in other parts of the UK, the conception of formal eligibility criteria for social services, introduced under community care, has increasingly dominated work with adults. The Unified Assessment Framework in Wales, like *Fair Access to Care Services* (*FACS*) in England, contains four eligibility bands ranging from *critical, substantial, moderate,* to *low*. Only two out of the 22 social services authorities in Wales now provide the full range of services (i.e. from *low* to *critical*), with the majority focusing on *critical* and *substantial* only. From a social work perspective, as others have rightly emphasised, such institutional constraints make reconciling users' and carers' priorities much more complex and intractable (Holloway and Lymbery, 2007). Such constraints clearly can undermine preventative agendas, but encouragingly, the Chief Inspector of Social Services in Wales in his Annual Report (SSIW, 2006) makes the important point that Unified Assessment Guidance gives equal consideration to risk as well as to current need. He suggests that services such as supported housing and the use of technological equipment provide ways of supporting increased independence. The Report emphasises that an effective range of preventive services calls for a wider approach than from social services alone. The Report also acknowledges evidence to show that several authorities have been raising the threshold of eligibility to balance demand with resources. The result, as the Chief Inspector argues, is that individuals who might benefit from early intervention do not receive a service, leading possibly to more serious problems later on. The Chief Inspector suggests that provision of an aid to prevent falls at the first sign of risk may help an older person manage without more intensive services later (paras 4, 17–18). One in two women and one in five men over 50 years of age will experience an osteoporotic fracture. Over 12,000 such fractures occur in Wales each year, of which over 4,200 are hip fractures. Of patients who receive this injury, 70% die within a month, with 25% dying within the following year. Half of the survivors fail to regain their pre-fracture level of independence (DH, 2006a: 109).

Social work and older people

At the outset, it is worth pointing out, as others have done, that the term 'social care' is not widely recognised outside the UK; elsewhere 'social work remains the only descriptor' (Holloway and Lymbery, 2007: 385). The emergence of different terminology in the UK to describe aspects of

social services activity is not without significance, in that it mirrors accounts which suggest that, particularly in the context of practice with older people, managerialism, bureaucratisation, form-filling, and financial assessments have brought an end to the traditional activities of social work (Sharkey, 2000). The debate over whether care management has undermined social work or should be regarded as essentially different from social work (Carey, 2003) is clearly beyond the scope of this chapter. Instead, discussion will be predicated by an assumption that the agreed purpose is to raise social work's professional profile with older people by focusing on the complexity of the social work task (Crawford and Walker, 2004; Lymbery, 2005; Marshall, 1983; Phillips et al., 2006; Stevenson, 1989) and some of the challenges in relation to practice with older people.

All the major texts listed above highlight a need to address ageist social work practice, for example, labelling individuals as belonging to one homogeneous group, such as 'the elderly'. Stevenson (1989: 11) draws attention to a particularly unpleasant and pervasive form of ageism which suggests that older people only require their basic physical needs to be satisfied, rather than a combination of physical, social, emotional, and spiritual:

> I am ashamed to say that I have heard this said by social workers: *all they really need is to be warm, comfortable and well fed*. Whilst physical infirmity may make physical care of great significance to the older person and mental infirmity may limit their capacity to give and receive other kinds of care, the efforts we take to relate to the whole person are critical if we are to avoid the stigmatising and depersonalising process which insults the integrity of the older person.

Social work texts contain less information about work with older people than about some other service user groups (Lymbery, 2005). In the context of an anti-ageist agenda, categorising older people as a separate group and different from other adults might be seen as a contributory factor in the stigmatising process. Whilst it needs to be emphasised that many older people will not need social workers or social services, some older people, for example those with dementia, have complex needs that certainly warrant expertise. Tibbs (2001: 71–2) argues that a lack of specialised knowledge might lead to inappropriate or ineffective intervention: 'difficulty in making the initial contact with the person, achieving the balance between the person's right to autonomy, their need for help, and their need for emotional support throughout the process'. The skills alluded to are no doubt generic to all social work, but the justification for the special focus on social work and older people is, in our view, well founded given the knowledge base required to facilitate a sensitive, appropriate, and holistic response.

An illustration of this point is taken from Lymbery's comprehensive text, *Social Work with Older People* (2005) where, for example, a detailed outline of the manifestations of dementia is provided. Dementia, apparently, is not in itself an illness but a syndrome caused by a number of other illnesses, Alzheimer's being but one of a number of causes. It is important to establish the nature of the dementia, as the cause will affect the nature of the treatment provided. It would be impossible to construct a viable care plan without clarity about the likely progress and effects of the medical condition (Lymbery, 2005: 29). The fact that much day-to-day social work practice continues to be carried out by staff with little or no qualifications is in itself a reflection of an ageist perspective, and despite the welcome improvement in workforce development, there is still an unacceptably low level of skills and qualifications in adult care. The *Strategy for Social Services in Wales* (WAG, 2007), for instance, suggests that despite significant improvement that has taken place in recent years, some half of the care staff employed by social services authorities in Wales still lack formal qualifications (WAG, 2007: para 2.17). Significantly, the Guidance relating to Community Care Assessments in Wales is non-specific about minimum qualifications. The UFSAMC Guidance relating to necessary qualifications is vague or non-committal. However, considerable skill and experience are necessary even at the early stages of assessment.

PQ can help social workers to penetrate what others have described as 'the mask of ageing' (Biggs, 1997). This is illustrated in the excellent example below taken from the *Report of the Chief Inspector* (SSIW, 2006).

Practice example: Mr M

Social services undertook a general assessment, which concluded that Mr M was managing quite well at home and could not be considered a priority. The assessor used information provided by Mr M but did not check its validity. Mr M complained about the assessment outcome and was reassessed by a very experienced, qualified social worker. On the second occasion, issues about Mr M's difficulties were explored more fully. It became clear that his wish to appear independent was greater than his ability to do everything for himself. The social worker then arranged a package of support at the local day centre. He was very pleased with this service (adapted from Swansea Adult Services Review).

Critical application of theory to PQ practice is essential if older people are to be provided with appropriate services, and if social workers are to understand their function and be able to reflect critically on the quality of their practice. A wide range of theoretical approaches is appropriate, as Phillips, Ray and Marshall (2006) and others demonstrate. Phillips et al. touch on the feminisation of ageing (2006: 12), a theme which Lloyd (2006: 1181) explores in some detail, arguing that 'the feminist ethics of care provides a strong argument for challenging the abstract ideal of the independent, autonomous individual', which has become the standard against which the quality of life is measured.

The complexity of social work with older people provides scope for a range and combination of different perspectives including what Payne (1996) succinctly describes as *individualist-reformist*, *socialist-collectivist*, and *reflective-therapeutic* perspectives. In essence, what Payne and Lymbery (who successfully builds on Payne's analysis) suggest is that it is often unrealistic to construe social work as simply about a process of social reform, because older individuals in genuine need often need immediate assistance. To perceive social work as an account of individual cases is to ignore older people's collective experiences. Lymbery (2005: 51) concludes that 'a skilled social work practitioner must be able to identify the approach that most suits the circumstances with which s/he is confronted, being sufficiently flexible to respond to them in different ways according to their nature and their cause'.

The practice example below illustrates how both collective and individualistic approaches can be successfully combined.

Practice example

In response to the *Strategy for Older People* (2003), a North Wales social services authority, in partnership with several voluntary organisations, developed small lunch groups (rather than clubs) in which three or four older people have lunch together at a local café or restaurant. Initially this was supported by the authority's Strategy Officer, who assisted in tasks of finding a suitable location, putting individuals in contact with one another, and arranging taxis or community transport for participants in a lunch group. Referrals were received mainly from social workers, but once established, referrals were increasingly received from older people themselves, and the groups took over organisational arrangements and became self-regulating.

The same authority brokered a door-to-door shopping service for older people with the community transport service and a local voluntary organisation. The service operates from a different location each day. Individuals are collected from home and taken to a supermarket for their weekly shopping as well as lunch or a snack, if they wish. The service provides, in addition to the driver, an escort to assist the frailer older people and, where necessary, to take shopping into a person's house. The service is primarily aimed at individuals who can no longer drive themselves, or get about on their own, and who are at risk of becoming housebound. The service has proved so popular that there is now a waiting list.

The organisers claim that the service helps to reinforce community and interpersonal links. They cite some encouraging examples: on one occasion, two sisters who lived about 10 miles apart and who, because of illness and disability, had not seen each other for some years, found they were on the same shopping trip. This chance meeting resulted in weekly contact via the scheme. Another example involves a man who had been caring for his wife who had Alzheimer's. Consequently, they had not left the house for some months. The scheme enabled both to travel on the bus and, with the escort's support, for the man to do his shopping as well as meet and socialise with other participants. Funding for the scheme came mainly from *Supporting People* with the Local Health Board contributing through the purchase of two minibuses.

Conclusion

Social work with older people is both challenging and varied. Empowering older people is possible and necessary (Thompson and Thompson, 2001). As Phillips, Ray and Marshall (2006: 4) suggest, 'social workers who choose this field cannot be shrinking violets – older people are not well served by social workers who do not question attitudes, resources, and priorities – they also need to be confident that they have something to say'. The tradition in Wales, would be to say 'Amen' to all that.

Questions for reflection

1. To what extent do you agree with Baruch's contemplative reflection, cited at the beginning of this chapter?

2. As the chapter indicates, there are conflicting views about the efficacy and heuristic advantages associated with promoting individual budget regimes. Do you favour their introduction? What dangers or advantages, if any, might arise from their widespread application?

3. One of the stipulations in *The Approval and Visiting of Post Qualifying Courses for Social Workers (Wales)* Rules (CCW, 2007) is that the content of any training programme should reflect 'current research and evidence, the service user and the carer perspective, current legislation, current policy and the inter-professional context, the Code of Practice and the Welsh context of social work'. Deliberate and reflect on your practice in the light of the above aspiration. To what extent do you think that practice across the UK addresses cultural, linguistic, and ethical considerations?

Further reading

Clements, L. and Thompson, P. (2007) *Community Care and the Law* (4th edition). London: Legal Action Group.

This is the 'Bible' on community care – the book is beginning to resemble the traditional family Bible in both size and weight. The scholarship is astonishing and the authors do not limit discussion to the provision and regulation of residential and domiciliary services, but also address issues of continuing care, mental capacity, adult protection, hospital discharge, Direct Payment regimes, carers' rights, and the legality of eligibility criteria. Emerging differences between Wales and England are acknowledged and partially confronted.

Lymbery, M. (2005) *Social Work with Older People: Context, Policy, and Practice*. London: Sage.

This book very successfully combines theory, social work history, policy and practice and, as the publishers claim, is suitable for a wide range of readers. Its clearly written style and analytical depth ensure a stimulation of interest at PQ levels. Drawing on sociological and philosophical theories, it also addresses key practice issues, such as the relationship between care management and social work and the interrelationship between social work and health care. The approach is reflective and balanced, and the content guaranteed to add to practitioners' understanding of key issues and dilemmas.

Phillips, J., Ray, M. and Marshall, M. (2006) *Social Work with Older People* (4th edition). Basingstoke: Palgrave.

This book addresses many topics and debates. It is very well written, addresses social work values, and provides cogent examples of the application of different theories and methodologies, including task-centred and person-centred approaches, biographical and cognitive behaviour therapy, and attachment theory in the context of bereavement. This excellent book confines itself to English legislation and UK government policies alone, suggesting that 'most of these apply to Wales too' (2006: 6).

Chapter 7

Engaging with the social model of disability

Bob Sapey

Introduction

Chapter 7 begins with critical reflections on the role of social work and social workers' understandings of disability as it is important to set the context for discussions about the PQ requirements of social workers to work with disabled people. The starting point is what is meant by 'disability' and 'disabled people'. The chapter suggests that PQ candidates will need to rethink and reconstruct their views of professionalism so that they are consistent with the social model of disability.

Understanding disability

This is the fifth time that I have been asked to contribute on the topic of disability to a social work textbook. Each time my chapter has appeared alongside several others with titles reflecting the dominant ways in which social workers define and compartmentalise their work. This would always include other service user groupings based on the body, such as older people and children, but perhaps also by functional need such as fostering and adoption. Writing as I do from a social model perspective (Oliver and Sapey, 2006), an approach that examines the social construction of material and attitudinal barriers to disabled people's participation in society, this always presents a dilemma as I am loathe to sign up to a definition of disability that is based on the current UK social services' administrative category. Not only does this potentially impose a label and deny people the opportunity of self-definition, it also changes over time and from one area to another.

In local authorities, the term 'disabled people' is still used by social workers in the sense of the National Assistance Act 1948, to refer to adults under retirement age with substantial and permanent physical impairments. Alongside this term, social workers will distinguish other groups such as: older people; sensorially impaired people; adults with learning difficulties; disabled children; children with learning difficulties; mentally ill adults below retirement age; children and adolescents with mental

health problems; elderly mentally 'infirm' people; and patients with chronic illnesses. The precise wording of each group may vary from one authority to another, but the first point to be made is that social workers and their managers use the term 'disabled' to describe a functional division of their roles within local authority employment, rather than as a biological or even legal description of a group of people. Elsewhere within UK disability policy, all these different groups are afforded protection under disability discrimination legislation and therefore the term 'disabled people' has quite a different meaning.

Section 1 of the Disability Discrimination Act 1995 (DDA) defines a disabled person as a person with 'a physical or mental impairment which has a substantial and long-term adverse effect on his [*sic*] ability to carry out normal day-to-day activities'. In recognition of the difficulty in identifying impairments, the government states that they should be understood in their ordinary sense, and that the important factor is that they have an effect on a person's ability to carry out normal day-to-day activities. Furthermore, unlike social welfare enactments, this definition of disability is inclusive of impairments that may arise through old age and it will include long-term problems, rather than just those that are permanent. Disability can also arise from a wide range of causes and this was a significant feature of the Disability Discrimination Act 2005, which amended the 1995 Act. The following are listed in the guidance to the 2005 Act:

- Sensory impairments, such as those affecting sight or hearing;
- Impairments with fluctuating or recurring effects such as rheumatoid arthritis, myalgic encephalitis (ME)/chronic fatigue syndrome (CFS), fibromyalgia, depression and epilepsy;
- Progressive, such as motor neurone disease, muscular dystrophy, forms of dementia and lupus (SLE);
- Organ specific, including respiratory conditions, such as asthma, and cardiovascular diseases, including thrombosis, stroke and heart disease;
- Developmental, such as autistic spectrum disorders (ASD), dyslexia and dyspraxia;
- Learning difficulties;
- Mental health conditions and mental illnesses, such as depression, schizophrenia, eating disorders, bipolar affective disorders, obsessive compulsive disorders, as well as personality disorders and some self-harming behaviour;
- Produced by injury to the body or brain (Secretary of State for Work and Pensions, 2006: 4).

The DDA definition differs from definitions used in the welfare field in that it tries to be more precise and in the main is concerned with the effects of impairment, rather than the impairment itself. However, the Act also recognises that discrimination may occur when a person's ability to carry out day-to-day activities is not affected and, as such, people who have cancer, HIV infection, multiple sclerosis, or people who are blind or partially sighted do not have to show that their condition affects them in this way. Equally, there is a list of conditions and behaviours that are specifically excluded from protection under the DDA:

- Addiction to, or dependency on, alcohol, nicotine, or any other substance (other than in consequence of the substance being medically prescribed);
- The condition known as seasonal allergic rhinitis (e.g. hay fever), except where it aggravates the effect of another condition;
- Tendency to set fires;
- Tendency to steal;

- Tendency to physical or sexual abuse of other persons;
- Exhibitionism;
- Voyeurism (Secretary of State for Work and Pensions, 2006: 6).

The meaning of disability used by social workers not only reflects a particular administrative category, it is also much more rigidly defined than that used elsewhere in the UK. However, from a social model perspective all official definitions have their problems. Their focus on impairments, or even the effects of impairment, is only part of the issue. There are also the impacts of disabling material and attitudinal environments, and of the psycho-emotional effects of disablism (Thomas, 1999). In social work itself, evidence suggests that barriers to disabled people's inclusion as social workers remain strong (Baron et al., 1996; Crawshaw, 2002; James and Thomas, 1996; Sapey et al., 2004) and this is accompanied by a pathologising rejection of disabled people's self-definitions, especially in relation to identity and need (Oliver and Sapey, 2006).

Role of social work

As Higham points out in Chapter 1, the UK National Occupational Standards for social work include an international definition of social work (Topss UK Partnership, 2002) as a key purpose, which has achieved wide acceptance in the UK. However, is it also true for people who use services? I should like to discuss three aspects of this definition:

1. Whether social work should be a profession;
2. Whether social work can promote empowerment; and
3. That social workers see themselves as intervening 'at the points where people interact with their environments' rather than being part of those environments.

Finkelstein (1981a) has long argued that there is a need for a change in the professional role within rehabilitation services – that professionals must change from expert definers of need and rationers of services and become a resource which disabled people use as they choose:

Finkelstein's argument

The endemic squabbles between rehabilitation workers about professional boundaries and the familiar farce of professional 'teamwork' can only be put at an end when all the workers and facilities in rehabilitation become resources in a process of self-controlled rehabilitation. (Finkelstein, 1981a: 27)

He also argued for the end of professions allied to medicine in favour of professions allied to the community (Finkelstein, 1999a, 1999b). The education of this new occupational group would be

based on disability studies and workers would need to be immersed within disability culture and politics if disabled people are to achieve real change.

In Canada, Nelson, Lord and Ochocka (2001) argued that to achieve a genuine shift in the paradigm of community mental health, professionals must abandon their role as experts and work in partnership with service users. For them, the transfer of services from institutional settings into the community simply represents moving the locus of a traditional medical approach to treatment, care and support. What is required to bring about real change is that service users have genuine control and service professionals do not.

Thompson (2002) calls for radical change and like Nelson et al. argues for working in partnership with service users.

Thompson's challenge to professionalism

In some respects, this user participation movement has had the effect of challenging the complacency of a traditional model of professionalism based on the notion of 'we know best'. ... The challenge social work faces ... is to develop forms of professionalism which are consistent with, and welcoming of, user participation and a commitment to equality and social justice – that is, professionalism based on partnership. (Thompson, 2002: 717)

Whether such change is possible is questionable. Whilst the British Association of Social Workers (BASW, 1980) may have argued for a similar change in the past, this approach was not included in their subsequent policies other than those relating to social work records (BASW, 1983; Øvretveit, 1986). The real pressure for change in practice has come from disabled people. For the last 30 years since the publication of *The Fundamental Principles of Disability* (UPIAS, 1976), disabled activists and academics have been trying to persuade social workers to change their practice with disabled people to one based on a social model of disability. One of the main proponents of such a change, Professor Michael Oliver, has recently concluded the following.

The social model of disability

...has had no real impact on professional practice, and social work has failed to meet disabled people's self-articulated needs. Twenty years ago I predicted that if social work was not prepared to change in terms of its practice towards disabled people it would eventually disappear altogether. Given the proposed changes by the New Labour government in respect of modernising social services, it seems likely that that forecast is about to come true. We can probably now announce the death of social work at least in relation to its involvement in the lives of disabled people. (Oliver, 2004: 25)

It is arguable therefore that for social workers to change so radically as to work in partnership with disabled people, they would not only need to abandon their attempts at professionalisation, but also abandon being part of an occupational group called social work.

The second issue that needs consideration in the international definition of social work is whether social work can be empowering. Freire's (1970) argument would be that as social workers are part of the powerful state, they should have that power taken away by disabled people. The idea that empowerment can be achieved by the powerful gifting certain resources may seem attractive in social work education and training, but it fails to recognise the control that remains with those powerful people over the resources that have been gifted.

Practice example

Whilst evaluating the implementation of direct payments in one English county, Sapey and Pearson (2004) observed that the local authority supported a care manager's decision to veto a disabled person spending part of their direct payments on a mobile phone contract. The care manager's argument was that this was a luxury item as opposed to a care service, whereas the disabled person wished to use the phone as a means of summoning help in an emergency. On the one hand, the local authority and care manager were involved in providing this person with direct payments which are designed to give greater control and choice; on the other, they wished to ensure the money was only used on traditional care services. The disabled person will not be fully in control unless the care manager's authority is completely and irrevocably removed.

The third point was social work's claim to be working 'at the points where people interact with their environments'. There is an assumption of neutrality on the part of social work in this statement. However, far from being neutral in relation to the social problems of service users, Holman (1993) argues that the ideology that underpins the BASW Code of Ethics (see Chapter 2) is intensely individualistic and 'minimizes considerations of mutual obligations, of environment and structures'.

Holman's view of the BASW Code of Ethics

...it opens the door to explanations of human problems which stress the inadequacy of individuals regardless of their circumstances. ... It diminishes the resolve to campaign against poverty and other societal forces, for they are regarded as outside the real scope of social work, which is just to deal with individuals. Not least, the climate that social work is to do with a professional coping with an individual client is a barrier to social workers acting collectively with user organizations and residents of communities. (Holman, 1993: 51–2)

For Holman, the solution lies in the development of mutuality as the basis of the relationship between welfare recipients and the state, but it also illustrates the extent to which social work is part of the problem. Social work is one part of the environment of welfare that disabled people have to interact with in order to gain assistance and unfortunately, they cannot call upon social workers to help them negotiate the problem that is social work (Davis, 2004).

PQ requirements

Whilst the international definition of social work as a 'professional' activity has been incorporated within occupational standards, in all four UK countries, the GSCC and the Care Councils reinforce the idea of social work as a state-sponsored occupational group by closely linking their requirements for PQ social work with adults to current government policies. This is important for what it implies about the Department of Health's, the GSCC's, and the Care Councils' views of social work's status – that social work is not an occupational group that can or should aspire for a conventional professional status, or one that involves the self-government of standards. Rather, social work is a range of tasks that are undertaken within a particular social context, and in the early twenty-first century that context is one in which the recipients of those tasks have control over how they are performed.

So what are the values that are required within PQ education and training?

Independence, Well-being and Choice (DH, 2005) and *Our Health, Our Care, Our Say* (DH, 2006c) are in line with English government policy, that disabled people are informed about the services available to assist them and enabled to participate as active and expert partners in their own care. So too are the Disability Discrimination (Northern Ireland) Order (DDO) 2006 that has made changes to disability discrimination law across a range of different fields; Scotland's support of the DDA; and the Welsh Assembly Government's funding of the Disability Wales 'Equality in Action' project to develop knowledge, skills and values for mainstreaming the social model of disability in service planning and delivery throughout Wales.

Recommendations

The GSCC in England states that in order to achieve partnership working, social work practice must be based on a social model of disability.

> ## The GSCC view of adult services
>
> The appropriate model for thinking about and engaging with this 'partnership of expertise' is the social model of disability. This model emphasises the disabling nature of the environment and institutions rather than a person's condition itself, capabilities rather than limitations and ways of enhancing citizenship and full participation in society by combating all forms of social exclusion. It is linked to equalities training and a comprehensive understanding of, and commitment to, challenging discrimination in all its forms. The social model requires social workers to overcome barriers to inclusion and reach out to marginalised groups. Programmes will need to foster a critical engagement with, and scrutiny of, the social model of disability. This should involve critically examining the impact of all models and approaches and terminologies used by other professions and disciplines. (GSCC, 2005b: 8)

This clearly raises a number of questions: first, about how social work education can encourage social workers to incorporate the social model of disability in their practice; and second, about how social workers might develop a 'critical engagement with, and scrutiny of, the social model of disability'. Indeed, many disabled people might argue that whilst social work practice must be based on the social model, it is not the place of social workers to criticise or scrutinise that model.

Incorporating the social model in practice

Some social work programmes have extensive experience of teaching from a social model perspective. A precondition of doing this effectively is to start not with social work, but with disablement, and this is best approached through disability studies (Oliver and Sapey, 2006). Disability studies has been defined as seeking 'to advance teaching, research and scholarship that is concerned with:

- the analysis of disability and the exclusion of disabled people as a social consequence of impairment;
- the identification and development of strategies for fundamental social and political changes that are necessary for the creation of an inclusive society in which disabled people are full participants, and are guaranteed the same rights as non-disabled people.' (www.disabilitystudies.net/dsaconf2003/dsa 2003.htm)

The incorporation of disability studies in social work education would require PQ programmes to start by critically analysing the ways in which disabled people are socially excluded by the lack of access to education, housing, health and welfare services, the economy and the political processes of British society. This would include the ways in which different occupational groups, including social

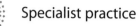

workers, have contributed to the construction of legal and professional boundaries that assist them in rejecting the responsibility to help disabled people holistically. Hence social workers commonly refer people to housing, benefits, or employment advisers and to paramedical therapists, whilst restricting their own involvement to matters concerned narrowly with personal (and sometimes domestic) care. Those institutionalised processes would need to be examined as social responses to people with impairments, as part of the attitudinal and material barriers to inclusion and as the prejudices that create psycho-emotional disablement (Thomas, 1999). At this beginning stage PQ candidates must learn to reflect critically about the effects of oppression on disabled people and the ways in which these are supported by state policies and their own actions.

Oliver and Bailey (2002) drew up a schema that typified three approaches to welfare. These are helpful for understanding how agencies that appear either to be benevolent or to be complying to the rules may be contributing to the oppression of disabled people.

Three different approaches to the delivery of welfare

Humanitarian approach: Services are provided out of goodwill and the desire to help individuals and groups perceived as less fortunate. Producers are in control of services and users are expected to be grateful. The outcome is often that producers think they are doing a good job but users are critical and seen as ungrateful.

Compliance approach: Services are driven by government policy and legislation. ... Producers adopt a minimalist approach, both to the principles and practice of service delivery, and do only what is necessary to comply with the law or government regulations. Service users often feel disgruntled because they think they are being denied something they are entitled to.

Citizenship approach: This requires disabled people to be seen as: full citizens with rights and responsibilities; as contributing members of society as both workers and valued customers (users); and to be recognised as empowered individuals (voters).

Only then will the relationship between providers and users of services be a truly harmonious one. (Oliver and Bailey, 2002)

Services to disabled people are still largely provided under the humanitarian and compliance approaches. Some local authorities are moving in the direction of a citizenship approach for other minority groups, for example by setting targets for the employment of people from ethnic minorities (Oliver, 2004), but in terms of social work services there is a deeply embedded professional resistance to a citizenship approach. In one English county studied by Sapey and Pearson (2004), the implementation of direct payments had been led by the Chief Executive's Department in conjunction with disabled people as they understood the implications that this system had for the broader citizenship agenda, whereas in the Social Services Department, this approach was not appreciated. In contrast, the Derbyshire Centre for Inclusive Living, which is run by disabled people and which takes a social model approach to service provision, argued for a reversal of traditional collaborative arrangements.

> ### Reversing traditional collaboration
>
> The people [DCIL] supports are not to be constructed as *users*, because such a role has constraints on what people might want to say about the purpose, direction and inclusiveness of public services. And it does not purport to *involve users*, because historically it's an organisation in which disabled people 'involved workers'. (Gibbs, 2004: 157–8)

Current changes being introduced as a result of *Independence, Well-being and Choice* (DH, 2005), especially in terms of disabled people being given greater authority to assess their own needs, will have a direct impact on how social care is managed and provided. I have argued elsewhere (Sapey, 1993) that the local authority role as the assessor of need within the NHSCC Act 1990 represents the continuity of an ideology of control over disabled people first seen in the Poor Laws. Disability equality training and disability awareness education can help social workers to engage positively with the social model of disability and the consequences for their practice. However, that can only be a start, and people are going to have to be quite strongly committed to working in new ways if they are also going to engage critically with the social model. The next section of this chapter will outline what a critical engagement might involve.

Critical engagement with the social model of disability

The origins of the social model of disability are inextricably linked to the development of the disabled people's movement in the UK. While disability activism can be traced back to the nineteenth century, the modern movement is generally thought to have started with Paul Hunt, a resident in Le Court Cheshire Home, who in the 1960s edited a collection of essays by disabled people intended 'to explore the experience of disability rather more realistically and in greater depth' than the 'sentimental autobiography' or writings 'preoccupied with the medical and practical details of a particular affliction' (Hunt, 1966: ix). In the 1970s Hunt went on to form, with other disabled people, the Union of Physically Impaired Against Segregation (UPIAS). Whilst segregation applied to all areas of social life, its most visible form was the nursing and residential homes to which disabled people were usually admitted by social workers. In 1976 UPIAS published *The Fundamental Principles of Disability* as a result of debates between themselves and Disability Alliance, a grouping of organisations *for* disabled people, but controlled by non-disabled professionals. It was this paper that voiced clearly for the first time, the principal definition of what would later be called the social model of disability (Oliver, 1983).

Definition of the social model

Disability is something imposed on top of our impairments by the way we are unnecessarily isolated and excluded from full participation in society. To understand this it is necessary to grasp the distinction between the physical impairment and the social situation, called 'disability', of people with such impairment. Thus we define ... disability as the disadvantage or restriction of activity caused by a contemporary social organisation which takes no or little account of people who have physical impairments and thus excludes them in the mainstream of social activities. Physical disability is therefore a particular form of social oppression. (UPIAS, 1976: 3–4)

Oliver (1983) argued that disability is a relationship between people with impairments and the restrictions imposed upon them by society. Finkelstein also argued that: 'Society disables people with different physical impairments. The cause, then, of disability, is the social relationships that take little or no account of people who have physical impairments' (Finkelstein, 1981b: 34).

In one of the more constructive critical engagements with debates about the social model of disability, Thomas (2003) emphasised the need to retain sight of the original idea, that disability was a social relationship. She countered those critics who had called for an abandonment of the social model on the grounds that it denied the disabling role played by impairment, by recalling and emphasising the importance of impairment to the originators of the model. Thomas went on to set out her agenda for the development of disability studies in the UK and I believe that this can and should form the basis of how social workers undertaking PQ can themselves critically engage and scrutinise the social model of disability.

Thomas's agenda for disability studies

I'd like to see our discipline rediscover the importance of the social relational understanding of disability that the early UPIAS pioneers introduced – disability as a form of social oppression – and to make this the foundation, the underpinning, of our work. We need such a firm foundation if we are to think creatively and with a purpose about a theoretical agenda for the future of our discipline.

So, ... here are my top four priority themes:

To develop a contemporary political economy of disability,
To understand the psycho-emotional dimensions of disability,
To theorise difference,
To theorise impairment and impairment effects. (Thomas, 2003: 6)

Thomas wants to update and extend the materialist examination of the relationship between political economies and disablement that had been at the centre of the thinking that originally defined and refined the social model. She wishes to set this in the context of the globalisation of capital and to examine the consequences of such changes for disabled people and the creation of disability. For social workers, these issues are reflected in the economic and institutional structures within which they work and which are intended to deliver services to disabled people.

The creation of purchaser–provider splits in local authorities, the development of economic outcome measures of effectiveness and the liquidation of community care assets into direct payments all represent different strands of the culture in welfare managerialism in an age of inequality, at a time in which dependency is no longer respected (Sennett, 2003). Abberley (1997) has argued persuasively that traditional economic theories, both liberal and Marxist, have always excluded disabled people because of their emphasis on a person's worth being based on their productivity. Sennett (2003) argues that in the post-war welfare systems of western societies, dependency was to be expected and it was not devalued in quite the way it is today in our current individualistic economic and social culture. Ellis and Rogers (2004) found that social workers not only believe the promotion of self-reliance to be a virtue, but they also perceive rights-based approaches to welfare as a threat to their professional authority.

I have argued elsewhere (Sapey, 2000, 2001, 2004a) that we are witnessing an historical shift from a situation dominated by what Finkelstein (1980) described as the hegemony of care, in which both the stigmatisation and deservingness of disabled people are accepted, to a time when disabled people are socially excluded from welfare if they are unable or unlikely to use that support to achieve a state of self-reliance. Morgan (2005) argues that the relationship with employment and productivity has been central to European Union concepts of citizenship. Entitlement to move throughout the EU is still based on being economically active or self-sufficient. Social workers need to understand what is happening to the structures and systems that exist to assist disabled people and their own role as part of the problem.

Thomas (1999, 2007) has argued that the psycho-emotional effects of disablism be added as a further dimension of the social model. This has been taken up with some enthusiasm within disability studies because it is seen as a constructive response to some critics, particularly feminists who had argued for the inclusion of personal experiences within the social model's politicised theorisation of disablement. Reeve (2002) describes psycho-emotional effects as having three main forms. First, there is an emotional cost to be paid when a person is socially excluded by, for example, segregated education, a lack of employment opportunities and a whole host of social and leisure pursuits. Second, there is the 'gaze' to which disabled people are subjected. This causes shame and over time people can come to believe they are at fault. Third, there is internalised oppression, the acceptance by disabled people of the prejudices against them. This leads to the acceptance of all kinds of abuse, justified by their perceived lack of worth.

Morris's (1997) work on the neglect and abuse of disabled children in care and her analysis concerning the collusion of social workers in this process illustrates very clearly how this is a concern for practitioners. But equally, it may be that the offence is experienced by disabled people because of the insistence of social workers and their employers on categorising and labelling different groups of people in ways that entirely disrespect their own self-definitions of identity.

This then overlaps with critically examining difference and differences. The construction of oppressed groups as 'other' has a long history and has been used to justify slavery, patriarchy and ethnic cleansing.

In Germany in the 1930s, state health service employees assessed disabled people to determine their fitness to survive. Many of the criteria used to decide if disabled people should be sent to camps were concerned with their functional ability, judged through an assessment of their domestic and social skills (Burleigh, 2001). Barnes (1991) has argued that the oppression of disabled people often consists of society deciding it is going to treat people with particular impairments in ways in which they would never consider treating others. This finding is reiterated in studies of disabled people's lives, ranging from violence and abuse (Rioux et al., 1997) to community care (Morris, 1993).

For social workers, the construction of 'other' is central to their own professionalising ambitions. Social work is an activity where the career path is traditionally away from practice, hence reflecting an ambivalent attitude towards service users. Social workers would like to claim that somehow their value base is one that allows them to confer more dignity and respect on people than do other occupational groups in health and social welfare. However, it is difficult to think of another group of 'people workers' who so rapidly move out of direct contact with their own clients. The question here is whether in the future PQ education will change or reinforce the hierarchical differences that exist between social workers and disabled people.

The final part of Thomas's agenda for disability studies requests that the academy theorise impairment and impairment effects. She argues that this is appropriate because impairments are central to the social relationship of disability and also because 'the particular character of our impairments plays a critical role in shaping the forms and degrees of disablism that we [disabled people] encounter' (Thomas, 2003: 15). It is difficult for non-disabled people to join in here, particularly those in occupations like social work that has done so much to promote an individual model in which impairment is seen as the cause of disadvantage and disablement.

It will clearly be a difficult task to get social workers to adapt to the role of overcoming barriers to inclusion and reaching out to marginalised groups. Essential to this will be the requirement that they also develop a critical view of impairments and impairment effect, but it will test practitioners' commitment to the social model.

Conclusion

In a study looking at disabled people's access to social work education (Sapey et al., 2004), our key finding from the review of literature was that social workers saw disabled people as *clients*, not as *colleagues*. This is a barrier to inclusion. In another study of research literature on disability that could be useful to social work practice (Sapey, 2004b), only one in eight papers or reports were from social work journals. More than half were published in the one journal which aims to represent the importance of the voices of disabled people, *Disability & Society*, and a further 20% were funded and disseminated by the Joseph Rowntree Foundation.

Engaging with the social model of disability does not mean having to set up alternative social work activities to these. It means joining in, even if to some extent that means rejecting much of what social work has been and has come to represent. PQ candidates must critically reflect on these issues, begin to reconstruct their traditional views of professional identity towards one that is consonant with the social model of disability, and change their practice accordingly.

Questions for reflection

1. Can you identify an alternative definition of 'professionalism' that fits with the social model's perspective?

2. How would you reorganise social work services to reflect Finkelstein's (1981a) argument that professionals must change to become a resource which disabled people use as they choose?

3. What should be a social worker's role in a user-run agency that offers support to disabled people receiving direct payments?

Further reading

Oliver, M. and Sapey, B. (2006) *Social Work with Disabled People* (3rd edition). Basingstoke: Palgrave Macmillan.

This book has been essential reading for students and professionals in the field of disability studies for 20 years, providing a comprehensive introduction to the social model of disability and its implications for practitioners. Extensively revised and updated, the third edition reconstructs social work practice with disabled people in the light of the latest legislation and policy changes. It provides a substantial challenge to traditional approaches by promoting a citizenship approach to social welfare. Above all, it stresses the importance of thinking critically about the welfare response to disability and urges students and professionals to reflect on and improve their practice.

Swain, J., French, S., Barnes, C. and Thomas, C. (eds) (2004) *Disabling Barriers: Enabling Environments* (2nd edition). London: Sage.

Part 1. *Perspectives of disability and impairment*: this first part describes some key theoretical issues within disability studies which form the book's conceptual framework.

Part 2. *In our own image*: these chapters set a developing agenda concerned with disabled people reclaiming the right to determine their own identities.

Part 3. *Controlling lifestyles*: this part covers some of the most significant barriers to participation – employment, housing, education, independent living, leisure, technology, communication, family life, ageing and childhood – and the way towards enabling is largely due to disabled people taking control.

Part 4. *In charge of support and help*: these chapters focus on social care services and the roles of disabled people and social care workers. The theme is the need for better partnership working and for recipients of welfare to take control away from providers.

Part 5. *Creating a society fit for all*: the final part focuses on aspects of achieving fairer societies that are inclusive in design, in which disabled people are valued citizens.

Thomas, C. (2007) *Sociologies of Disability and Illness: Contested Ideas in Disability Studies and Medical Sociology*. Basingstoke: Palgrave Macmillan.

Thomas has made significant theoretical contributions to disability studies, both in the UK and internationally. In this book, she provides an informed and informative overview of the development of the theorisation of disability within disability studies and medical sociology, as well as setting out clearly the ways in which these sometimes competing fields could find more common ground.

Throughout the last 30 years a few key texts in the field of disability studies in the UK have led the way in advancing our understanding of the social model of disability and setting out the conceptual frameworks within which the rest of us work. For me, this has included: Vic Finkelstein – *Attitudes and Disabled People* (1980); Mike Oliver – *The Politics of Disablement* (1990); Jenny Morris – *Pride Against Prejudice* (1991); Colin Barnes – *Disabled People in Britain* (1991); and Carol Thomas's own *Female Forms* (1999). Others may feel that I should have included certain other books in this list, but few would be likely to disagree that these volumes contain seminal ideas that have contributed positively to the development of disability studies. This book is the latest to join that list as essential reading for anyone wishing seriously to understand the current state of our understanding of disability.

Chapter 8

Learning disability

Kathy Boxall and Speakup Self Advocacy and Eastwood Action Group

Introduction

Chapter 8 offers a starting point for social workers who wish to study for a specialist post-qualifying award in work with people who have learning difficulties. It has been written by Kathy Boxall (who is a lecturer at Sheffield University) and the following members of Speakup Self Advocacy and Eastwood Action Group in Rotherham: Bryan Adams, Mariane Alexander, Chris Andrews, Joe Atkinson, Katie Beck, Trevor Cheetham, Janice Chicken, Carole Clarke, Richard Davis, Trev Duxbury, Roy Farnsworth, Vicky Farnsworth, Rob Flute, Annette Flynn, Christine Gervis, Shelley Leigh Hadfield, Laura Hitchin, Barry Hoden, Susan Lister, Kathy Masterman, David McCormick, Fayaz Mohammed, Alan Padfield, Shaida Parveen, Naheeda Razaq, Rabeena Sadiq, David Storey, Ernest Waring, Kerry Widdison and Naila Yousef. Two people who act as supporters to the self-advocacy groups (who have chosen not to be named) also contributed to the chapter.

Our chapter begins by looking at definitions of learning disability, the historical development of learning disability services, specialist learning disability social work, user-involvement and advocacy. We then go on to consider the voices of people from Speakup Self Advocacy and Eastwood Action Group who discuss their experiences of social work and offer suggestions for post-qualifying training, which we link to recent developments in policy and practice. Finally, we raise questions about social work's role in the changing world of social care and conclude by arguing that if post-qualifying social workers are to defend specialist learning disability social work, they will need to draw on learning disability research and literature that does not have a social work focus.

Our chapter is concerned with social work with *adults* who have learning difficulties, however references related to work with children who have learning difficulties are included in the section on further reading and resources at the end of the chapter.

What is learning disability?

The categorisation of service users into discrete 'service user groups' is fundamental to the organisation of modern social work practice. Although boundaries may be tested by resource constraints or by service users whose 'complex needs' traverse categories, the necessity for categorisation is taken as given and its legitimacy is rarely questioned. It is assumed, for example, that 'learning disability' exists and that there is at least some consensus about who should (or should not) be included in the learning disability category. Within the research literature, however, learning disability has long been a contested category and there is far from universal agreement about meanings attributed to the category or those who fall within its bounds (Jenkins, 1998). Conventional understandings of learning disability often refer to lack of intelligence, chromosome disorders and other clinically defined abnormalities. These ideas are consistent with an individual model understanding of learning disability (Oliver, 1996), which locates 'the problem' within the individual and frequently attributes biomedical causes to any difficulties they experience.

Official definitions of learning disability also tend to adopt an individual model approach; for example, the *Valuing People* White Paper, which sets out the government's strategy for learning disability for the twenty-first century, offers the following definition:

> Learning disability includes the presence of:
>
> - A significantly reduced ability to understand new or complex information, to learn new skills (impaired intelligence), with
> - A reduced ability to cope independently (impaired social functioning)
> - Which started before adulthood, with a lasting effect on development. (DH, 2001: 14)

A note that: '"learning disability" does not include all those who have a "learning difficulty" which is more broadly defined in education legislation' (DH, 2001: 15) further qualifies this definition. The term 'learning difficulties', however, is the preferred term of many Self Advocacy groups (see, for example, Emerson et al., 2005; Learning Difficulties Research Team et al., 2006). In these contexts, and within this chapter, 'learning difficulties' is used synonymously with 'learning disabilities' but only in the sense that the same people might be included by the use of either term.

Despite the stated preferences of many people with learning difficulties, the 'field' of learning disability is defined and controlled by those responsible for research, policy and practice in this area; acknowledging this, we use the term 'learning disability' in this chapter to denote the administrative category of contemporary policy and practice, and we refer therefore to *learning disability services*. However, when referring to people who are the 'subjects' or 'users' of learning disability policies or services, we use the term *people with learning difficulties*. In so far as our discussion includes people eligible to receive a learning disability social work service and does not extend to people who have a specific learning difficulty (such as dyslexia), we follow the Department of Health (DH, 2001) convention regarding boundaries to the learning disability category. However, the focus of our chapter is learning disability policies, practices and research, rather than any perceived 'deficit' of individuals with learning difficulties (see the section on the social model of disability below).

Historically, the individual deficit of people with learning difficulties was used to justify their segregation and institutionalisation (Potts and Fido, 1991; Ryan and Thomas, 1987). Social workers working with adults resettled from long-stay hospitals will be only too aware that during the first half of the last century it was not only people with learning difficulties who were removed from mainstream society and sent to mental deficiency institutions; people were also incarcerated for a range of other 'defects', including their different physical appearance or 'immoral' behaviour (Potts and Fido, 1991). Some of these people still receive learning disability services and continue therefore to be categorised in this way. Charlotte Davies (1998) argues that contact with the learning disability service system is inextricably bound up with an individual's identity as a person with learning difficulties. This 'pragmatic' definition of people as having learning difficulties by virtue of their receipt of learning disability services is, however, changing as inclusive education policies and integrated services blur the boundaries of the learning disability category. As Jan Walmsley and John Welshman (2006: 6) have argued, it is now possible for people to be in receipt of a range of services and benefits which are not learning disability specific and 'unless defined by their past as more traditional service users, they cease to be readily identifiable as people with learning difficulties'.

However, ideas of 'difference' are also powerful in everyday life and people with learning difficulties have argued that even in situations where they are not visibly associated with learning disability services they are viewed as 'different' by members of the public (Docherty et al., 2005: 38). Social workers also work within the norms, values and structures of the society in which they are situated. Children and adults with learning difficulties are rarely regarded as valued citizens in our society and they frequently face social exclusion (Emerson et al., 2005); many also face worse health treatment than people without learning difficulties (Mencap, 2007; Nocon, 2006). In the UK, abortion can normally be carried out only up to 24 weeks. However, it is permissible to terminate a pregnancy on the grounds of foetal abnormality right up to full term (Louhiala, 2004; Morris, 1991). Permitting late abortion where the foetus is identified as having Down's syndrome or other chromosome anomalies associated with learning difficulties conveys a message that the lives of people with learning difficulties are of lesser worth than the lives of people *without* learning difficulties (Ward, 2002). Learning disability social workers work within a society, therefore, where ideas about the lesser worth of people with learning difficulties are prevalent (Wolfensberger, 2000). They also sometimes have a role in supporting parents who have made a difficult decision to terminate an affected pregnancy. However, through their work to integrate and include children and adults in the mainstream, social workers also strive to promote the rights of people with learning difficulties and in so doing to influence societal norms and values, although their specialist role and the learning disability services of which they are frequently a part may also serve, ironically, to reinforce ideas of people with learning difficulties' 'difference' (Van Maastricht, 1998; Wolfensberger, 2000).

Normalisation and social role valorisation

Wolf Wolfensberger's (1972) principle of normalisation highlights the way in which people with learning difficulties have been devalued throughout the western world and points to some of the consequences of such devaluation, including being cast into roles such as 'non-human', rejection by families and communities and subsequent congregation and segregation within institutions. Wolfensberger (1972) argues that in order to break the cycle of devaluation, people with learning difficulties need 'normal' opportunities for 'ordinary' lives. This means that working practices or

individual behaviours which are not regarded as 'normal' need to be discouraged. However, Wolfensberger also acknowledges that the term 'normalisation' is particularly susceptible to misinterpretation and in 1983 he proposed a new term for his principle – 'Social Role Valorisation' or 'SRV' (Wolfensberger, 1983). This promotes the view that if people with learning difficulties occupy valued social roles (for example, having a job or being a tenant in their own home), then other people's perceptions of them will be enhanced and good things may follow. On the other hand, if they are congregated with other people with learning difficulties in segregated settings, they will be perceived negatively by others and will be denied the 'good things in life' (Wolfensberger, 1983, 2000). Wolfensberger's work has subsequently been criticised for shoring up dominant group ideas about what is regarded as 'valued' and negative attitudes about the 'acceptability' of people with learning difficulties (Bano et al., 1993; Brown and Smith, 1992).

However, in the late 1970s and early 1980s, Wolfensberger's ideas gave staff working in long-stay hospitals in the UK 'permission' to treat people with learning difficulties as human beings. Viewed in retrospect, this may seem obvious but to have acted without this 'permission' at that time would have entailed going against a working culture of deprivation and degradation (with all its in-built sanctions). This served to both deny people with learning difficulties individual humanity and worked to maintain a system upon which the denial of their collective humanity depended (Martin, 1984; Ryan and Thomas, 1987). Wolfensberger's ideas encouraged a service-level response which viewed people with learning difficulties as individuals rather than 'the mentally handicapped', and also offered a model or way of working with those individuals which promoted inclusion and an 'ordinary life' (Kings Fund, 1980).

Although Wolfensberger (2000) argues that his ideas can be applied to a range of 'devalued people', they have not been widely applied in work with other service user groups, nor have they been popular with the UK disabled people's movement (Oliver, 1999). The social model of disability (Oliver, 1990, 1996), on the other hand, has been enthusiastically embraced by many people with physical and sensory impairments but, until recently, has been less readily adopted by learning disability services (Race et al., 2005).

The social model of disability

The social model of disability (see Chapter 7) is perhaps most readily understood in relation to people with physical impairments; wheelchair users, for example, may be disabled by physical barriers such as steps as well as by the attitudinal barriers of others. The social model is concerned with *barrier removal*: if physical and attitudinal barriers can be removed – for example, through improved access to buildings, public transport, education and employment – people with physical impairments will be more fully included in the mainstream and hence will be 'less disabled' by our society (Oliver, 1990, 1996). However, some disabled people have criticised the social model, pointing to its failures to account adequately for their experiences of pain or suffering (Crow, 1996). Others have argued that the experiences of disabled women, black and minority ethnic communities and other minority groups have been neglected within social model discussion (Morris, 1991, 1996; Vernon, 1998). Other authors (for example, Chappell, 1998; Goodley, 2000) have argued that the

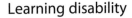

experiences of people with learning difficulties have similarly been marginalised. However, a number of people with learning difficulties (Aspis, 1999; Docherty et al., 2005) have now contributed to the discussion themselves and have argued that the lack of access has led to their marginalisation within the social model:

> We might want to study the social model ourselves but we can't because it isn't accessible. It should be in pictures and large print. (Docherty et al., 2005: 34)

Where such access has been facilitated, people with learning difficulties have argued that they are disabled by barriers to inclusion in mainstream activities. For many people with learning difficulties, the lack of access to information is a key barrier:

> Anything that's been printed isn't accessible if people don't read. The things that they've got out now, texting and the web and things, they don't make them accessible. That's a barrier. (Docherty et al., 2005: 35)

They are also concerned about the over-focusing of attention on things they 'can't do' and the effect that this can have on their self-esteem:

> When you say we can't do this, we can't get a job, we can't get a house, we can't have a baby, it makes our self-esteem go down, our morale go down. It makes you feel like you're worthless. It makes you feel sick. It's a type of bullying. And you get it drummed and drummed in all the time; that you're stupid, you can't get a job, you won't have a relationship or a house. Once people have told you that, that's how it looks and feels. (Docherty et al., 2005: 39)

However, people with learning difficulties have also argued that the removal of barriers would result in their being less disabled:

> If we could get rid of all the negative ideas that other people have and think of the positive ideas, that would help. Everything would be a whole lot easier and a whole lot better. (Docherty et al, 2005: 40)

The people with learning difficulties – Daniel Docherty, Richard Hughes, Patricia Phillips, David Corbett, Brendan Regan, Andrew Barber and Michael Adams – who contributed to the above discussions are all articulate members of Self Advocacy groups. This raises questions about the relevance of the social model to people with more severe learning difficulties. However, if social model arguments extend only to people with mild or moderate learning difficulties, then those with severe or 'profound' learning difficulties risk being 'left in the realms of static, irreversible, individualised biology' (Goodley, 2001: 213). The social model highlights the separation of perceived impairment (which is individually based) from socially created disability (which is imposed 'on top of' an individual's perceived impairment). Thus, whatever the degree or extent of an individual's learning difficulties, their experience of disability (that is, socially created restriction) is imposed on top of this (Barnes et al., 2002). Within this chapter, therefore, our discussion of the social model extends to all people with learning difficulties, including those identified as having severe or profound learning difficulties.

Specialist social workers

Although people from Speakup Self Advocacy and Eastwood Action Group are clear that social workers have played an important part in their lives (see Boxes 8.1 and 8.2 below), this area of work has not usually been prioritised within social work education: 'In general social workers have not been central to the lives of people with learning disabilities. Their professional education also reflects a lack of sustained contact with people with learning disabilities ... [and] specialist social workers are few' (Manthorpe, 2003: 266).

Qualifying-level programmes which offer dual qualifications in learning disability nursing and social work do provide some specialist training. However, the learning disability specialism is located in the nursing element of these programmes. The specialist social work path is therefore far from well trodden and there are few signposts or pointers available for social workers who wish to work towards a post-qualifying award in this area.

Part of the explanation for the lack of specialist social work in this area lies in the policies of institutionalisation of people with learning difficulties which dominated during the first half of the last century in all the constituent countries of the UK and throughout the western world (Wolfensberger, 1975). Removing people from their local communities was viewed as a more efficient means of dealing with 'social problems' than community-based social support and within the institutions, segregation of the sexes also served the eugenic ideal of preventing the procreation of those deemed 'mentally defective' (Thomson, 1998). Despite UK policies that provided for deinstitutionalisation from the 1960s onwards, resettlement programmes were delayed and for many adults with learning difficulties, reintegration into their communities of origin did not take place until the last two decades of the century (Race, 2002). Social workers played a key part in this resettlement process (Cambridge et al., 2005). However, historically, people working in a social work role also supported the earlier institutionalisation policies. For example, workers from the Charity Organisation Society and other voluntary organisations set up residential training centres for the permanent care and protection of 'feebleminded women' in the early part of the last century (Jackson, 1996; Thomson, 1998). More recently, social workers have supported and facilitated community-based provision for children and adults with learning difficulties and have, for example, developed family placement schemes and promoted Direct Payments (Dagnan and Drewitt, 1988; Leece and Leece, 2006). Developments such as *In Control* (Poll et al., 2006 – see below) and other initiatives that have followed the *Valuing People* White Paper (DH, 2001) have also included social workers, but have not generally been social work-led.

Specialist social work in this area has been further complicated by 'care management', originally introduced to manage the transfer of people and resources from long-stay hospitals to the community (Cambridge et al., 2005). Care management roles continue to be filled by people from a range of backgrounds, including community nurses and occupational therapists as well as social workers (Cambridge and Carnaby, 2005). Alongside the development of care management within wider community care services, learning disability services have also seen parallel requirements related to Person Centred Planning (DH, 2001), and recent moves towards Individual Budgets (Poll et al., 2006; SCIE, 2007). This raises questions about the relationship and relative status of these different approaches and has resulted in fragmentation, inconsistencies and the blurring of agency responsibilities (Cambridge et al., 2005).

Many people with learning difficulties and their families do not have ongoing social work involvement in their lives. They may, however, have regular contact with a range of health, education and voluntary sector workers as well as other social *care* staff who provide essential support. Self advocacy groups such as Speakup and citizen advocacy projects also play an increasingly important role in people's lives (Boxall et al., 2002). It can be difficult, therefore, to separate the roles and tasks of social workers from those of others who offer advice, support and assistance to people with learning difficulties and their families. It could also be argued that recent developments such as *In Control* (Poll et al., 2006) and Self-directed Support (SCIE, 2007) will serve to further blur the roles and boundaries of those involved in providing support to people with learning difficulties and their families.

The legislative context of social work with people with learning difficulties has not supported specialisation. Whereas specialist mental health social work has embraced the Approved Social Worker role, social work with people with learning difficulties does not fit well with mental health legislation. Section 1 of the Mental Health Act 1983 defines both 'mental impairment' and 'severe mental impairment' and makes provision for the detention of those people covered by these definitions who also display 'abnormally aggressive or seriously irresponsible conduct'. The inclusion of this latter phrase clearly indicates that legal detention in hospital should not be the norm for people with learning difficulties. However, since many people with learning difficulties have never been legally detained but have been placed 'voluntarily' in hospital by their families or carers, their legal status is unclear. This is because some people with learning difficulties are deemed to 'lack capacity' to consent to admission to hospital. Since they were admitted without their consent and without being compulsorily detained under the Mental Health Act, their status is ambiguous. However, the Department of Health (DH, 2006b) recently proposed an amendment to close what has become known as the 'Bournewood gap' through a Bill linked to the Mental Capacity Act 2005.

Service user involvement and advocacy

A key agenda in current social work education and in social care services more generally is increased commitment to the involvement of service users (Carr, 2004). The sea-change in the expectations of service users which such involvement entails is particularly marked in the case of people with learning difficulties, some of whom, in the space of 50 years, have moved from institutions where they were deemed incapable of caring for themselves to communities where they are involved in making choices about the services they receive (Walmsley and Welshman, 2006). They may also be expected to contribute to wider service development through involvement in Partnership Boards (set up to oversee the implementation of *Valuing People* in local areas) and in university teaching and research (DH, 2001; see also Boxall et al., 2004). However, service user involvement is not a one-way process and just as other disabled people have argued collectively for their right to equal treatment, so too have people with learning difficulties come together to form Self Advocacy groups such as Speakup Self Advocacy and Eastwood Action Group (www.speakup.org.uk) to campaign for change and speak out about discrimination (Goodley, 2000).

Although at first sight service users, service providers, policy-makers and university researchers and educators all appear to support user involvement, the power dynamics remain heavily weighted against service users, who may face poor access, confusing terminology and a lack of feedback when they are 'involved' (Branfield et al., 2006; Carr, 2004). As Simone Aspis (1997: 652) has argued, if

Self Advocacy is reduced to responding to requests for 'user expertise', service providers may effectively 'dictate what people with learning difficulties should be speaking up about'. However, people with learning difficulties have their own ideas and agendas and are increasingly speaking and writing about these (Docherty et al., 2005).

Citizen Advocates, who are independent of service providers but usually supported by an advocacy office, stand alongside people with learning difficulties and support them to get their point of view across, or speak on their behalf (Boxall et al., 2002). The Mental Capacity Act 2005 introduces statutory decision-specific advocacy (similar to Citizen Advocacy but restricted to support to make a particular decision) in England from April 2007 and in Wales from October 2007. This is the first time there has been a statutory basis or significant funding commitment for independent advocacy in England and Wales. It has also been proposed that 'specific key provisions of the Mental Capacity Act 2005 should be adopted in Northern Ireland, with minimal amendment' (McClelland, 2007: 14). In Scotland, the Adults with Incapacity (Scotland) Act 2000 was implemented between April 2001 and October 2003 but does not include provision for a statutory decision-specific independent advocacy service. In England, the Independent Mental Capacity Advocate (IMCA) Service was in place by April 2007 and IMCA advocates or 'case-workers' are expected to provide decision-specific advocacy in situations where a person is deemed to 'lack capacity'. The definition of 'lack of capacity' offered in Section 2 of the Mental Capacity Act 2005, like the definition of learning disability we refer to at the beginning of this chapter, locates the 'problem' in the individual due to 'an impairment of, or a disturbance in the functioning of, [their] mind or brain'.

A recent report commissioned by the Department of Health (Redley et al., 2006) revealed a lack of awareness of the Mental Capacity Act among social care practitioners, many of whom were also unhappy about the expectation within the Act that they are responsible for assessing a person's decision-making capacity. The report also emphasises the importance of social care practitioners understanding and supporting the IMCA case-worker's role, if decision-specific advocacy is to work effectively (Redley et al., 2006).

Voices from Speakup Self Advocacy and Eastwood Action Group

This part of our chapter is based on transcripts of two group discussions held in January 2007 with people with learning difficulties from Speakup Self Advocacy and Eastwood Action Group in Rotherham. The comments in the boxes below are direct quotes from people (whose names are listed at the beginning of the chapter) who participated in the group discussions. The two group discussions have, however, been merged in order to avoid linking individuals to particular comments. Contributions from people from Speakup who were acting in a support role have not been included in the boxes but have been incorporated into the text of the chapter.

Given the limited amount of social work support that is available to people with learning difficulties and their families, and the overlapping roles between social workers and other occupational groups, it would not be surprising if people with learning difficulties themselves were unclear about the roles and tasks of social workers. However, the people involved in the discussion groups had no difficulty in identifying what social workers did and the kinds of things that they could help with (Box 8.1).

Box 8.1: Social workers

- Social workers help you with your problems and they listen to your problems.
- They help you to do things – you discuss it with them about what you want to do, then they help you to do it.
- They sort out your funding and money.
- They take you to hospital appointments and back to the day centre afterwards.
- They help you when your kids are in foster placements – they check and make sure everything is OK with the placements and make sure that the kids aren't being bullied or anything like that.
- They give you a lot of help with your children – arrange it with you when you can see your kids. They can arrange access or contact so that your kids can come to your house, so that you don't always have to go to their place.
- They help you in court.
- They help you with relationships and sorting out arguments.
- They help you to move or get your own place.
- They can help you get a job as well.
- They give you support when you need it, like if you need a bit of support doing your shopping or dealing with money, they help you out.
- If you've split up with your family, they give you support and help you understand what's happening and where you go from there. (Speakup Self Advocacy and Eastwood Action Group, 2007)

Not surprisingly, people in the discussion groups viewed social work support as something which was time-limited. Despite this, it had clearly had an impact on their lives and many people could remember social workers who had worked with them over the years. Some also spoke very appreciatively of the help they had received (Box 8.2).

Box 8.2: Helpful social work

I don't have a social worker – I used to have one. He was good. He's been good to me. He helped me do things I can't do. I can read but I can't write at all. The social worker helped me to write forms.

My social worker was lovely, she was lovely. She did her job alright. She helped me sort out things.

They helped me to get out of Calderstones [long-stay hospital]. They talked to me and found out what I wanted. They found me somewhere to live.

A social worker helped me when my mum was alive and I lived at home. I was very worried about my mum at the time. I've never been a big drinker but my mum used to like to drink a lot. I wanted my mum to be careful, to go steady with her drinking. I told

(Continued)

(Continued)

the social worker about my mum and I had to go into a hostel. I didn't want to go because I was worried about my mum. The social worker came to the centre to have a talk to me.

The lady who I had, she was OK, she was fine, she talked to me, she didn't tell me what to do or force me into anything. The only reason why she was there was because of my baby's dad who's not involved any more. [...] The social worker used to come and see me and then she sent me a letter saying that she doesn't need to come no more. There was no reason for her to come because she realised that I could bring up my child just like any other mother or parent. I was pleased about that but I still get scared about it sometimes. But I listened to what she had to say and it turned out fine. (Speakup Self Advocacy and Eastwood Action Group, 2007)

Given that media representations often focus on the negative aspects of social work, it is good to report positive stories. It is also helpful to hear from parents who have had positive experiences of social work, as there is research evidence to suggest that parents with learning difficulties may face discrimination within the child protection system (Booth and Booth, 2005; SCIE, 2005a). In an attempt to help counter such discrimination, a recent report (Tarlton et al., 2006) outlines strategies for positive practice with parents with learning difficulties and the government has also published recent practice guidance in this area (Morris, 2007). Speakup Self Advocacy have also been involved in producing a video information pack – *Keeping Children Happy* – which contains excellent, easy-to-understand information about parenting skills (available from www.speakup.org.uk).

Although there were lots of positive comments about social workers, not everyone who participated in the discussion groups was happy about social work involvement in their lives. It is important to acknowledge that social workers have to manage the competing demands of government, employers, local communities, families and carers, as well as the needs of service users and may not always be able to act in the best interests of service users (Jones, 2001). Parents and carers may also speak more loudly than people with learning difficulties and where parental concern coincides with negative social attitudes towards their sexuality and parenthood, the voice of adult children with learning difficulties may effectively be silenced (Carson and Docherty, 2002). Hopefully, the new Independent Mental Capacity Advocate service will provide the positive support of an independent advocate in situations such as those described in Box 8.3.

Box 8.3: Unhelpful social work

I had a social worker a long time ago and she wasn't a very good social worker. When me and my husband started living together we were discussing having kids. The social worker came and my mum and my brothers and sisters and her had a meeting in the kitchen. They said I couldn't have any kids because I wouldn't be capable. They said if they turned their backs they wouldn't know if we'd have kids or not, so she made me have the operation. She wouldn't let me live my life by my choice.

Some social workers tell you should just have one baby. They try to, in a way, bully you and talk you into having a coil when you might not want to. Some people with learning difficulties feel a bit scared to say anything or do anything if something like that happens, just in case the social worker tries to force them into something else they don't want to do, or tries to bully them again. (Speakup Self Advocacy and Eastwood Action Group, 2007)

The combination of time-limited social work intervention and the need for continued involvement at key points in their lives meant that some members of the discussion groups had worked with several different social workers. There was general agreement in the discussion groups that some social workers were more skilled than others and people had a number of ideas and suggestions about the sorts of things they would like social workers to learn about at post-qualifying level. These fell into three main areas:

- Transport;
- Listening and communication;
- Choice, risk and protection.

In making these suggestions, we do not wish to imply that all social workers need to improve their skills and knowledge in all of these areas – as we have already mentioned, many social workers are already doing a great job.

Transport

For some people who participated in the discussion groups, getting out and about was a real problem. Those people who did not travel independently felt strongly that social workers should help with transport and should learn about it in their post-qualifying studies. It was clear that this was a very big issue and there was general agreement that the lack of transport could lead to people feeling lonely and left out (see Box 8.4).

Box 8.4: Transport

- Social workers should help us with transport.
- They need to take people out more, so they can meet more friends.
- Social workers should be able to drive and they need cars.
- They should take people out in their cars, people who can't drive. (Speakup Self Advocacy and Eastwood Action Group, 2007)

The identification of transport as a priority for PQ social work training is perhaps a little surprising. However, many people with learning difficulties are unable to access public transport without support. For others, current public transport is inaccessible, even with support. Budgetary constraints may mean that social workers' concerns to ensure that service users are safe take priority over issues such as transport to attend leisure or recreational activities. The concerns of people with learning difficulties from Speakup Self Advocacy and Eastwood Action Group, however, point to the importance of social workers highlighting the central role of transport in facilitating social inclusion, whenever they undertake assessments. Social workers can also direct service users and their families to welfare rights services and benefits which can be used to pay for support when using public transport, or in some situations to purchase a car and pay someone to drive it (Greaves, 2007). The introduction of Individual Budgets (SCIE, 2007) means that social workers' knowledge of different funding streams and ways in which funding can be used to support people to participate fully in community life will become increasingly important.

In common with other western nations, the UK government is moving away from traditional service-bound social care towards the provision of more personalised forms of support (SCIE, 2007). These developments build upon Direct Payments schemes that were introduced during the 1990s in all of the constituent countries of the UK (Leece and Leece, 2006). However, despite government guidance to local authorities to increase the numbers of service users in receipt of Direct Payments, take-up of Direct Payments among people with learning difficulties remained low. This was partly because of the mistaken belief that people with learning difficulties would be unable to direct their own care and support but also because of the legal requirement for service users to consent to receive Direct Payments and concerns about some people with learning difficulties' 'lack of capacity' to consent. This issue has now been resolved and there is clear government guidance that people with learning difficulties should be included in Direct Payments (DH, 2004c).

The *In Control* pilot project, spearheaded by the Valuing People Support Team and Mencap, was established in 2003 to encourage local authorities to set up new systems of social care support (Poll et al., 2006). The project has been looking at ways of tailoring support to the individual needs of people with learning difficulties and promoting *Valuing People*'s (DH, 2001) key principles of rights, choice, independence and inclusion, through the use of Individual Budgets or 'self-directed support'. An Individual Budget contains all the money a particular individual is entitled to from several different funding streams. At present, this includes funding from:

- Council-provided Social Care services (including Direct Payments)
- Supporting People
- Independent Living Fund
- Disabled Facilities Grant
- Integrated Community Equipment Services
- Access to Work.

In the *In Control* pilot, a single assessment process based on the principles of *self-assessment* (Qureshi, 2006) is being used to cover all the above funding streams. An 'independent broker' supports the individual to develop a support plan which looks beyond traditional services to what they would need for inclusion in the mainstream of society. There have been some suggestions that social workers, rather than 'independent brokers', would be well placed to take on the role of supporting service users' self-assessment (Beresford, 2007: 51). Once assessment is complete, the local authority allocates the agreed funding and provides 'light touch' monitoring. The individual can then spend this pot of money in a more flexible way, choosing who they wish to provide support, equipment or facilities, including private companies (Poll et al., 2006).

Early indications suggest that the new arrangements have been received favourably in the pilot areas (Poll et al., 2006). Funding has been used flexibly in a range of ways, including support to travel 'on the bus, just like everyone else' (Brindle, 2006). Building on this success, the *In Control* project has now been extended to other service user groups (Poll et al., 2006). However, self-directed support has also been subject to critique: there is an acknowledged agenda to 'save the state money' (SCIE, 2007: 4) and it is also likely that, just as with Direct Payments, a 'two-tiered system' will develop where take-up will be found disproportionately among the affluent middle classes (Leece and Leece, 2006).

Listening and communication

People from Speakup Self Advocacy and Eastwood Action Group also felt strongly that social workers should learn about listening and communication in their post-qualifying studies. Their conviction about the importance of this issue is evident from the comments in Box 8.5.

Box 8.5: Listening and communication

- Social workers should listen to us.
- They need to learn to listen to us more and find out what we have to say and then see what they can do about it, if they can help us.
- That's really a big thing – listening to us and talking to us, not talking over us, not talking to the person who's next to us. Talk to the person themselves with a learning difficulty, that's a really big thing.
- They need to remember to ask us if we've got anything on our minds, any problems.
- And give us time to say what we want to say.
- They should speak up clearly and tell us how we can get in touch with them.
- They need to know about different cultures.
- Social workers should make sure they tell us if arrangements have been changed, so we aren't left waiting ages for them to turn up.
- Be friendly, don't treat people bad. Treat people equal. (Speakup Self Advocacy and Eastwood Action Group, 2007)

There are a number of readily available resources on communicating with people with learning difficulties. For example, The *Easy Info* website (http://easyinfo.org.uk) collates advice from a range of organisations offering advice on communicating with people with learning difficulties. Speakup

Self Advocacy (www.speakup.org.uk) can also offer specific advice on how to make your information friendly, and Phoebe Caldwell's work on intensive interaction provides straightforward suggestions for communicating with people who don't use speech or a recognised signing system (Caldwell and Horwood, 2007). However, most of the concerns identified in Box 8.5 are relevant to respectful communication with any service user group or individual. Listening and communication skills are key aspects of the social work role (Topss/Skills for Care, 2002) and the requirements for service user involvement in qualifying-level social work education should hopefully mean that respectful communication with service users is included in these programmes (Advocacy in Action et al., 2006; DH, 2002). There is also a role for post-qualifying social workers in actively promoting user involvement in service development and training (GSCC, 2005a).

The Statement of Expectations from service users and carers (part of the National Occupational Standards for Social Work) includes expectations that social workers will:

- Involve users and carers in decision-making;
- Share records with users and carers;
- Build honest relationships based on clear communication (Topss/Skills for Care, 2002).

Current social work practice involves a considerable amount of text-based work that is inaccessible to many people with learning difficulties (Docherty et al., 2005) and text-based materials may pose particular challenges when sharing records with people with learning difficulties. However, plans and records can be produced in more accessible formats. Customised graphics packages can be purchased from the following websites:

- Access2Pictures www.peoplefirstltd.com;
- Change Picture Bank http://www.changepeople.co.uk;
- Valuing People ClipArt collection www.inspiredservices.org.uk;
- Photosymbols www.photosymbols.com.

These graphics packages have been designed specifically for people with learning difficulties who may have difficulty reading and consist of pictures or photographs rather than symbols. They cover a range of subject areas, including choice and control, home life, relationships and sexuality and, in addition to being a useful supplement to written records, they may also provide a valuable aid to face-to-face communication with people with learning difficulties. However, they are no substitute for the basics of good communication that Speakup Self Advocacy and Eastwood Action Group highlight above: *individual attention, good listening* and *time*.

A supporter from Speakup with close links to families of people with learning difficulties from black and minority ethnic communities spoke of the way in which 'language barriers' and 'misunderstandings' had resulted in lengthy delays in the provision of services to these families. The supporter felt that social workers could do more to make families feel comfortable about getting in touch and could also offer more support in situations where parents face 'language barriers' when accessing services. Two publications that accompanied the *Valuing People* White Paper (DH, 2001) highlight the needs of families of people with learning difficulties: *Family Matters* (Ward, 2001) and *Learning Difficulties and Ethnicity* (Mir et al., 2001). The framework for action which followed

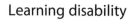

(DH, 2004b: 7) acknowledges that services are failing to meet the needs of people with learning difficulties from black and minority ethnic communities and makes a range of recommendations for improving services. One such recommendation argues that:

> Understanding and promoting cultural competence can be achieved by including people with learning disabilities from minority ethnic communities and their family carers in training and development of staff. (DH, 2004b: 45)

This important training role will require substantial support from those with responsibility for workforce development as well as from staff attending such training. As mentioned previously, there is also a role for post-qualifying social workers in providing and facilitating training and it will be important to include service users and families from black and minority ethic communities in any such initiatives.

Choice, risk and protection

Although few of the people from Speakup Self Advocacy and Eastwood Action Group had a current social worker, they felt there was an ongoing role for social workers in their lives, particularly in relation to protection from harm or abuse. People participating in the discussion groups wanted to ensure that post-qualifying social workers understood the importance of this protective role. They also recognised that effective social work requires skills and knowledge, and the comments in Box 8.6 indicate their understanding of the complexities of the social work role and also their expectations of social workers.

Box 8.6: Choice, risk and protection

- Social workers need to learn about choices. They should let us have a choice of what we want, and let us say what we want to say, and treat us with respect, and let us bring our children up.
- They need to learn how to solve problems, so they can help us solve our problems.
- When we make a mistake social workers should respect us and understand because everyone makes mistakes and they should give us a chance.
- They should be positive, not negative.
- Social workers need to look after us so we don't get hurt.
- If we are doing OK it doesn't mean they can stop helping us, they need to stay until we are sure we can do it for ourselves.
- They need to learn about abuse – sexual molestation and things like that. They need to understand that it does happen to people and they need to find ways of finding out about it and stopping it happen.
- Some social workers don't know about complex needs, they only know some things. They need to learn more about complex needs, so they can help us. (Speakup Self Advocacy and Eastwood Action Group, 2007)

The people who participated in the discussion groups were all adults. Until relatively recently, there has been little acknowledgement of abuse or the need for policy guidance related to the protection of adults with learning difficulties. Although now well documented, the abuse of disabled children, including children with learning difficulties, was also slow to be acknowledged (National Working Group on Child Protection and Disability, 2003). Policies designed to protect adults who may be vulnerable to abuse have lagged behind those aimed at protecting disabled children, but Adult Protection policy guidance is now in place in England (*No Secrets* – DH, 2000), Wales (*In Safe Hands* – National Assembly for Wales, 2000) and Northern Ireland (*Safeguarding Vulnerable Adults* – Social Services Directorate, 2006); and the Adult Support and Protection (Scotland) Act received Royal Assent in March 2007.

The protection of vulnerable adults requires complex, multi-agency collaboration in order to translate policy guidance into practice. Research undertaken by Ruth Northway and colleagues (2007) in Wales found inconsistencies among agencies regarding their interpretation and implementation of the *In Safe Hands* policy guidance, with variation as to what might be considered abuse or who might be regarded a perpetrator. Their findings also highlight the problem of 'policy overload' and suggest that although aware of their existence, individual staff may have limited understanding of adult protection policies.

A review of research evidence relating to the perceptions and management of risk in adult social care (Mitchell and Glendinning, 2007) suggests that staff working with adults with learning difficulties may be familiar with normalisation ideas and, as a consequence, may view risk and risk-taking as a normal part of everyday life. However, the studies reviewed also indicate that the views of risk which are held by staff sometimes conflict with those of parents and carers, who may be more concerned to protect people with learning difficulties from what they perceive as the dangers of everyday life. Mitchell and Glendinning (2007) also note the greater attention given in the studies they reviewed to reporting the views of parents and carers, compared to those of adults with learning difficulties. It will be important that space is left for the voices of people with learning difficulties and their views of choice and risk-taking when implementing adult protection policies. Those people with learning difficulties who do not use speech or a recognised signing system will also need time and space to convey their perspectives and feelings about these issues (Edge, 2001). Speakup Self Advocacy (www.speakup.org.uk) has made an excellent video about abuse – *Abuse is Bad* – which provides straightforward information about abuse and protection.

The concepts of choice, risk and protection are central to the social work role. There is a considerable learning disability literature which relates to choice and people with learning difficulties (for example, Edge, 2001; Smyth and Bell, 2006), but literature related to adult protection is less well developed and it will be important for PQ social workers to keep up to date with resources related to recent changes in this area, as and when they are published (for example, DH, 2007a; Pritchard, 2007). We also need to remember that there has been a long history of abuse and neglect in hospitals and residential provision for people with learning difficulties (Martin, 1984). There have also been several recent reports (see, for example, Healthcare Commission, 2006, 2007) of abuse in residential settings. It is important, therefore, that social workers are mindful of the possibility that staff employed to protect people with learning difficulties may neglect their responsibilities or may themselves be guilty of abuse.

Conclusion

The changes in social care which have occurred in the last few years have contributed to a legislative background which could support specialist social work with people with learning difficulties. In particular, the policy guidance surrounding adult protection (DH, 2000; National Assembly for Wales, 2000; Social Services Directorate, 2006; the Adult Support and Protection (Scotland) Act) and mental capacity (Mental Capacity Act 2005, Adults with Incapacity (Scotland) Act 2000) provides a legislative context for work with vulnerable adults, though this is not specific to work with people with learning difficulties and does not identify an exclusive social work role. Post-qualifying social workers may therefore wish to consider how learning disability social work – such as that described by people from Speakup Self Advocacy and Eastwood Action Group (above) – differs from informal supports or the interventions of other occupational groups. Critical engagement with the social work role is regarded as an essential aspect of PQ level study (GSCC, 2005a) and recent documents relating to the General Social Care Council's research into the professional role of the social worker (for example, Blewett et al., 2007) may provide a helpful starting point for such deliberations. The issue of the extent to which social work with people with learning difficulties is distinctive from social work with other adult social care service users is, however, another question.

As we stated at the beginning of this chapter, the boundaries of the learning disability administrative category are becoming increasingly blurred. Many children with learning difficulties now attend mainstream schools and may not receive social care services until they leave school – if at all. On reaching adulthood, some people with learning difficulties' contact with the service system will be limited to assessment for Direct Payments or self-directed support. Others will use more traditional social care services but some may 'slip through the net' because they have no one to assist them in obtaining services or support. People from Speakup Self Advocacy and Eastwood Action Group have a clear understanding of the social work role and its importance at key points in their lives. However, the most significant English learning disability policy document for 30 years, the *Valuing People* White Paper (DH, 2001), which set out the government's strategy for learning disability for the twenty-first century, pays little attention to social work; in its entire 149 pages it includes the words 'social worker' only three times. Post-qualifying social workers may therefore wish to consider arguments for a specific learning disability social work role.

Given the lack of previous commitment to training for specialist social work in this area, there are few specialist learning disability texts for social workers. Prior to the publication of Paul Williams's (2006) *Social Work with People with Learning Difficulties* (which is aimed at qualifying level students) it would probably be necessary to go back to the 1980s for examples of specialist learning disability social work texts (for example, Browne, 1982; Hanvey, 1981). When considering arguments for learning disability social work, post-qualifying students may therefore need to consult learning disability texts which do not have a specific social work focus as well as more general disability studies literature based on a social model understanding of disability (see the recommended reading and resources at the end of the chapter). As Michael Oliver and Bob Sapey (2006: 185) have argued, although much disability studies research has clear implications for practice strategies, the impact of disability studies on social work practice has been limited. Social model activists and academics, however, counsel against focusing on specific impairment groups, arguing instead for collective approaches which focus on disabled people's commonalities, rather than on individual impairments

such as learning difficulties (Barnes, 1998; Campbell and Oliver, 1996). Such arguments also appear to advocate a generic approach to social work with disabled people (including people with learning difficulties) which is not impairment-specific (Oliver and Sapey, 2006). Post-qualifying social workers may, however, wish to consider the extent to which such a generic adult social work approach would risk marginalising service users who have learning difficulties.

The Health and Social Care White Paper *Our Health, Our Care, Our Say* (DH, 2006c) indicates a clear role for social work with people who have ongoing needs, and the Green Paper on which it was based emphasises 'the role that skilled social work will continue to play in assessing the needs of people with complex problems and in developing constructive relationships with people who need long-term support' (DH, 2005: 10). The challenge for post-qualifying social workers will be to fulfil this role in relation to people with learning difficulties by drawing upon learning disability research and literature (much of which does not have a social work focus) in order to build a strong foundation for specialist social work in this area. The involvement of people with learning difficulties and their families will also be crucial to the development of a specialist learning disability social work role.

Questions for reflection

1. In your experience, how does learning disability social work differ from the support of informal carers or the intervention of other occupational groups in the lives of people with learning difficulties?

2. What are the arguments for and against specialist learning disability social work as opposed to generic adult social work?

3. How could *you* encourage the involvement of people with learning difficulties and families/carers from black and minority ethnic communities in staff training?

Further reading and resources

Books

Brown, K. (ed.) (2006) *Vulnerable Adults and Community Care*. Exeter: Learning Matters.

Grant, G., Goward, P., Richardson, M. and Ramcharan, P. (2005) *Learning Disability: A Life Cycle Approach to Valuing People*. Maidenhead: Open University Press.

McDonald, A. (2006) *Understanding Community Care: A Guide for Social Workers* (2nd edition). Basingstoke: Palgrave Macmillan.

Race, D. (2002) *Learning Disability: A Social Approach*. London: Routledge.

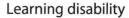

Read, J., Clements, L. and Ruebain, D. (2006) *Disabled Children and the Law: Research and Good Practice* (2nd edition). London: Jessica Kingsley.

Swain, J., French, S., Barnes, C. and Thomas, C. (eds) (2004) *Disabling Barriers: Enabling Environments* (2nd edition). London: Sage.

Mental Capacity Act training materials

In May 2007, the Department of Health, in partnership with the Welsh Assembly Government and the Social Care Institute for Excellence (SCIE), published online training materials to support the implementation of the Mental Capacity Act 2005. The materials include hyperlinks to the Act, case studies, exercises and audio clips and can be accessed from the SCIE website at: www.scie.org.uk/publications/misc/mca.asp.

Websites

Department of Health webpages on Vulnerable Adults: www.dh.gov.uk/en/Policyandguidance/Healthandsocialcaretopics/Socialcare/Vulnerableadults/index.htm

Department of Health webpages on learning disabilities and autism: www.dh.gov.uk/learningdisabilities

Every Child Matters website – contains useful information on safeguarding disabled children: www.everychildmatters.gov.uk

Research in Practice for Adults (RIPFA) website: www.ripfa.org.uk

Speakup Self Advocacy website – contains an order form for all the videos which Speakup have produced: www.speakup.org.uk

Chapter 9

European skills and models: the relevance of the social pedagogue

Jacob Kornbeck and Eunice Lumsden

Introduction

Chapter 9 considers issues related to the social pedagogue profession in three European countries – Belgium, Denmark and Germany – and the implications of this professional role for PQ social work practice in the UK. A key concern is whether PQ frameworks can offer social workers opportunities to adopt social pedagogy as a distinct role, particularly in England. This discussion does not imply that British social workers should embrace uncritically a paradigm that lacks a UK tradition, but suggests they would benefit from 'looking over the fence'. Social pedagogues apply their professional education and training to a range of professional roles in ways that differ from UK social work traditions. Yet despite differences, an implicit European social pedagogue model could provide a source of inspiration for new roles within children's services and adult social care.

The chapter is not aimed solely at providing more insight or satisfying academic curiosity about social work in European countries. Examples from Belgium, Denmark and Germany provide social workers with opportunities to reflect critically on their own roles and skills and how qualifying and PQ learning might converge. The discussion about European branches of social work, and how social work education relates to professional roles, may help social workers develop into critically reflective practitioners (Schön, 1983).

What is a social pedagogue?

To UK readers, it may seem puzzling that this book includes a chapter on 'pedagogues', a word suggesting the world of education rather than that of social work. Yet a look at social work and social pedagogy in European countries reveals that social pedagogues (including professionals with alternative

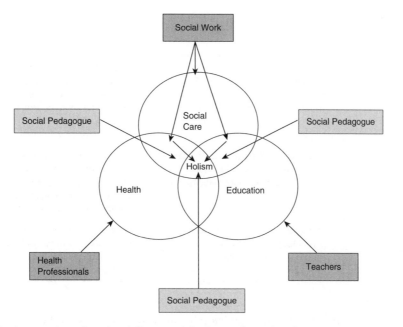

Figure 9.1 Intersection of service delivery and the locus of social pedagogues
(Source: Lumsden, 2005)

titles but similar profiles) constitute an important social profession. Whilst the idea of one social work profession is still prevalent in the UK, despite increasingly specialised practice, in most European countries different professions co-exist within a shared professional space of social work, conceptualised as 'social professions' (Otto and Lorenz, 1998). The 'social professions' often include a 'social work profession' strongly based on psychology, sociology and therapy, and a 'social pedagogue' profession whose competence profile resembles those of teachers and allied disciplines. Some social pedagogue curricula contain modules traditionally present in teacher training, but not in social work

Figure 9.1 identifies social pedagogy as a holistic professional practice, which could be located at the exact intersection of social care, health and education, or in fields where only two of these overlap. This intersection implies a variety of roles that deal with social problems from an educational perspective. It may appear strange at first that all these should contain common features, yet social pedagogy is a well-known concept in most European countries (although the name may vary), which actually covers all the fields shown in Figure 9.1. Social pedagogy is not exactly social work and not exactly education – it is an intriguing blend of both (Courtioux et al., 1986; Crimmens, 1998; Davies Jones, 1994a, 1994b; Hämäläinen, 2003; Kornbeck, 2001). Although differences between countries can be substantial, some shared characteristics are shown below.

The term 'social pedagogy' is not always used in social work literature, and that is why some relevant books with chapters about social pedagogical practice – for example, with looked-after children (Petrie et al., 2006) or with children and families (Freitas et al., 2005) in various European countries – cannot be identified easily with social pedagogy. Much social pedagogical practice and many social

Table 9.1 Professional designations

	Social Work	Social Pedagogy
Typical names of the profession	*Sozialarbeiter* (Germany, Austria, Switzerland), *assistant social* (France, Belgium, Switzerland), *asistente social* (Spain), *socionom* (Sweden), *socialrådgiver* (Denmark), *pracownik socjalny* (Poland).	*Sozialpädagoge* (Germany, Austria, Switzerland), *éducateur* (France, Belgium, Switzerland), *educator especializado* or *educator social* (Spain), *social pædagog* (Denmark), *Pedagog socjalny* (Poland).
Traditional practice strongholds	Social service departments of local authorities, children and families' services, occupational rehabilitation.	Residential care for children and young people, work with offenders (different age groups), work with people with various disabilities in residential settings (all ages), youth work in the community.
Typical curriculum	Strong elements from sociology, psychology, psychotherapy. In some countries, numerous law courses and law exams.	Education and some psychology, many elements in common with some branches of teacher training, many practical modules (drama, art, even cookery).

pedagogues do not carry the actual title, so that it becomes difficult to answer the questions 'what is social pedagogy?' and 'what is a social pedagogue?' in a clear-cut way. It may be said that social pedagogue professionals who practise in most of Europe would be, in the UK, associated sometimes with social care; in other situations, associated with education; and in yet others, with health. Social pedagogues tackle social problems in a holistic manner, drawing heavily on educational practices, but it must be borne in mind that British social work comprises many roles and is practised in a variety of settings. Children, young people and families, adult service users, and people with mental health problems are three typical practice settings that usually require rather different roles.

Table 9.1 summarises the main differences between social workers and social pedagogues in most European countries. (For reasons of brevity, the double forms (masculine/feminine) found in many European languages are not shown, but normally should be included in an English text committed to anti-oppressive practice, for example, *Sozialarbeiter/Sozialarbeiterin*.) Other specialisations that practise in France, Belgium, Spain and Switzerland include 'socio-cultural animators'. In Britain, social work traditionally is regarded as taking a lead role in meeting the care needs of a range of different groups, including older people and children and families. However, the complex roles in which British social workers find themselves means that they constantly have to grapple with and debate the nature of social work, and its place and acceptance in society.

European social pedagogy: inspiration for UK social work?

The model that emanates from these cursory descriptions and Table 9.1 may be termed 'European social pedagogy' – not a term used widely by academics or by official documents, but intended to guide critical reflection. The main question for reflection is whether PQ practice in the United Kingdom can use European social pedagogy as a source of inspiration – a question both practical and timely because the notion of 'social work' in Britain is not something given once and for all.

The British definition of social work has changed many times since the inception of the British Association of Social Workers (BASW), and the emergence of generic social services/social work departments with a unified, generic social work profession. Nothing should be taken for granted. Changes have taken place in the organisational structures of social work, with a divide between the roles of the state, the private, voluntary and independent sectors (PVI) becoming more prevalent in all areas of service provision. Consequently, it is not surprising that social work finds itself constantly searching for direction in a changing landscape of service provision. Thompson (2000: 12) provides a useful reminder about why this is the case, arguing that 'social work is a political entity and so, of course, how it is defined, conceptualized and implemented is therefore a contested matter'.

This debate is not restricted to the United Kingdom, but comprises a European and international dialogue (Gray and Fook, 2004; Powell and Geoghegan, 2005) about what the role of social work is and should be. This debate is integral to discussions about service provision and the professionals who provide services. As previous discussion illustrated, European social care provision is complex, and social pedagogues, as well as social workers, provide services in a range of settings.

British social work has faced numerous challenges, including a shift in relationships between purchasers and providers and, as previously discussed, PVI sector growth as a major provider of care. For some, social work's move to more regulated provision (Munro, 2004) has become too bureaucratic (Statham et al., 2006). Whilst there is debate about how to classify direct contact with service users, social workers indicate that actual contact time with service users has reduced. Administrative tasks have become more dominant as the social worker strives to become more accountable for how services are delivered. Need for accountability is fuelled further by the ways that safeguarding and child protection have been managed. Parton (2006) suggests a current repositioning in relation to safeguarding. One of the legacies of Victoria Climbie's death in 2001 and the subsequent Laming inquiry (2003) is reaffirming of the importance of multi-professional practice (see Chapter 10) for those involved with children and young people. The *Every Child Matters* agenda (DfES, 2004) provides considerable direction for how services will be provided and asserts the need for shared professional skills (DfES, 2005, 2006a). These developments include the English government beginning to engage with understanding the role of social pedagogy in Europe.

Within the climate of change, the United Kingdom sought to develop further the skills of social workers. The 'licence to practise' as a social worker at the point of qualification previously evolved from the completion of a certificate to a diploma. Today intending professional social workers must study their subject to degree level and beyond. The PQ frameworks that began from September 2007 (CCW, 2005; GSCC, 2005a; NISCC, 2005a; SSSC, 2004) could provide opportunities for offering pedagogy routes so that social work practitioners might develop their skills more holistically and place themselves at the forefront of a British pedagogic qualification framework. Changes in other areas of children's services, particularly in England, could offer social workers a way forward. Social work is not alone in redefining its future; other areas of provision for children, young people and families are experiencing a growth of academic qualifications aimed at developing a skilled multi-professional workforce (Lumsden, 2005). Chief among these is the unprecedented development of

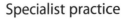

the Early Years Professional Status (EYPS) (CWDC, 2007) that could offer some social workers an opportunity to develop pedagogical skills.

Despite a move towards integrated services, professionals still need to retain their own distinct identities as well as being able to practise across traditional professional boundaries. This is where European social pedagogy has much to offer. An excerpt from a Belgian publication, below, is typical of a possible cross-over of the concept of social pedagogy.

A voice from Belgium

Educateurs work in and with everyday life and they fulfil their mission via everyday tasks. Often within a team, they are present round the clock and they help with most of the activities which everyday life may involve, by paying attention to the learning needs which are crucial and the autonomy of the persons with whom they work. *Educateurs'* work needs a certain direction and a sense of coherence, not a specific technical competence. The success of an intervention does not depend on the level of technical difficulties involved, but on the degree to which the professional manages to induce the required direction and a sense of coherence. If *educateurs* start being satisfied with the simple execution of tasks – be it the preparation of a meal, helping a child with its homework, organising a leisure activity, accompanying a person through an administrative procedure and advocating for that person, listening to an adolescent who is going through a personal crisis or caring for a young child – then these professionals will not evoke much interest. But if they begin to talk about why and how they carry out their tasks, then they will give rise to questions and debates about the values involved in relation to human development and participation in social life. (Gaspar, 2000: 2, Kornbeck's translation)

What is said about the *éducateur* profession (social pedagogues) would not apply to their social worker (assistants socieux), colleagues who are a smaller, more exclusive profession. Social work posts in Belgium are usually reserved for social workers, but social workers can also take social pedagogue posts.

Voices from Denmark

The range of posts that Danish social pedagogues may occupy is largely similar to the range of posts that could be drawn up for Belgium, whilst the range might be somewhat narrower for Germany. The brochure *Et godt tilbud* (*A Good Offer*) contains articles and job profiles for ten different social pedagogical settings in Denmark (SL, 2006, Kornbeck's translation):

These are:

- Children in residential care;
- Infants in residential care;
- Children with autism and ADH;
- Young people in secure units (youth prison equivalent);
- People with learning difficulties living on their own;
- People with learning difficulties living in a community;
- Adults with brain damage;
- Drug users;
- Adults with mental health problems;
- Homeless people.

The brochure lists many professional roles that British social workers would probably not instantly think of as being so closely related that the same profession should or could carry them out. The only problem with this diversity is that the generic principle has been almost too successful for its own good. Unlike Belgium, Denmark does not have one single study route for social pedagogy, which merged in 1992 with two other programmes (nursery and leisure pedagogy), initially in an effort to save money on the public budget. This means that Danish professionals involved in highly specialised social pedagogy tasks have the same initial education as nursery and leisure staff, creating a gap between professionals' skills and the demands made on them in practice. As a result, pedagogical graduates in Denmark are now reluctant to begin employment after attaining their bachelor's degree, and increasingly proceed to self-funded masters' courses.

New graduates increasingly prefer taking up new studies rather than going into practice straight away. According to Torsten Erlandsen, Education Policy Officer in the *Socialpædagogernes Landsforbund* (SL) secretariat, this is not a sign of elitism: 'They don't aim at moving upwards within the formal hierarchy to get into management posts, but rather at being promoted within the professional hierarchy. Many of those who consulted us would like a post with expert status' (Bengtsen Blem, 2006).

Is this a sign that they all want to become senior practitioners? Not necessarily, as Professor Kirsten Weber of the University of Roskilde points out. Her research is concerned with professions and their education and training, and her projects have a special focus on the pedagogue profession. 'I think on the contrary that the newly graduated pedagogues are realistic. They "read" the job market and question whether the amount of professional education they have obtained is sufficient in a life-span perspective' (Bengtsen Blem, 2006).

It may not come as a surprise that young colleagues have high ambitions, as Professor Weber reminds us: 'What is new is that, although they have taken a BA, they don't just accept that now they are going to work with that for the next forty years' (Bengtsen Blem, 2006). For a British reader, this may seem curious, given that the Danish BA in pedagogy takes three and a half years to complete (half a year more than the British honours degree in social work). One could argue that almost everyone in Denmark (and in Germany) studies longer than their counterparts in England, so that expectations about what constitutes sufficient professional education would vary. But it might also be, as Professor Weber says, that the young graduates 'read' the job market. Perhaps it does not make much sense to prepare for a highly specialised profession by studying on a strongly generic programme. This is a debate that relates to fundamental discussions in British social work education since 1970 – the year when generic social work education was introduced, replacing a series of old, specialised programmes. For SL, the trade union, the discussion is not closed. Vice Chair Marie Sonne remarks: 'I see this as an indication that professional specialisation is needed on the BA course – specialisation in social pedagogy. [...] Because if people who have just finished a three and a half years course still ask for more studies, then something must be missing on the course they just completed' (Bengtsen Blem, 2006, Kornbeck's translation).

Voices from Germany

The European social pedagogy model is clearly an abstraction because of differences between social pedagogy countries. Denmark and Belgium have a recognisable professional group of social pedagogues with well-defined higher education programmes. There, training usually took place in colleges that

lacked university status, but recently social pedagogy has developed into a more academic discipline. The German situation is diametrically opposite. A strong academic tradition has existed since the mid-nineteenth century, but there is no recognisable social pedagogue profession. Since 2001, the relevant framework regulation at federal level that defines the basics of German social work training does not mention social pedagogy, a development accompanied by lengthy academic debates since the 1960s.

'Convergence theory' has become increasingly powerful in German social work literature. Social work (*Sozialarbeit*) and social pedagogy (*Sozialpädagogik*) are two professions based on historical developments. Social work grew out of work with poor people in the nineteenth century and social pedagogy out of work in orphanages, as well as academic discussions about the role of education in society. Yet since the late 1960s, the use of a 'slash' to combine the two notions has become recurrent, reflecting a situation in professional practice where borders can be increasingly difficult to identify. Gradually, higher education programmes have followed this trend. 'Convergence theory' is today therefore the most influential model to describe the relationship between social work and social pedagogy, but it is important to note that it still represents one of several theories and that it does not stand unchallenged. Libraries could be filled with literature about the question, how social work and social pedagogy relate to each other, but Mühlum (2001: 12–14) attempted to simplify the many theoretical positions of social work authors and group them in clusters. As a result, at least six different 'schools' emerged. The three most important are:

- *Divergence theory* – claiming that social work and social pedagogy are profoundly different and neither can nor will merge;
- *Convergence theory* – according to which, social work and social pedagogy are two sides of the same thing. Their merger is unavoidable, although it may take some time. This theory is represented by the famous 'slash';
- *Subordination theory* – which implies that one of the two disciplines/professions must have a leading role in relation to both of these and build common theoretical models. It is usually university teachers in social pedagogy who follow this theory, which tends to be opposed by social work academics.

In Germany, by the mid-nineteenth century, social pedagogy (*Sozialpädagogik*) developed via the thinking of Karl Mager (1820–1858) and Adolph Diesterweg (1790–1866), first as a corrective to 'individual pedagogy' as an implicit model in school education. Then it became a philosophical model for broad questioning of the human condition, based on an appreciation of the individual's embeddedness in a community. This concept, promoted by Paul Natorp (1854–1924), was replaced in the 1920s by an interpretation that linked social pedagogy to specific professional roles, especially in work with children and young people. This rather anti-intellectual approach was epitomised in a famous definition coined by Gertrud Bäumer (1873–1954): 'everything that is education but is neither family, nor school' (Kornbeck's translation).

Social work (*Sozialarbeit*) by contrast, grew out of welfare work with poor people in the nineteenth century, but since the 1960s, social work and social pedagogy have virtually merged. German BA programmes are integrated in most states, and employers often advertise for a 'social worker/social pedagogue'. Curiously, the original notion of social pedagogy appears most strongly threatened in its country of origin.

Great Britain

This change in the nature of postgraduate study is reflected in Britain. The growth of post-1992 universities in the UK brought an expansion in the range of degrees, with work-based learning becoming an integral part of the British government's commitment to life-long learning. Foundation degrees were introduced in England in 2000, with the expectation that these qualifications would provide progression routes to honours degree programmes and beyond (HEFCE, 2000). The challenge for professions like social work is that qualification routes are complex, and in most of the UK countries, the licence to practise at the point of qualification is set both at honours degree level and masters level.

Inspiration for the United Kingdom?

Because the social work qualification is offered at both degree and masters levels in the UK, a PQ framework has to be flexible and meet competing needs and demands. It has to provide both a CPD framework and academic qualifications at honours and masters levels. Equally important are the roles of the employers who have to fund and release staff to pursue professional development. PQ frameworks are further complicated by rapid changes occurring in services for children, young people and families (DfES, 2006a). The challenge is to ensure that education, health and social care work come together to create the British government's vision of a multi-professional workforce with an integrated qualifications framework.

Accompanying these changes in the UK is the growth of research into whether social pedagogy has a place in the landscape of education, health and social care provision. Cameron (2006) and Petrie et al. (2006) provide interesting insights into the benefits and challenges of incorporating social pedagogy into UK courses and qualifications. There are no easy answers about how the tapestry of British professional qualifications can embrace and interweave the training afforded to the European pedagogue, although the benefits of such a role for addressing current policies are clear. This role can cut across traditional boundaries, allowing continued professional autonomy but producing something new to occupy the space of intersection where holistic approaches could benefit service users needing well organised inter-professional service delivery (Figure 9.1). One must recognise that social workers already work in these intersections and that knowledge and understanding of different professional roles and responsibilities are often vital in meeting the needs of, for instance, older people who receive care services. As discussed in the next section, social workers are skilled at working across professional boundaries and removing some of the existing barriers. Figure 9.1 illustrates that social workers can practise in all the areas that the social pedagogue occupies, but also have a place where disciplines come together to provide a holistic response to need.

We argue that the climate for social work practice is at a point where it needs to recognise social pedagogy's unique role in providing services. It could put itself forward as a profession that is ready to move beyond looking 'over the fence' in relation to social pedagogy by building opportunities for developing social pedagogical roles within the PQ framework. However, future provision for children, young people and families in England and the rest of the UK, and determining where professional boundaries start and end, and who does what, is a rapidly changing scenario.

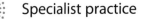

Early Years Professional Status

Despite engagement with European models of provision, the British government recently failed to use a unique opportunity in England to embrace the benefits of a holistic approach through a social pedagogic professional practitioner. The 'Early Years Professional with Early Years Professional Status (EYPS)' (CWDC, 2007) provides an opportunity for a radical approach to meet the needs of children from birth to age 5. The nature of this role, its relationship with early years teaching and other professionals, including social work, still needs to be negotiated, but what is certain is that the divide between education and social care in England has been removed. The Childcare Act 2006 (DfES, 2006b) lays down future development for viewing early years provision and how services will be provided. The EYPS has a pivotal role in ensuring the Act's successful implementation. National Occupational Standards for this professional role are evolving. An initial consultation process led to change because of a perceived bias towards education within the Standards. The revised draft Standards were piloted but concern remained about education remaining as the dominant strand. There was also debate about how to assess the Standards (Hevey and Lumsden, 2007) and how a range of professionals could embrace the role.

The Early Years Professional with EYPS is the first time an English government prescribed a professional role at degree level rather than allowing a role to evolve out of the need to improve services. The EYPS National Occupational Standards have a multi-professional and interdisciplinary dimension. Despite current uncertainty about the impact of EYPS on the early years workforce, the Early Years Professional's importance in forging a new professional role is evident. Embracing CPD (including PQ) for this role can be commended for social workers. The required knowledge, understanding and skills (CWDC, 2006) complement and extend the social work portfolio towards a greater understanding of education's and health's contributions. A social work PQ route towards EYP status would offer an opportunity for social work to embrace a holistic approach consistent with the European professional social pedagogue. At a time when English service provision for children and families, particularly for early years, is going through unprecedented change and financial investment, social workers might reflect on how their roles in early years provision might become more than just the final stop when all other intervention fails. The EYPS offers a route for social work to secure a role akin to social pedagogy and a new direction that promotes preventative work for those children and families who find themselves at the intersection of social care, health and education. A qualified social worker with EYPS could be a real contender in England for the title of social pedagogue, at the same time adhering to the core principles of social work.

At a time when British social work reflects on its location and importance in the provision of services, perhaps its starting point should be in relation to the commonalities of UK social work and social pedagogy and the additional learning needed for social workers to become social pedagogic workers. For example, adoption, safeguarding children, and mental health draw upon multi-professional knowledge, understanding and skills. The PQ frameworks can provide opportunities for the inclusion of modules that impart the knowledge and skills of European social pedagogy.

International and European dimensions

Bodies like the International Federation of Social Workers (IFSW), the International Association of Schools of Social Work (IASSW) and the European Association of Schools of Social Work (EASSW) share a belief in a shared core of social work values, knowledge and skills. Whether these are universal and transferable, or whether they are culture-specific and difficult to export, is an issue that occupies the attention of social work academics. It may be that social pedagogy is not so easy to export (Kornbeck, 2002). Whilst evaluating a new BA in Curative Education Programme in Scotland, which draws inspiration from social pedagogy, Jackson (2006: 69) emphasised an essential difference: 'The notion of "service users" as individuals to whom things are done is rejected by the programme. The learning relationship between student and child is characterised by *mutuality*, defined here as the respectful give-and-take between and among persons.' Given the centrality of the service user notion in social work, professionals can conclude that Curative Education contains content that could be common to social work and social pedagogy.

Conclusion

This chapter has argued that social work may be constructed differently in different national contexts, and that these differences are reflected in theoretical concepts that underpin professional skills and roles. Social workers' perceptions of UK social work roles must be revised when confronted with the reality of social workers' roles in other countries. But whilst this diversity might have surprised a British practitioner 20 years ago, it should not really be surprising today. Remember that since the 1990s, social work in England, Wales, Scotland and Northern Ireland developed country-specific traditions that since 2003 are under the regulatory leadership of Care Councils for each of the four UK countries. Each country-specific Care Council has developed its own PQ framework. Reflecting on European diversity should also lead to an enhanced reflection on social work diversity within each country of the United Kingdom.

Looking at professional profiles and roles in other countries should also help social workers understand current debates about the possibility of introducing a new professional role based on the European tradition of social pedagogy, which builds on social work's skills, roles and qualifications, and develops particular specialisms for practice. Although there is no direct reason why Britain should adopt models from other countries, UK social workers (particularly in England where social services departments have divided into adult social care and children's services) may be able to identify the merits of practising a version of the social pedagogue model.

Questions for reflection

1. Does a shared core of values, knowledge and skills, which could unite all social work roles in different countries, exist?

2. If a shared core exists, how does it relate to the different traditions of social work and social pedagogy?

3. How could these two traditions, social work and social pedagogy, co-exist in the UK in the future?

Further reading

Campanini, A. and Frost, E. (eds) (2004) *European Social Work: Commonalities and Differences*. Rome: Carocci.

This book provides a general but very short overview in English of the professions in Belgium, Denmark and Germany as well as other countries.

Gustavsson, A., Hermansson, H.E. and Hämäläinen, J. (eds) (2003) *Perspectives and Theory in Social Pedagogy*. Göteborg: Daidaloan.

This is an edited book with chapters (all in English) about social pedagogy.

Petrie, P., Boddy, J., Cameron, C., Wigfall, V. and Simon, A. (2006) *Working with Children in Care: European Perspectives*. Maidenhead: Open University Press/McGraw-Hill.

This is an anthology of texts comparing social pedagogical practice in Denmark, England and Germany as well as other countries.

Part Three

PQ functions

Patricia Higham

Part Three (Chapters 10–13) considers functions that traverse all the specialisms: inter-professional learning and multi-professional practice; research and reflective practice; enabling the learning of others; and leadership and management skills.

All four UK countries emphasise inter-professional education and enhancing skills for multi-professional practice (CCW, 2005; GSCC, 2005a; NIPQETP, 2005: 20; SSSC, 2004: 5). Practising in multi-professional teams may lead some social workers to fear that social work's distinctiveness is being watered down. Payne (2006) attributes their fears to trends towards more fragmented inter-professional service delivery arrangements, but argues that fragmentation provides opportunities for social workers to develop wider varieties of specialist practice.

The service user group and carer group that the editor visited to consult about the book emphasised how they valued multi-professional services. Chapter 10 *Inter-professional learning and multi-professional practice for PQ*, by Roger Smith, discusses challenges for practitioners who work across occupational boundaries, specific issues for social work, developments in training and learning for multi-professional practice, and the value and potential limitations of good-quality inter-professional learning.

To use research and other forms of knowledge effectively as 'evidence' that informs practice, social workers must develop critical reflective practice (Schön, 1983, 1987) that includes knowledge from a variety of sources. Chapter 11, *Research and reflective practice*, by Eithne Darragh and Brian Taylor, discusses the links between research, evidence, and critical reflection for developing expertise at PQ levels, using examples from Northern Ireland.

Chapter 12 *Practice education*, by Patricia Higham and Mavis Sharp, critically evaluates practice education's contributions to social work practice, arguing that it is an essential skill. The chapter considers how practice educators' knowledge and skills contribute to social workers' development within learning organisations.

Most leadership and management programmes for social workers focus on 'management' rather than 'leadership'. Chapter 13 *Leadership and management*, by Victoria Stewart, Laurence Taylor Clarke and Joyce Lishman, reviews a Scottish initiative that provided a postgraduate CPD distance-learning course in leadership for middle managers in social services. Its key motivation was to provide participants with the appropriate knowledge, skills and confidence to deliver effective leadership in current contexts of change.

Inter-professional learning and multi-professional practice for PQ

Roger Smith

Introduction

Chapter 10 provides a guide for practitioners and others concerned with developing professional knowledge and skills at PQ levels by focusing on questions relating to inter-professional working and its ever-changing terrain. The chapter addresses some persistent challenges facing practitioners who work across occupational boundaries; specific issues for social work; the demands placed on training and learning programmes; some promising developments in this regard; and, finally, the potential value (and limitations) of good quality inter-professional learning experiences in promoting better practice.

Having discrete tasks increasingly closely defined and subdivided into specialist areas of activity is perhaps an inevitable consequence of modern forms of organisation. Weber's (1957) formative work anticipated the emergence of distinctive and tightly prescribed roles in large-scale public bureaucracies. Baumann (1992) suggested that the proliferation and fragmentation of roles and functions are features of the postmodern world.

These trends are evident in social work, where the continual designation of new functions and job titles results in a need to differentiate the specific duties attached to each role. Some relatively recent innovations ('care manager' or 'family support worker') have become recognised specialist activities relatively quickly. The emergence of new social work roles and functions is mirrored by similar trends in health and education. The consequences are an increasing complexity and an uncertainty of working relationships, on the one hand, and a proliferation of new challenges for training staff to work together, on the other.

When considering these trends, the reversion to genericism in qualifying-level social work education and training from 2003 is an interesting and significant anomaly. Genericism indicates a

continuing commitment to core values, knowledge and skills that delineate social workers' professional identity, cutting across the boundaries determined by user 'categories', sectors or practice settings. However, PQ frameworks across the UK are specialist in nature. These wider developments generate new challenges for social workers in negotiating diverse, complex working environments and inter-professional relationships. In England, the separation of strategic responsibility for adults' and children's services from 2006 compounds the challenge. The question of whether or not inter-agency working is desirable is much less significant than the immediate practical task of developing holistic approaches to meeting service users' needs, which requires a commitment to effective joint working. In short, in the present era, social workers cannot avoid multi-professional practice. One feature of a contemporary professional toolkit for PQ practice is a capacity to work flexibly and effectively across a range of functional, agency and even sector boundaries, in the ultimate interests of benefiting service users.

Inter-professional working: challenges and possibilities

The drive both to specialise and to integrate has been apparent probably since the emergence of a modern welfare state with its formalised responsibilities and service delivery arrangements. A series of recurrent themes, representing persistent challenges to effective interdisciplinary working, include:

- Boundary disputes: 'whose job is this?';
- Status issues: 'you don't have the right to tell me what to do';
- Language barriers: 'is this individual a patient or a service user?';
- Competing practice models: 'which is more valid, the "social" or "medical" model?';
- Complex accountabilities: 'who will take the blame if this goes wrong?';
- Decision-making rights: 'who takes the lead here?'; and
- Social factors: gender, ethnicity, and culture, for example.

Certain inbuilt challenges must be considered as well as others that are more contingent, such as the potential for personal conflict and uncertainty, and acknowledged generic problems of effective teamworking.

When contemplating inter- or multi-professional working as a preferred operational strategy, some key issues should be addressed. One such comprises the obvious structural impediments to good working relationships between professionals with different histories and mutual expectations (doctors, nurses and social workers), where status differences and implicit professional hierarchies are accepted almost routinely, and the 'older' more established medical profession carries more authority and credibility than the 'newer' social care professions. Lymbery (2006: 1124) illustrates the challenges to social workers in achieving credibility for services to older people: the 'uncertain professional status of social work creates a particular problem in relation to the development of collaborative working'. Lymbery suggests that social workers' opportunities to contribute their distinctive professional skills and knowledge still depend on doctors' approval. Improved collaborative practices have been achieved only in the face of this status and power imbalance, a problem that may be associated with the importation of widely held conventional assumptions into the practice sphere. Ingrained beliefs are as likely to affect practitioners as well as those on the outside. Other, more tangible signs of difference, such as gender, ethnicity, or the relative value of cars parked outside the office may reinforce underlying assumptions.

Almost inevitably, perceived differences will be imported into specific working environments that require joint assessments and shared decisions about people's lives and the services provided. *Professional* differences must be recognised and valued, since these distinctive orientations will each have something unique to offer to the collective task. These differences should not lead to implicit hierarchies or a particular model's dominance. Tensions between professional perspectives are inevitable, perhaps desirable, but their roots and inbuilt dynamics can generate problems.

Potential conflict

Sources of potential conflict can be structural, policy driven, organisational, procedural, professional, or personal.

1 Structural

Differences of perspectives and priorities arise from how tasks and accountabilities are organised. A core activity for one professional grouping – for example, social workers' safeguarding of children – may be a marginal concern for education, health and police. This may account for some historic difficulties in mobilising partner agencies to take active roles in situations that social workers perceive as urgent and serious. These problems may be compounded to the extent that implicit professional hierarchies result in particular groups' interests becoming progressively marginalised. For example, a social worker may not be in a very strong position when seeking to negotiate the readmission of an excluded pupil on 'social' rather than 'educational' grounds.

2 Policy

Similarly, well-rehearsed arguments about policy 'silos' reflect the continuing experience of parallel developments that create tensions and potential disruption between professional spheres. At organisational levels, continual processes of restructuring, reinventing or dismantling service organisations reflect this tendency, leading to confusion about mutual responsibilities and roles.

Substantive policy initiatives can have the unintended consequence of measures to resolve one problematic issue having undesirable effect elsewhere. Attempts to end 'bed blocking' in health settings may lead to a mismatch of mutual perceptions between professionals. As Lymbery (2006: 1128) notes, this type of policy development intensifies tendencies on the part of health colleagues to over-emphasise one aspect of the social work role: 'social workers have always been valued in hospitals in relation to the speed with which they could enable beds to be cleared – a task which they have often resented'. Similarly, social workers in the youth justice sphere are likely to think that their professional standing and assessment skills are being under-valued when policy-led drives seek to 'reduce delay' in the administration of justice.

3 Organisational

Some problems for inter-professional working may be associated with the forms of engagement for practitioners from different disciplines – an issue in situations where they come together on an *ad hoc* basis around the needs and wishes of a particular service user, and also where they are delegated or seconded to work in more formally constituted multi-agency teams. In both instances, a lack of clarity about 'rules of engagement' and where decision-making authority lies can lead to misunderstandings and conflicts about sharing information or resources.

4 Procedural

Policy differences are reflected in varying and sometimes conflicting procedural requirements. The examples cited above illustrate the frustrations experienced by other agencies and practitioners when social workers insist on carrying out assessments thoroughly, according to their own professional standards. Boundary disputes may arise over rule conflicts, such as the circumstances in which information legitimately can be shared, or where competing definitions of eligibility might apply. Person-Centred Planning (PCP) and the Common Assessment Framework (CAF) represent recent attempts (DfES, 2004) to develop shared processes and tools for use across disciplinary boundaries. However, some procedural issues persist, such as the question of when to apply a particular assessment tool, and which takes precedence, demonstrated by the youth justice system's reluctance to adopt the CAF.

5 Professional

In some instances, inter-disciplinary conflict can be associated with a failure to recognise the legitimate professional perspectives of practitioners from other disciplines. Social workers should not underestimate the persistence of traditional stereotypes, but should be aware that external influences, such as the media, help to generate and sustain stereotypes and misconceptions.

Practice example: social and medical models

The strengths and limitations of the 'social' and 'medical' models of disability have been well rehearsed by now (Beresford et al., 2005; Chapters 7 and 8), but polarised views of their relative legitimacy and value still may surface. Equally, professionals from different disciplines may attribute beliefs to their peers that do not necessarily reflect their views or understandings. For instance, a medical student I met at an inter-professional learning event recently stated that the medical model would not prejudice every 'medic'.

6 Personal

Additionally, differences that are essentially personal may become 'professionalised' and transformed into apparently legitimate reasons for non-cooperation. As professions become more diverse, these differences are also likely to reflect gender bias or ethnic and cultural variations. The interplay between personal differences and conventional stereotypes is complex, but stereotypes may reinforce each other, leading to apparently justifiable 'professional' reasons for non-cooperation.

Practice example: child protection in Cleveland

Although occurring some time ago, one particularly graphic example of this kind of tendency was the consequence, in Cleveland in the late 1980s, of a communication breakdown between senior representatives of at least three professional groupings: the police, social services and health (Cleveland Report, 1988). As a result, mechanisms in place for responding to allegations of child sexual abuse became dysfunctional, leading to extremely high-profile and damaging confrontations between different approaches that had failed children and families in the area.

This brief summary suggests some potential concerns, on several levels, about the feasibility of inter-professional working. Obstacles can be identified that lead to strongly expressed doubts about its value. Effective mechanisms, including appropriate training and learning opportunities, should be made available to facilitate good practice in multi-professional environments.

Lessons from past experience?

For a number of years, research studies have explored inter-professional and inter-agency working across a wide range of substantive practice areas, including mental health, learning disabilities, the safeguarding of children and youth justice. Recurrent themes have emerged.

For example, Carpenter et al. (2003; Chapter 5) found that social workers expressed concerns about possible threats to their professional standing when working in multi-disciplinary mental health settings. This finding conveys a sense that social workers perceive that colleagues from health apparently do not appreciate the 'culture' and values of social work because social workers see themselves as different from health professionals rather than recognising potential differences *within* health. Social workers may be more inclined to recognise complexity and uncertainty as being natural parts of the practice terrain. In this respect, inter-professional misunderstandings and conflict may reflect cultural differences in seeking 'certainty' and closure.

White and Featherstone (2005: 215) make this point in other ways, suggesting that 'professionals working at the multi-agency interface operate with robust social identities, which they take for granted as members of particular occupational groups, organizations or teams'. Similar information conveys contrasting meanings according to participants' alternative perspectives, especially where uncertainty or 'ambiguity' is evident in receiving referrals (2005: 213). White and Featherstone provide concrete illustrations of variable practice (and underlying assumptions) in the time and depth given to the assessment of need, where initial paediatric consultations might last 10 to 15 minutes, whereas similar consultations by Child and Adolescent Mental Health Services (CAMHS) might last two hours, presumably covering a much wider range of issues. The definition of service users' needs, according to their research, reflects a tendency to differentiate needs according to professional disciplines, rather than to see needs as being shared across occupational boundaries. White and Featherstone (2005: 211) claim that a psychiatrist may define a young woman's needs as 'social', whilst a social worker identifies concerns that the psychiatric system does not meet obvious 'mental health needs'.

Frost, Robinson and Anning (2005: 189) identify similar problems of perspective and definition in the sphere of youth crime. Here, in multi-agency youth justice teams, a clear distinction is seen between social workers' 'emphasis on the young person's wider social and family context' and 'law-related' professions' concern with the 'impact on the victim/complainant' of reported offences. This contrast reflects a more fundamental difference of opinion about the most important considerations in any particular situation. Frost et al.'s study observed similar conflicts across a range of children's services.

One social worker in a health-based team commented that medical colleagues did not seem to understand the purpose or value of social work inputs. Associated with this rather exclusive view of the primacy of one particular discipline, evidence is also found of procedures, language and attitudes that compound a sense of them and us, leading to a 'circle of exclusion'. Despite this evidence, misunderstandings and inbuilt professional hierarchies do not mean that *practices* are fundamentally incompatible, but rather that polarising attitudes and processes should be challenged through 'joint training and co-practice' (Frost et al., 2005: 191).

The findings of Frost et al.'s research also highlight an important distinction between settings staffed by practitioners from a variety of disciplines, which are nominally multi-professional, and those that encourage or require genuinely collaborative working. In the field of learning disabilities, various attempts over the years have promoted joint working, but policy initiatives of this kind have not necessarily led to substantive changes in practitioner behaviours. Thompson (2005: 185) argues that:

> Even where health and social care staff had moved into the same building, few … agencies addressed effectively the combined issues of inter-agency and multi-disciplinary assessment … moving in together without adequate team development did not make for successful joint working.

In common with other contributors, Thompson suggests that one solution might be to identify core elements of joint professional training that would develop the knowledge and skills necessary for effective collaboration.

These examples identify constraints and challenges for effective collaborative practice at PQ levels, with a common belief that the challenges can be addressed, and that it is both desirable and achievable to promote and develop better ways of working together. Some solutions appear to lie in better structures, policies and procedures, and some in more 'joined-up' approaches to learning and practice development.

Benefits of joint working

Whilst substantial pitfalls may be evident, the search for effective multi-professional practice specifies its distinctive benefits: increased efficiency, more holistic interventions, creative and innovative forms of practice, responsive services, and, above all, improved outcomes for user-centred and user-led services.

1 Increased efficiency

Agreeing joint procedures for common practice requirements (such as information gathering, assessments and planning) should result in substantial savings in employers' and practitioners' time and effort, and a reduction in confusion, delay and duplication. Service users would avoid unhelpful and possibly counterproductive experiences such as having to repeat the same information time and again for a series of practitioners following different agency procedures. Tools such as the Common Assessment Framework (DfES, 2004) are intended to assist in achieving this aim.

2 More responsive services

A collaborative approach to practice should open up a wider range of services without the need for repeated referrals to individual agencies, and should enable practitioners to identify and access appropriate services more easily. Success depends on sharing organisational resources, and enabling practitioners to 'passport' service entitlements across a range of provision – a necessary element of a shared approach, since common assessment is of little use if it does not also promise entitlement to appropriate services in due course.

3 More holistic interventions

The argument is relatively straightforward: pooling skills, knowledge, and resources should enable services collectively to address more aspects of individual need at once, in ways that do not conflict or overlook key issues. Sharing information and ideas should offer increased certainty that all aspects of service users' needs and wishes will be considered, and the most appropriate interventions offered, rather than simply interventions that are most easily available.

4 Creative and innovative forms of practice

Collaboration should provide fuller considerations of need, which may open up possibilities that would not be available to an organisation acting in isolation. New ways of considering service user situations may emerge from sharing ideas. A common sense of purpose enables practitioners to feel more comfortable about making risky decisions and challenging roadblocks within parent organisations. Because conventional barriers are removed, practitioners find themselves developing new and original ways of addressing problems.

5 Improved prospects for user-centred and user-led services

The focus shifts in collaborative practice from singleton agency perspectives to perspectives that centre directly on the person who uses services – this person *is* the rationale for establishing a multi-agency team. In certain circumstances where inter-professional partnerships emerge on an *ad hoc*

basis, frameworks for delivering services may be specific to the one individual concerned – the intention behind initiatives such as Person Centred Planning (PCP) and the lead professional role advocated by *Every Child Matters* (DfES, 2004).

Inter-professional working: encouraging evidence

Research studies back aspirations for inter-professional working, to the extent that multi-professional practice has delivered tangible benefits. Examples of effective multi-professional practice provide some evidence that successful collaborative practice is achievable. Although their findings were often ambiguous, Frost, Robinson and Anning (2005) believe that some positive achievements can be associated with the development of multi-agency teams. Joint working in the youth crime arena involves distinct challenges in relation to clashes of belief and culture, but positive outcomes ensue from constructive engagement and respect for each other's differences. Multi-agency teams have scope to contain alternative perspectives and draw on these to test their ideas about good practice: 'Joined-up working does not necessarily mean doing away with difference' (Frost et al., 2005: 190).

In a different practice setting, practitioners jointly developed an information-sharing protocol (rather than use agency guidelines to block information exchange) because they were required to find a common basis for interventions (2005: 193). Frost et al.'s review of inter-professional practices concluded that the place of social work is particularly significant, especially in children's services (2005: 195): 'Arguably social work is *the* joined-up profession … that seeks to liaise, mediate, and to negotiate between professions and between the professions and the children and their families'.

Social workers' essential characteristics ensure that they are particularly suited to inter-professional working, and can make a distinctive contribution. Their inherently holistic, user-centred and networking aspects mean that they have a natural affinity with the key aspirations of collaborative agendas.

Examples of effective multi-agency arrangements can be found across the practice spectrum. For instance, Gardner (2003) identifies a fairly well-established model of collaborative working based around early years' services for children, where centres have been established to bring resources together and provide a range of non-stigmatising service provision for families. This kind of arrangement may be valued because services are organised around children's and families' expressed needs, but successful examples of this model exhibit specific features, including a joint, agreed 'meta-strategy', 'allowing for differences', effective 'dissemination' of shared aims and objectives and a willingness to learn from each other on the part of both practitioners and their employers (Gardner, 2003: 151).

Leiba (2003) suggested that collaborative working is likely to enhance practice precisely because it brings together different understandings and aptitudes; as a result, narrow assumptions originating from one perspective can be challenged and new thinking introduced. The process may be uncomfortable, but a spirit of critical reflection and mutual challenge is ultimately beneficial, as long as it is takes place within a cultural framework of trust and cooperation. In this way, practice assumptions can be reframed and horizons broadened, especially if service users and carers are included in a collaborative process. Douek (2003: 129) argues that close working relationships between social workers and health professionals can identify unmet needs, such as the impact of caring for an individual with dementia.

As these examples illustrate, the exact form and content of inter-professional practice may vary, from a willingness to share referrals at one end of the spectrum, to complex interactive processes of 'assessment, provision and coordination of care, monitoring and evaluation' (Evers et al., 1994: 150). Leiba and Weinstein (2003: 78) assert that certain elements, including: 'joint training and shared learning', 'trusting relationships', respect for 'differences', valuing your own and others' contributions, sharing tasks where necessary, and having both explicit 'protocols' and good 'informal' communications are essential for constructive joint working.

Social workers' contributions

Although social workers may face obstacles because of their professional history and identity, their specific contributions to collaborative practice are significant for a number of reasons. Social workers' perceived places in professional hierarchies have implications for their credibility with colleagues from other organisations, and the extent to which their contributions are valued. Research studies identify social workers as feeling marginalised, partly because they often have to operate on other professionals' terrain, partly because social workers believe that their professional knowledge and skills are not valued, or because other professions perhaps *over-value* their own contribution. Frost et al. (2005: 192) report a social worker in one study being 'aggrieved that some [medical] consultants seem to think highly of their status'.

A sense of one's place in an assumed hierarchy can flow in both directions. Frost et al. (2005) also report that part-time staff and early years staff in Britain feel themselves excluded from key discussions and processes. Social workers' hesitancy could be associated with ambivalence about their place in a professional hierarchy, but also about the distancing effect that any claim to professional authority and expertise might have on relationships with people who use services and carers. The question is not just one of whether or not full professional status is achievable, but also whether professional status is desirable if it prevents practitioners from demonstrating solidarity with service users, and results in them distancing themselves from service users.

Social workers' relatively tentative hold on professional status problematises prospects for effective collaborative practice. A concentration on practice with marginalised and socially excluded groups leads to social workers' sense of difference and distance. Social workers' focal concerns may be relatively peripheral to those of other 'mainstream' services; and, at the same time, social workers may encounter the challenge of representing the interests of undervalued groups (older people, people with learning difficulties) or groups that are perceived apparently as socially unacceptable (young offenders or asylum seekers). Here, the challenge for effective inter-professional practice at PQ levels is to ensure that colleagues from other disciplines recognise and act on these groups' legitimate claims. Lymbery (2006) argues that the task of establishing effective forms of multi-disciplinary practice in the interests of marginalised groups is highly problematic because of the coincidence of specific service users' powerlessness and the precariousness of social workers' professional standing.

If they are to assume lead roles in promoting collaboration from social work's own distinctive perspectives and in the interests of service users, social workers have to lay explicit claim to attributes that should be seen as essential components of multi-disciplinary service delivery. Lymbery suggests

that social workers can demonstrate at least three qualities that may not be exclusive, but are perhaps more central to their practice than that of other groups. These are:

- Social work's value base;
- Its 'relational nature'; and
- Its skills in service coordination.

Social workers are probably committed to a holistic view of needs and to anti-oppressive practice to a greater extent than other disciplines, for example (Lymbery, 2006: 1129). Collaboration is also based fundamentally on the time-consuming but essential task of building relationships with service users and carers. Perhaps because of this, social workers are well placed to identify and connect the important elements of potentially complex care plans. The idea that social workers are key agents in linking and coordinating interventions for older people is similar to that expressed about social workers' capacity to cement in place a range of services for children and families (Frost et al., 2005: 195). These ideas resonate with Blewett, Lewis and Tunstill's (2007) discussion of the roles and tasks of social workers in England.

Two other distinctive features of professional social work practice demonstrate the specific contributions social workers might make towards collaborative practice. The first of these is social work's 'social' nature, and its explicit function to link individual circumstances and needs and the social systems and contextual factors that impact on these needs. More than other professionals, social workers are expected to carry out assessments that make these connections, and then to act on them (for instance, in applying the assessment framework in children's services). Second, and linked with this, is social workers' (sometimes underplayed) responsibility to advocate on behalf of service users. Social workers are expected to respect the rights and promote service users' wishes according to the Code of Practice (GSCC, 2002a). The Code suggests that social workers should take an active part in advocating on service users' behalf (discussed in Chapter 3). This, in turn, necessitates their readiness to engage with other services and professional groups to promote the interests of those with whom they work. In this sense, social workers no longer have an option to think solely in terms of working within uni-professional boundaries, since social workers hold a core responsibility to cross boundaries where necessary, and engage with professionals who work in other service areas.

Social work and inter-professional learning

Previous discussion established the importance of PQ candidates engaging in learning that equips them for effective practice in multi-agency and collaborative settings. A number of principles should inform this learning experience to ensure it is consistent with social work's aims and objectives. Within a variegated working environment, certain aspects of inter-professional learning may coincide more readily with the prior experiences and orientations of specific groupings, but the overall aim should be to promote effective mutual understanding – not to teach practitioners to do each other's jobs, but to enable them to appreciate different skills and knowledge, and to develop capacity for practising alongside each other without 'giving up' any core principles or practices specific to their own professions. For example, the legitimacy of social workers' advocacy roles should be acknowledged and valued through the learning process.

The Centre for the Advancement of Inter-Professional Education (CAIPE) formulated the underlying principles of inter-professional education that articulate a vision of shared learning that is largely consistent with social workers' values. These principles unproblematically express the view that social workers should commit themselves to improving the quality of care, notably referring to the value of 'holistic' working. The principles emphasise placing service users' and carers' interests at the heart of educational experiences, with service users and carers being involved in the planning, delivery and assessment of learning activities (see Chapter 3).

The CAIPE model of inter-professional learning also emphasises the importance of mutual respect, and advocates interactive processes through which members of different disciplines should learn 'with, from and about each other' (CAIPE, 2006). The aim of inter-professional learning should be to utilise joint learning to promote 'mutual trust and respect, acknowledging differences, dispelling prejudice and rivalry and confronting misconceptions and stereotypes'. These aspirations are compatible with social work values, whilst also offering helpful benchmarks against which to evaluate models of inter-professional education.

Over the years, a considerable number of attempts have been made to develop effective approaches to inter-professional learning (Barr, 2002, for example), but detailed evaluations have yet to demonstrate a clear influence on practice quality and its impact on service users (Cooper et al., 2001; Zwarenstein et al., 2005). Claims can be made about improvements in participants' 'knowledge, attitudes, skills and beliefs' (Cooper et al., 2001: 236), but perhaps understandably, it is more difficult to trace these through into clear-cut benefits at the point of service delivery (Chapter 15 discusses PQ evaluation issues).

Barr (2002) claims that early examples often focused on perceived problems in practice settings and were targeted at professionals in their early careers. These efforts to promote shared understandings seemed to concentrate on the aspect of learning 'about' each other. Subsequent initiatives concentrated more explicitly on bringing experienced practitioners together to learn collaboratively, with a view to promoting better 'collaboration in practice' (Barr, 2002: 13). More recent developments have focused on qualifying practitioners, drawing together a wide, varying range of disciplines, partly because of the growing emphasis in most qualifying programme frameworks on the importance of inter-professional education (IPE), and an acceptance that this must be a joint learning experience.

An IPE model

Some IPE models (including the one with which the chapter's author is most familiar) have consciously sought to develop inter-professional learning in practice settings (Lennox and Anderson, 2007), which has meant that service users and carers can be involved in teaching and learning processes as active participants. Typically, this IPE model provides a framework within which multi-professional groups of students can meet with current service users, explore with them their needs, wishes and experiences of the services provided for them, and critically evaluate both the quality of collaborative practice and the service outcomes. This model is now well established in the East Midlands region of England, and a substantial number of qualifying students from different disciplines and different institutions are now involved each year.

This IPE programme has been evaluated from a variety of perspectives, including students, community tutors, service users and participating agencies. Findings suggest that each of these groups reports positively on its involvement (Smith et al., 2007). In particular, service users have welcomed opportunities to share their 'expertise', and participating students report a more positive view of other disciplines and professions. The model appears to be particularly effective in offering 'real-life' insights into both the strengths and shortcomings of collaborative practice, specifically from the point of view of the intended beneficiaries, and therefore should be readily transferable to additional disciplines and to other phases of professional development, including the PQ frameworks. The underlying questions and challenges remain the same: how can practitioners best achieve effective inter-professional working that meets the aspirations and needs of those who use services?

Conclusion: the value of inter-professional learning for PQ

Whilst the idea of collaborative working is attractive, many potential obstacles stand in the way of its effective realisation within PQ practice. Barriers are likely to result from structural, organisational, professional and, indeed, personal differences. For social workers in particular, their uncertain relationships with the notion of professionalism further compound the problem. Social workers are ambivalent about distancing themselves from service users by claiming professional authority and expertise; at the same time, there has been considerable scepticism from elsewhere about the validity of social workers' claims for professional authority and expertise. Here social workers undertaking PQ would benefit from reflecting critically (Schön, 1983, 1987, 1991b; Eraut, 1994, see Chapter 1) on how they perceive themselves contributing to multi-professional teams, and then could use opportunities for learning within PQ to begin to think differently about themselves and ultimately construct a more confident approach to multi-professional practice.

The task of becoming accepted as full partners in collaborative practice is therefore bound up with the equally important job of articulating and promoting the distinctive qualities and skills that social workers can contribute at PQ levels: their distinctive approaches to user-centred, holistic and empowering interventions, which social workers hold as centrally important principles, and which can also be identified as specific *professional* attributes at PQ levels. As a consequence, PQ approaches to inter-professional learning that are based around the 'real-life' experiences of service users and carers and draw on their knowledge and expertise are likely to be particularly productive, whilst also reflecting core social work values, and enabling social workers to recognise and appreciate their own distinctive contributions to collaborative practice.

Questions for reflection

1. As a practitioner working in inter-professional settings, you may feel that you are being asked to 'give up' authority over certain aspects of your work. What do you think it is acceptable to give up, in this

sense, and what aspects of your distinctive professional role should never be relinquished?

2. In your experience, do you think that your own professional standing has helped to ensure that power imbalances in inter-professional settings have been (or can be) minimised?

3. Reflect critically on the most important element of good inter-professional working. Is it a clear understanding of each other's roles and responsibilities, or the quality of your relationships with practitioners from other disciplines?

Further reading

Frost, N. (2005) *Professionalism, Partnership and Joined-up Thinking*. Dartington: Research in Practice.

This book is an extremely helpful review of existing examples of collaborative practice, essentially in children's services, which incorporates a number of useful ideas about the potential for improving joint working 'on the ground'.

Leathard, A. (ed.) (2003) *Interprofessional Collaboration from Policy to Practice in Health and Social Care*. London: Routledge.

This book contains an important collection of chapters linking policy and practice concerns relevant to inter-professional working from a variety of perspectives, including service users, child and adult health and social care service providers, and some international reflections.

Weinstein, J., Whittington, C. and Leiba, T. (eds) (2003) *Collaboration in Social Work Practice*. London: Jessica Kingsley.

This edited collection provides a focused view of what inter-professional practice feels like from the social work perspective. It is not uncritical and offers a number of helpful accounts of some of the potential shortcomings of inter-professional working as well as its possible benefits. The book also includes some interesting and important observations from the carer's perspective.

Chapter 11

Research and reflective practice

Eithne Darragh and Brian Taylor

Introduction and definitions

Chapter 11 discusses linked key factors of research, evidence, and critical reflection for developing capability and expertise at PQ levels. PQ social work practice needs to make effective use of research and other forms of knowledge as 'evidence' to inform practice. To acquire this capability, social workers must develop skills in critical reflective practice so that their learning includes knowledge from a variety of sources in a cycle of continuing professional development (CPD).

An emergent consensus within social work and other human service professions argues that professionals should strive to attain 'evidence-based practice' (EBP). Some academics prefer the term 'evidence-informed practice' to emphasise service users' views and professional judgements as well as a received knowledge base. Whilst acknowledging these views, this chapter retains 'evidence-based practice' (and its acronym 'EBP') because this term is now well established internationally across professions and within a wide range of human services, including criminal justice, education, health, and social care (Campbell Collaboration, 2007).

A critical appraisal of practice inevitably raises questions. Why should practitioners do things a certain way? How can social workers improve their current practice? These questions remind social workers of the limits of their knowledge. Social workers must make judgements on the 'best evidence' available from a variety of sources – research, professional experience, legal, policy, and procedural requirements – and incorporate this evidence with service users' own accounts of their situations, needs and aspirations (Pawson et al., 2003). The chapter examines how research can inform practice, provides examples of evidence informing practice, and explains how CPD can develop the relevant knowledge and skills that will help practitioners, trainers, managers and policymakers to base their decisions on 'best evidence'.

Issues in evidence-based practice

Not everyone supports EBP wholeheartedly. (For a different view, see Chapter 5.) Some scholars express concern that EBP initiatives will lead to restricted visions (Gray and McDonald, 2006), neglect of service users' perspectives (Webb, 2001), or the loss of human and ethical contexts of practice (Williams and Fulford, 2007). Others appear overwhelmed by the scale of knowledge available, and daunted by the new skills required for computer-based database searching (Taylor, 2003), appraising research quality, and synthesising research.

Where do the experiences and views of people who use services and their carers fit with EBP (McNeish et al., 2002)? Calder and Hackett (2003) argue that use of social work methods must be negotiated with service users and take account of service users' own understandings of their needs and goals. Proponents of EBP do not suggest that professionals should disregard service users' views because of particular research findings (Haynes et al., 2002). People who use services expect social workers to be as well informed as reasonably possible, to draw on sound knowledge, share relevant knowledge appropriately, and engage with the 'best evidence' in relation to making shared decisions about care and support.

Although experience is a valuable source of knowledge, social workers who rely solely on personal experiences to inform their practice run the risk of bias. Research on effective interventions provides some pointers to assist choices about which intervention is most appropriate for a particular situation (Gambrill and Gibbs, 1999; Gibbs, 2003). Research data, when available, give social workers some indication of the likelihood of 'success' (however defined) as a result of using a particular intervention within a particular context. These findings are increasingly developed into guidelines for informing practice (Rosen and Proctor, 2003).

Three types of questions for EBP must be addressed:

- *Social work effectiveness*: What works in social care interventions? Which aspects of an intervention make it effective? For which types of situation is a particular intervention most effective? How much does a particular intervention cost compared to an alternative that is equally effective?
- *Social work processes*: How do helping processes work? Are the processes acceptable to people who use services? What causes social problems, and how can knowledge of causes improve practice?
- *Social work decisions*: How *do* social workers make judgements and decisions? How *should* social workers make judgements and decisions? Can evidence improve decision-making? How should evidence best be used? What makes decision-making effective in a particular type of situation?

What works? Effectiveness in social work

Much of the effort in EBP to date has focused on addressing 'best evidence' for effective interventions, particularly to inform professional practice and expenditure on publicly funded services. In general, the quest for evidence of effective interventions leads to experimental studies where 'similar' service users receive different interventions so that research can observe different outcomes. To

rule out other factors that might influence the outcome (such as family factors, age, and changes in society more generally), the best approach is to assign participants randomly to two groups, one (the 'experimental' group) that receives the intervention being studied and one (the 'control' group) that does not. This basic design is known as a randomised controlled study. There are practical and ethical challenges to undertaking such studies in social work. When is it morally justifiable to allocate individuals to receiving a new treatment or no treatment? Is the alternative of 'delayed treatment' more easily justified in some contexts? Considering the potential waste of resources on ineffective interventions from not knowing about effectiveness puts the dilemma into a different perspective. But who should decide whether we 'know' that an intervention is worth using – the researcher, the profession as a whole, or should this be through some as yet undeveloped mechanism (Weijer et al., 2000)?

Parental mental health: example of using research findings

Research findings suggest that concerns for parents with depression in respect of their relationships with their children include the quality of attachment, engagement, sensitivity, emotional availability, ability to cope with the child's distress and appropriate behaviour management.

- *Child Protection: Messages from Research* (DH, 1995) was a key social work research document that highlighted the potential impact of parents' mental health on their parenting abilities and the possible negative consequences for their children.
- Cleaver, Unell and Aldgate (1999) and Harbin and Murphy (2000) identified the potential impact of mental health problems, substance misuse, domestic violence and social exclusion on children, their parents and carers.
- Fellowes-Smith (2001) claimed that clinical observations, borne out by research, suggest that children of parents with anxiety disorders are more vulnerable to anxiety disorders and a range of related problems.
- A Social Exclusion Unit report (2004) drew attention to research in the 1980s and 1990s that highlighted the impact of parental mental health on their children, claiming that nearly half of adults using mental health services are parents.

Practice example: Ms Collins

Ms Collins is a 28 year-old woman living alone with her two children. She had experienced a previous violent relationship and was known to mental health services since 1999 following the stillbirth of her second child. She attended the outpatient clinic since 1999, but in early 2005 the consultant psychiatrist referred her to the community mental health social work team because of her depression, panic attacks and distress. A social history was requested and completed. Professional input included monitoring Ms Collins's mental health; interface work with children's services, including attending case conference meetings; liaising with other professionals, primarily the children's services social worker, education welfare officer and general practitioner; therapeutic input, including grief work; and work with the older child, Jerry, in understanding his mother's mental health.

Because Jerry, Ms Collins' son, was not attending school regularly, he was subject to area child protection committee procedures. As part of this work, I attended a core group meeting to review the child protection plan and attended the review case conference. At the case conference, the focus of concern was on Ms Collins's parenting. Because Jerry recently had transferred to secondary school, I was particularly interested in interventions to promote Jerry's responsibility and independence. My view influenced the conference's decision to allocate a social work assistant to the family with specific responsibility to encourage and support Jerry in attending school.

In addition, I shared my research-based learning with the children's services' social worker to enhance her understanding of the significance of parental mental ill-health on children. As well as monitoring Ms Collins's mental health and promoting positive mental health, I agreed to explore her son Jerry's understanding of his mother's illness with him, drawing on Bamford's findings (2005) that stigma may prevent children who encounter difficulties at home from discussing these at school, and that families fear the unknown because of their lack of knowledge about the illness and its effects. (Source: Darragh, 2007)

This example illustrates the need for effective joint working arrangements between children's services and mental health social workers. A local community health and social care trust in Northern Ireland developed a protocol for joint working through extensive consultation with service users and professionals from various disciplines. The protocol was disseminated at inter-programme seminars where practice examples and research data illustrated the importance of joint working, information-sharing, referrals in situations of concern, and inter-programme meetings for providing streamlined family services. The joint working protocol is an example of using research findings to promote 'best practice' that aims to meet service users' needs.

A knowledge explosion, combined with a desire for the effective use of research resources and ethical concerns about imposing unnecessary and sometimes risky research on participants, has led to a number of organisations making commitments to finding, appraising and synthesising the best studies of effective interventions, and making systematic reviews of this evidence widely available. Internationally, these include the Cochrane Collaboration (2007) for health and social care, and the Campbell Collaboration (2007) for social welfare (broadly defined), education and criminal justice. In the UK, organisations include the Centre for Reviews and Dissemination (CRD) (2007) in health care, and the Evidence for Policy and Practice Information and Coordinating Centre (EPPI) (2007) for social sciences and public policy, particularly including educational and public health interventions.

A growing number of national organisations seek to distil and disseminate 'best evidence' into a digestible format for busy practitioners and policy-makers. In the UK, the Social Care Institute for Excellence (SCIE) (2007) promotes 'better knowledge for better practice' in social work.

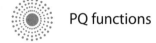

> ## Questions for reflection
>
> 1. Is it worthwhile for a social worker working with older people with dementia to arrange a physical activity programme in a residential unit, supported housing scheme, or day centre?
>
> 2. What effects might the social worker reasonably expect this intervention to have on the functioning, mood, cognition, behaviour or mortality of the older people participating?
>
> 3. What views do older people have of hospital discharge arrangements?

If a social worker reads one research study, would that be sufficient evidence? He or she might ask whether the study sample was representative of the older people they work with, or whether there were other flaws in the study. Perhaps a social worker might have more confidence in a systematic review of research with an explicit (and replicable) approach to identifying studies, an explicit (and challengeable) approach to deciding which studies were of good enough quality to include, and an explicit approach to synthesising studies (see Forbes et al., 2007 for the effectiveness question above and Fisher et al., 2006 for the process question).

Informing effective helping processes

Whilst most EBP attention has focused on studies of effectiveness, it is also important to review helping processes. Understanding service users' views of experiences of being helped can sensitise professionals to critical issues. Social workers should consider and combine multiple sources of evidence to create models for practice in particular situations. Qualitative studies of service users' perspectives provide information that informs the ways services are delivered. Correlation studies (usually surveys) help social workers to understand individual and family problems, make better assessments, engage more sensitively with service users' situations, and propose more effective care plans of jointly agreed interventions (Taylor and Devine, 2005).

For example, whilst comprehensive knowledge of children is essential for practising with children, to promote positive family environments social workers also should understand parents' needs. A growing body of research and evaluation evidence demonstrates the importance of positive working relationships between families and professionals in jointly producing good outcomes for children and young people. Studies in the UK support the notion that the quality of the relationship between the child's family and professionals is paramount to successful outcomes (DH, 1991, 1995). In the USA, family involvement is associated with positive outcomes in the 2001 and 2002 Child and Family Service Reviews and Outcome Indicators (Milner, 2003).

Family group conferences, based on Maori traditions, were developed in New Zealand as a model that enables partnership and empowerment through placing decision-making in the hands of service users and their families. Since its first legislated appearance in New Zealand in 1989 in the Children and Young Person's Act, family group conferencing gradually spread throughout the world. Because PQ practice requires social workers to share power with, consult with, engage with, and support users of services, the family group conference model can demonstrate good practice in working in partnership with service users and carers.

Practice example: family group conferences

Until 2002, in Northern Ireland, family group conferences remained a mechanism for decision-making only in child protection and safeguarding. As an independent coordinator for a local community trust during the early 2000s, I was fully committed to the model and recognised its value for other programmes. Having moved to mental health services in 2005, I was keen to introduce this approach for services users with mental health problems. Before introducing the family group conference model to mental health services, I had to explain the model and its principles to senior managers. Fortunately, the North Essex mental health partnership had already introduced the model to mental health service users, and had evaluated their approach with extremely positive outcomes, asserting that most conferences enabled families to become active partners in planning and identifying the most appropriate resources to meet their needs (Mutter et al., 2002). This evaluation provided a basis for discussion at a seminar with senior managers. Using research to support the proposal demonstrated the model's worth, the potential for positive service user and family outcomes, and its cost-effectiveness.

Designing a pilot project founded on research and 'best practice' principles was essential for gaining senior management support and funding. Sharing the research findings and raising awareness with all multi-disciplinary professionals in the field of mental health ensured that all parties understood the model and could make appropriate referrals. To secure the pilot as core business, it was essential to use research techniques to evaluate the pilot. Evaluation/research tools that focused on service users' mental health state before and after the process, communication within the family, and the views of all participants were agreed. This practice example illustrates how research can be used to promote and move 'best practice' into mainstream programmes. (Source: Darragh, 2007)

Supporting decision-making

Social workers make many decisions every day, covering diverse situations such as assessing the risks inherent in a proposed care arrangement following hospital discharge, whether a name should be placed on the child protection (safeguarding) register, or selecting a practice method for intervention with a particular family. Some decision-making (generally where consequences are more serious) is formalised into group or organisational processes (Duffy et al., 2006), such as reviews, case discussions and court hearings. Other joint decisions are more informal, such as a practitioner checking a decision with the team leader as he or she is dashing down the corridor to another meeting.

The public requires accountability in the stewardship of public expenditure. Increasing demands on health, adult social care and children's services focus social workers' attention on ways to achieve good decisions (Taylor, 2006a). Reports of inquiries into tragedies refer frequently to decision-making (Laming, 2003). Because aspects of risk management (including plans to 'take risks', and the monitoring of these) have become an increasingly central feature of social work practice (Kemshall and Pritchard, 1996; Taylor, 2006b), better tools to support decision-making are required.

Evidence from research can help social workers to analyse risk and harm (Taylor and Donnelly, 2006a, 2006b), but this still leaves them with the task of deciding which evidence is relevant to particular situations, and which situations may be harmful or risky (Calder, 2003). No amount of research will take these responsibilities away from the professional or the organisation. In PQ practice, the social worker has to decide what is to be done, even if it is to accept, reject or adapt a synthesis of research produced by others. Even where studies show overwhelmingly that a particular approach is 'effective', there will still (normally) have been individuals in a 'control' group who have improved more than some individuals in an 'experimental' group, even though the average improvement was greater in the experimental group.

Using 'best evidence' to shape practice will never prescribe a 'correct' solution for every circumstance. All that can be achieved from effectiveness studies is information about the situations in which a particular intervention has been found to be effective in general for people with that type of problem or issue to face. An EBP philosophy is not intended to discourage a critical, reflective approach to practice; on the contrary, it contributes to the substance on which such reflections may be based.

Developing critical reflective practice

As Chapter 1 discusses, critical reflection on practice (Schön, 1983, 1987, 1996) is a key component for developing capability and expertise, as social workers seek to apply theory and research to the 'problem-solving' challenges that they and service users face. Reflection is an essential component in learning how to learn (Taylor, 1996) with challenges in considering how social workers gather (and 'filter') information from spoken words, non-verbal cues, and written materials, and become more critically aware of how they combine these disparate items of information into a problem-solving process with the person who uses services (Moffatt, 1996).

Question for reflection

1. In what ways do social workers create a 'working model' of the problem or challenge facing an individual or family, and then seek to envisage possible ways forward to address key issues?

As discussed in Chapters 1 and 2, critical reflective practice can help social workers to formulate this 'working model'. Chapter 1 established that different authors use the term 'reflection' differently to explain how reflection can help to develop practice, and warn against adopting too simple an approach – reflection must be critical. Chapter 2 argued that critical reflection can assist social workers to develop more confidence to assert their values in practice.

Boud, Keogh and Walker (1985: 19) define reflection as 'a generic term for those intellectual and affective activities in which individuals engage to explore their experiences in order to lead to new understandings and appreciations'. Schön (1996: 26) explains reflective practice as 'thoughtfully considering one's own experiences in applying knowledge to practice while being coached by professionals in the discipline'. Reiterating some of the discussion in Chapter 1, Schön's 'reflection-in-action' is sometimes described as thinking on one's feet, involving looking to personal experiences, connecting with personal feelings, and attending to theories in use, whilst 'reflection-on-action' (1983: ix) entails building new understandings that inform individual actions in the situations that unfold, with the new understandings emerging after the encounter. Eraut's (1994) and Usher, Briant and Johnson's (1997) critiques of reflective practice – that reflection-in-action as a separate process may not be possible in rapidly occurring situations, that the two kinds of reflection should be interrelated, and that reflection must take place within a context (see Chapter 1) – can be countered by flexibly applying Schön's concepts to practice, and by social workers' customary concern to take into account the social, personal, and political contexts of service users' situations.

Later, when social workers talk through their actions with a supervisor and write up their reports, the art of 'reflecting-on-action' enables them to spend time exploring why they acted as they did, and what happened in a particular situation. In so doing, practitioners develop sets of questions and ideas about their practice.

Kolb's model for adult learning processes (Kolb, 1984; see Chapters 1 and 2; Kolb and Fry, 1975), inspired by the work of Lewin (1948) and Dewey (1933, 1938, 1997), can help social workers to understand the processes of critical reflective practice (Figure 11.1). The model suggests four successive stages: *concrete experience* is followed by *reflective observation* on that experience on a personal basis. This may be followed by the derivation of general rules describing the experience, or the application of known theories to it (*abstract conceptualisation*), and hence to the construction of ways to modify the next occurrence of the experience (*active experimentation*), leading in turn to the next *concrete experience*. All this may happen 'in action' or as 'reflection-on-action' over time, depending on the situation.

The process of reflection may also take place at team and organisational levels (Dimmock, 1996) when groups of professionals seek to relate wider issues of research and professional knowledge to their practice. Reflection is an aspect of mentoring and supervision that is key to social work accountability and professional development. For the social worker undertaking PQ, a critical reflective process should link back to the workplace and the mentor/supervisor, as well as being facilitated in a learning group. Compiling a portfolio of practice for a PQ award (see Chapter 2) provides evidence of reflection-on-action and should ensure that the social worker has demonstrated skills of critical reflective practice.

Developing social work research capacity

A major challenge for the social work profession over the next decade is to develop its capacity to undertake robust research and to also develop the knowledge and skills for making connections between research and practice. Social work must create a sound evidence base that will inform choices of decisions in complex practice situations.

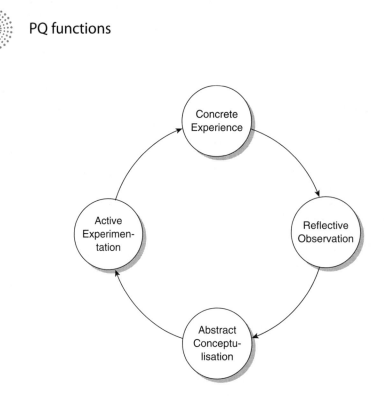

Figure 11.1 Model of adult learning processes (Kolb, 1984)

The UK has recognised this challenge. Concerns in the late 1990s (e.g. Smyth, 2002) led to a SCIE-commissioned review (Shaw et al., 2004) of the actual and potential coverage of social work and social care research within programmes of the Economic and Social Research Council (ESRC), the main research funding body for UK social work. This review in turn led to the JUC/SWEC Research Strategy for Social Work (JUC/SWEC, 2006) that points out a lack of investment in social work research in relation to the size of its workforce, the scale of services delivered and public funding expenditure.

As part of PQ education and training, all professional social workers should regard themselves as users of research and as contributors to the production of knowledge that informs practice and service developments. Each service user and carer can be regarded as one practice example among many that (with their active consent and appropriate ethical safeguards) can be used to inform future practice.

In Northern Ireland, an example of support for research skills development is the range of schemes offered by the Research and Development Office for Health and Social Services that is part of the Department of Health, Social Services and Public Safety for Northern Ireland. These include:

1 Fellowships providing three years secondment on salary for staff up to a certain grade to undertake a PhD.
2 Bursaries to support attendance at research methods training, normally towards a Masters' degree.
3 Studentships that are funded through the universities to employ a research assistant who undertakes one year of research methods training followed by a three-year PhD.

All proposals funded under these schemes have to be relevant to the health and social well-being strategy for Northern Ireland, must offer opportunities for an individual to develop sound research knowledge and skills, and should contribute to the development of the service, the profession and the critical mass of research expertise.

Discussions are taking place in various places in Northern Ireland about the possibility of a professional doctorate (PD), sometimes called a 'taught doctorate' (see Chapter 15). PDs are less common in the UK than in the USA, where Doctorate in Social Work (DSW) programmes are popular. The PD usually explores a work-related practice topic through taught modules, each with their own assignment, which together with a final dissertation equate in effort, complexity and length with a traditional PhD by research. Another opportunity for a professional doctorate is the DGov doctorate that can embody clinical and social care governance within broader governance agendas, or the DBA (Doctorate in Business Administration), exploring a leadership or management issue relevant to social work. The PD, DGov, or DBA can provide a means of developing some social workers to a non-medical consultant level (see Chapters 12, 14, and 15).

Practice example: using research to inform practice

A social work mental health team leader recently returned from Queen's University, Belfast, where he had studied with the support of the Research and Development Office, having completed a comparative research study on the benefits of Assertive Outreach approaches in Mental Health (Davidson and Campbell, 2007). He made a presentation to senior managers highlighting the research's key findings and its implications for future policy development. The findings confirmed the value of small caseloads, a team approach to practice with the key worker system and the importance of worker continuity. These findings will also influence the Community Mental Health team leaders across the directorate.

Developing knowledge and skills for using evidence to inform practice

The dissemination of research and professional knowledge is built into PQ requirements in areas such as 'enabling others' and 'contribute to the performance of professional and interprofessional groups, teams and networks' (NIPQETP, 2007). Social workers are expected to share their learning with others at a team level and beyond. A range of approaches supports this process. Dissemination is sometimes undertaken centrally by seminars or publications. However, increasing opportunities exist for social workers to share their learning at journal clubs, practice groups or lunchtime seminars. These fora highlight the necessity of social

workers using research to inform their practice with service users. In Northern Ireland, the British Association of Social Workers (BASW) plays an important role in promoting research-based seminars, conferences and practice focus groups. A number of Voices in Practice groups (including children and families, mental health, learning disabilities, and addictions) actively promote research discussions.

Positive outcomes of EBP gradually are becoming evident:

- Promoting evidence-informed policy development by employers that supports social workers making the best possible practice decisions;
- Determining appropriate uses of research for identifying risks, assessing behaviours, and making well-informed social work decisions;
- Increasing social workers' competence and confidence, particularly in multi-professional working environments;
- Helping social workers to include critical reflection and reference to research in their assessment reports and practice reviews.

Social work as a profession needs to develop knowledge and skills in each aspect of EBP, although each individual and organisation will not undertake all areas. Major skill areas relate to systematic research reviews (Coren and Fisher, 2006; Dempster, 2003), the dissemination of research and the application of professional knowledge to practice. Skills areas within systematic reviews include:

- Identifying relevant research through searching electronic databases (Taylor, 2003; Taylor et al., 2003);
- Appraising the quality of research and understanding its limitations (*Critical Appraisal Skills Programme (CASP) and Evidence-based Practice* (www.phru.nhs.uk/casp/casp.htm>; Taylor et al., 2007);
- Systematically synthesising research with diverse designs (Fisher et al., 2006).

More fundamentally, the social work profession must improve the infrastructure of effective databases (Taylor et al., 2006, 2007) and knowledge about the potential and limitations of systematic reviews.

Social workers undertaking PQ education and training should be able to demonstrate the basic skills of EBP, including retrieving research from electronic databases and appraising its quality, approaching a literature review using an explicit method that seeks to avoid bias, and reflecting on how research and reviews of research challenge their current practice and thus help them to identify concrete ways to improve their post-qualifying practice. They should be able to reflect on how their practice experiences and service users' and carers' views inform their critique of research reviews, for example by highlighting aspects that reviews had not considered. They should be able to reflect on the ways that research studies confirm or contradict each other, particularly in their practice implications.

Conclusion: incorporating research into practice through reflection

To move from 'competence' to 'expertise' (Benner, 1984; see Chapter 1), the social work profession must grasp the nettle of creating, accessing, understanding and applying sound research to practice through a critical reflection process. This does not imply a derogation of professional judgement. On the contrary, it implies greater challenges in embracing a robust research base integrated with ethical, legal, theoretical, policy and practice issues when making decisions in situations of uncertainty and conflict.

Macdonald (2001) argues that the accumulation of research findings makes integrating knowledge based on 'best evidence' into practice increasingly complex for practitioners. Higgins and Pinkerton (1998) state that more systematic approaches are now required to develop the most effective services. The virtues of using the best available evidence to inform practice are self-evident in three ways. Social workers must seek:

1 The best practice in a particular circumstance for the service user's benefit;
2 The best use of resources; and
3 Decisions based on professional knowledge rather than dominated by organisational 'requirements' (Webb, 2001).

However, Gambrill (2006) draws attention to issues in pursuing a sound research base to inform social work practice. With the introduction of clinical and social care governance (DH, 2005; DHSSPS NI, 2001, 2002) there is now a widespread impetus towards basing practice and policy decisions on sound research. Sound systems for developing EBP are required (Ferguson, 2003; Simmons, 2007; Webb, 2002) in the context of contemporary risk societies (Power, 2007).

Social workers undertaking PQ education and training should develop skills in undertaking, supporting, accessing, appraising, synthesising, disseminating and applying research as a reference point for effective practice and decisions, and as a knowledge base for involving service users and carers as better-informed participants in making decisions about their own care and support. Robust research and readable reviews of research will provide the essential food for critical reflection that helps to improve social work practice for the ultimate benefit of people who use services and carers. It can be argued that social workers whose PQ education and training include the application of research and critical reflection to practice will be able to undertake decisions that are better founded and judged than those without this kind of learning.

Further reading

Brown, K. and Rutter, L. (2006) *Critical Thinking for Social Work*. Exeter: Learning Matters.

This book, written specifically for social workers undertaking PQ studies, enables readers to develop their critical thinking ability and apply this to everyday decision-making as well as to reflect on their skills.

Newman, T., Moseley, A., Tierney, S. and Ellis, A. (2005) *Evidence-Based Social Work: A Guide for the Perplexed.* Lyme Regis: Russell House.

The book is a straightforward guide to essential steps in evidence-based practice, including creating a practice evidence question, understanding basic statistics and appraising the quality of research.

Roberts, A. and Yeager, K.R. (eds) (2006) *Foundations of Evidence-Based Social Work.* New York: Oxford University Press.

Despite its comprehensive scope, this is a practical and readable manual providing a guide to the ever-expanding world of evidence-based practice, written by a range of eminent authors.

Chapter 12

Practice education

Patricia Higham and Mavis Sharp

Introduction

Chapter 12 critically evaluates practice education's contributions to practice. Enabling others work-based learning is an essential PQ skill, but an under-valued one. Despite trainers' and academics' support of practice education, many managers and practitioners pay it little attention. This chapter considers reasons for this neglect, and argues that practice educators' knowledge and skills can help to develop new social work roles and promote quality. The chapter notes the importance of a learning organisation culture to sustain practice. The authors draw on their experience of practice education, *inter alia*, as an external assessor and a practice teacher.

Definitions

The terminology used to describe different roles for developing and assessing work-based learning is not straightforward. Where formerly the 'practice teacher' fulfilled multiple roles in relation to work-based learning, now it is acknowledged that more than one person may be involved in developing and assessing practice. Line managers, for example, are likely to play an important role in PQ awards. The GSCC's National Practice Learning Strategy Group, whose membership includes representatives of NOPT (National Organisation of Practice Teachers), JUC/SWEC (Joint University Council Social Work Education Committee), SfC (Skills for Care England), CWDC (Children's Workforce Development Council) and BASW (British Association of Social Workers), developed a 'benchmark' (quality assurance) statement (GSCC et al., 2007) for practice learning. This, however, provides guidance rather than specific definitions, and acknowledges local variations in terminology. The chapter's definitions draw on, but are not synonymous with, the GSCC et al.'s benchmark. Variation from the GSCC benchmark is prompted by its failure (so far) to discuss practice learning at PQ levels.

- *Practice teacher* – Trained to be competent in five areas (values, management, teaching, assessment and reflective practice), the practice teacher role was introduced around 1990 to take responsibility for judging whether a social work qualifying student attained competence at the point of qualification. The designation of '*practice assessor*' or '*practice mentor/assessor*' (PMA) is gradually replacing '*practice teacher*' (although contested by the NOPT, the National Organisation of Practice Teachers) but a more apt designation might be '*practice educator*'.
- *Practice assessor* – This term, introduced when the social work qualifying degree was being planned in 2002, denotes an assessor of social work qualifying students' work-based learning. When first introduced, it was not clear whether the role would be as broad as that of a practice teacher, or whether the changed terminology indicated a narrower role.
- *Practice mentor* – Supports, encourages, and provides informal 'teaching' to a student practitioner, PQ candidate or other learner. The role can be combined with that of practice assessor.
- *Practice supervisor* – Usually refers to a work-based supervisor of a social work student on a placement. The practice supervisor provides on-site, day-to-day support and supervision, in close collaboration with a designated 'long arm' practice teacher, who usually is not employed directly by the placement agency and is therefore not available on-site throughout all the placement days. However, the practice teacher is responsible for the pass/fail decision on the students' practice.
- *Practice mentor/assessor* – A skilled and trained mentor and assessor of the work-based learning of social work degree students, PQ candidates, and other learners – increasingly used in place of '*practice teacher*'.
- *Practice educator* – Introduced by the GSCC's (2005a) designation of the new PQ practice specialism of Practice Education, this term signifies a social worker who is able to carry out all the functions of practice education (mentoring, teaching, assessing, and developing support systems), exercise a high level of leadership, and work at a strategic level. (Confusingly, the GSCC et al.'s (2007a) benchmark suggests both the broad definition given here and a more general use of this term to denote a qualified social work practitioner contributing to a social work students' learning and assessment alongside more experienced qualified colleagues.)
- *Practice learning opportunity* – a new designation for a 'placement'.

Enabling others: a core social work role

Employers' workforce strategies aim to develop a skilled workforce, and work-based learning and assessment play an essential part in achieving this aim. Without the contributions of practice mentors and assessors, the social work profession would have no evidence of whether social workers in their various roles are appropriately knowledgeable, skilled and helpful to people who use services and carers.

Academics and trainers assert that good quality practice education is crucial for improving practice (Parker, 2007; Slater, 2007). A PQ practice education specialism confirms that social workers have extended their competence to capability and (perhaps) expertise in work-based assessment, teaching and management of support systems for teaching and assessment (GSCC, 2006c: 6, 7). However, relatively few social workers have attained this level of capability. Why? A review of practice education's development may provide some explanations.

The development of practice education

Before 1990, placement supervisors of social work students did not observe practice formally, but provided supervision in which theory was identified retrospectively and abductively (Blaikie, 1993) from the students' detailed written accounts of practice, which formed the basis of supervision. Often, the written accounts were 'process recordings' that analysed psychodynamic thinking and motivation.

The Central Council for Education and Training in Social Work (CCETSW) (the UK-wide predecessor body to the country-specific GSCC and Care Councils) introduced the UK-wide Practice Teaching Award (PTA) (CCETSW, 1989) when the Diploma in Social Work (CCETSW, 1989) became the qualifying award for intending social workers. The Practice Teaching Award (GSCC, 2000: s5) prepared practice teachers to assess students' competence through direct observation of practice. Following the introduction of the PTA, process recordings all but disappeared, and interest in encouraging students to understand motivations and defence mechanisms (Freud, 1936) declined.

The Practice Teaching Award was located at a higher education level that is equivalent to the final year of honours degree study, and was assigned 60 'professional' (e.g. non-academic) credits, equivalent to half a year of full-time study, or one year's study on a part-time basis. The PTA also was equated to NVQ level 4, possibly NVQ 5.

Forty-four programmes (UK-wide) were approved to offer the Practice Teaching Award. These PT programmes varied in length, content, volume of assessment, amount of credits, and whether or not they offered an academic award as well as a professional award. The PTA's entry requirements differed from other PQ awards because it was open to non-social workers as well as experienced social workers. Candidates who had completed a D32/33 VQ (vocational qualification) award were offered some exemption from the assessment part of the PTA.

The PTA's strengths and weaknesses

The PTA exhibited strengths but also weaknesses. Looking across other professional groups, the PTA was arguably the major award of its type specifically designed to support practice learning for a professional qualification. The PTA created an elite cadre of skilled social work practitioners who are able to develop and assess work-based learning. Generally credited with success in raising the quality of social work students' practice learning experiences, the PTA prepared PQ candidates to teach and assess the practice of students on qualifying social work programmes, but did not prepare them to assess the practice of experienced practitioners who were candidates on PQ programmes.

An adequate supply of practice teachers was never achieved (Lindsay and Tompsett, 1998). Insufficient numbers of practitioners were willing or were sponsored by their employer to take the Practice Teaching Award, and of those who did, relatively few continued in that role. The wastage was very high. Despite some employers paying an increment to practice teachers, many practice teachers took only one student, and subsequently did not continue in the role. Some practice teachers moved into management roles, thus improving their career pathways – evidence that their employers valued their skills, but also an indication that employers had not considered the role of practice teacher as a career path in itself. The complexity of some PTA programmes and the lengthy portfolios of evidence required of those taking the award were additional barriers to expanding the supply of practice teachers. Most PT programmes had small intakes, and some did not recruit every year – thus the numbers of newly trained practice teachers combined with an inability to retain practice teachers failed to keep pace with rising demand. CCETSW had intended that all qualifying students would have a practice teacher qualified via the Practice Teaching Award by 1995 (CCETSW, 1991: 4), but this date kept being put back and was eventually dropped. *Community Care* (Samuel, 2007) drew attention to the continuing problem – despite a performance indicator for local authorities that measured the number of placements offered, 39 of 150 councils in England offered 10 or fewer placement days for each social worker in 2005–6.

Although practice teaching sought to develop social workers who could reflect critically on their actions, the competence-driven Diploma in Social Work impeded attainment of this aim. Practice teachers' assessment of competence overshadowed the functions of teaching and mentoring. Criteria for evidencing competence were similar to those used by vocational qualifications (VQs): currency, validity, authenticity and sufficiency (QCA, 2007). Students' portfolios that comprised the evidence for the practice teacher's report had to include the many Diploma in Social Work competences; in some instances, the amount of detail impeded overall coherence.

Some practice portfolios for the qualifying social work programmes lacked comprehensive narratives of practice with individual service users, and instead featured cross-referenced charts of competences and lists of separate tasks that were intended to provide evidence of competence. The portrayal of the students' relationships with service users and carers was not always evident. In contrast, some universities designed a portfolio that enabled the student and practice teacher to present integrated accounts that succeeded in evidencing competence but also the humanity of their practice. For example, the University of Bristol required students to write 'student accounts of practice' (SAPs) that illuminated students' understanding as well as their actions, and these, together with the direct observations of practice, resulted in meaningful portfolios.

The introduction of the practice teacher role and the requirement for observed practice initially led to some quality assurance tensions with universities' assessment systems. The CCETSW DipSW statement that the practice teacher's judgement should 'stand in their own right as recommendations to the programme assessment board' (CCETSW, 1991: 26) was sometimes mistakenly interpreted that a practice teacher's pass/fail judgement could not be moderated or challenged at the university's Board of Examination. This misinterpretation ignored one of the basic elements of assuring fairness in marking – the principle of internal and external moderation, whereby one marker's view is second marked or double marked, scrutinised by an external examiner, and debated by the Board of Examiners.

'Practice Assessment Panels' (PAPs), with a membership comprised of practice teachers, were meant to assure the quality of the student portfolios, but some panels interpreted their role as undertaking a counting exercise to check whether all the competences were included. The relationship of the practice-focused PAP to university Boards of Examiners was not always clear – in most instances the PAP became a Board sub-panel that reported its recommendations to the Board for confirmation. The PAPs' typical designation of a 'good', 'average' and 'less good' practice teacher report sometimes judged the completeness of the practice portfolio and the efforts of the practice teacher, rather than the quality of the students' practice, although arguably, if the report was not full and clear, the nature of the practice also was not clear. The use of an additional 'second opinion' practice teacher (later replaced by 'concerns' procedures) when a students' practice was considered likely to fail was an effective means of moderating a crucial decision (CCETSW, 1989, 1991).

Incentives for change

A number of incentives led to the reworking of the Practice Teaching Award into different kinds of practice education module, programme, and award:

- The reform of social work education (DH, 1998), and the success of social work qualifying degree (which requires more placement days) in recruiting increased target numbers of intending social workers, exacerbated the demand for work-based learning and assessment;
- Social workers' registration requirements for post-registration training and learning (PRTL) led to a wider demand for continuing professional development (CPD) opportunities, including PQ, and as a consequence increased the need for skilled mentors and assessors of work-based learning;
- The consequent decision to improve both the supply and retention of social workers able to contribute to others' work-based learning and assessment of others;
- Moves to transform social work and social care employers into learning organisations (Senge, 1990; Chapters 1, 6, and 14), thus creating additional demand for mentors and assessors of work-based learning;
- Within the reform of social work education, debate about the Practice Teaching Award's scope and 'fitness for purpose' to meet the increased demands for mentors and assessors of work-based learning.

The Practice Learning Task Force

In 2003, the Department of Health established the Practice Learning Task Force (PLTF) in England for a two-year period to increase the numbers of practice assessors and quality of practice education. The PLTF provided infrastructure support for the national intake of the social work degree (increased in England to 500 extra places each year to remedy the shortage of qualified social workers). The PLTF promoted the introduction of two-day and five-day short courses to prepare an expanded range of practice assessors and supervisors, aiming to attract more practice learning opportunities in the voluntary and independent sectors (PLTF, 2005).

The Practice Learning Task Force drew attention to the need for skilled mentors and assessors of work-based learning, but did not succeed in solving the problem of the insufficient supply of practice learning opportunities for social work degree students. Whilst the value of work-based learning and the need for skilled assessors was clearly recognised, the National Association of Practice Teachers (NOPT) remained wary of efforts that apparently diminished the role of the practice teacher. It continued to advocate for high standards in practice education. Its website retains the title of 'practice teacher' (NOPT, 2007). The NOPT wanted to keep the 'gold standard' represented by the soon-to-disappear Practice Teaching Award. But the time was right for reform – numbers of mentors and assessors had to be increased or the new social work degree would fail to achieve its target numbers.

Changed practice education expectations across the UK

All four UK countries stipulated changes in their arrangements for practice assessment and practice education, with a comparative matrix available on the GSCC website (GSCC, 2007b).

Northern Ireland reconfigured the Practice Teaching Award to meet the requirements of the NISCC Practice Learning Standards 2006 and the NI PQ Framework.

In Wales, the PQ Rules include a statement explaining how assessment is relevant to practice modules. The Care Council Wales published a 'good practice' guide, *Ensuring Consistency in Learning to Practice* (CCW, 2004)

Two of the four UK countries, Scotland and England, developed detailed strategies for practice education, which parallel each other by embedding developments for practice learning and practice education within the wider framework of learning organisation networks.

Scotland

The Scottish Practice Learning Project (SPLP), a joint initiative between the Scottish Social Services Council (SSSC) and SIESWE, the Scottish Institute for Excellence in Social Work Education (now IRISS) (reporting to the PLIG – Practice Learning Implementation Group) agreed objectives to promote a learning culture, establish learning centres, work with key stakeholders to increase the quality, variety and quantity of practice learning opportunities, review the practice teaching award, and develop an alternative modular award. Its ongoing objectives are now mainstreamed into the Scottish Social Services Council's work.

A key message that underpinned the SPLP's work was that it is everybody's business to support practice learning. As Chapter 1 noted, Scotland's replacement for the Practice Teaching Award is a suite of qualifications (SIESWE, 2005) consisting of a four-stage modular framework at different levels based on the Scottish Credit and Qualifications Framework (SCQF, 2006). Resources were made available not only to support practice learning for the social work qualifying degree, but also to support employees who contribute to others' learning, including the induction of newly appointed staff, supporting staff taking training programmes, mentoring, assessing practice and/or adopting a strategic or management role in training. Service users and carers and practitioners from other professions are encouraged to contribute to social workers' work-based learning.

England

In England, practice education and enabling others are integral to the PQ framework. Registered social workers must take part in PQ assessment based on actual practice. Practice assessment draws on the GSCC Code of Practice, relevant specialist standards and the *Guidance on the Assessment of Practice in the Workplace* (GSCC, 2002b). The GSCC did not stipulate a stand-alone practice education award at Specialist Award level, but instead introduced a required module 'Enabling Others' within each Specialist Award. This module carries an expectation that PQ candidates will contribute to the learning and assessment of a social work student whilst taking their Specialist Award – a strategy intended to increase the numbers of PMAs for social work and social care.

The English PQ framework represents a major change in thinking about practice education in relation to the newly qualified social worker. Instead of viewing practice education as a role for an elite practice teacher, the GSCC requires that all social workers, no matter where they are located and employed, should make a transition from being a learner, enabled by others, to enabling others' learning. The requirement for 'enabling others' applies to work with social work students and qualified social workers, but also may include supporting, mentoring, teaching and assessing other staff (GSCC, 2006c: 11). Enabling others and recognising their achievements are viewed as evidence of professional self-development. Functions that support students or colleagues include planning, finding practice learning opportunities, learning, and assessment.

The Specialist level module 'Enabling Others' focuses on good practice in assessment, supported by teaching, whilst the Higher Specialist and Advanced award levels focus on teaching and management in support of assessment (GSCC, 2006c: 15). At the two higher PQ award levels (2006c: 19), practice education candidates 'should seek to become champions of the learning organisation'. Although the GSCC claims that the higher award levels in practice education can help a social worker gain recognition as an expert who can lead colleagues, teams, other communities, or represent their employers in local, regional and national training networks (2006c: 16), this recognition depends on employers developing a human resources strategy that establishes career pathways for practice educators.

The modular structure of the GSCC PQ framework enables practice education to be integrated within other specialisms (2006c: 22–4). A particularly apt integration is with leadership and management.

Practice example: Mix and Match awards

The University of Birmingham decided to offer a Leadership and Management Higher Specialist Award with a three-module Practice Education pathway, thus meeting the further learning needs of social workers who had previously completed the Practice Teaching Award.

The GSCC encourages synergy between practice education PQ and a learning and development qualification structure at VQ 3/4/5, based on the Employment National Training Organisation development standards catalogue, that provides training for VQ assessors and verifiers. The three core domains for practice education (GSCC, 2006c: 12; GSCC/Topss, 2002) – A and B (teaching and assessing the practice of student social workers) and C (mentoring and supporting students or colleagues) – were developed to provide some compatibility with the vocational qualification structure (GSCC, 2006c: 25), thus giving scope for shared learning.

The GSCC announced that it would explore with the Higher Education Academy the possibility of mapping the practice education awards for accreditation purposes (GSCC, 2006c: 28). However, although the GSCC encourages course designers to draw the underpinning standards for practice education from relevant academic educational theory contained in the work of the Higher

Education Academy, Universities UK, the Standing Conference of Principals, the Department for Employment and Learning, and the Higher Education Funding Councils (GSCC, 2006c: 18), the GSCC made no mention of seeking synergy between PQ practice education (2006c: 19) and the part-time academic teaching qualification for higher education (Certificate in Education) that is now required of all newly appointed social work lecturers (2006c: 19), despite the overlap of curricula. This oversight perpetuates a previous inequality when the GSCC's predecessor body, CCETSW, had gained recognition of the PTA for automatic membership of the Higher Education Academy (HEA, 2007), but ignored the Certificate in Education obtained by qualified social workers who were university teachers of social work.

Changes in practice

Because social workers increasingly practice in multi-professional teams, the GSCC stipulates that those who complete approved practice education awards should be able to contribute to the teaching and assessment of other professionals (GSCC, 2006c: 26). Practice education with skilled mentoring and assessment can promote partnership working (Bell, 2006) across professional boundaries and traditional service provider demarcations. The roles social workers trained for 30 years ago are tending to disappear as new roles take over (Cree, 2003; Higham, 2006). Practice education can play an important part by supporting practitioners who adopt new roles. It also can help social workers to recognise and challenge the effects of institutional regimes by valuing, empowering and involving service users and carers (discussed in Chapter 3) as contributors to service planning.

Reviews of social work

Chapter 3 discussed the reviews of social work conducted by all four UK countries, which resulted in recommendations that need the contributions of practice educators to achieve the reviews' goals. Of particular interest is the Scottish Executive Report *Changing Lives* (2006c) from the *Twenty-first Century Review of Social Work* (2005), which identified five change programmes (performance improvement, service redesign, practice governance, leadership, and workforce development). *Changing Lives* recommended four tiers of social work practice, with social workers directly involved in the more complex top two tiers, and a new social care paraprofessional assisting the social worker by directly engaging in the less complex areas of practice of the bottom two tiers, thus enabling social workers to focus on appropriately demanding areas of practice.

The English government report *Options for Excellence* (DH/DfES, 2006) proposed a workforce development strategy with four stands (perception, partnership, professionalism and participation) that was followed by a GSCC-led review of social workers' roles and tasks. *Options for Excellence* referred to the potential development of 'consultant/expert practitioners' that use practice-related research skills and knowledge to support the professional development of multi-professional team members, and to champion evidence-based and evidence-informed practice. The consultant/expert practitioner could offer an alternative to a management career pathway for social workers who prefer to remain in practice (see Chapters 11, 14 and 15).

The mentor role

The mentor role has been part of PQ since 1992, when CCETSW required PQ candidates to have mentoring support. This requirement was reiterated in the 1998 guidance on approaches to mentoring: PQ candidates were to receive accurate advice on the awards and adequate support to complete the awards. Mentoring was viewed either as a separate support role or as contributing to a PQ candidate's assessment. CCETSW used the generic term 'mentor' but recognised that other terms such as 'practice supervisor' could be used locally, seemingly encouraging the previously noted confusion over terminology. These guidelines are now superseded by country-specific PQ frameworks offering opportunities to develop mentoring and assessment skills, which can lead to career progression into roles where social workers develop the learning of others at more strategic levels.

PQ candidates who have been away from formal education for a period of time may need mentoring support to help them successfully re-enter education and contain the possible tension between lack of confidence in undertaking formal learning and confidence in their practice experience. Mentors can play an important role in supporting newly qualified social workers, acting as role models, enabling students and novice social workers to 'shadow' experienced practitioners, and contributing to staff retention strategies (see Chapter 14) by advising on career development. Bourn and Bootle (2005) identify how mentors can use IT systems to link geographically isolated students or candidates to a learning community, and how in some organisations, mentors form groups to promote anti-oppressive practice.

Line managers

Arguably, line managers play essential roles in PQ as learning facilitators, despite debate about whether the mentor role should be undertaken by the candidates' line manager or by an independent mentor (Bourn and Bootle, 2005; Clutterbuck, 2001; Rumsey, 1995; Thompson, 2006; Turner, 2000). Small-scale studies (Bourn and Bootle, 2005; Rumsey, 1995) of PQ award programmes suggest that PQ candidates rated independent mentors' support as very good, but line managers' mentoring support was rated much lower. When line managers undertook the mentor role, there were conflicts of interest and inadequate preparation, exacerbated by a lack of interest, time and objectivity (Turner, 2000). This should not obscure the potential benefit of line managers undertaking a mentor role that focuses on supportive supervision, provided they are prepared appropriately. PQ leadership and management awards include modules on practice education that could address training for line managers' involvement as mentors.

Rumsey (1995) argues that separating the roles of assessor and mentor, although important, can pose problems, particularly in situations where PQ candidates face heavy work pressures, as it takes additional time for building relationships with mentors. Two separate roles carried out by different people could be confusing, and would require contracts of learning to establish clarity of function and responsibility – this would be particularly important in situations where a PQ candidate's progress is potentially one of failure (Sharp and Danbury, 1999). A close partnership and learning agreement between the line manager and mentor would offset any possible manipulation by the PQ candidate. Turner (2000) discusses a shared approach where line managers provide work-based support and mentors provide specialist knowledge.

East Midlands Skills for Care's work-based learning and assessment strategy for PQ (SfC, 2007) included the proposal that line managers should undertake a PQ verification and mentoring role, including formative direct observations. Whilst verification was a feature of the previous PQ framework, it is not yet evident that universities will adopt the principle of line manager mentoring/observation.

The learning organisation

Thompson (2006) argues that there seems to be little point in debating which is the best approach to mentoring because any approach will only work in a learning organisation with processes that support shared mentoring roles. A learning organisation culture (see Chapters 1, 3 and 14) needs to support the essential PQ skill of enabling others' work-based learning. Line managers' difficulties in combining mentoring, supervisory, and practice assessment functions reflect their own CPD needs to acquire knowledge and skills that sustain a learning organisation.

A learning organisation provides an environment where social workers are expected to acquire skills in enabling others. Dale (1994) defines a learning organisation as one that facilitates and transfers the learning of its constituent members with a culture of unwritten rules and assumptions that support learning. This kind of organisation emphasises the value of supervision and CPD, and minimises barriers to learning by building staff members' strengths. In an organisation that recognises learning as ongoing, a practitioner will be able to question and reflect on their uncertainties without feeling threatened.

Developing a learning organisation presents challenges for managers, but also enhances their leadership. A learning organisation will undertake to address line managers' potential difficulties in assuming a mentoring role by providing support through CPD.

Practice example: a jointly run CPD workshop

Mary is a line manager of a multi-professional children's services team. Together with Darryl, a senior practitioner who had completed a practice education PQ award, Mary organised jointly run CPD workshops for all team members (social workers, occupational therapists, occupational therapy assistants, children's services workers, and temporary agency staff). Some team members were taking a part-time distance learning social work degree, others were taking VQs, and some team members had completed PQ or CPD awards. The purpose of the workshops was to promote higher standards of multi-professional practice. The workshops enabled participants to share their practice experiences from their different perspectives, link their experiences to relevant knowledge and theory, and develop shared understandings of what constitutes good practice.

At the time of writing, employers as a whole have not developed learning organisations. Social workers who want to undertake PQ awards or modules should explore the availability of mentoring and work-based support. Potential gaps in provision could be offset by informal support arrangements with colleagues or candidate support groups.

Practice educators who confidently fulfil all the practice education functions will become champions of the learning organisation within their local and regional training and development frameworks (GSCC, 2006c: 38). Practice educator champions will use their knowledge to promote a critical understanding of workforce planning and development and contribute to training strategies.

Conclusion

Practice education arguably should become the most important part of PQ training and education, because it serves as a lynch-pin for raising practice and service standards, but some impediments must be addressed before practice education can make its rightful contribution:

- Clarify the confusing terminology for different practice education roles, the differences between the roles, and each role's relationship to the other roles.

In an effort to increase practice education's bank of skills, PQ frameworks now feature flexible provision – from modules to full PQ awards – for developing practice education skills. Flexible provision has led to a variety of confusingly labelled roles in practice education, some of which practise only one aspect of the full range of skills. The confusing terminology that tries to explain different practice education roles does not help practice education's cause. Further, the interconnection between the roles and their relationship to each other is not yet fully established. The GSCC benchmark for practice learning opportunities (GSCC et al., 2007) may be useful for doing this, but it fails to take account of expectations for PQ practice learning.

- Establish career pathways for practice educators, including standards for those undertaking practice mentoring and assessment at qualifying and post qualifying levels.

Employers could establish a career pathway for practice educators, and stipulate standards required for different roles in practice mentoring and assessment. The GSCC et al.'s National Practice Learning Strategy Group will consider issuing a national statement (England) regarding the experience and minimum training for 'practice assessors' in relation to PQ (GSCC et al., 2007: 10).

- Clarify the differences between assessing PQ level practice, qualifying level practice and vocational practice.

A further challenge is how to assess PQ candidates' practice with expectations that differ from those for social work qualifying students. As Chapter 1 argued, PQ candidates have already been judged as competent, so they must demonstrate more than a beginning level of competence – they should be aiming for capability and expertise. Care must be taken not to assess social workers' practice with the same expectations as for social work students. Assessment at every level of practice will need carefully designed practice-level descriptors.

- Take forward the best achievements of the Practice Teaching Award into the new frameworks and win the commitment of line managers and practitioners.

Each country's PQ framework should take forward the PTA's best achievements into the design of new practice education awards. The cadre of experienced qualified practice teachers must be convinced that newer, more flexible arrangements will not diminish the standards of practice education. Parker (2007: 764) identifies a 'clear need to begin to capture a wider stakeholder perspective and systematically consider how we might develop effective approaches to practice learning that respond to current policy shifts and workforce agenda whilst inculcating critical perspective and engagement with these views'. Without line manager and practitioner backing for practice education, the PQ frameworks and also the qualifying degree will flounder rather than flourish. Practice education provides a potential solution to the problem of workforce retention, so it is surprising that so far it has not won more widespread support. The development of a more populist and flexible approach to practice education rather than an elitist approach may be more likely to succeed, although it is not without inherent issues.

Questions for reflection

1. What are the three most challenging aspects of a practice educator role?

2. How should the rights of users and carers be protected when a practice educator intends to observe the practice of a PQ candidate, given that the observation and the subsequent written report could represent an intrusion into the confidentiality of the service user relationship?

3. How can line managers prepare for mentoring and assessing PQ candidates?

Further reading

Dunworth, M. (2007) 'Joint assessment in inter-professional education: a consideration of some of the difficulties', *Social Work Education*, 26, 4: 414–22.

This article discusses a Scottish university's attempt to assess nurses and social workers jointly where professional and academic qualifications were involved. It recounts efforts to integrate assessment in a multi-disciplinary academic course with PQ assessment, and examines tensions between different academic disciplines and the mechanisms used to resolve them.

Williams, S. and Rutter, L. (2007) *Enabling and Assessing Work-Based Learning for Social Work: Supporting the Development of Professional Practice*. Learn To Care Publication 10: Baurnemouth.

This book, which considers the implications of PQ frameworks, is aimed at PQ candidates undertaking the 'enabling others' aspect of specialist workforce development.

Chapter 13

Leadership and management

Victoria Stewart, Laurences Clarke and Joyce Lishman

Introduction

Chapter 13 reviews critically a Scottish innovative initiative to provide a postgraduate, continuing professional development distance-learning course in leadership for middle managers in social services. The programme is designed to inform participants from the statutory, voluntary and private social services sectors about current change agendas, and to provide them with the appropriate knowledge, skills and confidence for delivering effective leadership in the current contexts of change in social work and social services.

Why did the Scottish Executive commission a course in leadership (rather than management)? Research by the Scottish Leadership Foundation (Van Zwanenberg, 2003) revealed a lack of confidence and training among middle managers about undertaking their professional leadership role. They doubted their ability to articulate confident professional perspectives in interdisciplinary and multi-professional teams – perspectives about social work's and social services' unique contributions towards achieving improved user and carer outcomes with their voices listened to and acted upon.

Leading to Deliver, a postgraduate certificate in leadership, is a leadership development programme commissioned by the (then) Scottish Executive after competitive tendering. The Taylor Clarke Partnership (a leadership and organisational development consultancy based in Scotland) delivers the programme in partnership with The Robert Gordon University in Aberdeen. For The Robert Gordon University, the programme has involved two innovative partnership arrangements, the first between a private consultancy and the university's Faculty of Health and Social Care and the second between Aberdeen Business School and the School of Applied Social Studies, a hitherto unlikely alliance!

The Taylor Clarke Partnership provides expert consultancy and teaching in leadership development. The Robert Gordon University holds responsibility for accrediting the programme and marking candidates' submitted assessments, which are based on taught modules from the Taylor Clarke

Partnership that involved integrating and applying ethics, knowledge and theory into practice in a leadership role.

So far, 400 students from the whole of Scotland have undertaken this programme over four years, and a further 100 are completing in the fifth cohort. They have begun to provide a critical mass in relation to leadership and bringing about change in the organisations in which they work. The Leadership and Management Group, one of six groups leading the *Changing Lives* Implementation Plan (Scottish Executive, 2006c) is currently considering how leadership can continue to be better embedded in public service reform to ensure that services are joined up, personalised (Leadbetter, 2004) and focus on early intervention and prevention rather that crisis management. However, a tension exists (not fully addressed by Leadbetter) deriving from the increasing focus on users' and carers' requirements: many users of services in child protection (and in Scotland, criminal justice) are involuntary and 'control' is more of an issue than 'care'.

This chapter first will examine the literature relevant to leadership and management in social work and social services, then present *Leading to Deliver* as a case study of a leadership and change programme, and finally draw together the challenges and lessons learned.

Literature review

Defining leadership and management

To understand the interest in management and leadership approaches in social services, it is necessary to understand something of their content and history. Should leadership and management be differentiated? What do they mean for social services?

Thinking about management and leadership has developed through some fairly distinct phases since the early twentieth century. Classical management theorists such as Taylor (1947), Fayol (1949) and Weber (1957) focused on planning, formal organisational structures and a clear division of responsibility to optimise performance, with an assumption of rational, consistent behaviour on the part of employees. The technical structure of the organisation was seen as the key to efficiency (measured through increased productivity) with financial incentives providing the remaining necessary driver for workers.

A new school of thought emerged to address weaknesses in the classical theories. Human relations theorists such as Mayo (see Gillespie, 1991) and Argyris (1957) realised the importance of the informal, social aspects of the organisation. They identified the unpredictability and complexity of group and individual behaviour, including motivation, which Maslow (1954), McGregor (1960) and others studied further.

Similarly, theories of leadership developed and evolved over time, and whilst there is no single agreed definition of leadership or a good leader, there is general agreement that leadership is concerned with interactions between leaders and their followers to achieve goals. Leadership could therefore be said to involve an understanding of group and individual behaviour and motivation. Key debates on definitions of leadership revolve around questions of origin. Are leaders born or made? Trait theorists, such as Stogdill (1974), attribute good leadership to characteristics, qualities and attributes that are inherent in an individual and cannot be learnt, whereas behaviourist theorists, such as Tannenbaum and Schmidt (1958) and Blake and Mouton (1964), conclude that good leadership consists of particular behaviours or 'styles' which can be learnt.

This theory of learned behaviour has been taken further in recent years with the development of thinking about transformational leadership. This links leadership heavily to change and the personal transformations that are necessary to be able to lead effectively. Reflective learning and continuing personal and professional development are central to this process of change. Implicit in theories of transformational leadership is reliance on other people's reactions – the followers. Theories of dispersed leadership and 'followership' build upon the idea of leadership as a social process, making the leader a facilitator of leadership in others rather than a figurehead as such. The idea of 'followership' resonates with Heifetz's (1996) idea that leadership mobilises people to tackle tough problems. Heifetz suggests that leaders should refrain from providing solutions to problems and instead, facilitate others to find and implement solutions for themselves.

Ideas of dispersed leadership suggest that leadership need not be located at the top of a hierarchy – it can come from all levels and from with out the organisation. The latter applies particularly to the public sector where citizen and community leadership are promoted.

Hartley and Allison (2000) conclude that individual leaders have a clear role in shaping future visions and encouraging local authority employers to see beyond immediate pressures. They identify two features of note from their observations. First, those at the managerial apex played a crucial role but were not always the visible leaders of change – they often delegated the leadership role to others. Second, the leadership role passed from individual to individual as time went by and perceptions changed. Hartley and Allison conclude that leadership is no longer about command and control at the top, although formal power exercised through a directive style was seen to be important for unlocking potential sticking points. Much of the observed leadership was about influencing, and not just within a department or unit, but also across departments, organisations and sectors. This calls for an understanding of the contexts of different units and their interrelationships.

Distributed leadership, promoted through an emphasis on community and citizen leadership, has great potential. How does this sit with concentrated leadership that is promoted through increased accountability, the responsibilities placed on chief social work officers, and others at the top of the tree?

Emergent themes

Certain themes emerge from reviewing the literature on leading and managing people that appear particularly pertinent to issues around how best to develop leadership and management capability. (This assumes, of course, that leadership and management are 'good things' in the first instance.) First, there is debate around the need and relevance of controlling workers as opposed to engaging their commitment (Walton, 1985 in Lawler, 2007). Second, there is debate about leadership's location – is it an attribute of the organisation or the individual (Grint, 2001)?

Leadership versus management

Distinctions between leadership and management are perhaps most apparent if we look at certain aspects of management that relate to control, rigidity and planning, as opposed to the softer aspects now associated with leadership: interpersonal relationships, influence and empowerment. It is not this simple,

however, as previous discussion has perhaps indicated. The human relations school of management promotes theories and styles of management more akin to the interpersonal approach linked to leadership. Similarly, leadership may be partly about the use of interpersonal skills to gain results through others, yet a leader may also be in a situation that requires a more directive, controlling approach.

Kotter (1990) identifies management as being about transactions (controlling, budgeting, organising, planning, staffing, problem-solving) and leadership as being about transformation (establishing vision and direction, communicating the direction, inspiring and motivating people and producing change). Hence, management is about efficiency and regulation, and leadership is about motivation and change (Barker, 1997). These ideas and those of other theorists are reflected in a leadership–management continuum (SfC, 2006b), which identifies separate and distinct leadership and management skills and a number of common skills:

- Skills for management involve: control, planning, performance, supervision, delegation, performance, accountability, finance, monitoring and evaluation, teamwork and team-building;
- Skills for leadership involve: inspiration, transformation, direction, trust, empowerment, creativity, innovation and motivation;
- Overlapping skills and leadership and management are: communication, development, decision-making, integrity, role model, negotiation, knowledge, professional competence, setting standards, flexibility and focus.

Having identified that commonly accepted definitions suggest a difference between management and leadership, why is it that leadership appears to be the emerging favourite?

The swing from management to leadership

In 2005 the Interim Report of Scotland's *Twenty-first Century Social Work Review* suggested that 'the need for effective leadership in the public sector as a whole has arguably never been greater, with increasing complexity of need and a continuing shift towards service integration and user centred delivery. Increasingly that requires that professionals are led rather than managed, enabled and empowered rather than controlled (Scottish Executive, 2005: 38).

With an increasingly complex political and social environment, change is viewed as the only constant. Increased numbers of government programmes, initiatives, and academic commentary identify leadership as a crucial component of improved public sector performance. Modernising government initiatives appear to favour leadership training over management training. National and regional leadership programmes in recent years have developed in many public sector departments, including social (work) services, the prison service, the probation service, the fire service and the NHS. Social services are a little behind other service professionals, such as the NHS, in developing formal frameworks and competences as a backbone to these leadership development programmes.

The definitions of leadership and management implicit in the quotation above, and the apparent preference for leadership in the public sector, indicate that the term 'management', in these circles, tends to be defined in relation to classical theories. This could be attributed partly to the historical context of management interventions in social work, a context that has been similar across the public sector. Management and management development were prominent themes in social services by the 1990s, with a similar increase in the number of academic publications on aspects of management and management development in social work.

The roots of this managerialism are complex, but firmly grounded in political responses to changing public expectations. Management was seen as a means to make public sector organisations more effective, accountable and transparent. However, whilst social work managerialisation may have gone some way to meet public and media needs, internally the term seems to have negative connotations nowadays and is often used to indicate the conflicting values in running social services as a market-driven, quasi-capitalist business (Harris, 2003).

Management's formal, rational aspects are not seen to fit well with the complexity of human lives, and social services cannot be controlled and measured within the tight boundaries often promoted through management theory. As discussed earlier, not all management theory focuses on top-down control. Theory and understanding have evolved from central controlling hierarchies, ruthless pruning and strict measurement of outputs to flatter empowering structures, and an understanding of individual and group motivation and recognition. This has been described as a move from masculine to feminine management – a development that seems to resonate with the core social work values of concern for people and honest, open relationships (Coulshed and Mullender, 2006). 'The challenge is to incorporate business ideas about valuing, developing and listening to staff, listening and responding to 'customers', managing diversity rather than imposing conformity, and trying to build flexibility throughout, rather than copying the negative stereotypes of commercial business' (Coulshed and Mullender, 2006).

Ironically, pressures from stakeholders, including the public and media, have made it difficult for social services to operate in this flexible manner, and there is pressure to be seen to measure and control inputs and outputs. It has been suggested that no single management theory or concept is able to encompass social services' complexity, or meet stakeholder expectations. Perhaps the inspirational vision of strong leaders is seen as a means of enabling individuals to cope with change and maintain focus on the one constant – the need for better public services – and allow a flexibility of delivery within supportive, empowering environments. Conversely, it may be that leadership is another means of control whilst moving away from the negative implications of (business) management. Some suggest that social work values are needed to counterbalance managerialism (Healy, 2002); thus leadership is needed to promote social work values.

Why are leadership and management needed?

In 2003, the Scottish Leadership Foundation (SLF) published the results of its study (Van Zwanenberg, 2003) into the career paths, training, development needs, and experiences of leaders and managers in Scottish social services. Its sample, which included both statutory and voluntary sectors, was relatively small, but was sufficient to be representative. The sample highlighted several common challenges facing leaders and managers in their professional careers:

- Leading with confidence in professional knowledge, skills and values – reiterating the unique contribution of social work to the spectrum of care professionals;
- Leading multi-professional and multi-organisational teams, with a clear focus on achieving successful outcomes for users and carers;

- Developing greater understanding, skill and experience in planning, commissioning and managing services with a multiplicity of providers;
- Developing the skills and experience of service design and delivery in an increasingly competitive and growing market;
- Leading change and transition where there is no specified end state;
- Leading for continuous improvement and learning both within the profession and across linked professions;
- Maintaining and developing the skills in and focus on the individual model of care;
- Maintaining and developing the drive for quality outcomes in terms of the individual, the family and the community;
- Taking the lead in collaborative ventures such as community planning and community participation at a locality level;
- Meeting personal challenges, such as maintaining motivation, identifying how leadership should look, and how this would sit with personal and professional goals and values.

Underpinning all of these was a need for robust management skills in areas such as planning, commissioning, budgeting, financial management, human resource management and change management. These challenges suggested a need that was not currently being met. The *Leading to Deliver* course was a direct response to this. However, Lawler, in his insightful review of literature on leadership in social work (2007), offers some concluding thoughts that encourage the recognition and development of social workers' existing skills, such as group work, including group leadership, openness, tolerance and support – all qualities generally associated with good leadership. Perhaps the leadership skills gap is not as wide as first thought.

How are these leadership and management needs being met?

Various writers on leadership in the social services (Gellis, 2001; Rank and Hutchison, 2000) have commented on the lack of any leadership development in social work training. In the Diploma in Social Work (the previous qualifying course now replaced by the social work degree), management was not a required competence. In the new degree in Scotland, it is a standard. Scotland-wide, SVQs in Social Care, including the Level 4 Managing Social Care and the Registered Managers Award, were the only competency, professional management or leadership model in use in Scotland. This lack was seen to inhibit the progression and movement of staff (Van Zwanenberg, 2003).

The launch of the qualifying honours degree in social work saw a significant change to the content of qualifying programmes, although just two years later, further changes were called for. The report of Scotland's National Review of Social Work, *Changing Lives* (Scottish Executive, 2006c: 56), called for 'universities and service providers ... to work together in a planned way to meet existing gaps in skills' and *Social Work: A 21st Century Profession* (Scottish Executive, 2006a) called for the new degree to ensure that the 'skills, knowledge and understanding of social workers are equal to the task being asked of them' (Scottish Executive, 2006c: 2).

Encouragingly, results from the SLF study indicated quite high proportions of management had undertaken leadership and management training though without a development or standards framework this was necessarily of an *ad hoc* nature. Chief social work officers and senior managers from both the statutory and voluntary sectors were more likely than first and middle managers to have undertaken leadership and management training in areas such as change management, partnership working, cross-organisational working, multi-professional teams, stress management and personal impact. Interestingly, a higher proportion of first, middle and senior management in the voluntary sector had engaged in this training than first, middle and senior management in the statutory sector.

Major questions arise from the literature about leadership and management in relation to the *Changing Lives* agenda in particular: how is a distributed leadership style (which may ensure greater autonomy as well as accountability of front-line staff) compatible with the *Changing Lives'* requirement for greater accountability for chief social work officers?

Leading to Deliver: a case study

We present this as a case study of how leadership training was provided to a significant group of middle managers in social services in Scotland. The programme content focused around four assessed modules, each delivered during a three-day residential course. A fifth assessed module was run as a distance-learning module through The Robert Gordon University Virtual Campus. On the uccessful completion of all five assessments, the student is awarded the Postgraduate Certificate Social Services Leadership, carrying 60 SCOTCAT credits at SVQ Level 5. This award allows those gaining it to satisfy aspects of the Registered Managers Award, an important SSSC registration requirement in Social Services in Scotland.

Content

As a starting point for developing the programme content, *Leading to Deliver* took the major challenges identified by Van Zwanenberg (2003) – the need for strong management skills in planning, commissioning, budgeting, financial management, human resource management and change management.

Four taught modules were designed to meet these challenges:

Module 1 – Changing to Lead. This module covers personal refection on the appropriateness of participants' existing leadership approach through 360° feedback, comparison with others via discussion in syndicate groups and critical analysis of leadership theories. A personal development plan is produced at the end of the module.

Module 2 – Leading and Influencing Change. This module introduces the context for change and assesses various models of change for their applicability in social services. Participants identify skills and behaviours needed to influence and lead change and how to increase the acceptance of change. The syndicate is introduced as a laboratory for learning about and experimenting with team dynamics.

Module 3 – Leading Change in Service Delivery.   This module is the most unfamiliar for participants as it covers the nature and practice of strategic management as well as introducing the concepts of services and process management, and ends with the application of a balanced scorecard approach to performance management.

Module 4 – Leading Delivery through Effective Relationships.   This module is about how to provide a seamless delivery to users and carers through effective partnerships. Collaborative working is the module's key outcome. Participants develop confidence in leading and participating in multi-disciplinary/organisational teams and examine rationales for decisions and the impact of ethics in these situations.

Module 5 – Practice Analysis.   This assignment-based module requires participants to reflect critically on their learning and development in reference to a key piece of practice in leading change and demonstrate how this has influenced their management and leadership.

The Scottish Executive was keen to have as much cross-fertilisation as possible. As a result, the programme was designed for 100 participants at a time, divided into eight syndicate groups, each with one learning support facilitator. Care was taken to mix syndicates across statutory and voluntary sectors, professional backgrounds, and geography. Each cohort of 100 takes roughly ten months to complete the programme.

The programme has a specific underlying teaching and learning philosophy to effect lasting personal change and ongoing personal and professional development. The use of 360° assessment, Myers Briggs (Myers and Myers, 1980), personal development plans and other relevant self-assessment tools encourages participants to take charge of their own development needs and increase their awareness of their personal impact.

The award of a Postgraduate Certificate validated the unique leadership context and capabilities in this sector and aimed to develop enthusiasm and commitment to further study. The five assessed modules required participants to reflect critically on their personal change and development and evidence these, thus strengthening reflective practitioner skills and evidence-based practice.

Many aspects of the programme design also reinforced learning against key sector priorities: for example, using large mixed cohorts facilitated interaction across professional and organisational boundaries, encouraging networking and knowledge-sharing, and helping to promote understanding and awareness of differing practices and approaches in a variety of fields and sectors. This idea of learning from others in a supportive network was further strengthened through using facilitated, cross-syndicate action learning sets.

Support for participants' development, which included personal one-to-one support provided by trained facilitators, was a crucial aspect of the programme. Syndicate group membership was fixed throughout, and this, together with the intensity of the three-day residential modules, led to strong bonds being formed between participants and with their facilitator. It was, however, equally important that participants received support on their return to work so that they entered an environment conducive to the application of learning. To this end, line managers and senior managers within participants' organisations were involved in the progress of the programme through emails, newsletters and feedback on participants' overall progress and development. Participants were also encouraged to identify and use a mentor throughout the programme and beyond.

Content was contextualised through 'mini-lectures' delivered to the entire cohort by the coordinating facilitator: management and social work concepts were introduced during these mini-lectures using relevant examples. The programme development team were mindful of the need to provide credible, expert input in a diverse range of fields and sectors to accommodate the cohort's needs. As such, guest speakers were used in each module to provide expert input on subject matter (e.g. service design) in particular fields (e.g. children and families) and from particular perspectives (e.g. voluntary sector).

More specifically, contextualisation of material was provided through facilitated group work that applied concepts to participants' own work-based practice examples. Given that the programme operates at postgraduate level and aims to encourage participants to undertake further study and self-directed learning, participants were provided with copies of, or direction to, relevant contextualised reading material. This aims to provide evidence and examples of leadership and management concepts in action within their specific social services context, often providing an alternative perspective about material covered in detail during the programme. This self-directed learning was compounded in module assignments that asked participants to apply their learning to work-based scenarios and strongly encouraged them to undertake further reading and study in that specific area.

Some flexibility was built into the programme content by using short workshops delivered on one evening in each module. These were optional, and introduced additional topics of interest not covered directly in the module content, such as budgeting, dealing with the press, business planning, assertiveness, and stress management. Participants were encouraged to run their own workshops where appropriate. A cohort 1 graduate returned to deliver a workshop to cohort 3 on the application of the Bridges' Model of Change (1995) at work.

Issues

The involvement and commitment of participants' managers was, at first, somewhat patchy, coming from an arms' length relationship with their organisations. Because the Scottish Executive wholly funded the programme, participants were selected from applications submitted by their organisation, but not necessarily forming part of the strategic development of that organisation. Hence, when cohort 1 was asked at the end of Module 4 what the greatest difficulties were in applying their learning, most participants cited reasons to do with a lack of organisational and manager commitment. By cohort 5, much greater commitment from the participants' organisations was required, in the form of a change project that a senior officer deemed of strategic importance to the organisation, and a 1½ day pre-session for participants' managers. Participants are now required to produce an outcome scorecard that tracks their progress on their objectives for being involved in *Leading to Deliver*.

Limiting beliefs and how they are challenged

Whilst the programme was originally designed to tackle the sector's lack of leadership confidence, particularly with respect to partnerships with health and education, several other 'limiting beliefs'

(resonating with attitudes expressed in Chapter 10) have emerged as the programme has matured. These limiting beliefs can be expressed as follows.

Practice example: limiting beliefs

'We're not worthy.'

'We know best.'

'They [establishment] don't know what they're talking about.'

'Intuitive decision-making is best for social services.'

'We aren't given the resources to do the job.'

These self-limiting beliefs are important for all of social work and social services to address. Are these what influence professional relationships with senior colleagues in social work and other disciplines? The 'safe' environment of the syndicate group is critical for creating challenges to these limiting beliefs and helping participants to adapt their beliefs and be supported in attitudinal change.

Within the syndicates, these limiting beliefs are challenged in the context of transformational change, and transformed in the following ways.

Practice example: transforming limiting beliefs

'We're not worthy' becomes transformed to 'we need to build greater confidence.'

'We know best' to 'how do we empower users, carers, and staff, including involuntary users?'

'They don't know what they're talking about' to 'I need to take responsibility.'

'Intuitive decision-making is best for social services' to 'we need to use evidence-based practice.'

'We aren't given the resources' to 'how may we prioritise better and more clearly?'

Impact

As of August 2007, three extensions to the contract for two cohorts have been made, making five cohorts of approximately 100 participants each. A majority of participants on cohorts 1–4 have now completed the programme and graduated (90%). Whilst it is very difficult to assess the full implications and outcomes of such a large and complex programme, an assessment of how the programme has thus far met its intended aims for cohort 1 has been carried out.

This indicates that the programme is extremely well received by participants. Their peers, staff and managers all perceive that they have made changes in the way they lead and manage (statistically significant changes were found using a repeat 360° feedback). There are many examples of organisational impact and evidence of community benefit. In terms of the residential periods of learning, 96% of those participants who started the programme attended Module 4 some six to nine months later. Each cohort of roughly 100 graduates adds to a growing group of change agents in the Scottish social services sector. It is emerging that this population and its managers represent a critical mass of managers committed to Scotland's *Changing Lives* agenda and are acting to implement the agenda.

Lessons learnt

Focus groups of potential participants, their managers, their organisations and users and carers, were carried out prior to cohort 1 to inform the approach and content of the programme. These groupings were revisited after cohort 1 to ascertain the impact of the programme. Each module was evaluated with an exit-level questionnaire which created a continuous improvement orientation for the project, with changes in approach being effected for the next module, and changes to content and teaching process for the same module in the next cohort. Each cohort was surveyed after the completion of Module 5 and asked to retake the 360° feedback. Their managers were also surveyed after cohort 1. Nine participants from cohort 1 have been followed in a longitudinal study to determine the long-term impact of the programme.

The syndicate group work is critical for helping participants surface and deal with their 'limiting beliefs' resulting in changed behaviours. The syndicate also acts as a safe environment to admit and work on weaknesses and to receive feedback, support, challenge and encouragement from other syndicate members and the facilitator.

The combination of intensive skills development with academic assignments at a postgraduate level has been an extremely effective combination. The forced review, deeper reading, understanding and reflection of the assignments have increased the use and retention of skills and knowledge developed in the residential periods of learning. The experience of Taylor Clarke is that where there is no requirement for assignments, participants are much more likely to revert to original behaviours and have difficulty recalling content and evidencing the use of new skills or techniques six to twelve months later.

Bonding within syndicates was marked, with many continuing to keep in contact and indeed help each other well after the end of the programme. This contrasts with the idea in cohort 1 of having cross-syndicate action learning sets to create greater networking. These action-learning sets found it impossible to develop the trust and openness that participants had in the syndicates. As such, they proved to be quite superficial in nature and attendances dropped off dramatically. Whilst in cohort 1 an attempt was made to mix geographically, and in cohort 2 by type of work, in cohort 3 and thereafter, the sets were coincident with the syndicate. This worked much more effectively. In

cohort 5, participants were asked to carry out a change project that supported their organisation's response to Scotland's *Changing Lives*. Here cross-syndicate groupings of similar projects did have some success, although it was noticeable that many participants preferred to work only with those in their own syndicate who had similar projects.

How did participants experience the impact? The following examples illustrate how participants experienced undergoing a transformation leadership change.

Practice example: leadership change

'Gaining an understanding of the climate of change and the drivers behind that which has allowed me to participate and bring my team into the planning of services locally.'

'I have demonstrated my ability to lead change by leading the team through exercises when we vision the future and put change into a wider context and in relation to other agencies, and in managing individual responses to change and making the transition a to the new services.'

'I have a better understanding of how I as an individual can influence what goes on rather than seeing myself as a cog in a wheel – how I can actually have quite a lot of influence. Again, that links to confidence, but it is more than that. It's about realising you have influence if you want it and taking a more positive outlook. There has also been a re-injection of energy and enthusiasm into the job. I certainly feel that.'

'Emotionally, I am more mature, because I can understand the bigger, picture, even if I don't always agree with it – I now know why my directors make the decisions they make, and I don't now get angry and upset, or get disheartened, or take it personally. Now I've channelled that energy in a different way – I am solution-orientated. It's a more balanced approach. There was no similar focus on strategy in previous training.'

'It makes me more efficient and able to participate in discussions, for example responding to evaluation questionnaires for our service. I would not have known where our project would have needed a goal to comply with funding requirements, and especially, I see the long-term strategy behind that, that is to get it to work in partnership – that it's not the case of putting in buzzwords, it's a case of understanding the key drivers – of understanding why these things are asked for, for funding applications.'

Conclusion

The previous section reviewed the ongoing and continuous review and learning that the Taylor Clarke Partnership and The Robert Gordon University, in consultation with the Scottish Executive, engaged in whilst developing and refining the programme over five cohorts.

What were the overall major challenges? As the previous section stated, an early one was getting the buy-in of participants' managers and organisations. Social workers know that going away on a course that transforms them personally may have limited value when they return to the organisation (or indeed family) who have not joined up to the change project.

In the initial programme development, two local challenges in delivery seemed possible. Neither materialised. The collaboration of a business school and a social work school in a university originally meant that stereotypes (encapsulated by the initial interchange: business school – 'I have never met a social worker'; social work school – 'I don't wear sandals and we do a much wider range of work than child protection') had to be and were easily abandoned. There was mutual learning about social work's context, values, policy and practice, and useful lessons from business that social work could learn in relation to leadership and management.

Again, the potential challenge for a social work school of working with a private business consultancy quickly proved non-existent. The Taylor Clarke Partnership had considerable experience of consultancy in the public sector. More importantly, values, ethics and teaching and learning preferred strategy coincided extremely well, and the private–public partnership was able to negotiate and problem solve – for example, when the assessment process appeared, at times, problematic to a few participants, and when, for the syndicate leaders, the assessors seemed rather distant from the teaching and learning (a justifiable view). Perhaps this tension was resolved by mutual trust and respect between the three authors of this chapter and their willingness to address problematic issues and where necessary, resolve them.

A further challenge for all of us was running a very high-profile programme on behalf of the Scottish Executive. This involved, and still does, uncertainty about the future and funding, but more problematically adapting to changes in the Scottish Executive (now the Scottish Government) policy, in particular in relation to the balance of leadership and management and in relation to budgeting and financial management (huge policy developments and changes which we and participants had to embrace at short notice) and the *Changing Lives* (Scottish Executive, 2006c) report with its emphasis on leadership and management as one of its change streams.

Social work education inevitably is an activity with a potentially high level of government scrutiny of how well or badly social work helps service users achieve the outcomes they want or, for involuntary users, society wants. Delivering a programme on leadership in social work and social services inevitably is, if anything, an even more political activity. The chapter authors have therefore appreciated the debate and mutual interchange with the Scottish Executive (now the Scottish Government) and also with the Scottish Leadership Foundation in monitoring and developing the programme. It has been a good model of partnership (with all its contributions) and their continuing support is appreciated.

Questions for reflection

1. Reflect on your own work experience: how do you see the difference between leadership and management?

2. How do you integrate leadership into your delivery of personalised services?

Further reading

Harris, J. (2005) *The Social Work Business*. London: Routledge.
This book offers a critical examination of managerialism in social work services.

Kotter, J. (1990) *A Force for Change*. London: Free Press.
This book provides an introduction to transformational leadership.

Lawler, J. (2007) 'Leadership in social work: a case of *caveat emptor?*', *British Journal of Social Work*, 37: 123–41.
The article provides a careful critique of leadership in social work.

Martin, V. (2003) *Leading Change in Health and Social Care*. London: Routledge.
This is a helpful text which examines leadership in health and social care.

Part Four

Learning organisations and criticality

Patricia Higham

The last two chapters, 14 and 15, take a step back from direct practice to consider organisational issues for PQ.

Social work practice takes place within a world of employment, either in organisations or on a self-employed basis. Chapter 14 *Employment perspectives and learning organisations,* by Nicholas Blinston and Patricia Higham, discusses social work recruitment and retention, arguing that employers should develop learning organisations that support PQ as a way of addressing recruitment and retention and ensuring that practice is fit for purpose. This chapter builds on Chapter 13's discussion of leadership.

The attainment of PQ qualifications logically should lead to career progression, but a significant impediment is the absence of a UK-wide career ladder for social work. Chapter 15, *PQ issues, career development and criticality,* by Patricia Higham, discusses issues and opportunities for PQ, including career ladders, and considers the concept of criticality in relation to critical reflective practice before reprising the question posed in Chapter 1: *How will a social worker in possession of a post-qualifying award – at any level – be expected to be different from a social worker without one?*

Chapter 14

Employment perspectives and learning organisations

Nicholas Blinston and Patricia Higham

Introduction

Chapter 14 argues that employers should become learning organisations and recognise that PQ can help with recruitment and retention issues by enhancing professional identity, morale, and social workers' capacity to deal with change. Rather than competing for staff locally and regionally, strategic regional partnerships between employers and universities are best placed to agree strategies for recruitment, retention and professional learning.

Recruitment and retention

Chapter 1 established that the recruitment of qualified social workers is a longstanding issue (CCW, 2003, 2007; NISSC, 2002; Scottish Executive, 2002b; SfC, 2005). An equal challenge for UK employers is retention (JISC, 2005; *Personnel Today*, 2003). Social workers cite stress (Collings and Murray, 1996), low morale (Jones et al., 1991), and changing role expectations that devalue the professional role (Dominelli, 1996) as reasons for leaving their employment.

Changing role expectations

A significant reason for leaving social work is social workers' perceptions of changes in their roles. Employers, employees and independent practitioners articulate a range of concerns about care management that apparently routinises adult services, and policy directions that promote service users' and carers' views, thus evoking professional anxiety in some social workers (Atkins, 1998).

As organisations become more user-led, with Direct Payments (DH, 2004c; Leece and Leece, 2006) and individual budgets (Clements, 2007; SCIE, 2007), who should define social workers' roles? Some social workers may still see themselves as gatekeepers of scarce resources, rather than as skilled professionals with distinctive roles in specialist multi-professional services. Some social workers may not be certain which organisations they will work for, or who their colleagues will be. Uncertainties caused by organisational changes have led many social workers to question their traditional values and the qualities they bring to service delivery (see Chapter 2).

A study of PQ candidates (GSCC/CWDC/SfC, 2006) noted multi-professional practice's impact on social workers (see Chapter 10), suggesting that social work might become dissipated as a minority profession in organisations whose primary task is not social work (Postle et al., 2002: 157). The study envisions PQ as a potential means of countering this negative outcome. However, given the uncertainty of change, it is not entirely surprising that some disillusioned social workers leave the profession altogether.

The 2003 National Employers' Skills Survey (DfES/LSC/SEMTA, 2004) revealed that vacancy levels in social care, including social work, were approximately twice the level for all types of industrial, commercial and public sector employment in England, and that vacancy and turnover rates indicated a national average for all directly employed social services staff as 11%. This rate showed some improvement from 2001–2, but London was worse, with a 17% vacancy rate, and regional variations showed a higher rate in southeastern England (16.7%) and between regional authorities. The report concluded that some employers had more success than others in retaining their staff.

Steps to improve retention

The reform of social work education (DH, 2002) that led to the introduction of the social work degree, social work registration, and new PQ frameworks, was intended, *inter alia*, to address recruitment and retention. Governmental reviews of social work like *Options for Excellence* (DH/DfES, 2006), and the *Twenty-first Century Review of Social Work* in Scotland (Scottish Executive, 2006c) called for a review of social workers' roles (Blewitt et al., 2007).

Local authorities' workforce planning strategies adopted different strategies for the retention problem, typically positioning themselves with differential pay and conditions in competition with each other. The Social Services Inspectorate's Annual Report for 2003 (DH, 2003b) drew attention to the lack of capacity and workforce issues as underlying themes in the recruitment and retention crisis. Although noting the positive impact of the government's social work recruitment drive, there were too few social workers to meet workforce demands, notwithstanding innovative initiatives to increase role flexibility.

Workforce development in Scotland

Under the Regulation of Care (Scotland) Act 2001, the Scottish Social Services Council (SSSC) has a responsibility to address recruitment and retention challenges. The Council promotes workforce development – a coherent education and training strategy that underpins the delivery and development of social work, social care and related activities. Workforce development aims to raise service standards and create a more highly skilled workforce by improving training for social workers and care staff.

Other UK countries

Other UK countries recognise, in principle, the importance of workforce development, which is one of the principles of a learning organisation. Therefore if social services organisations were to become learning organisations that undertook workforce development in a more systematic way, they would be better equipped to address their recruitment and retention problems. The next part of this chapter explores learning organisations.

Learning organisations

Chapter 1's discussion of PQ frameworks in the four UK countries noted that that one purpose of the Wales PQ framework is to allow social care organisations to develop as learning organisations. Chapter 1 explored Schön's and Argyris's theories on organisational learning (Argyris and Schön, 1978, 1996), based on the premise that rapid societal change forces organisations to adapt their working practices. A learning society that promotes continuous ongoing learning is particularly suited for dealing with pressures for change. Learning organisations and PQ share characteristics – both enable employers to tackle change. Learning organisation theory (Pedlar et al., 1997; Poell et al., 2004) can contribute to increased understanding of how to tackle recruitment and retention issues.

Single-loop and double-loop learning

The concept of double-loop learning (Argyris, 1976) is characteristic of learning organisations. Senge (1990) suggests that single-loop learning, a method of trying to improve on what is already being done, is often practised by organisations that respond to crises by aiming for short-term improvements in a single area without considering wider contexts. Senge argues that in the short term, organisations may try to ignore feedback loops, but feedback can reappear to exacerbate longer-term organisational problems. Senge portrays learning as a dynamic process that recognises cause and effect, requiring organisations to engage in systematic thinking that links separate processes. Accordingly, he promotes 'system maps' that portray connecting systems.

Double-loop learning (Argyris and Schön, 1978) is more sophisticated than single-loop learning because it adopts a questioning attitude to taken-for-granted assumptions and values, and looks beyond established structures and processes. Double-loop learning is essential for a learning organisation because its characteristic questioning style is more likely to lead to change than single-loop learning.

Shared characteristics with PQ

Learning organisation theory contains features that are consistent with the PQ frameworks. For example, evidence-based practice, discussed in Chapter 11, is important for a learning organisation whose learning is based on experience. Leadership, a new emphasis for PQ, is also an important concept for a learning organisation. Schein (1992) promotes problem-solving leadership that encourages an organisation to reflect on itself, self-diagnose problems, and then self-manage transformational change. Schein

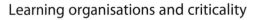

considered the possibility of developing a set of assumptions that could encourage perpetual learning and change, whilst at the same time becoming stable parts of organisational culture. Leadership (see Chapter 13) is crucial for developing a learning organisation – according to Schein, leaders serve as stewards of an organisation's vision as well as mentors of that vision in relation to others.

Conceptualising a learning organisation

Iles and Sutherland (2001) identified five features of a learning organisation in relation to change management in the NHS, which are transferable to social work organisations.

1. *Organisational structures* – managed hierarchies that enhance stakeholder involvement in decision-making and support networking and teamwork.
2. *Organisational culture* – openness, creativity and experimentation; freedom to try new approaches.
3. *Information systems* – the processing and sharing of complex information to enable effective knowledge management.
4. *Human resource practices* – appraisal and rewards that promote long-term learning, and the acquisition and sharing of new skills and knowledge.
5. *Leadership model* – communicating the vision of a learning organisation with openness and reflection on learning; making certain the organisation has capacity to learn, change and develop – stewardship of the vision (Senge, 1990).

Organisational learning and improvement

Nevis, DiBella and Gould (1995) defined organisational learning as organisational capacity, based on experience, to maintain or improve performance, but also acknowledged a complex chain of processes in which this learning must take place. Nevis et al. suggested facilitating factors for the improvement in learning.

- *Scanning imperative* – gathering information, curiosity and awareness.
- *Performance gap* – shared perception of gaps between actual and desired performance levels.
- *Concern for measurement* – effort to define key factors (metrics, specific quantifiable measures).
- *Experimental mindset* – support for new ventures, using changed work processes, policies and structures as continuous learning opportunities.
- *Climate of openness* – open organisational communications, sharing rather than hiding problems, using debate as a problem-solving activity.
- *Continuous education* – ongoing commitment to education and development at all organisational levels.
- *Operational variety* – an appreciation of diversity, pluralistic definition of competences.
- *Multiple advocates* – more than one champion, all employees advancing new ideas.
- *Involved leadership* – leaders implementing an organisational vision, interacting frequently with employees, and involved in educational programmes.
- *Systems perspective* – problems and solutions viewed as systemic relationships among processes, connections between different teams' needs and goals and the overall organisation.

Discussion

This systematic thinking about learning organisations poses challenges to social work employers who work in contexts of annual inspections, target-setting and political scrutiny where too often effort is directed towards short-term gains rather than longer-term improvements. Social work organisations in the UK might struggle to organise themselves along the lines of fluidity advocated by a learning organisation, especially when an organisation has to manage statutory risk. Within social work's scrutinised responsibilities, these changes, if put into practice, would threaten centralised systems of planning and control. A local authority employer, working within a regional framework with other local authorities, might worry about where accountability would sit in a crisis.

In a social work environment, employers may perceive that potential risks are so great that social workers should err on the side of caution. In those situations, social workers' actions should be scrutinised through supervision, but also supported when they take risks based on appropriate knowledge. The culture of a learning organisation should be such that it seeks to win social workers' commitment to learning from experience (Gould, 2000).

Another crucial factor for a learning organisation's success is the amount of time social workers are given for critical reflection, both in the immediate practice situation and for adopting good practice models from the wider practice community. Critical reflection (see Chapters 1, 2 and 4) is difficult for employers to promote when faced with staff shortages and enduring work pressures, but it helps create improved motivation among social workers.

Social work's image

Social work's poor image in the media has not helped employers to recruit and retain staff. Roche and Rankin (2004) argue that for many years social services were regarded as peripheral, ranking low in the welfare state hierarchy. The public's perception was that social work was unskilled, poorly paid and therefore not for them.

Practice example

An online debate (Community Care, 2004) produced these comments on what would make social work more attractive:

Social workers risk their careers if a child protection case goes wrong ... people want a job where the value systems are clearer and responsibility is something that can be clear.

Retaining staff can be better achieved when social workers are adequately supported in a learning culture within their workplace.

Employer responses

To deliver change agendas, employers recognised the need to work hard to recruit qualified social work staff. Some have introduced enticements to attract staff, but the question arises of whether these are simply add-ons and a means of disguising the lack of investment in workforce development (Thorpe, 2004).

In England, the Children's Workforce Strategy (DfES, 2006a) seeks to build a world-class workforce for children and young people by addressing workforce planning issues, including those of social workers. The Strategy identified the importance of addressing supply, retention and quality issues facing children's social work. Pay and status were highlighted, but factors of poor supervision and management and insufficient training were also identified.

Sector Skills Councils within adult social care (Skills for Care) and children and young people's services (the Children's Workforce Development Council) in England, together with national initiatives on reshaping services around service users, resulted in a drive for regional workforce planning, illustrated by the establishment of learning resource centre networks (LRCN) under Skills for Care England's regional offices. LRCNs had regional responsibility for improving social work practice placements and NVQ provision, requiring employers and universities to collaborate in addressing problems. The Association of Directors of Adult Social Services (ADASS) has taken some responsibility for workforce planning, which has led to a regional approach in some areas. The introduction of the PQ social work framework in England requires regional collaboration under the joint leadership of Skills for Care and the Children's Work Development Council (although at the time of writing organisational arrangements may change).

Investigating recruitment and retention

What makes some employers more successful in recruiting and retaining social work staff? In 2004, a number of local authority employers in England were awarded Beacon status (CSCI, 2004) for supporting social care workers (including social workers). A small research project (Blinston, 2005) sought to discover whether Beacon Authority employers could be considered learning organisations by comparing two social services employers in England (Employers X and Y) – how they applied organisational cultures to practice, senior managers' leadership styles, recruitment and retention rates, and specific policies designed to ensure good performance in this sphere.

The two employers

Employer X

At the time of the research, Employer X, which had Investors in People status, had been a three-star authority for three years and saw itself as having a high profile at the forefront of national developments. Its well-resourced spending plans were linked to service planning and audit trails. Located in inner London, during weekdays its population increased to over 1 million because of an influx of commuters. Employer X had areas of significant affluence, but also some of severe deprivation. The unemployment rate was 7.5%, above the national average. The black and minority ethnic population was about 10.9%, with over 100 recognised languages spoken.

Employer X developed a corporate strategy of an integrated approach for recruitment and retention, with a vision of becoming an employer of choice and setting new standards for the public sector, prompted by its staff turnover in 2003/04, which was 19.1% compared to an inner London average of 14.1%. Vacancy rates were high at 22% compared with an inner London average of 18.3%. Housing costs were a major issue. Many social workers commuted to work with a typical journey taking over one hour. The keyworker housing scheme was seen as complicated, and had little effect on housing costs. It was thought that in ten years' time, unless housing was properly addressed, the staffing crisis would become critical.

Children and families reception teams employed large numbers of agency staff who generally stayed only a short while. Because of high turnover, inexperienced young social workers were appointed to highly complex critical environments, which led to stress and exacerbated staff turnover. Temporary social workers from agencies (typically, social workers from Australia, New Zealand or South Africa on working holidays) were appointed to fill vacancy gaps.

Employer X reviewed its 'brand', revising and streamlining key messages to target potential applicants. An introductory bonus of £1,000 and an annual retention bonus of £1,000 after two years service were paid to professionally qualified social work staff and care management staff. An improved starting salary was introduced for children and families social workers. A new corporate pay structure shrank pay bands from 14 to eight, with expectations that staff would move through salary bands based on performance management and assessment processes. The integrated strategy included recognising and rewarding staff contributions and exceptional performance with discretionary pay, and schemes that recognised the need for a work/life balance.

Employer X benchmarked itself against leadership and management standards. Its flat management structure sought to convey a clear understanding of roles and responsibilities and it developed competences that emphasised leadership and consultation for all management layers. It invested significantly in a coaching programme for aspiring black and minority ethnic staff, which improved their career prospects. A role of assistant team manager was created to support newly qualified staff and offer one-to-one supervision.

With a background in research and evidence-based practice, the director expected the new initiatives to be based on evidenced outcomes, where managers operated with moral and ethical perspectives within an incremental change philosophy. Formal workforce planning was an element of service planning, but managers sometimes confused workforce planning with workforce development. However, employer X recognised that changes in legislation would require more rigorous approaches to workforce planning.

Corporate and departmental objectives were linked to individuals' performance management plans. Key objectives were linked to performance and pay. Training plans set explicit targets for teams and individuals, who were encouraged and supported to attain their training requirements. To retain good staff, Employer X was open to individual requests for a range of development opportunities.

Analysis

Young, single, newly qualified social workers were attracted to Employer X because of its reputation for being well organised, its systematic approach to service development, and its variety of social work experience. Exit interviews with staff indicated the main reasons for leaving were career moves, promotion and moving out of London for housing, rather than overt dissatisfaction with Employer X.

Employer X was confident in performance, demonstrating maturity as an organisation, with a sense of knowing where it was going, and expecting to build on previous innovation, successful management and service delivery. Employer X scored highly on organisational structure and culture, with a commitment to learning and innovation. Despite evidence that Employer X based its performance and initiatives on hard facts, and benchmarked itself against other successful authorities, it was difficult to gain specific information on how Employer X acquired, processed and shared knowledge.

Employer X's holistic and integrated strategic planning processes, linked to organisational learning and development, were consistent with many characteristics of a learning organisation. However, an area for concern was its lack of strategic partnerships with neighbour employers. Although London employers could have managed the labour market more successfully if they took a regional approach, there was no evidence that Employer X considered this.

Employer Y

Employer Y, a two-star unitary authority with promising prospects whose overall common performance assessment in 2004 was 'good', was in a relatively affluent area of southwest England, with a growing population, low unemployment, a mix of rural and urban centres, and a black and minority ethnic population of 2.4%. Employer Y split its social services department to form a children and young people's department and a community care department. A unit within the community care department provided workforce development functions for all social work staff under a service level agreement.

Employer Y became a Beacon Authority for its workforce recruitment principally because of its trainee social worker scheme. The other aspect that helped Employer Y to become a Beacon Authority was its evidence-based practice network, whose aim was to translate the results of existing research into service and practice developments. Despite this commitment to reflection and learning, it was said that the network went through peaks and troughs in activity and engagement.

Employer Y was the first employer in the region to gain single status, which resulted in pay rises for experienced social workers. The pay rises had a potential positive effect for recruiting experienced workers, and a potential negative effect for not attracting 'new blood', except for their trainee social worker scheme. (A neighbouring employer then introduced social worker career progression, giving the rival employer an edge on pay for newly qualified social workers.)

Individual social workers underwent an annual performance and development review that set objectives linked to departmental service plans, which fed into teams' staff development plans, that in turn informed the workforce development unit of training needs and requirements. Employer Y introduced a qualifications framework (not linked to pay) that stipulated qualifications criteria and core training requirements for each post, and explained how the department would support social workers to gain these qualifications.

Analysis

Employer Y developed a good reputation for service planning and delivery on performance measures, but lacked specific workload management policies, although staff carried realistic workloads that enabled them to meet performance targets. Employer Y's trainee social work scheme, although highly regarded within the department, was a stand-alone scheme with seemingly few links to workforce planning as a whole and no links to wider workforce plans or wider planning processes, despite

Employer Y having a strong culture of service planning that linked strategic plans to team and individual needs. Leaders were role models, communicating a vision, planning and giving direction. A 2004 employee satisfaction survey found that 94% of staff were aware of their section/team aims and purposes, 88.5% felt they had a clear purpose, and 67% said that Employer Y was effectively managing changes to its services and structures.

As a relatively new organisation, Employer Y worked hard at its planning processes, giving time and space for managers to get the job done, and was proud of its reputation locally of delivering what it promised. One of its characteristics seemed to be 'control', but this was balanced by a view that leaders were open to new ideas, encouraging creativity and allowing experimentation.

Overall, Employer Y displayed a linear approach to learning rather than double-loop learning. Some of Employer Y's processes and initiatives did not appear to be interconnected – although worthwhile, these contributed to the overall plan by serendipity as much as intent. Employer Y had a vision of its future direction, was confident that it was performing well, supported by external measures such as the star rating and its Investors in People award, but there was no evidence that Employer Y reflected on its processes, perhaps because it was a new organisation.

Employer Y adopted a pragmatic approach to recruitment and retention rather than a conceptual approach, paid social workers well, and provided a planned environment and a qualifications framework. Social workers seemed to like working for Employer Y. Like other local authorities, Employer Y did not work in regional partnerships to tackle recruitment and retention issues.

Comparison

A matrix based on Iles and Sutherland's five principles of a learning organisation (2001) and Nevis, DiBella and Gould's ten facilitating factors (1995) compared the two employers' strategies.

What contributes to social workers' retention in employment?

The comparison revealed that social workers were attracted to well-run, successful organisations, where they could gain high levels of satisfaction. Neither employer mentioned PQ as a possible motivator for retention. Understanding motivation is essential for improving staff retention. Motivating factors include:

1 Appraisal systems coupled with good communication.
2 Involvement in decision-making processes, particularly with staff affected by change.
3 Good induction.
4 Time and space to reflect.
5 Support from supervision.
6 Personal development.
7 Career progression and pathways seen as open and fair.
8 Enhanced responsibility.
9 Flexible working hours that recognise work/life balance.
10 Access to 'state of the art' communication tools.
11 Good working environments.
12 Clear policies and procedures.

Table 14.1 Learning organisation matrix: Employers X and Y

Principles	Characteristics	Employer X Evidence	Employer Y Evidence
Organisational structure	*Stakeholder involvement. Team working. Able to adapt new structures.*	*Stakeholder involvement:* Consultation; committee reports. Stakeholders' views considered. Internal/external/trade unions focus groups. Consultation with community. Partnership groups relating to service areas.	*Stakeholder involvement:* Annual employee satisfaction survey, management 'walkabouts', 'sounding board' forum, Investors in People.
		Team working: Individual aims and objectives linked to those of the team. Organised and systematic.	*Team working:* Team development days, members support managers and devolve decision-making.
		New structures: Leadership works hard to enable change. Transformational. Flat management structure. Clear understanding of roles. Incremental change.	*New structures:* Staff survey on effectively managing change.
Organisational culture	*Openness, creativity and experimentation. All levels able to offer innovations. Commitment to learning at all levels.*	*Openness, creativity and experimentation:* Very open. Always encourages creativity. Neutral regarding experimentation. Failure is not encouraged. Culture of risk assessment. Councilors 'love us to do new things, as long as the press and publicity are good'.	*Openness, creativity and experimentation:* Very open to change and new ideas. Encourages creativity and allows for experimentation.
		Innovations: Key performance objective for managers. Likes to be at the forefront of national developments.	*Innovations:* Trainee social worker scheme.
		Commitment to learning: Training plans linked to business plans. Well resourced.	*Commitment to learning:* Evidence based practice network.
Information systems	*Support practice:* Acquisition, processing and sharing of knowledge. Awareness of internal/external environment.	*Support practice:* Performance management based on hard facts.	*Support practice:* Information systems project board. Process owners group. User group.
		Acquisition, processing and sharing of knowledge: New initiatives based on evidence.	
		Awareness of internal/external environment: Benchmarks itself against other 'successful' authorities	

(Continued)

Table 14.1 (Continued)

Principles	Characteristics	Employer X Evidence	Employer Y Evidence
Human resource practices	*Support individual learning and acquisition of new skills. Appraisal and rewards.*	*Individual learning:* Personal training plans linked to personal management plan. *New skills:* Pathways for unqualified staff. *Appraisal and rewards:* Development and training key to appraisal.	*Individual learning:* Induction, supervision, annual performance and development review, support for CPD. *New skills:* Staff development action plans. Qualification framework. *Appraisal and rewards:* Annual performance and development review linked to service plan.
Leadership	*Role model. Communicates the vision. Performance improvement through learning.*	*Role model:* Always open to new learning. Innovative. Moral and ethical perspective. Energy and imagination. *Communicates the vision:* Enthusiastically communicates vision. Gives direction. *Performance improvement through learning:* Sets standard and manages performance.	*Role model:* Always open to new learning. Approachable. Sets standards. *Communicates the vision:* Enthusiastically communicates the vision. *Performance improvement through learning:* Gives direction. Very good at planning. Time and space given to service planning. Supportive of training through budget provision.

Many of these, link with the overall purposes of continuing professional development and PQ, and some might be the outcomes of PQ and CPD.

Does being considered a learning organisation help employers with recruitment and retention?

Employer X saw recruitment and retention as part of its wider strategy and planning framework rather than as a stand-alone activity. Employer Y took a more compartmentalised approach. Its recruitment and retention strategy, although successful, was a discrete activity that did not appear to link with wider strategies. Although both employers displayed some characteristics of learning organisations (with Employer X demonstrating more of these), neither had developed a workforce development strategy that was fully fit for the future.

Current situation

Time has now moved on from when this comparison was undertaken. What has changed? Some progress in recruitment is reported. According to the Pay and Workforce Strategy Survey 2006, the number of authorities reporting difficulties in recruiting social workers (children and families) decreased from 89% to 78% between 2004 and 2006 (I& DeA Knowledge, 2007). Recruitment issues may ease as more social work graduates join the social work workforce. Bursaries for qualifying training, trainee social worker schemes and the legacy of the Practice Learning Taskforce (see Chapter 12) may also benefit recruitment, but it continues as a worrying issue. The percentages of employers reporting recruitment difficulties are still sufficiently high to cause alarm.

Depressingly, the overall problem of retention does not seem to have improved markedly since 2005. In 2006, *Options for Excellence* (DH/DfES) reported that 49% of English local authorities found retention of children's social workers difficult or very difficult, and that the same was probably true for social workers practising with adults. A 2006 survey from the Chartered Institute of Personnel and Development (CIPD) found a significant increase in employers struggling to retain staff – almost eight in ten finding retention a problem in 2006 compared to nearly seven in ten during 2005. In contrast, the Welsh Local Government Association stated that during 2006–7, the number of staff employed in social services in Wales increased by 3% compared to 2005–6, but also acknowledged that recruitment and retention remained an issue for which no quick solution was possible (Dagnell, 2007).

Steps to address retention

The PQ frameworks, if supported by employers, potentially could enhance motivation and increase job satisfaction, thus contributing to a recruitment and retention strategy.

The Department of Health, Skills for Care England and the Care Councils in Scotland, Northern Ireland and Wales published 'good practice' examples of recruitment and retention strategies on their websites – for example, the University of Salford, in partnership with employers, offers a short course for those returning to social work, which updates their professional knowledge on practice changes that have occurred since they left the profession.

All the UK countries recognised in 2003 that comprehensive up-to-date workforce data for social care and children's services workers were very limited. Consequently, an ongoing project has compiled national minimum data sets (NMDS–SC) to understand trends and make suitable predictive plans as part of workforce development strategies (SfC, 2006a). The Scottish Government developed a Core Minimum Data Set (CMDS) (Scottish Government, 2007) to improve the quality of data available on the social services workforce in Scotland. However, because of the rapidly changing nature of the workforce, with sizeable numbers of eastern Europeans and other migrants gaining employment in the personal social services, there is some doubt whether an accurate picture of the workforce is possible.

Conclusion

Change Consultancy and Training's report on recruitment and retention in the West Midlands care sector (SfC West Midlands, 2007) usefully summarises national trends. Of local authorities, 81% reported difficulties in the recruitment and retention of social workers, but only 43% reported diffi-culties in retaining occupational therapists and environmental health officers, and 28% experienced problems retaining teachers. The report criticises the typical 'knee-jerk' response of some London local authorities to increase pay as a response to retention issues, pointing out that this attracts staff from neighbouring boroughs, which then triggers other employers to raise pay or else cope as best they can with increased vacancies. The problem lies in an insufficient supply of social workers rather than with insufficient pay.

The report recommends that social worker shortages be addressed nationally (although acknowl-edging regional variations). Its recommendations echo Blinston's small-scale (2005) study and implicitly support learning organisation values by concluding that pay is not the primary solution – employees are said to want knowledge and personal development. Employers who link their work-ers' personal and career goals with organisational goals will attract and motivate employees, a conclusion that fits well with this chapter's premise that becoming a learning organisation and pro-moting PQ will address recruitment and retention. The future will reveal whether employers will recognise PQ's value in relation to recruitment and retention and whether employer collaboration on a regional basis becomes an accepted strategy.

Questions for reflection

1. Think of a social work organisation that you know. To what extent is it a learning organisation?
2. What motivates social workers to continue in their employment?
3. Why should employers support social workers' PQ?

Further reading

Coulshed, V., Mullender, A., Jones, D.N. and Thompson, N. (2006) *Management in Social Work* (3rd edition). Basingstoke: Palgrave Macmillan.

This classic text's updated content includes a discussion of learning organisations.

Gould, N. (2000) 'Becoming a learning organisation: a social work example', *Social Work Education*, 19, 6: 585–96.

Gould explores, *inter alia*, knowledge hierarchies, the role of supervision and coaching, action research, reflective practice and informal learning.

Gould, N. and Baldwin, M. (eds) (2004) *Social Work, Critical Reflection and the Learning Organisation*. Aldershot: Ashgate.

This book contains useful chapters that explore learning organisations in relation to critical reflective practice, supervision and organisational learning.

Chapter 15

PQ issues, career development and criticality

Patricia Higham

Introduction

Although drawing the book to a close, the discussion in Chapter 15 is a beginning, not an ending because PQ is a developing endeavour. The chapter discusses issues (academic levels of PQ awards, award portability, the absence of career ladders, the shortfall of social work educators and researchers) and opportunities (organisational collaboration, professional doctorates, consultant social workers and outcome evaluation). Finally, the chapter reiterates the theme of critical reflective practice by considering criticality in relation to PQ.

Organisational aspects

The qualifying social work degree, registration, and post-registration training and learning (PRTL) are building blocks of professional social work, but successful PQ frameworks are essential for social work to become fully recognised as a profession. At the time of writing, PQ has yet to prove its success with practitioners and employers. This book argues the merits of PQ – to help practitioners move from competence to capability and then to expertise (Chapter 1), to develop critical reflection that sustains morale, and to enable social workers to construct and reconstruct their vision of practice (Chapters 1, 2 and 4).

There are inbuilt problems in the PQ frameworks. A perceived insufficiency of resources for employers to fund awards and release social workers for study is exacerbated by recruitment and retention problems (Chapter 14). Line managers are agnostic about, or unaware of, PQ's worth. Employers as a whole have not yet become full-fledged learning organisations that undertake integrated workforce planning for PQ (Chapter 14).

Along with these potential barriers to PQ's success lies an unanswered question of whether social workers as a whole want to undertake PQ. PQ study requires effort, commitment, and the investment of personal resources. Informally, employers mention social workers who, under the previous UK-wide PQ framework, 'had to be dragged kicking and screaming to PQ' because they did not perceive any beneficial outcomes from PQ study. If that remains the situation, the PQ frameworks will fail, thus weakening social work's claim to be a profession. PQ contains opportunities for employers to collaborate on workforce planning, tackle recruitment and retention, and become learning organisations. Most importantly, PQ provides social workers with opportunities to become critically reflective practitioners, whose practice differs from those without PQ.

Barriers

A number of issues pose potential barriers to PQ.

Appropriate academic levels

Agreeing appropriate academic levels for the CPD/PQ frameworks is problematic. The majority of current social workers lack an undergraduate degree. Until the qualifying degree was introduced in 2002, most social workers qualified with a two-year Diploma in Higher Education/Diploma in Social Work at sub-degree level, or previously had qualified with a Certificate of Qualification in Social Work or a Certificate in Social Services, which were not linked to any academic award (although a minority of social workers traditionally were able to qualify via a degree or masters degree). Over time, social work graduates will become the majority and will undertake PQ studies at postgraduate masters level, but currently many experienced practitioners arguably are not ready for postgraduate-level study. This is a significant issue when considering choices of award.

Some employers are ambivalent about postgraduate PQ awards, fearing that too many experienced social workers will not be able to study at this level. They are reluctant for social work to become 'academic', recalling that the regulatory body had not previously required PQ awards to be academic awards.

Only Northern Ireland has specified that its PQ framework will be postgraduate (PG) throughout. Specialist awards in England (which are the awards that most social workers will take) are set at a level equivalent to the final year of an undergraduate degree so that social workers without a degree can attain one, although these awards can also be delivered at PG level. To succeed, PQ must find ways of meeting the CPD needs of all social workers – newly qualified, experienced, graduates and non-graduates. However, catering to the educational and practice diversity of potential PQ candidates adds to PQ's costs.

Lack of portability

Chapter 1 criticised the country-specific PQ frameworks for their lack of UK-wide portability. Social workers moving from one UK country to another will find the transfer of PQ learning difficult, unless steps are being taken to enable each country's PQ qualifications and accreditation of prior learning to be recognised across the UK.

Career ladders

The PQ frameworks are aspirational – but if PQ practice succeeds in gaining employers' support and attracts more candidates, questions will be asked about how PQ attainment will impact on roles and careers. An unclear link between PQ learning and career advancement will undermine the PQ frameworks.

The main focus for social workers' advancement has been into management. In this context, expert social work practitioner skills have been seen as less important than management training. Social workers hoping to advance have often found themselves on generic management courses that have not always met their specific needs particularly well.

Because of its combined health and social care administration, Northern Ireland has applied career ladders that were proposed by the NHS *Agenda for Change* (NHSMA, 2006) and *Knowledge and Skills Framework* (NHSMA, 2004b) to its social workers. Elsewhere, social workers have no agreed national career ladder or 'skills escalator'. In England, this omission is significant because the children's workforce in England is constructing its own career ladder (DfES, 2006a). Without a career ladder, social workers' motivation to undertake PQ may falter, and employers may be uncertain about how to use the frameworks to benefit the workforce. Although it might not be possible to agree a national career ladder for Scotland, Wales, or England, regional workforce development agreements could begin to establish career ladders linked to PQ attainment.

What is a skills escalator?

The Changing Workforce Programme (CWP, 2004), which is part of the NHS Modernisation Agency, examined the need for new roles and for working in different ways. The resulting 'skills escalator' is a generic analysis of job roles that categorises roles on a hierarchical scale. Workers' decision-making becomes more autonomous and responsible the further up the scale they are placed. Using this concept makes it possible for the NHS in England to rethink the roles of non-medical health professionals and enable them to develop responsibilities up to consultant level supported by appropriate CPD. The skills escalator (NHSMA, 2004a) provides a career ladder template for further developing new roles and new ways of working, linking pay and rewards to clearly defined roles and responsibilities.

Despite having no national career ladder for social work, some local employer agreements recognise PQ for particular roles. However, without a national career ladder the onus falls on practitioners to search for career opportunities following PQ.

Addressing the shortfall of social work educators and researchers

Lack of investment in the supply of social work educators and researchers is a significant issue. Arguably, social work education and training can only attain higher standards and meet the demands of expanded numbers for PQ learning and the qualifying degree through developing more research-active social work educators and practitioners.

The demographic profile of university social work staff suggests that a policy for replacement and development is a matter of urgency. StLaR (Strategic Learning and Research) is a DH- and DfES-funded Human Resources Plan Project (DfES/DH, 2004) that began in November 2002 to develop a human resources plan for the educator and researcher workforce in health and social care, in recognition of the difficulties of recruiting, retaining and developing the career paths of professionally qualified health and social care (social work) researchers and lecturers, many of whom are currently approaching retirement. Increased academic demands have disadvantaged the career opportunities of social work practitioners who typically enter academic life at a later stage without research experience. Once employed within an academic setting, these professionals rapidly lose their practice credibility. A StLaR Project Team prepared a final report in 2004 for the Department of Health and Department for Education and Skills, but the issue is not yet resolved. Regretfully, the PQ frameworks currently do little to encourage a solution.

PQ opportunities

On the positive side, PQ provides organisational development opportunities. Employers' collaboration in planning PQ provision (Chapter 14) could foster collaborative workforce planning for becoming learning organisations and addressing recruitment and retention issues – both potential barriers to the successful take-up of PQ.

Another opportunity, although not yet part of PQ frameworks as such, is the provision of professional doctorates and advanced research training for social workers (see also Chapter 11). The professional doctorate should be part of the PQ frameworks – but only the Northern Ireland framework mentions it (NISCC, 2005a).

Practice example: a candidate for the professional doctorate (ProfD)

Mary is a senior social worker employed as a team leader with children and young people. She previously completed a specialist PQ award, and now wants to develop her career through additional CPD. She considered a leadership and management programme, but instead became interested in the professional doctorate (ProfD) (Scott et al., 2004). Mary wanted to develop skills for researching outcomes for care leavers. Her local university informed her that the ProfD was part-time over 3–4 years. She could undertake a study of care leavers as a practice-related research topic to develop and apply knowledge in a professional setting – changing and improving practice as well as understanding it.

After enrolling for the ProfD, her first step was to develop her research skills. Then, with the help of her supervisors, she designed a staged research project that explored aspects of her research question about outcomes for care leavers. Each stage of learning culminated with a written assessment that together comprised the doctorate thesis.

Mary enjoyed the ProfD because learning was part-time and divided into stages, with supportive class contact provided through workshops, supervision and learning sets throughout all the stages. Mary's research was conducted in partnership with her employer, her colleagues, and with people who use services and carers. Her learning generated applied outcomes that were relevant for social work practice. Although the aims of Mary's research potentially could have been designed to enable her to meet professional body PQ requirements, the professional regulatory body did not recognise the ProfD.

Consultant social workers

Social work consultants are social workers who continue to practise, rather than move to management posts, but who demonstrate and are rewarded for their expertise, skills, specialist knowledge, and leadership of practice. In itself, such a role would involve 'leadership' but not necessarily line management responsibilities. (Chapter 13 provided an account of a pioneering PQ leadership programme.) An alternative way of looking at this proposed role is to envision the consultant social worker as a critically reflective practitioner who exercises leadership, mentoring and expert support to other professional colleagues. The consultant social worker would benefit from taking a professional doctorate.

At the end of November 2007, the London borough of Hackney advertised for a consultant social worker to lead its *Reclaim Social Work* initiative for children's social work (*Guardian Jobs*, 2007). Growing interest is expressed for social workers to adopt the mental health role of 'responsible clinician' (DH, 2007b) that is similar to the non-medical consultant roles currently being developed within health (NHSMA, 2004a). Another possibility for a consultant social worker is to join GP-style practices of social workers which, under the Children and Young Persons Bill 2007 *Care Matters: Time for Change* (DCSF, 2006), could become regulated providers of services intended to strengthen the support given to children and young people in the care system – a new model of social work provision to be piloted by local authorities in England.

Evaluating PQ outcomes

To gain full acceptance, PQ frameworks must demonstrate favourable outcomes for practice, the essential question being 'what is the difference between a practitioner with PQ and one without? Carpenter's study for SCIE (Carpenter, 2005), on evaluating social work education's outcomes, exposed a general lack of rigour in how social work programmes are evaluated. All universities undertake module and programme evaluations by gathering and collating learner feedback into an annual programme review that is scrutinised at arm's length in the university and externally by professional regulators. This kind of evaluation usually does little more than give a view of learners' short-term reactions to lecturers' teaching performance, and fails to capture longer-term practice changes as a result of learning.

To identify what kind of outcomes should be sought for social work education, Carpenter reviewed Barr et al.'s (2000) development of Kirkpatrick's (1987) classification of outcomes. Its six levels comprise:

1. Learners' reactions.
2a. Modification in attitudes and perceptions.
2b. Acquisition of knowledge and skills.
3. Changes in behaviour.
4a. Changes in organisational practice.
4b. Benefits to users and carers.

The usual learner feedback and assessment processes provide evidence of achieving outcome levels 1–2b, but outcome levels 3–4b, which are especially desired by employers, cannot be gathered by conventional means. Although direct observation of practice might affirm whether or not certain higher-level outcomes are achieved, direct observation's 'single snapshot' characteristic provides a limited view, which needs to be balanced by additional methods of evaluation.

Kraiger, Ford and Salas (1993) suggest three hierarchical levels of skill-based learning outcomes: initial skills acquisition, skill compilation, and eventually practice 'automaticity'. These correspond to Benner's (1984) progression from novice to expert practice, and Schön's (1983) reflection-in-action (Chapter 1). There are difficulties in knowing how to measure automaticity outcomes. Carpenter (2005: 14) suggests that automaticity might be detected when students become less self-conscious when performing complex actions.

Outcomes of motivation (determination to change) and self-efficacy (belief in self) also can be measured using standard self-rating scales. Krieger, Ford and Salas (1993) suggest that self-efficacy is a good predictor of subsequent performance. Carpenter (2005) argues that the design of modular learning outcomes should be reviewed to improve the likelihood of discovering whether outcomes are achieved. Evaluation techniques could become more rigorous by noting the number of times a particular practice intervention is used, and the results of those interventions. Carpenter gives examples of using pre-learning and post-learning questionnaires with natural comparisons across two groups; repeated measures of evaluations across two groups that receive different kinds of input; or repeated measures of the same learner before, during, and after the formal learning takes place. These techniques could yield better data but can be time-consuming and resource-intensive. Collaborative evaluation of outcomes across universities is a little-used strategy, but regional workforce planning could encourage this broader approach.

Carpenter (2005) argues the importance of engaging social workers in systematically evaluating their learning. Users and carers also must be involved in evaluating outcomes. They are particularly interested in the quality of social worker/user/carer relationships, although this is a process rather than an outcome *per se*.

Theorising criticality

At this point, the discussion reiterates and expands Chapter 1's discourse on critically reflective practice. In 1997, Barnett theorised 'criticality' (which may lead to positive as well as negative judgements) as an alternative to 'critical thinking' in higher education, providing a rounded template that complements Schön and Eraut (Chapter 1) on how practice can become thoughtful. Barnett argues that 'critical thinking' should be replaced by 'critical being', which embodies three forms of criticality – critical reason, critical self-reflection and critical action – spread across three domains – knowledge, self and the world.

Forms of criticality		*Domains of criticality*
1. Critical reason	↔	knowledge
2. Critical self-reflection	↔	self
3. Critical action	↔	the world

Each form of criticality takes place at four levels:

Level 1: Critical skills
Level 2: Reflexivity
Level 3: Refashioning of traditions
Level 4: Transformatory critique.

These levels generally correspond to the different levels of PQ learning and support the notion that social workers progress from competence to capability and expertise.

Criticality and PQ

At Level 1 of criticality, the 'critical skills' level is characterised by social workers systematically questioning and thinking through work situations, checking that their practice is consistent with the Code of Practice, codes of ethics and agency policy, and solving problems associated with their day-to-day practice. This is the level that might be expected of recently qualified social workers.

Level 2 finds social workers reflecting critically on their understanding of social work knowledge, on their practice, and on how to develop flexible practice suitable for the organisational and societal structures they encounter. Although there can be no hard-and-fast designation, this level is probably appropriate for social workers undertaking a specialist PQ module or award.

Level 3, refashioning of traditions, suggests that social workers increasingly will question and re-evaluate their particular professional approach to practice, and become more innovative. This third level is characteristic of experienced social workers undertaking more advanced PQ awards, and who perhaps are engaged in developmental projects where they exercise leadership.

Level 4, the transformatory critique, finds social workers questioning in a deeper way the bases of social work knowledge, reconstructing their personal and professional self, and involving themselves as leaders in collective action strategies to address societal injustice and problems. Not all social workers may attain this level of emancipatory criticality, which is characteristic of some masters-level study and is central to professional doctoral study.

Social work education has made some use of Barnett's theory. Ford et al. (2004) juxtaposed Barnett's criticality, Bailin et al.'s (1999) conceptualisation of critical thinking, and Adams,

Dominelli and Payne's (2002) thinking about critical practice for social workers for an ESRC-funded research project on developing criticality among social work and modern languages under-graduates. Ford et al. found Barnett's theory of criticality accorded well with higher education's expectations of social work students, although the project engaged only with undergraduates on the social work degree. Barnett's criticality aligns strongly with PQ's goals and provides a useful analytical tool for developing practice.

Barnett criticises Schön's reflective practice (Chapter 1) for being too individualistic (Barnett, 1997: 132), focusing too much on action and therefore limiting the potential of professional decision-making (1997: 137). Criticality can help create a learning society (1997: 167–9) within a university – a concept similar to the learning organisation (Chapters 1 and 14).

Conclusion

This chapter has considered issues and opportunities for PQ's ongoing development. The key question posed in Chapter 1 was: 'how will a social worker in possession of a post-qualifying award (at any level) be expected to be different from a social worker without one?' Chapter 1 suggested that PQ practice should demonstrate more autonomy, original thinking, creativity and responsibility, resulting in a critical understanding of practice issues, the appropriate exercise of professional judgement, and problem-solving in unfamiliar contexts. Discussion in subsequent chapters affirmed that critical reflection and criticality are crucial for developing PQ practice beyond competence. PQ practice must be seen as developmental, moving towards capability and expertise.

Critical reflective practice, social work capability and expertise, criticality and the learning organisation contain overlapping features that can shape PQ practice. However, it must be recognised that achieving the goal of social workers becoming critically reflective practitioners is likely to lead to tension between that goal and employers' needs to deliver efficient services under resource constraints. Employers may not always welcome the challenges that critical reflective practitioners would raise about policies that fail to deliver person-centred, user-led services. Barnett (1997) acknowledged that a university that promotes the concepts of a learning society will trigger some discomfort for learners and other stakeholders because of criticality's challenges to traditional thinking. These issues must be debated as PQ develops.

In time, the relative success of four very different PQ frameworks across the UK can be compared, taking into account each country's differences in legislation and policies. Will the PQ frameworks be flagships for social work reform or sinking ships? Answering this question with evidence that affirms the beneficial outcomes of PQ will determine whether employers provide continuing support. Being able to answer the question depends on adopting a better means of evaluating the outcomes of PQ learning, as Carpenter (2005) advocates. PQ must aim to develop practice beyond competence. Of all the issues facing PQ, perhaps the most essential are to develop social workers' capability and expertise, and to adopt better techniques to evaluate PQ's outcomes.

This book is solidly on the side of PQ as a means of raising practice standards and benefiting the people who use services and carers. The future success of PQ over time is the responsibility of all stakeholders – social work practitioners and managers, educators and trainers, employers, social work regulators, users and carers and other individuals or organisations.

Questions for reflection

1. Consider the different forms, levels and domains of criticality discussed above. Where would you place yourself, and where would you want to be?

2. What is the most important issue for PQ's development in your own region/country?

3. How might this issue be addressed?

Further reading

Ferguson, H. (2003) 'Outline of a critical best practice perspective on social work and social care', *British Journal of Social Work*, 33: 1005–24.

Ferguson proposes a different view of critical practice, research and learning in social work, moving beyond a deficit approach to a critical best practice perspective that can provide key learning in areas such as engaging with service users, advocating on their behalf, promoting protection, establishing empowering relationships and undertaking longer-term anti-oppressive therapeutic work. Critical theory provides an interpretative framework for an operational definition of 'excellence' and what is 'best'.

Scott, D., Brown, A., Lunt, I. and Thorne, I. (2004) *Professional Doctorates: Integrating Profession and Academic Knowledge*. Maidenhead: Open University Press.

This book explores the format and purpose of professional doctorates.

Stepney, P. (2005) 'Mission impossible? Critical practice in social work', *British Journal of Social Work*, 36, 8: 1289–308.

Stepney provides a response to the predicament of social work being compromised and failing to speak out on issues by arguing that critical practice offers a potential for combining a protective role with prevention, and incorporating possibilities for critical reflection and change. He uses a structural modernist analysis that is informed by aspects of critical postmodernism.

Glossary

ADASS	Association of Directors of Adult Social Services
AMHP	Approved Mental Health Professional
APCL	Accreditation of prior certificated learning
APEL	Accreditation of prior experiential learning
APL	Accreditation of prior learning
ASD	Autistic Spectrum Disorder
ASW	Approved Social Worker
AYE	Assessed Year in Employment (Northern Ireland)
BASW	British Association of Social Workers
BSL	British Sign Language
CAF	Common Assessment Framework (children)
CAIPE	Centre for the Advancement of Inter-Professional Education
CAMHS	Child and Adolescent Mental Health Service
CASP	Critical Appraisal Skills Programme
CCETSW	Central Council for Education and Training in Social Work
CCW	Care Council for Wales
CFS	Chronic Fatigue Syndrome
CIPD	Chartered Institute of Personnel and Development
CMHT	Community Mental Health Team
Competence	A combination of values, knowledge and skills
CPD	Continuing professional development
CRD	Centre for Reviews and Dissemination
CSCI	Commission for Social Care Inspection
CWDC	Children's Workforce Development Council (England)

CWP	Changing Workforce Programme
CYPFC	Children, young people, families and carers
DBA	Doctorate in Business Administration
DCIL	Derbyshire Centre for Independent Living
DCSF	Department of Children, Schools and Family
DDA	Disability Discrimination Act
DDO	Disability Discrimination (Northern Ireland) Order
DfES	Department for Education and Skills
DGov	A form of professional doctorate
DH	Department of Health
DHSS	Department of Health and Social Security
DHSSPS NI	Department of Health, Social Services and Public Safety Northern Ireland
DipSW/DipHE	Diploma in Social Work/Diploma in Higher Education, the previous social work qualifying award
EBP	Evidence-based practice
EPPI	Evidence for Policy and Practice Information and Coordinating Centre
ESC	Ten Essential Shared Capabilities, mental health
ESRC	Economics and Social Research Council
EYPS	Early Years Professional Status
GSCC	General Social Care Council, regulator of social work education in England
HEC	Higher Education for Capability
IMCA	Independent Mental Capacity Advocate
IPE	Inter-Professional Education
IRISS	Institute for Research and Innovation in Social Services
JUC SWEC	Joint University Council Social Work Education Committee
LINks	Local Involvement Networks
LRCN	Learning resource centre network
ME	Myalgic Encephalitis
MHO	Mental Health Officer

NHS	National Health Service
NHS CCA	NHS and Community Care Act
NIMHE	National Institute for Mental Health (England)
NIPQETP	Northern Ireland Post-Qualifying Education and Training Partnership
NISCC	Northern Ireland Social Care Council
NMDS–SC	National Minimum Data Set, Social Care
NOPT	National Association of Practice Teachers
NOS SW	National Occupational Standards, which comprise some of the required Standards for PQ
NSF	National Service Framework
NVQ	National Vocational Qualifications (England and Wales)
PAP	Practice Assessment Panel
PCGMHW	Primary Care Graduate Mental Health Workers
PCP	Person-centred planning
PG	Postgraduate
PD	Professional doctorate
PLTF	Practice Learning Taskforce
PMA	Practice Mentor/Assessor
PPIP	Patient and Public Initiative Programme
PQ	Post-qualifying social work, sometimes refers to PQ education and training
PQ candidate	A student on an approved post-qualifying award
PQ1	A Requirement within the previous post-qualifying award in social work (PQSW)
PQ6	A Requirement within the previous post-qualifying award in social work (PQSW)
ProfD	Professional doctorate
Professional credit	A credit system used by the previous PQ awards
PRTL	Post-registration training and learning
PT	Practice Teacher
PVI	Private, voluntary and independent organisations

QAA	Quality Assurance Agency for Higher Education
RCT	Randomised controlled trials
Registration on the Social Care Register	Required for qualified social workers and social care staff
RGU	Robert Gordon University
SCIE	Social Care Institute for Excellence
SCQF	Scottish Credit and Qualifications Framework
SE	Scottish Executive
SfC	Skills for Care
SG	Scottish Government
SIESWE	Scottish Institute of Excellence in Social Work Education
SiSWE	Standards in Social Work Education (Scotland)
Skills escalator	A career ladder for the NHS (England)
SLE	Systemic Lupus Erythematosus (Lupus)
SLF	Scottish Learning Foundation
SRV	Social Role Valorisation
SSI	Social Services Inspectorate
SSIW	Social Services Inspectorate for Wales
SSSC	Scottish Social Services Council
Standards	GSCC standards for each PQ specialism, comprised of National Occupational Standards, relevant legislation, and other quality standards
StLaR	Strategic Learning and Research Project
STR	Support, Time and Recovery
SVQ	Scottish Vocational Qualification
SWAP	Social Policy and Social Work subject centre, Higher Education Academy
SWSPD	Social Work Services Policy Division Scotland
UN	United Nations
UPIAS	Union of Physically Impaired Against Segregation
VQ	Vocational Qualifications
WAG	Welsh Assembly Government

References

Abberley, P. (1997) 'The Limits of Classical Social Theory in the Analysis and Transformation of Disablement', in L. Barton and M. Oliver (eds), *Disability Studies: Past, Present and Future*. Leeds: The Disability Press. pp. 25–44.

Adams, R., Dominelli, L. and Payne, M. (2002) *Critical Practice in Social Work*. Basingstoke: Palgrave Macmillan.

Administration for Children and Families http://www.acf.hhs.gov/programs/cb/cwmonitoring/changing_culture.htm

Advocacy in Action with Staff and Students from the University of Nottingham (2006) 'Making it our own ball game: learning and assessment in social work education', *Social Work Education*, 25, 4: 332–46.

Age Concern, England (2007) *The Age Agenda*. London: Age Concern.

Aldridge, K. (2006) *Changing Times for PQ in the West Midlands*. Birmingham: West Midlands Regional Post Qualifying Consortium.

Argyris, C. (1957) *Personality and Organisation*. New York: Harper & Row.

Argyris, C. (1976) *Increasing Leadership Effectiveness*. New York: Wiley.

Argyris, C. and Schön, D. (1978) *Organisational Learning: A Theory of Action Perspective*. Reading, MA: Addison-Wesley.

Argyris, C. and Schön, D. (1996) *Organisational Learning II: Theory, Method and Practice*. Reading, MA: Addison-Wesley.

Arnstein, S.R. (1969) 'A ladder of citizen participation in the USA', *Journal of the American Institute of Planners*, 35: 216–24.

Aspis, S. (1997) 'Self-advocacy for people with learning difficulties: does it have a future?', *Disability & Society*, 12, 4: 647–54.

Aspis, S. (1999) 'What They Don't Tell Disabled People with Learning Difficulties', in M. Corker and S. French (eds), *Disability Discourse*. Buckingham: Open University Press. pp. 173–82.

Asquith, S., Clark, C. and Waterhouse, L. (2005) *The Role of the Social Worker in the 21st Century: A Literature Review*. Edinburgh: Scottish Government.

Atkins, J. (1998) 'Tribalism, loss and grief: issues for multi-professional education'. *Journal of Interprofessional Care* 12,33: 303–7.

Bailin, S., Case, R., Coombes, J.R. and Daniels, L.B. (1999) 'Conceptualising critical thinking', *Journal of Curriculum Studies*, 31: 285–302.

Bamford Review of Mental Health and Learning Disability (N. Ireland) 2007 *A Comprehensive Legislative Framework*. http://www.rmhldni.gov.uk/index/contactus.htm, website accessed 15/04/2008.

Bamford, D. (2005) *A Strategic Framework for Adult Mental Health Services*. Belfast: DHSSPS.

Banks, S. (2004) *Ethics, Accountability and the Social Professions*. Basingstoke: Palgrave Macmillan.

Banks, S. (2006) *Ethics and Values in Social Work*. 3rd edition. Basingstoke: Palgrave Macmillan.

Bano, A., Crosskill, D., Patel, R., Rashman, L. and Shah, R. (1993) *Improving Practice with People with Learning Disabilities: A Training Manual (Anti-racist Social Work Education: No.5)*. London: CCETSW.

Barker, R.A. (1997) 'How can we train leaders if we do not know what leadership is?', *Human Relations*, 50, 4: 343–62.

Barnes, C. (1991) *Disabled People in Britain and Discrimination: A Case for Anti-Discrimination Legislation*. London: Hurst & Company.

Barnes, C. (1997) 'A Legacy of Oppression – A History of Disability in Western Culture', in L. Barton and M. Oliver (eds), *Disability Studies: Past, Present and Future*. Leeds: The Disability Press. pp. 3–24.

Barnes, C. (1998) 'The Social Model of Disability: A Sociological Phenomenon Ignored by Sociologists?', in T. Shakespeare (ed.), *The Disability Reader: Social Sciences Perspectives*. London: Cassell. pp. 65–78.

Barnes, C., Oliver, M. and Barton, L. (eds) (2002) *Disability Studies Today*. Cambridge: Polity Press.

Barnett, R. (1997) *Higher Education: A Critical Business*. Buckingham: SRHE/Open University Press.

Baron, S., Phillips, R. and Stalker, K. (1996) 'Barriers to training for disabled social work students', *Disability & Society*, 11, 3: 361–77.

Barr, H. (2002) *Interprofessional Education: Yesterday, Today and Tomorrow*. London: CAIPE.

Barr, H., Freeth, D., Hammick, M., Koppel, I. and Reeves, S. (2000) *Evaluating Interprofessional Education: A United Kingdom Review for Health and Social Care*. London: BERA/CAIPE.

BASW (British Association of Social Workers) (1980) *Clients are Fellow Citizens*. Birmingham: BASW.

BASW (1983) *Effective and Ethical Recording*. Birmingham: BASW.

BASW (2002) *The Code of Ethics for Social Work*. Birmingham: BASW.

Bateman, N. (2000) *Advocacy Skills for Health and Social Care*. London: Jessica Kingsley.

Bauman, Z. (1992) *Intimations of Postmodernity*. London: Routledge.

Beckett, C. and Maynard, A. (2005) *Values and Ethics in Social Work: An Introduction*. London: Sage.

Bell, C. (2006) *New Types of Worker – Overview*. Leeds: Skills for Care.

Bengtsen Blem, K. (2006) '*Hurtigt videre til næste skolebænk*', *Socialpædagogen*, 2, 27 January http://www.sl.dk/Socialpædagogen/Arkiv.aspx (accessed 23/04/2007).

Benner, P.E. (1984) *From Novice to Expert: Excellence and Power in Clinical Nursing Practice*. Menlo Park, CA: Addison Wesley.

Beresford, P. (1994) 'Advocacy', in *Speaking Out for Advocacy – A Report of the National Conference*. Haworth: Labyrinth.

Beresford, P. (2005) 'Social Approaches to Madness and Distress: User Perspectives and User Knowledge', in J. Tew (ed.), *Social Perspectives in Mental Health: Developing Models to Understand and Work with Mental Distress*. London: Jessica Kingsley. pp. 32–52.

Beresford, P. (2007) *The Changing Roles and Tasks of Social Work from Service Users' Perspectives: A Literature Informed Discussion Paper*. Shaping Our Lives. http://www.gscc.org.uk/NR/rdonlyres/072DD7D6-B915-4F41-B54B-79C62FDB9D95/0/SoLSUliteraturereviewreportMarch07.pdf (accessed 28/11/2007).

Beresford, P., Branfield, F., Maslen, B., Sartori, A. and Jenny, Maggie and Manny (2007) 'Partnership Working: Service Users and Social Workers Learning and Working Together', in M. Lymbery and K. Postle (eds), *Social Work: A Companion to Learning*. London: Sage. pp. 215–27.

Beresford, P., Shamash, M., Forrest, V., Turner, M. and Branfield, F. (2005) *Developing Social Care: Service Users' Vision for Adult Support*. London: SCIE.

Best, L. (2007) *Rationale for PQ Programmes*. Unpublished account. Northampton: University of Northampton.

Bichard, M. (2004) *Final Report: An Independent Inquiry Arising from the Soham Murders*. London: Home Office.

Biggs, S. (1997) 'Choosing not to be old: masks, bodies and identity management in later life', *Ageing and Society*, 18, 5: 553–70.

Blaikie, N. (1993) *Approaches to Social Enquiry*. Cambridge: Polity Press.

Blake, R.R. and Mouton, J.S. (1964) *The Managerial Grid*. Houston, TX: Gulf.

Blewett, J., Lewis, J. and Tunstill, J. (2007) *The Changing Roles and Tasks of Social Work*: *A Literature Informed Discussion Paper*. London: GSCC.

Blinston, N. (2005) Does Being Considered a 'Learning Organisation' Assist Social Service Departments in the Recruitment and Retention of Professionally Qualified Social Care Staff? Unpublished MSc dissertation. Nottingham: Nottingham Trent University.

Blinston, N., Higham, P. and Sharp, M. (2006) Post-Qualifying Social Work Education: Flagships for Social Work Reform or Sinking Ships? Paper for Crossing Boundaries: Personal, Professional, Political, 8th UK Joint Social Work Education Conference. Cambridge: Homerton College, Cambridge University, 13 July. http://www.swap.ac.uk/quality/Docs/Crossing%20Boundaries%20Conference%20Workshop%20Paper%20on%20PQ%20Final%20Version.pdf (accessed 30/11/2007).

Booth, T. and Booth, W. (2005) 'Parents with learning difficulties in the child protection system', *Journal of Intellectual Disabilities*, 9, 2: 109–29.

Boud, D., Keogh, R. and Walker, D. (1985) 'Promoting Reflection in Learning: A Model', in D. Boud, R. Keogh and D. Walker (eds), *Reflection: Turning Experience into Learning*. London: Kogan Page. pp. 18–40.

Bourn, D. and Bootle, K. (2005) 'Evaluation of a Distance Learning Post Graduate Advanced Award in Social Work Programme for Children and Families Social Work', *Social Work Education*, 24, 3 (April): 343–62.

Bowey, L. and McGlaughlin, A. (2007) 'Older carers of adults with a learning disability confront the future: issues and preferences in planning', *British Journal of Social Work*, 37, 1: 39–54.

Boxall, K., Carson, I. and Docherty, D. (2004) 'Room at the academy? people with learning difficulties and higher education', *Disability & Society*, 19, 2: 99–112.

Boxall, K., Jones, M. and Smith, S. (2002) 'Advocacy and Parents with Learning Difficulties', in D.G. Race (ed.), *Learning Disability: A Social Approach*. London: Routledge. pp. 171–88.

Brandon, D. and Brandon, T. (2000) *Advocacy in Social Work*. Birmingham: Venture Press.

Branfield, F. and Beresford, P., with contributions from others (2006) *Making User Involvement Work: Supporting Service User Networking and Knowledge*. York: Joseph Rowntree Foundation.

Bridges, W. (1995) *Managing Transitions: Making the Most of Change*. London: Nicholas Brearley.

Brindle, D. (2006) 'Joe Public leading a welfare revolution', *The Guardian*, 11 October. http://www.society.guardian.co.uk (accessed 22/04/2007).

Brown, H. and Smith, H. (1992) *Normalisation: A Reader for the Nineties*. London: Routledge.

Browne, E. (1982) *Mental Handicap: The Role for Social Workers*. Sheffield: Sheffield University/Community Care.

Burleigh, M. (2001) *The Third Reich: A New History*. London: Pan Books.

CAIPE (2006) 'Interprofessional Education'. http://www.caipe.org.uk/index.php?&page=define&nav=1 (accessed 10/08/2007).

Calder, M.C. (2003) 'The Assessment Framework: A Critique and Reformulation', in M.C. Calder and S. Hackett (eds), *Assessment in Child Care: Using and Developing Frameworks for Practice*. Lyme Regis: Russell House. pp. 3–60.

Calder, M.C. and Hackett, S. (eds) (2003) *Assessment in Child Care: Using and Developing Frameworks for Practice*. Lyme Regis: Russell House.

Caldwell, P. and Horword, J. (2007) *From Isolation to Intimacy: Making Friends Without Words*. London: Jessica Kingsley.

Cambridge, P. and Carnaby, S. (2005) *Person Centred Planning and Care Management with People with Learning Disabilities*. London: Jessica Kingsley.

Cambridge, P., Carpenter, J., Forrester-Jones, R., Tate, A., Knapp, M., Beecham, J. and Hallam, A. (2005) 'The state of care management in learning disability and mental health services 12 years into community care', *British Journal of Social Work*, 35: 1039–62.

Cameron, C. (2006) *New Ways of Educating: Pedagogy and Children's Services. Final Report to the Esmee Fairburn Foundation*. London: Thomas Coram Research Unit, Institute of Education, University of London.

Campbell, J. and Oliver, M. (1996) *Disability Politics: Understanding Our Past, Changing Our Future*. London: Routledge.

Campbell Collaboration (2007) http://www.campbellcollaboration.org/ (accessed 13/06/2007).

Carers Northern Ireland (2007) http://www.carersni.org/Newsandcampaigns/Newsreleases/ 1185445341 (accessed 19/11/2007).

Carers UK (2006) 'Carers in Wales win campaign for a champion', 14 June 2006. http://www.carersuk.org/Newsandcampaigns/News/1150300828 (accessed 14/10//2007).

Carey, M. (2003) 'Anatomy of a care manager', *Work, Employment, and Society*, 17: 121–35.

Carpenter, J. (2005) *Evaluating Outcomes in Social Work Education: Evaluation and Evidence.* Discussion Paper 1. London: SCIE/SIESWE.

Carpenter, J., Schneider, J., Brandon, T. and Wooff, D. (2003) 'Working in multidisciplinary community mental health teams: the impact on social workers and health professionals of integrated mental health care', *British Journal of Social Work*, 33: 1081–103.

Carr, S. (2004) *Has Service User Participation Made a Difference to Social Care Services?* London: SCIE.

Carson, I. and Docherty, D. (2002) 'Friendships, Relationships and Issues of Sexuality', in D.G. Race (ed.), *Learning Disability: A Social Approach.* London: Routledge. pp. 139–53.

Carter, T. and Beresford, P. (2000) *Age and Change: Models of Involvement for Older People.* York: YPS, for the Joseph Rowntree Foundation.

CCETSW (Central Council for Education and Training in Social Work) (1989) *Improving Standards in Practice Learning: Regulations and Guidance for the Approval of Agencies and the Accreditation and Training of Practice Teachers.* Paper 26.3. London: CCETSW.

CCETSW (1989, 1991) *Rules and Requirements for the Diploma in Social Work* (DipSW). Paper 30. London: CCETSW.

CCETSW (1991) *Improving Standards in Practice Learning: Requirements and Guidance for the Approval of Agencies and the Accreditation and Training of Practice Teachers.* Paper 26.3 revised edition. London: CCETSW.

CCW (Care Council Wales) (2003) *Skills Foresight Plan for the Social Care Sector in Wales.* Cardiff: CCW.

CCW (2004) *Ensuring Consistency in Learning to Practice.* Cardiff: CCW.

CCW (2005) *The Modular PQ Framework Rules and Requirements.* Discussion Paper. November. Cardiff: CCW.

CCW (2006) *Post Qualifying Learning and Development for Social Workers: Report for Care Council.* March. Cardiff: CCW.

CCW/Cyngor Gofal Cymru (2007) *The Approval and Visiting of Post-Qualifying Courses for Social Workers.* Cardiff: CCW.

Chappell, A.L. (1998) 'Still Out in the Cold: People with Learning Difficulties and the Social Model of Disability', in T. Shakespeare (ed.), *The Disability Reader.* London: Cassell. pp. 211–20.

Children's Bureau (2008) *Reports and Results of the Child and Family Service Reviews (CFSRs).* http://basis.caliber.com/cwig/ws/cwmd/docs/cb_web/SearchForm (accessed 15/04/08).

Chisholm, J.S. (1996) 'The evolutionary ecology of attachment organization', *Human Nature*, 1: 1–37.

Clark, C.L. (2000) *Social Work Ethics: Politics, Principles and Practice.* Basingstoke: Palgrave.

Cleaver, H., Unell, I. and Aldgate, J. (1999) *Children's Needs – Parenting Capacity: The Impact of Parent Mental Illness, Problem Alcohol and Drug Use and Domestic Violence on Children's Development.* London: HMSO.

Clements, L.J. (2007) Individual Budgets and Carers. Unpublished opinion/scoping paper. clementslj@cardiff.ac.uk.

Clements, L.J. and Thompson, P. (2007) *Community Care and the Law.* London: LAG.

Cleveland Report (1988) *Report of the Inquiry into Child Abuse in Cleveland 1987.* Cmd 412. London: HMSO.

Clutterbook, D. (2001) *Everyone Needs a Mentor: Fostering Talent at Work* (3rd edition). London: Chartered Institute of Personnel and Development.

Cochrane Collaboration Website http://www/cochrane.org/ (accessed 15/04/08).

Collings, J.A. and Murray, P.J. (1996) 'Predictors of stress amongst social workers: an empirical study', *British Journal of Social Work*, 26: 375–87.

Community Care (2004) *Debate on making social work more attractive, 24 October.* http://www.communitycare.co.uk (accessed 16/11/2007).

Community Care (2006) *Skills Dilution Fear Over Framework.* 1 June. http://www.communitycare.co.uk/Article.aspx?liArticleID=54310&PrinterFri... accessed 07/06/2006.

Cooper, H., Carlisle, C., Gibbs, T. and Watkins, C. (2001) 'Developing an evidence base for interdisciplinary learning: a systematic review', *Journal of Advanced Nursing*, 35, 2: 228–37.

Coren, E. and Fisher, M. (2006) *Research Resource 1: The Conduct of Systematic Research Reviews for SCIE Knowledge Reviews.* London: SCIE.

Coulshed, V. and Mullender, A. (2006) *Management in Social Work* (3rd edition). Basingstoke: Palgrave Macmillan.

Coulshed, V. and Orme, J. (2006) *Social Work Practice* (4th edition). Basingstoke: Palgrave Macmillan.

Courtioux, M. et al. (eds) (1986) *The Socialpedagogue in Europe – Living with Others as a Profession.* Zürich: Fédération Internationale des Communautés Educatives (FICE).

Cowden, S. and Singh, G. (2007) 'The "user": friend, foe or fetish? A critical exploration of user involvement in health and social care', *Critical Social Policy*, 27: 5.

Coyle, D., Edwards, D., Hannigan, B., Fothergill, A. and Burnard, P. (2005) 'A systematic review of stress among mental health social workers', *International Social Work*, 48, 2: 201–11.

Crawford, K. and Walker, J. (2004) *Social Work with Older People.* Exeter: Learning Matters.

Crawshaw, M. (2002) 'Disabled people's access to social work education – ways and means of promoting environmental change', *Social Work Education*, 21, 5: 503–14.

CRD (Centre for Reviews and Dissemination) (2007) http://www.york.ac.uk/inst/crd/ (accessed 13/06/2007).

Cree, V. and Davis, A. (2007) *Voices from the Inside.* London: Routledge.

Cree, V.E. (ed.) (2003) *Becoming Social Workers.* London: Routledge.

Crimmens, D. (1998) 'Training for residential child care workers in Europe: comparing approaches in The Netherlands, Ireland and the United Kingdom', *Social Work Education*, 17, 3: 309–20.

Crow, L. (1996) 'Including All of Our Lives: Renewing the Social Model of Disability', in J. Morris (ed.), *Encounters with Strangers: Feminism and Disability.* London: The Women's Press. pp. 206–26.

CSCI (Commission for Social Care Inspection) (2004) *Star Rating Results 2004.* October 2004. http://www.csci.org.uk (accessed / /2007).

CSCI (2007) *Who Is An Expert by Experience?* http://www.csci.org.uk/get_involved/take_part_in_an_inspection/who_is_an_expert_by_experience.aspx (accessed 19/11/2007).

CSCI (2008) *Become one of our Experts by experience.* http://www.csci.org.uk/get_involved/take_part_in_an_inspection/join_our_experts_by_experience.aspx (accessed 11/01/2008).

CWDC (Children's Workforce Development Council) (2007) *Children's Workforce Strategic Update.* Phase 2 strategic report. London: CWDC.

CWDC (2006) Website. Early Years Professional. http://66.102.9.104/search?q=cache:FxMlWSnN45sJ:www.cwdcouncil.org.uk/projects/earlyyears.htm+Early+Years+Professional+Status+EYPS&hl=en&ct=clnk&cd=1&gl=uk (accessed 06/12/2007).

CWP (Changing Workforce Programme) (2004) *Role Redesign: Review of Activities 2003/04.* London: NHS Modernisation Agency.

Dagnan, D. and Drewett, R. (1988) 'Community-based care for people with a mental handicap: a family placement scheme in County Durham', *British Journal of Social Work*, 18: 543–75.

Dagnell, A. (2007) 'Wales Social Work Crisis', *Wales on Sunday*, 14 October. ICWales.co.uk (accessed 08/10/2007).

Dale, M. (1994) 'Learning organisations', in C. Mabey and P. Iles (eds), *Managing Learning*. London: Routledge with the Open University. pp. 22–23.

Davidson, G. and Campbell, J. (2007) *An examination of the use of coercion by assertive outrach and community mental health teams in Northern Ireland.* BJSW, 37, 3: 537.

Davies, C.A. (1998) 'Constructing Other Selves: (In)competences and the Category of Learning Difficulties', in R. Jenkins (ed.), *Questions of Competence: Culture, Classification and Intellectual Disability*. Cambridge: Cambridge University Press. pp. 102–24.

Davis, K. (2004) 'The Crafting of Good Clients, in J. Swain, S. French, C. Barnes and C. Thomas (eds), *Disabling Barriers: Enabling Environments* (2nd edition). London: Sage. pp. 203–5.

Davies Jones, H. (1994a) *Social Workers, or Social Educators?* London: National Institute of Social Work (NISW).

Davies Jones, H. (1994b) 'The social pedagogue in Western Europe', *Journal of Interprofessional Care*, 8, 1: 19–29.

DCSF (Department for Children, Schools and Families) (2006) *Care Matters: Transforming the Lives of Children and Young People in Care*. London: HMSO.

Dearden, C. and Becker, S. (1995) *Young Carers: The Facts*. Loughborough University: Loughborough.

Dempster, M. (2003) 'Systematic Review', in R. Miller and J. Brewer (eds), *The A to Z of Social Research*. London: Sage.

Dent-Brown, K. (1999) 'The Six-Part Story Method (6PSM) as an aid to assessment of personality disorder', *Dramatherapy*, 21, 2: 10–14.

Dewey, J. (1933) *How We Think: A Restatement of the Relation of Reflective Thinking to the Educative Process* (revised edition). Boston, MA: D.C. Heath.

Dewey, J. (1938) *Experience and Education*. New York: Collier Books.

Dewey, J. (1997) *How We Think*. Mineola, Long Island: Dover Books. (Originally published 1910.)

DfES (2004) *Every Child Matters: Change for Children*. DfES/1090/2004. London: HMSO.

DfES (2005) *Youth Matters*. Cm 6629. London: HMSO.

DfES (2006a) *Children's Workforce Strategy: Building a World-class Workforce for Children, Young People and Families*. Nottingham: DfES Publications.

DfES (2006b) *The Childcare Act*. http://www.opsi.gov.uk/acts/acts2006/ukpga_20060021_en.pdf (accessed 23/04/2007).

DfES/DH (Department of Health) (2004) *Strategic Learning and Research Advisory Group (StLaR) Human Resources Project Plan for the Future Learning and Research Workforce in Health and Social Care*. London: DfES/DH.

DfES/LSC/SEMTA (2004) *National Employers Skills Survey 2003*. Wath-on-Dearne: DfES/LSC/SEMTA.

DH (1991) *Care Management and Assessment: Practitioners' Guide*. London: HMSO.

DH (1995) *Child Protection: Messages from Research*. London: HMSO.

DH (1998) *White Paper: Modernising Social Care*. London: DH.

DH (1999) *National Service Framework for Mental Health*. London: DH.

DH (2000) *No Secrets: Guidance on Developing and Implementing Multi-agency Policies and Procedures to Protect Vulnerable Adults from Abuse*. London: DH.

DH (2001) *Valuing People: A New Strategy for Learning Disability for the 21st Century*. London: DH.

DH (2002) *Requirements for Social Work Training*. London: DH.

DH (2003a) *The Health, Social Care and Well-being Strategies (Wales) Regulations 2003*. London: The Stationery Office.

DH (2003b) CI (2003)10: *Modern Social Services: A Commitment to Reform: the 12th annual report of the Chief Inspector Social Services Inspectorate 2002–2003*. London: DH.

DH (2004b) *Learning Difficulties and Ethnicity – A Framework for Action*. London: DH.

DH (2004c) *Direct Choices: What Councils Need to Make Direct Payments Happen for People with Learning Disabilities*. London: DH.

DH (2004d) *The Ten Essential Shared Capabilities: A Framework for the Whole of the Mental Health Workforce*. London: DH.

DH (2004e) *The Community Care Assessment Directions 2004*. DH: London.

DH (2004f) *Fair Access to Care Services – Guidance on Eligibility Criteria for Adult Social Care*. DH: London.

DH (2005) *Independence, Well-being and Choice: Our Vision for the Future of Social Care for Adults in England*. London: DH.

DH (2006a) *National Framework for older people*. London: DH.

DH (2006b) *Mental Health Bill: Bournewood Safeguards*. Briefing sheet (Gateway reference: 6794). London: DH.

DH (2006c) *Our Health, Our Care, Our Say: A New Direction for Community Services.* Cm 6737. London: DH.

DH (2007a) *Independence, Choice and Risk: A Guide to Best Practice in Supported Decision Making.* London: DH.

DH (2007b) *Mental Health Act 2007.* London: DH.

DH (2007c) *Mental Health: New Ways of Working for Everyone: Developing and Sustaining a Capable and Flexible Workforce.* London: DH.

DH (2007d) *Public and Patient Involvement (PPI).* http://www.dh.gov.uk/en/Policyandguidance/Organisation policy/PatientAndPublicinvolvement/index.htm (accessed 14/10/2007).

DH/DfES (2006) *Options for Excellence: Building the Workforce for the Future – A Joint Report for the Departments of Health, Education and Social Care, Adult Social Care and Children's Workforce.* London: DH/DfES.

DHSS (Department of Health and Social Services) (1974) *Report of the Committee of Enquiry into the Care and Supervision Provided in Relation to Maria Colwell.* London: HMSO.

DHSSPS (NI) (Department of Health, Social Services and Public Safety for Northern Ireland) (2001) *Best Practice – Best Care.* Belfast: DHSSPS (NI).

DHSSPS (NI) (2002) *Departmental Guidance HSS(PPM) 10/2002 Governance in the HPSS – Clinical and Social Care Governance: Guidelines for Implementation.* Belfast: DHSSPS (NI).

Dimmock, B. (1996) 'Team and Management Consultation: Reflections on the World's Third Oldest Profession', in N. Gould and I. Taylor (eds), *Reflective Learning for Social Work.* Aldershot: Ashgate.

Docherty, D., Hughes, R., Phillips, P., Corbett, D., Regan, B., Barber, A., Adams, M., Boxall, K., Kaplan, I. and Izzidien, S. (2005) 'This is What We Think', in D. Goodley and G. Van Hove (eds), *Another Disability Studies Reader? People with Learning Difficulties and a Disabling World.* Antwerp: Garant. pp. 29–49.

Doel, M., Flynn, E. and Nelson, P. (2006) *Experiences of Post-Qualifying Study in Social Work.* Capturing the Learning series. Sheffield: Practice Learning Taskforce/Centre for Health and Social Care Research, Sheffield Hallam University. June.

Doel, M. and Shardlow, S.M. (2005) *Modern Social Work Practice: Teaching and Learning in Practice Settings.* Aldershot: Ashgate.

Dominelli, L. (1996) 'Deprofessionalizing social work: anti-oppressive practice, competencies and postmodernism', *British Journal of Social Work,* 26: 153–75.

Douek, S. (2003) 'Collaboration or Confusion? The Carers' Perspective', in J. Weinstein, C. Whittington and T. Leiba (eds), *Collaboration in Social Work Practice.* London: Jessica Kingsley. pp. 121–36.

Doyle, C. (1997) 'Emotional abuse of children: issues for intervention' *Child Abuse Review,* 6: 330–42.

Doyle, C. (2001) 'Surviving and coping with emotional abuse in childhood', *Clinical Child Psychology and Psychiatry,* 6, 3: 387–402.

Doyle, C. (2006) *Working with Abused Children* (3rd edition). Basingstoke: Palgrave Macmillan.

Doyle, C. and Lumsden, E. (2005) 'What Do Children Think about Surestart'. Conference paper. Reykjavik, Iceland: ECCERA Democracy and Society International Conference, 28 August–2 September 2006.

Dreyfus, H.L. and Dreyfus, S.E. (1986) *Mind over Machine: The Power of Human Intuition and Expertise in the Era of the Computer.* Oxford: Basil Blackwell.

Duffy, J., Taylor, B.J. and McCall, S. (2006) 'Human rights and decision making in child protection through explicit argumentation', *Child Care in Practice,* 12, 2: 81–95.

Dumfries and Galloway Child Protection Committee (2000) *Child Protection Inquiry into the Circumstances Surrounding the Death of Kennedy McFarlane.* Dumfries: Dumfries and Galloway CPC.

Dunkerley, D. (2007) 'Wales's changing population: a demographic overview', *Contemporary Wales,* 19: 116–25.

Dunn, J. (1988) *The Beginnings of Social Understanding.* Cambridge, MA: Harvard University Press.

Dunn, J. (1993) *Young Children's Close Relationships: Beyond Attachment.* Newbury Park, CA: Sage.

Dunn, J. and Kendrick, C. (1982) *Siblings: Love, Envy and Understanding*. Cambridge, MA: Harvard University Press.

Edge, J. (2001) *Who's in Control? Decision-Making by People with Learning Difficulties who have High Support Needs*. London: Values Into Action.

Edwards, R. (2002) *Devolution and Health*. London: The Nuffield Trust.

Ellis, K. and Rogers, R. (2004) 'Fostering a Human Rights Discourse in the Provision of Social Care for Adults', in H. Dean (ed.), *The Ethics of Welfare*. Bristol: Policy Press. pp. 89–110.

Emerson, E., Malam, S., Davies, I. and Spencer, K. (2005) *Adults with Learning Difficulties in England 2003/4*. London: NHS Health and Social Care Information Centre.

England, H. (1986) *Social Work as Art: Making Sense for Good Practice*. London: Routledge.

Eraut, M. (1994) *Developing Professional Knowledge and Competence*. London: Falmer Press.

Eraut, M. (2006) 'How Do We Represent Lifelong Professional Learning'. Conference Paper. EARLI SIG Professional Learning and Development Conference: Lifelong Learning of Professionals: Exploring Implications of a Transitional Labour Market. Heerlen, The Netherlands: Open University of the Netherlands.

Erikson, E.H. (1965) *Childhood and Society* (2nd edition). Harmondsworth: Penguin.

ESRC (Economic and Social Research Council) (2005) *Postgraduate Training Guidelines 2005* (4th edition). Cheltenham: ESRC publications.

Etzioni, A. (1968) *The Active Society: The Theory of Societal and Political Processes*. New York: Free Press.

Evans, S., Gately, C., Huxley, P., Katona, C., Kendall, T. and Mears, A. (2005) 'The impact of "statutory duties" on mental health social workers in the UK', *Health & Social Care in the Community*, 13, 2: 145–54.

Evers, H., Cameron, E. and Badger, F. (1994) 'Inter-professional Work with Old and Disabled People', in A. Leathard (ed.), *Going Inter-Professional*. London: Routledge. pp. 143–57.

Evidence for Policy and Practice Information and Coordinating Centre (EPPI Centre) (2007) Website. Social Science Research Unit. Institute of Education, University of London. http://eppi.ioe.ac.uk/cms/ (accessed 16/01/2008).

Fay, B. (2000) *Contemporary Philosophy of Social Science*. Oxford: Blackwell.

Fayol, H. (1949) *General and Industrial Management*. London: Pitman.

Fellowes-Smith, E. (2001) 'Impact of Parental Anxiety Disorder on Children', in P. Reder, M. McClure and A. Jolley (eds), *Family Matters*. London: Routledge. pp. 96–106.

Ferguson, H. (2003) 'Outline of a critical best practice perspective on social work and social care', *British Journal of Social Work*, 33: 1005–24.

Ferguson, I. and Lavalette, M. (2004) 'Beyond power discourse: alienation and social work', *British Journal of Social Work*, 24, 3: 297–316 (16).

Finkelstein, V. (1980) *Attitudes and Disabled People: Issues for Discussion*. New York: World Rehabilitation Fund.

Finkelstein, V. (1981a) *Disability and Professional Attitudes*. Sevenoaks: NAIDEX Convention.

Finkelstein, V. (1981b) 'To Deny or Not to Deny Disability', in A. Brechin, P. Liddiard and J. Swain (eds), *Handicap in a Social World*. London: Hodder & Stoughton. pp. 34–6.

Finkelstein, V. (1999a) *Professions Allied to the Community (PACs)*. www.leeds.ac.uk/disability-studies/archive uk/index.html (accessed 00/00/0000).

Finkelstein, V. (1999b) *Professions Allied to the Community: The Disabled People's Trade Union*. www.leeds.ac. uk/disability-studies/archiveuk/index.html (accessed 25/8/2007).

Firth, M.T., Dyer, M., Marsden, H., Savage, D. and Mohamad, H. (2004) 'Non-statutory mental health social work in primary care: a chance for renewal?', *British Journal of Social Work*, 34, 2: 145–63.

Fisher, M., Qureshi, H., Hardyman, W. and Homewood, J. (2006) *Using Qualitative Research in Systematic Reviews: Older People's Views of Hospital Discharge*. London: SCIE.

Fook, J. (2002) *Critical Theory and Practice*. London: Sage. pp. 30–9.

Fook, J. (2007) 'Uncertainty: The Defining Characteristic of Social Work?', in M. Lymbery and K. Postle (eds), *Social Work: A Companion to Learning*. London: Sage. pp. 30–9.

Fook, J., Ryan, M. and Hawkins, L. (2000) *Professional Expertise: Practice, Theory and Education for Working in Uncertainty*. London: Whiting and Birch Ltd.

Forbes, D.A., Forbes, S.C., Markle-Reid, M., Morgan, D., Taylor, B.J. and Woods, J. (2007) 'Physical Activity Programmes for Older Persons with Dementia (Protocol)'. *Cochrane Database of Systematic Reviews*, 2. Art. No.: CD006489. DOI: 10.1002/14651858.CD006489. http://www.mrw.interscience.wiley.com/cochrane/clsysrev/articles/CD006489/frame.html (accessed 21/10/2007).

Ford, P., Johnston, B., Mitchell, R. and Myles, F. (2004) 'Social work education and criticality: some thoughts from research', *Social Work Education*, 23, 2: 185–98.

Frank, J. (1995) *Couldn't Care More: A Study of Young Carers and Their Needs*. London: Children's Society.

Freire, P. (1970) *Pedagogy of the Oppressed*. New York: Continuum.

Freitas, M.J., Friesenhahn, G.J., Frost, E. and Michailidis, M.P. (eds) (2005) *Children, Young People and Families: Examining Social Work Practice in Europe*. Rome: Carocci.

Freud, A. (1936) *The Ego and Mechanisms of Defense*. New York: International University Press.

Frost, N., Robinson, M. and Anning, A. (2005) 'Social workers in multidisciplinary teams: issues and dilemmas for professional practice', *Child and Family Social Work*, 10: 187–96.

Furlong, M.A. (2003) 'Self determination and a critical perspective in casework: promoting a balance between independence and autonomy', *Qualitative Social Work*, 2, 2: 177–96.

Gambrill, E. (2006) 'Evidence-based practice and policy: choices ahead', *Research on Social Work Practice*, 16, 3: 338–57.

Gambrill, E. and Gibbs, L. (1999) *Critical Thinking for Social Workers: Exercises for the Helping Professions*. London: Sage.

Gardner, R. (2003) 'Working Together to Improve Children's Life Chances: The Challenge of Inter-Agency Collaboration', in J. Weinstein, C. Whittington and T. Leiba (eds), *Collaboration in Social Work Practice*. London: Jessica Kingsley. pp. 137–60.

Garthwaite, T. (2005) *Social Work in Wales: A Profession to Value*. Cardiff: ADSS Wales.

Gaspar, F. (2000) 'En remontant le temps. Regard sur l'éducateur', in F. Gaspar, M. Gilles, D. Wautier, A. Wéry, M. Davagle and J. Vanhaverbeke (eds), *Les carnets de l'éducateur: Exploration d'une profession*. Marchienne-au- Pont (Belgium): Rhizome. pp. 25–33.

Gellis, Z. (2001) 'Social work perception of transformational and transactional leadership in health care', *Social Work Research*, 25, 1: 17–26.

Gibbs, D. (2004) 'Social Model Services: An Oxymoron?', in C. Barnes and G. Mercer (eds), *Disability Policy and Practice: Applying the Social Model*. Leeds: The Disability Press. pp. 144–59.

Gibbs, L. and Gambrill, E. (2002) *Social Work: Critical Theory and Practice*. London: Sage,

Gibbs, L.E. (2003) *Evidence-based Practice for Helping Professions*. Pacific Grove, CA: Brooks/Cole.

Gillespie, R. (1991) *Manufacturing Knowledge: A History of the Hawthorne Experiments*. Cambridge: Cambridge University Press.

Glendinning, C., Challis, D., Fernandez, J.-L., Jones, K., Knapp, M., Manthorpe, J., Netten, A., Stevens, M. and Wilberforce, M. (2007) 'Evaluating the individual budget pilot projects', *Journal of Care Services Management*, 1, 2: 123–8.

Goodley, D. (2000) *Self-advocacy in the Lives of People with Learning Difficulties*. Buckingham: Open University Press.

Goodley, D. (2001) '"Learning Difficulties", the social model of disability and impairment: challenging epistemologies', *Disability & Society*, 16, 2: 207–23.

Gough, D. and Stanley, N. (2007) 'Implementing policies and procedures', *Child Abuse Review*, 16: 205–8.

Gould, N. (2000) 'Becoming a learning organisation: a social work example', *Social Work Education*, 19, 6 (December): 585–96.

Gould, N. (2006) 'An inclusive approach to knowledge for mental health social work practice and policy', *British Journal of Social Work*, 36, 1: 109–25.

Gower, D. (2004) 'Theraplay'. *Child Webmag*. http://www.childrenwebmag.com/ (accessed 08/10/2007).

Gray, M. and Fook, J. (2004) 'The quest for a universal social work: some issues and implications', *Social Work Education*, 23, 5: 625–44.

Gray, M. and McDonald, C. (2006) 'Pursing good practice? The limits of evidence-based practice', *Journal of Social Work*, 6, 1: 7–20.

Greaves, I. (2007) *Disability Rights Handbook: A Guide to Benefits and Services for All Disabled People, their Families, Carers and Advisers*. London: Disability Alliance.

Grint, K. (2001) *Strengthening Leadership in the Public Sector. Annex D: Literature Review*. London: Cabinet Office.

GSCC (2000) *Post Qualifying Social Work Education and Training PQ Handbook,* section 5, Practice Teaching Award. London: GSCC.

GSCC (2002a) *Codes of Practice for Social Care Workers and Employers*. London: GSCC. www.gscc.org.uk (accessed 04/06/2007).

GSCC (2002b) *Guidance on the Assessment of Practice in the Workplace*. London: GSCC.

GSCC (2005a) *Post-Qualifying Framework for Social Work Education and Training*. London: GSCC.

GSCC (2005b) *Specialist Standards and Requirements (Adult Services)*. London: GSCC.

GSCC (2006a) *Annual Quality-Assurance Report on Social Work Education and Training 2004–05*. London: GSCC.

GSCC Website (2006b) *PQ Handbook*. http://www.gscc.org.uk/Training+and+learning/Continuing+your+training/Post-qualifying+training/Post-qualifying+training+downloads.htm (accessed 15/6/07).

GSCC (2006c) *Specialist Standards and Requirements Practice Education* (March). London: GSCC.

GSCC (2007a) *Post-Qualifying Training*. http://www.gscc.org.uk/Training+and+learning/Continuing+your+training/Post-qualifying+training/ (accessed 23/04/2007).

GSCC PQ Matrix (2007b) Website http://www.gscc.org.uk/NR/rdonlyres/6ADC3FA5-2308-45C2-8624-FCBFC8084A3A/0/PQmatrix8feb07.pdf (accessed 15/10/2007).

GSCC (2007c) *Roles and Tasks of Social Work in England. Consultation Paper. Executive Summary*. http://www.gscc.org.uk/NR/rdonlyres/FCF0168C-FCE2-4AFE-AC1E-147522024828/0/Executive summaryv05final.pdf (accessed 28/11/2007).

GSCC (2007d) *Specialist Standards and Requirements for PQ Education and Training for Social Work in Mental Health Services* (January). London: GSCC.

GSCC (2008) *Social Work at its Best. A Statement of Social Work Roles and Tasks for the 21st Century*. London: GSCC.

GSCC/CSCI/Skills for Care/SCIE (2006) *Eight Principles for Involving Service Users and Carers*. London: GSCC.

GSCC/CWDC/SfC (2006) *Workforce Planning Guide for PQ: (8) Candidates Experiences of PQ Study*. Leeds: Skills for Care.

GSCC/NOPT/JUC/SWEC/SfC/CWDC/BASW (2007) *National Practice Learning Strategy Group Benchmark (Quality Assurance) Statement*. London: GSCC.

GSCC/Topss (2002) *Guidance on the Assessment of Practice in the Workplace*. London: GSCC.

Guardian Jobs (2007) *Consultant Social Worker. London Borough of Hackney*. http://jobs.guardian.co.uk/job/348951/consultant-social-worker (accessed 28/12/2007).

Hämäläinen, J. (2003) 'The concept of social pedagogy in the field of social work', *Journal of Social Work*, 3, 1: 69–80.

Hanvey, P. (1981) *Social Work with Mentally Handicapped People*. London: Heinemann Educational.

Harbin, F. and Murphy, M. (2000) *Substance Misuse and Child Care: How to Understand, Assist and Intervene when Drugs Affect Parenting*. Lyme Regis: Russell House.

Harris, J. (2003) *The Social Work Business*. London: Routledge.

Harris, P.L. (1989) *Children and Emotion*. Oxford: Blackwell.

Harrison, K. and Ruch, G. (2007) 'Social Work and the Use of Self: On Becoming and Being a Social Worker', in M. Lymbery and K. Postle (eds), *Social Work: A Companion to Learning*. London: Sage. pp. 40–50.

Hartley, J. and Allison, M. (2000) 'The role of leadership in the modernisation and improvement of public services', *Public Money and Management*, April–June: 35–40.

Hawkins, P. and Shohet, R. (2006) *Supervision in the Helping Professions* (3rd edition). Maidenhead: Open University Press.

Haynes, B.R., Deverau, P.J. and Guyatt, G.H. (2002) 'Clinical expertise in the era of evidence-based medicine and patient choice', *Evidence Based Medicine*, 7: 36–8.

Healey, K. (2002) 'Managing human services in a market environment: what role for social workers?', *British Journal of Social Work*, 32: 527–40.

Healey, K. (2005) *Social Work Theories in Context: Creating Frameworks for Practice*. Basingstoke: Palgrave Macmillan.

Healthcare Commission (2006) *Joint Investigation into the Provision of Services for People with Learning Disabilities at Cornwall Partnership NHS Trust*. London: HCC/CSCI.

Healthcare Commission (2007) *Investigation into the Service for People with Learning Disabilities provided by Sutton and Merton Primary Care Trust*. London: Commission for Health Care Audit and Inspection.

HEA (Higher Education Academy) (2007) Website. http://www.heacademy.ac.uk/ (accessed 15/10/2007).

HEC (Higher Education for Capability) (1994) 'Capability Manifesto', *Capability*, 1, 1.

HEFCE (Higher Education Funding Council for England) (2000) *The Foundation Degree Prospectus*. http://www.hefce.ac.uk/pubs/hefce/2000/00_27.htm (accessed 23/04/2007).

Heifetz, R. (1996) *Leadership without Easy Answers*. Cambridge, MA: Harvard University Press.

Hevey, D. and Lumsden, E. (2007) The Early Years Professional. Conference Paper. Second Annual CECDE on Vision into Practice, 9 February, Dublin.

Heyes, S. (1993) *A Critique of the Ideology, Power Relations and Language of User Involvement*. http://www.simon.heyes.btinternet.co.uk/essay (accessed 14/08/2008).

Higgins, K. and Pinkerton, J. (1998) 'Literature Reviewing: Towards a More Rigorous Approach', in D. Iwaniek and J. Pinkerton (eds), *Making Research Work: Promoting Child Care Policy and Practice*. Chichester: Wiley. pp.

Higham, P. (2006) *Social Work: Introducing Professional Practice*. London: Sage.

Higham, P.E. (2001) The Dilemma of Standardisation. Paper and presentation to GSCC PQ Assessors Standardisation Event, 27 November. London: GSCC.

Higham, P.E. (2005) *PQ Consortium Wales: 2004–05 External Assessor Report*. London: GSCC.

Hockey, J.L. and James, A. (2003) *Social Identities across the Life Course*. London: Palgrave.

Holloway, M. and Lymbery, M. (2007) 'Caring for people: social work with adults in the next decade and beyond', Editorial. *British Journal of Social Work*, 37, 3: 375–86.

Home Office Immigration and Nationality Directorate (2007) *Planning Better Outcomes and support for Unaccompanied Asylum Seekers*. Consultation Paper. Home Office IND: London.

Holman, B. (1993) *A New Deal for Social Welfare*. Oxford: Lion Publishing plc.

Hopkins, G. (2006) 'Duty, love and sacrifice', *Community Care*, 19–25 January. http/www.childrenuk.co.uk/chsep2004/chsep2004/theraplay.htm (accessed 19/08/07).

Hunt, Paul (1966) 'A Critical Condition' in P. Hunt (ed) *Stigma: The Experience of Disability* London: Geoffrey Chapman Available at http://www.leeds.ac.uk/disability-studies/archiveuk/archframe.htm [Accessed 15-4-08]

Hutton, A. and Partridge, K. (2006) *Say It Your Own Way: Children's Participation in Assessment*. Barkingside: Barnados/DfES.

Huxley, P., Evans, S., Gately, C., Webber, M., Mears, A. and Pajak, S. (2005a) 'Stress and pressures in mental health social work: the worker speaks', *British Journal of Social Work*, 35, 7: 1063–79.

Huxley, P., Evans, S., Webber, M. and Gately, C. (2005b) 'Staff shortages in the mental health workforce: the case of the disappearing approved social worker', *Health & Social Care in the Community*, 13, 6: 504–13.

Iles, V. and Sutherland, K. (2001) *Organisational Change. A review for healthcare managers, professionals and researchers*. London: SDO Service Delivery and Organisation Research and Development Organisation, National co-ordinating Centre for NHS.

I& DeA Knowledge (2007) *Recruitment and Retention of Staff in Social Work and Social Care*. http://www.idea.gov.uk/idk/core/page.do?pageId=6588132 (accessed 18/12/2007).

Jackson, M. (1996) 'Institutional Provision for the Feeble-minded in Edwardian England: Sandlebridge and the Scientific Morality of Permanent Care', in A. Rigby and D. Wrigth (eds), *From Idiocy to Mental Deficiency: Historical Perspectives on People with Learning Disabilities*. London: Routledge. pp. 161–83.

Jackson, R. (2006) 'The role of social pedagogy in the training of residential child care workers', *Journal of Intellectual Disabilities*, 10, 1: 61–73.

Jacobson, N. (2004) *In Recovery: The Making of Mental Health Policy*. Nashville, TN: Vanderbilt University Press.

James, A. and Prout, A. (1990) *Constructing and Reconstructing Childhood*. London: Falmer Press.

James, P. and Thomas, M. (1996) 'Deconstructing a disabling environment in social work education', *Social Work Education*, 15, 1: 34–45.

Jenkins, R. (1998) *Questions of Competence: Culture, Classification and Intellectual Disability*. Cambridge: Cambridge University Press.

Jernberg, A. (1999) *Theraplay: Helping Parents and Children Build Better Relationships through Attachment-based Play* (2nd edition). San Francisco, CA: Jossey-Bass.

JISC (Joint Information Systems Committee) (2005) *Briefing Paper – Retaining Staff*. April. www.jisc.ac.uk (accessed 22/07/2007).

Jones, C. (2001) 'Voices from the frontline: state social workers and New Labour', *British Journal of Social Work*, 31: 547–62.

Jones, C., Ferguson, I., Lavalette, M. and Penketh, L. (2004) *Social Work and Social Justice: A Manifesto for a New Engaged Practice*. http://www.liv.ac.uk/sspsw/manifesto/Manifesto.htm (accessed xx/xx/2007).

Jones, F., Fletcher, B.C. and Ibbetson, K. (1991) 'Stressors and strains amongst social workers: demands, supports, constraints, and psychological health', *British Journal of Social Work*, 21: 443–69.

Jordan, R. and Parkinson, C. (2001) 'Reflective practice in a process for the re-approval of ASWs: an exploration of some inevitable resistance', *Journal of Social Work Practice*, 15, 1: 67–79.

JUC/SWEC (Joint University Council Social Work Education Committee) (2006) *A Social Work Research Strategy in Higher Education 2006–2020*. London: Social Care Workforce Research Unit.

Karban, K. (2003) 'Social work education and mental health in a changing world', *Social Work Education*, 22, 2: 191–202.

Keith-Lucas, A. (1972) *Giving and Taking Help*. Chapel Hill, NC: University of North Carolina Press.

Kemshall, H. and Pritchard, J. (eds) (1996) *Good Practice in Risk Assessment and Risk Management 1*. London: Jessica Kingsley.

Kerr, B., Gordon, J., MacDonald, C. and Stalker, K. (2005) *Effective Social Work with Older People*. Edinburgh: Scottish Executive. http://www.scotland.gov.uk/social research (accessed 29/06/2007).

King's Fund (1980) *An Ordinary Life: Comprehensive Locally-based Services for Mentally Handicapped People*. London: King's Fund.

Kirkpatrick, D.L. (1987) 'Evaluation of Training', in R.L. Craig and L.R. Bittel (eds), *Training and Development Handbook*. New York: McGraw-Hill. pp. 87–112.

Kohli, R.K.S. (2007) *Social Work with Unaccompanied Asylum Seeking Children*. Basingstoke: Palgrave.

Kolb, D. (1984) *Experiential Learning: Experience as the Source of Learning and Development*. London: Prentice Hall.

Kolb, D.A. and Fry, R. (1975) 'Towards an Applied Theory of Experiential Learning', in C.L. Cooper (ed.), *Theories of Group Processes*. New York: Wiley. pp. 27–56.

Kornbeck, J. (2001) 'Sozialpädagogische Inhalte, unterschiedliche Formen: Drei Ansätze zum Standort der Sozialpädagogik in Europa', *Standpunkt Sozial*, Vol. 2001, no 3, pp. 80–88.

Kornbeck, J. (2002) 'Reflections on the exportability of social pedagogy and its possible limits', in *Social Work in Europe*, 9, 3: 37–49.

Kotter, J. (1990) *A Force for Change*. London: Free Press.

Kraiger, K. Ford and Salas, E. (1993) 'Application of cognitive, skill-based and affective theories of learning outcomes to new methods of training evaluation', *Journal of Applied Psychology*, 78: 311–28.

Lahad, M. (1992) 'Story Making and Assessment Method for Coping with Stress: Six Part Story and BASIC Ph', in S. Jennings (ed.), *Dramatherapy: Theory and Practice 2*. London: Routledge. pp. 150–63.

Laming, Lord W.H. (2003) *The Victoria Climbie Enquiry: Report of an Inquiry by Lord Laming Presented to Parliament by the Secretary of State for Health and the Secretary of State for the Home Department by Command of Her Majesty*. CM 5992 London: HMSO.

Lau, A. (1991) 'Cultural and Ethnic Perspectives on Significant Harm: Its Assessment and Treatment', in M. Adcock, R. White and A. Hollows (eds), *Significant Harm*. London: Significant Publications. pp. 149–62.

Lawler, J.J. (2007) 'Leadership in social work: a case of *caveat emptor*?', *British Journal of Social Work*, 37: 123–41.

Leadbetter, C. (2004) *Personalisation through Participation: A New Script for Public Services*. London: Demos.

Learning Difficulties Research Team, Bewley, C. and McCulloch, L. (2006) *Let Me In – I'm A Researcher! Getting Involved in Research*. London: DH.

Leece, D. and Leece, J. (2006) 'Direct payments: creating a two-tiered system in social care?', *British Journal of Social Work*, 36: 1379–93.

Leeding, A.E. (1976) *Child Care Manual for Social Workers* (3rd edition). London: Butterworths.

Leiba, T. (2003) 'Mental Health Policies and Interprofessional Working', in J. Weinstein, C. Whittington and T. Leiba (eds), *Collaboration in Social Work Practice*. London: Jessica Kingsley. pp. 161–80.

Leiba, T. and Weinstein, J. (2003) 'Who are the Participants in the Collaborative Process and What Makes Collaboration Succeed or Fail?', in J. Weinstein, C. Whittington and T. Leiba (eds), *Collaboration in Social Work Practice*. London: Jessica Kingsley. pp. 63–82.

Lennox, A. and Anderson, E. (2007) *The Leicester Model of Interprofessional Education*. London: HEA.

Lewin, K. (1948) *Resolving Social Conflicts*. New York: Harper & Row.

Lindsay, J. and Tompsett, H. (1998) *Careers of Practice Teachers in the London and South East Region*. London: CCETSW.

Lloyd, L. (2006) 'A caring profession? the ethics of care and social work with older people', *British Journal of Social Work*, 36, 7: 1171–85.

Lord, J. and Hutchison, P. (2003) 'Individualised support and funding: building blocks for capacity building and inclusion', *Disability & Society*, 18, 1: 71–86.

Louhiala, P. (2004) *Preventing Intellectual Disability: Ethical and Clinical Issues*. Cambridge: Cambridge University Press.

Lumsden, E. (2005) 'Joined Up Thinking in Practice: An Exploration of Professional Collaboration', in T. Waller (ed.), *An Introduction to Early Childhood: A Multidisciplinary Approach*. London: Paul Chapman. pp. 39–54.

Lymbery, M. (2001) 'Social work at the crossroads', *British Journal of Social Work*, 21: 369–84.

Lymbery, M. (2005) *Social Work with Older People*. London: Sage.

Lymbery, M. (2006) 'United we stand? partnership working in health and social care and the role of social work in services for older people', *British Journal of Social Work*, 36: 1119–34.

MacDonald, C. (2006) *Challenging Social Work: The Context of Practice*. Basingstoke: Palgrave Macmillan.

Macdonald, G. (2001) *Effective Interventions for Child Abuse and Neglect: An Evidence-based Approach to Planning and Evaluating Interventions.* Chichester: John Wiley & Sons.

Manthorpe, J. (2003) 'Book review: D. Race (2002) *Learning Disability – A Social Approach.* London: Routledge', *International Social Work*, 46, 2: 267–9.

Marshall, M. (1983) *Social Work with Old People.* Basingstoke: Macmillan.

Martin, J. (1984) *Hospitals in Trouble.* Oxford: Blackwell.

Maslow, A.H. (1954) *Motivation and Personality.* New York: Harper & Row.

Mayer, J. and Timms, N. (1970) *The Client Speaks.* London: Routledge and Kegan Paul.

McCrae, N., Murray, J., Huxley, P. and Evans, S. (2004) 'Prospects for mental health social work: a qualitative study of attitudes of service managers and academic staff', *Journal of Mental Health*, 13, 3: 305–17.

McCrae, N., Murray, J., Huxley, P. and Evans, S. (2005) 'The research potential of mental-health social workers: a qualitative study of the views of senior mental-health service managers', *British Journal of Social Work*, 35, 1: 55–71.

McGregor, D. (1960) *The Human Side of Enterprise*, Sydney: McGraw-Hill.

McMichael, A. (2000) 'Professional identity and continuing education: a study of social workers in hospital settings', *Social Work Education*, 18, 2: 175–83 (9).

McNeish, D., Newman, T. and Roberts, H. (eds) (2002) *What Works for Children: Effective Services for Children and Families.* Buckingham: Open University Press.

Means, R. (2007) 'Modernisation Muddles: What is the Future of Social Care for Older People in England and Wales?' Paper presented at Swansea University, 16 March 2007. Available as OPAN download.

Mencap (2007) *Death by Indifference.* London: Mencap.

Miller, E.J. and Gwynne, G. (1972) *A Life Apart.* London: Tavistock.

Milner, Jerry (2003) Changing the Culture of the Workplace Closing Plenary Session – Annual Meeting of States and Tribes, January 29.

Milsom, S. (2006) 'An Ageing Population and Research in Wales'. Paper presented at launch of OPAN Cymru, Swansea University, 17 May. Available as OPAN download.

Mir, G., Nocon, A. and Ahmad, W. with Jones, L. (2001) *Learning Difficulties and Ethnicity.* London: DH.

Mitchell, W. and Glendinning, C. (2007) *A Review of the Research Evidence Surrounding Risk Perceptions, Risk Management Strategies and their Consequences in Adult Social Care for Different Groups of Service Users* (Working Paper No. DHR 2180 01.07). York: University of York Social Policy Research Unit.

Moffatt, K. (1996) 'Teaching Social Work as a Reflective Process', in N. Gould and I. Taylor (eds), *Reflective Learning for Social Work.* Aldershot: Ashgate. pp. 47–62.

Morgan, H. (2005) 'Disabled People and Employment: The Potential Impact of European Policy', in A. Roulstone and C. Barnes (eds), *Working Futures? Disabled People, Policy and Social Inclusion.* Bristol: Policy Press. pp. 259–71.

Morris, J. (1991) *Pride Against Prejudice: Transforming Attitudes to Disability.* London: The Women's Press.

Morris, J. (1993) *Community Care or Independent Living.* York: Joseph Rowntree Foundation.

Morris, J. (ed.) (1996) *Encounters with Strangers: Feminism and Disability.* London: The Women's Press.

Morris, J. (1997) 'Gone missing? Disabled children living away from their families', *Disability & Society*, 12, 2: 241–58.

Morris, J. (1998) *Still Missing? Disabled Children and the Children Act.* London: The Who Cares Trust.

Morris, J. (2007) *Good Practice Guidance on Working with Parents with a Learning Disability.* London: DH/DfES.

Mühlum, A. (2001) *Sozialarbeit und Sozialpädagogik* (2nd edition). Frankfurt: Deutscher Verein für öffentliche und private Fürsorge.

Munro, E. (2004) 'The impact of audit on social work practice', *British Journal of Social Work*, 34: 1075–95.

Mutter, R., Judge, B., Flynn, L. and Hennessey, J. (2002) *Supporting People Together: Family Group Conference in Mental Health Services.* Dagenham: Northeast Essex Mental Health Trust.

Myers, I.B. and Myers, P.B. (1980) *Gifts Differing*. Palo Alto, CA: Consulting Psychologists Press.

Napier, L. and Fook, J. (eds) (2000) *Breakthroughs in Practice: Theorising Critical Moments in Social Work*. London: Whiting and Birch Ltd.

National Assembly for Wales (2000) *In Safe Hands: Protection of Vulnerable Adults in Wales*. Cardiff: National Assembly for Wales.

National Working Group on Child Protection and Disability (2003) '*It Doesn't Happen to Disabled Children': Child Protection and Disabled Children*. London: NSPCC.

National Statistics online http://www.statistics.gov.uk/CCI/nuggest 25p?10= (accessed 02/12/2007).

Nelson, G., Lord, J. and Ochocka, J. (2001) *Shifting the Paradigm in Community Mental Health: Towards Empowerment and Community*. Toronto: University of Toronto Press.

Nevis, E., DiBella, A. and Gould, J. (1995) 'Understanding organisations as learning systems', *Sloan Management Review*, Winter: 73–84.

NHSMA (NHS Modernisation Agency) (2004a) *A Career Framework for the NHS*. Discussion Document – version 2 (June). London: DH.

NHSMA (2004b) *The NHS Knowledge and Skills Framework (NHS KSF) and the Development Review Process* (October). London: DH.

NHSMA (2006) *Agenda for Change*. Resource Pack (March). London: DH.

NIMHE (National Institute for Mental Health England) (2005a) *NIMHE Guiding Statement on Recovery*. London: DH.

NIMHE (2005b) *The Social Work Contribution to Mental Health Services: The Future Direction*. A discussion paper. London: NIMHE.

NIPQETP (Northern Ireland Post-Qualifying Education and Training Partnership) (2005) *Draft Proposal for the Development of a NI Post-Qualifying Framework*. Consultation Document (November). Belfast: NIPQETP.

NIPQETP (2007) *The Northern Ireland Post-Qualifying Framework*. Belfast: NIPQETP.

NISSC (Northern Ireland Social Care Council) (2002) *Workforce Planning for Social Work: Supply, Demand and Provision of Newly Qualified Social Workers Required 2001/2–2003/4*. Belfast: NISCC.

NISCC (Northern Ireland Social Care Council) (2005a) *Rules for the Approval of Post-Qualifying Education and Training in Social Work in Northern Ireland*. Draft for Consultation (October). Belfast: NISCC.

NISCC (2005b) *Explanation of Social Care Workers' Roles*. Website. www.niscc.info/careers/faq.htm (accessed xx/05/2005).

NISCC (2006) *PSS Development and Training Strategy 2006–2016*. Belfast: NISCC.

NISW (National Institute of Social Work) (1982) *Social Workers: Their Role and Tasks*. London: Bedford Square Press.

Nocon, A. (2006) *Background Evidence for the DRC's Formal Investigation into Health Inequalities Experienced by People with Learning Disabilities or Mental Health Problems*', London: Disability Rights Commission.

NOPT (National Association of Practice Teachers) (2007) Website http://www.nopt.org/index.html (accessed 15/10/2007).

Northway, R., Davies, R., Mansell, I. and Jenkins, R. (2007) ' "Policies don't protect people, it's how they are implemented": policy and practice in protecting people with learning disabilities from abuse', *Social Policy & Administration*, 41, 1: 86–104.

Oliver, M. (1983) *Social Work with Disabled People*. Basingstoke: Macmillan.

Oliver, M. (1990) *The Politics of Disablement*. Basingstoke: Macmillan.

Oliver, M. (1996) *Understanding Disability: From Theory to Practice*. Basingstoke: Macmillan.

Oliver, M. (1999) 'Capitalism, Disability and Ideology: A Materialist Critique of the Normalization Principle', in R. Flynn and R. Lemay (eds), *A Quarter-century of Normalization and Social Role Valorization: Evolution and Impact*. Ottawa: University of Ottawa Press. pp. 163–73.

Oliver, M. (2004) 'The Social Model in Action: If I Had a Hammer', in C. Barnes and G. Mercer (eds), *Implementing the Social Model of Disability: Theory and Research*. Leeds: The Disability Press.

Oliver, M. and Bailey, P. (2002) Report on the Application of the Social Model of Disability to the Services provided by Birmingham City Council. Unpublished document.

Oliver, M. and Barnes, C. (1998) *Disabled People and Social Policy*. London: Longman.

Oliver, M. and Sapey, B. (2006) *Social Work with Disabled People* (3rd edition). Basingstoke: Palgrave Macmillan.

Onyett, S., Pillinger, T. and Muijen, M. (1995) *Making Community Mental Health Teams Work*. London: Sainsbury Centre for Mental Health.

Otto, H.U. and Lorenz, W. (1998) 'Editorial: the new journal for the social professions', *European Journal of Social Work*. 1, 1: 1–4.

Øvretveit, J. (1986) *Improving Social Work Records and Practice*. Birmingham: BASW.

Parker, J. (2007) 'Developing effective practice learning for tomorrow's social workers', *Social Work Education*, 26, 8: 763–79.

Parton, N. (2006) *Safeguarding Childhood: Early Intervention and Surveillance in Late Modern Society*. Basingstoke: Palgrave Macmillan.

Parton, N. and O'Byrne, P. (2000) *Constructive Social Work: Towards a New Practice*. Basingstoke: Macmillan.

Pawson, R., Boaz, A., Grayson, L., Long, A. and Barnes, C. (2003) *Types and Quality of Knowledge in Social Care*. London: SCIE.

Payne, M. (1996) *What is Professional Social Work?* Birmingham: Venture Press.

Payne, M. (1997) *Modern Social Work Theory*. Macmillan: Basingstoke.

Payne, M. (2005). *The Origins of Social Work: Continuity and Change*. Basingstoke: Palgrave Macmillan.

Payne, M. (2006) *Don't Live in Fear: Professional Social Work*. July. BASW: Birmingham. 14–15.

Pease, B. and Fook, J. (1999) 'Introduction: Postmodern Critical Theory and Emancipatory Social Work Practice', in B. Pease and J. Fook (eds), *Transforming Social Work Practice: Postmodern Critical Perspectives*. London: Routledge. pp. 1–22.

Peck, E. and Norman, I.J. (1999) 'Working together in adult community mental health services: exploring inter-professional role relations', *Journal of Mental Health*, 8, 3: 231–42.

Pedler, M., Burgoyne, J. and Boydell, T. (1997) *The Learning Company: A Strategy for Sustainable Development*. Maidenhead: McGraw-Hill.

Personnel Today (2003) 'Councils struggle to recruit and retain staff', *Personnel Today*, April. www.personneltoday.com (accessed 30/11/2007).

Petrie, P., Boddy, J., Cameron, C., Wigfall, V. and Simon, A. (2006) *Working with Children in Care: European Perspectives*. Maidenhead: Open University Press/McGraw-Hill.

Phillips, J. and Burholt, V. (2007) 'Ageing in Wales: policy responses to an ageing population', *Contemporary Wales*, 19: 180–97.

Phillips, J., Ray, M. and Marshall, M. (2006) *Social Work with Older People* (4th edition). Basingstoke: Palgrave.

Philpot, T. (2006) *Care Sector Guide: A Brief Introduction*. http://www.communitycare.co.ukArticles/2006/07/26/41871/a-brief-introduction.html (accessed 18/06/2007).

Piaget, J. (1983) 'Piaget's Theory', in P.H. Mussen (ed.), *Handbook of Child Psychology. Vol. 1: Theory and Methods*. New York: Wiley.

Pilgrim, D. (1997) 'Some reflections on "quality" and "mental health"', *Journal of Mental Health*, 6, 6: 567–76.

PLTF (Practice Learning Task Force) (2005) *New Approaches to Practice Learning*. Leeds: PLTF.

Plumb, S. (2005) 'The Social/Trauma Model: Mapping the Mental Health Consequences of Childhood Sexual Abuse and Similar Experiences', in J. Tew (ed.), *Social Perspectives in Mental Health: Developing Models to Understand and Work with Mental Distress*. London: Jessica Kingsley. pp. 112–28.

Poell, R., van Dam, K. and van den Berg, P. (2004) 'Organisation Learning in Work Contexts', *Applied Psychology. An International Review*, 53, 4 (October): 614–16.

Poll, C., Duffy, S., Hatton, C., Sanderson, H. and Routledge, M. (2006) *A Report on In Control's First Phase 2003–2005*. In Control. http://www.in-control.org.uk/ (accessed 19/04/2007).

Popple, K. (1995) *Analysing Community Work: Its Theory and Practice*. Maidenhead: Open University Press.

Post Qualifying Social Work Consortium for Wales (2003) *Handbook for completing PQSW Part II (PQ2-6) by Portfolio Route*. Swansea: Post Qualifying Consortium Assessment Board.

Postle, K. and Beresford, P. (2007) 'Capacity building and the reconception of political participation: a role for social care workers?', *British Journal of Social Work*, 37, 1: 143–58.

Postle, K., Edwards, C., Moon, R., Rumsey, H. and Thomas, T. (2002) 'Continuing professional development after qualification: partnerships, pitfalls and potential', *Social Work Education*, 21, 2: 157–69.

Potts, M. and Fido, R. (1991) *'A Fit Person to be Removed': Personal Accounts of Life in a Mental Deficiency Institution*. Plymouth: Northcote House.

Powell, F. and Geoghegan, M. (2005) 'Reclaiming civil society: the future of global social work?', *European Journal of Social Work*, 8, 2: 129–44.

Power, M. (2007) *Organised Uncertainty: Designing a World of Risk Management*. Oxford: Oxford University Press.

PQ Consortium for Wales (2005) 'Modernising PQ: the Care Council for Wales'. *PQ News in Wales Newsletter*, 5 (July): 1–2.

Preston-Shoot, M. (2006) 'Governmental Reviews of Social Work', Presentation to Social Work Assembly Forum, 22 May. Birmingham: BASW.

Pritchard, J. (2007) *Working with Adult Abuse: A Training Manual for People Working with Vulnerable Adults*. London: Jessica Kingsley.

QAA (Quality Assurance Agency) (2000) *Social Policy and Administration and Social Work Benchmark Statements*. Gloucester: QAA.

QAA (2001) *The framework for higher education qualifications in England, Wales and Northern Ireland*. Gloucester: QAA.

QCA (Qualifications and Curriculum Agency) (2007) *National Vocational Qualifications (NVQ) Assessment Strategy*. London: QCA. http://www.qca.org.uk/qca_4686.aspx (accessed 15/10/2007).

Qureshi, H. (2006) *Self-Assessment: How Does It Work, Is It Effective and How Can It Be Promoted*. Dartington: Research in Practice for Adults.

Race, D. (ed.) (2002) *Learning Disability: A Social Approach*. London: Routledge.

Race, D., Boxall, K. and Carson, I. (2005) 'Towards a dialogue for practice: reconciling social role valorization and the social model of disability', *Disability & Society*, 20, 5: 507–21.

Rafferty, J. and Steyaert, J. (2007) 'Social Work in a Digital Society', in M. Lymbery and K. Postle (eds), *Social Work: A Companion to Learning*. London: Sage. pp. 165–75.

Ramon, S. (2006) 'British Mental Health Social Work and the Psychosocial Approach in Context', in D.B. Double (ed.), *Critical Psychiatry: The Limits of Madness*. Basingstoke: Palgrave Macmillan. pp. 133–48.

Rank, M.G. and Hutchison, W.S. (2000) 'An analysis of leadership within the social work profession', *Journal of Social Work Education*, 36, 3: 487–512.

Rapaport, J. (2005) 'Policy swings over thirty-five years of mental health social work in England and Wales 1969–2004', *Practice*, 17, 1: 43–56.

Reder, P., Duncan, S. and Gray, M. (1993) *Beyond Blame: Child Abuse Tragedies Revisited*. London: Routledge.

Rees, O. (2007) *The Impact of the National Assembly for Wales on the Development of Family Law in Wales: Research Undertaken on Behalf of the North Wales Family Justice Council*. Bangor: Bangor University.

Reeve, D. (2002) 'Negotiating psycho-emotional dimensions of disability and their influence on identity constructions', *Disability & Society*, 17, 5: 493–508.

REU (Race Equality Unit) and SCIE (Social Care Institute of Excellence) (2006) *Doing It for Themselves*. London: REU and SCIE.

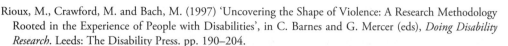

Rioux, M., Crawford, M. and Bach, M. (1997) 'Uncovering the Shape of Violence: A Research Methodology Rooted in the Experience of People with Disabilities', in C. Barnes and G. Mercer (eds), *Doing Disability Research*. Leeds: The Disability Press. pp. 190–204.

Roche, D. and Rankin, J. (2004) *Who Cares? Building the Social Care Workforce*. London: Institute for Public Policy Research.

Rogers, C.R. (1961/1967) *On Becoming a Person: A Therapist's View of Psychotherapy*. London: Constable.

Rose, R. and Philpot, T. (2005) *The Child's Own Story: Life Story Work with Traumatised Children*. London: Jessica Kingsley.

Rosen, A. and Proctor, E.K. (2003) *Developing Practice Guidelines for Social Work Interventions: Issues, Methods, and Research Agenda*. New York: Columbia University Press.

Rowland, M. (2003) 'Learning the hard way', *Community Care*, 30 (October): 32–4.

Rowland, M. (2006) 'Post Hoc Survey Evaluation: 2006'. Unpublished survey. Birmingham: West Midlands Regional Post-Qualifying Consortium.

Rumsey, H. (1995) *Mentors in Post Qualifying Education: An Inter-professional Perspective*. London: Central Council for Education and Training in Social Work.

Ryan, J. and Thomas, F. (1987) *The Politics of Mental Handicap*. London: Free Association Books.

Sage, H. and Allan, M. (2004) 'Sustaining Reflective Practice in the Workplace', in N. Gould and M. Baldwin (eds), *Social Work, Critical Reflection and the Learning Organisation*. Aldershot: Ashgate. pp. 87–100.

Samuel, M. (2007) 'Are students a cost or an investment?', *Community Care*, September: http://www.community care.co.uk/Articles/2007/09/27/105899/the-practice-placement-squeeze-whats-the-problem.html Website accessed 15/04/2007.

Sapey, B. (1993) 'Community care: reinforcing the dependency of disabled people', *Applied Community Studies*, 1, 3: 21–9.

Sapey, B. (2000) 'Disablement in the Informational Age', *Disability & Society*, 15, 4: 619–36.

Sapey, B. (2001) 'From Stigma to the Social Exclusion of Disabled People', in T. Mason, C. Carlisle, C. Watkins and E. Whitehead (eds), *Stigma and Social Exclusion in Healthcare*. London: Routledge. pp. 270–80.

Sapey, B. (2004a) 'Disability and Social Exclusion in the Information Society', in C. Barnes, S. French, J. Swain and C. Thomas (eds), *Disabling Barriers, Enabling Environments* (2nd edition). London: Sage. pp. 273–8.

Sapey, B. (2004b) 'Practice for What? The Use of Evidence in Social Work with Disabled People', in D. Smith (ed.), *Evidence-based Practice and Social Work*. London: Jessica Kingsley. pp. 143–60.

Sapey, B. and Pearson, J. (2004) 'Do disabled people need social workers?', *Social Work and Social Sciences Review*, 11, 3: 52–70.

Sapey, B., Turner, R. and Orton, S. (2004) *Access to Practice: Overcoming the Barriers to Practice Learning for Disabled Social Work Students*. Southampton: SWAPltsn.

Schein, E. (1992) *Organizational Culture and Leadership*. 2nd edn. San Francisco, CA.: Jossey Bass.

Schön, D. (1973) *Beyond the Stable State*. Harmondsworth: Penguin/New York: W.W. Norton.

Schön, D. (1983) *The Reflective Practitioner. How Professionals Think in Action*. London: Temple Smith.

Schön, D. (1987) *Educating the Reflective Practitioner*. San Franscisco, CA: Jossey-Bass.

Schön, D. (1991a) *The Reflective Practitioner: How Professionals Think in Action*. Aldershot: Ashgate.

Schön, D. (1991b) *The Reflection Turn: Case Studies In and On Educational Practice*. New York: Teachers Press, Columbia University.

Schön, D. (1996) *Educating the Reflective Practitioner: Toward a New Design for Teaching and Learning in the Professions*. San Francisco, CA: Jossey-Bass.

SCIE (Social Care Institute for Excellence) (2003a) *A Framework for Supporting and Assessing Practice Learning*. Position Paper No. 2. London: SCIE.

SCIE (2003b) *Types and Quality of Knowledge in Social Care*. London: SCIE.

SCIE (2003c) *Users at the Heart: User Participation in the Governance and Operations of Social Care Regulatory Bodies*. London: SCIE.

SCIE (2004a) *Has Service User Participation Made a Difference to Social Care Services?* Position paper No. 3. London: SCIE. http:/www.scie.org.uk/publications/positionpapers/pp03.asp (accessed 19/08/2007).

SCIE (2004b) *Involving Service Users and Carers in Social Work Education*. Resource Guide No. 2 (March). London: SCIE.

SCIE (2004c) *Learning Organisations: A Self-assessment Resource Pack*. London: SCIE.

SCIE (2005a) *Helping Parents with Learning Disabilities in their Role as Parents*. SCIE Research Briefing 14. London: SCIE.

SCIE (2005b) *Accessibility Guidelines* (July). London: SCIE.

SCIE (2005c) *Developing Social Care: The Past, the Present and the Future*. Position Paper No. 4 (July). London: SCIE.

SCIE (2005d) *Developing Social Care: Service Users' Vision for Adult Support*. Electronic Database Report No. 7 (September). London: SCIE.

SCIE (2006a) *Involving Children and Young People in Developing Social Care*. Practice Guide No. 6 (February). London: SCIE.

SCIE (2006b) *A Review of Carer Participation in England, Wales and Northern Ireland*. Position Paper No. 5 (April). London: SCIE.

SCIE (2007) *Choice, Control and Individual Budgets: Emerging Themes*. SCIE Research Briefing No. 20. London: SCIE.

Scott, D., Brown, A., Lunt, I. and Thorne, I. (2004) *Professional Doctorates: Integrating Profession and Academic Knowledge*. Maidenhead: Open University Press.

Scottish Executive (2002a) *It's Everyone's Job to Make Sure I am Alright: Report of the Child Protection Audit and Review*. Edinburgh: HMSO.

Scottish Executive (2002b) *Report of the Chief Inspector of Social Work Services for Scotland*. Edinburgh: SE.

Scottish Executive (2005) *Twenty-first Century Social Work Review: Interim Report*. April. Edinburgh: SE.

Scottish Executive (2006a) *Social Work: A 21st Century Profession*. Edinburgh: SE.

Scottish Executive (2006b) *National Training for Care Management: Practitioners Guide*. Edinburgh: SE.

Scottish Executive (2006c) *Changing Lives: Report of the 21st Century Review of Social Work*. Edinburgh: SE.

Scottish Executive (2007) *Better Health, Better Care: A Discussion Document*. Edinburgh: SE.

Scottish Government (2007) *Scottish Social Services Workforce: Core Minimum Data Set (CMDS)*. www.scotland.gov.uk/Publications/2007/02/12105705 (accessed 23/11/2007).

Scourfield, P. (2007) 'Social care and the modern citizen: client, consumer, service user, manager and entrepreneur', *British Journal of Social Work*, 37, 1: 107–22.

SCQF (Scottish Credit and Qualifications Framework) (2006) *Table of Main Qualifications*. http://www.scqf.org.uk/table.htm (accessed 30/06/2006).

Secretary of State for Work and Pensions (2006) *Disability Discrimination Act: Guidance on Matters to be Taken into Account in Determining Questions Relating to the Definition of Disability*. London: Department for Work and Pensions.

Seddon, D., Robinson, C., Reeves, C., Tommis Y., Woods, R. and Russell, I. (2006) 'In their own right: translating the policy of carer assessment into practice', *British Journal of Social Work*,

Senge, P. (1990) *The Fifth Discipline: The Art and Practice of the Learning Organisation*. London: Century Business.

Senge, P., Kleiner, A., Roberts, C., Ross, R. and Smith, B. (1994) *The Fifth Discipline Fieldbook: Strategies and Tools for Building a Learning Organization*. New York: Doubleday.

Sennett, R. (2003) *Respect: The Formation of Character in an Age of Inequality*. London: Allen Lane/Penguin.

SfC (Skills for Care) (2005) *The State of the Social Care Workforce 2004: The Second Skills, Research and Intelligence Annual Report*. Leeds: Skills for Care.

SfC (2006a) *Frequently Asked Questions: National Minimum Data Set.* Leeds: Skills for Care.

SfC (2006b) *Reprint of a 2004 Topss England Publication. Leadership and Management: A Strategy for the Social Care Workforce.* Leeds: Skills for Care.

SfC (2007a) *Developing and Delivering the New PQ Framework: Involving People Who Use Services and Carers.* Leeds: Skills for Care.

SfC (2007b) *What People Who Use Services Want To See in Post-Qualifying (PQ) Training for Social Workers.* Leeds: Skills for Care.

SfC (2008) *Skills Research & Intelligence Providing information about the social care workforce.* Leeds: Skills for Care http://www.nmdssc.org.uk/ (accessed 15/04/08).

Skills for Care East Midlands (2007c) *A Work-based Learning and Assessment Strategy for the new Post-qualifying Awards in Social Work in the East Midlands.* Derby: SfC EM.

SfC East Midlands (2006) *The Purpose of Social Work: Report* (Jane Houston). Derby: Skills for Care.

SfC West Midlands (2007) *Recruitment and Retention in the Care Sector in the West Midlands.* Final Report by Change Consultancy and Training (August). Leeds: Skills for Care.

Shakespeare, T.W. and Watson, N. (2002) 'The social model of disability: an outdated ideology?', *Research in Social Science and Disability*, 2: 9–28.

Shaping Our Lives (2007) National Service User Network Website. http://www.shapingourlives.org.uk/ (accessed 14/10/2007).

Sharkey, P. (2000) *The Essentials of Community Care.* Basingstoke: Macmillan.

Sharp, M. and Danbury, H. (1999) *The Management of Failing DipSW Students.* Aldershot: Ashgate.

Shaw, I., Arksey, H. and Mullender, A. (2004) *ESRC Research, Social Work, and Social Care.* London: SCIE.

Sheppard, M. (2006) *Social Work and Social Exclusion: The Idea of Practice.* Aldershot: Ashgate.

SIESWE (2004) *Scottish Voices: Service Users at the Heart of Social Work Education.* Dundee: SIESWE.

SIESWE (Scottish Institute for Excellence in Social Work Education) (2005) *Practice Learning Qualifications and Practice Learning Qualifications (Social Services).* December. Dundee: SIESWE.

Simmons, L. (2007) *Social Care Governance: A Practice Workbook.* Belfast: DHSSPS/London: SCIE.

SL (Socialpædagogernes Landsforbund) (2006) *Et godt tilbud.* Copenhagen: SL. http://www.sl.dk/upload/pjecer/et%20godt%20tilbud.pdf (accessed 23/04/2007).

Slater, P. (2007) 'The passing of the practice teaching award: history, legacy, prospects', *Social Work Education*, 26, 8: 749–62.

Smith, D. (ed) (2004) *Social Work and Evidence-Based Practice: Research Highlights in Social Work 45.* Jessica Kingsley: London.

Smith, R., Anderson, E. and Thorpe, L. (2007) 'Interprofessional Education', *SWAP*. http://www.swap.ac.uk (accessed 10/06/2007).

Smyth, C. (2002) *Promoting Research and Evidence-based Practice: From Rhetoric to Reality.* Belfast: NISSC.

Smyth, C. and Bell, D. (2006) 'From biscuits to boyfriends: the ramifications of choices for people with learning disabilities', *British Journal of Learning Disabilities*, 34, 4: 227–36.

Social Exclusion Unit (2004) *Mental Health and Social Exclusion.* London: Office of the Deputy Prime Minister.

Social Services Directorate (2006) *Safeguarding Vulnerable Adults: Regional Adult Protection Policy and Procedural Guidance (Northern Ireland).* Ballymena: Northern Health and Social Services Board.

SSIW (Social Services Inspectorate for Wales/Arolygiaeth Gwasanaethau Cymdeithasol Cymru) (2004) *Annual Report of the Chief Inspector 2002–2003.* Cardiff: SSIW.

SSIW (2006) *The Report of the Chief Inspector Social Services 2005–2006.* Cardiff: SSIW.

SSSC (Scottish Social Services Council) (2004) Continuing Professional Development for the Social Service Workforce. October. Dundee: SSSC.

SSSC (2005) *Rules and Requirements for Specialist Training for Social Service Workers in Scotland.* December. Dundee: SSSC.

Stanley, L. and Wise, S. (1993) *Breaking Out Again: Feminist Ontology and Epistemology*. London: Routledge/Taylor and Francis.

Statham, J., Cameron, C. and Mooney, A. (2006) *The Tasks and Roles of Social Workers: A Focused Overview of Research Evidence*. London: Thomas Coram Research Unit, Institute of Education, University of London. http://ioewebserver.ioe.ac.uk/ioe/cms/get.asp?cid=470&470_0=14109 (accessed 23/04/2007).

Stephenson, J. (1994) *Capability and Competence: Are They the Same and Does it Matter?* Leeds: HEC/Leeds Metropolitan University.

Stepney, P. (2006) 'Mission impossible? Critical practice in social work', *British Journal of Social Work*, 36, 8: 1289–307.

Stevenson, O. (1989) *Age and Vulnerability: A Guide to Better Care*. London: Edward Arnold.

Stogdill, R.M. (1974) *Handbook of Leadership*. New York: Free Press.

Stott, M. (1981) *Ageing for Beginners*. Oxford: Blackwell.

Sunderland, M. (2000) *Using Story Telling as a Therapeutic Tool with Children*. Bicester, Oxon: Speechmark.

Sure Start (2007) *Parents Surveys*. http://www.surestart.gov.uk/research/surveys/parentssurveys/ (accessed 14/10/2007).

Tannenbaum, R. and Schmidt, W.H. (1958) 'How to choose a leadership pattern', *Harvard Business Review*, 73 (March-April): 95–101.

Tarlton, B., Ward, L. and Horwath, J. (2006) *Finding the Right Support? A Review of Issues and Positive Practice in Supporting Parents with Learning Difficulties and their Children*. Bristol: Norah Fry Research Centre.

Taylor, B.J. (2003) 'Literature Searching', in R. Miller and J. Brewer (eds), *The A to Z of Social Research*. London: Sage. pp. 171–6.

Taylor, B.J. (2006a) 'Factorial surveys: using vignettes to study professional judgement', *British Journal of Social Work*, 36, 7: 1187–207.

Taylor, B.J. (2006b) 'Risk management paradigms in health and social services for professional decision making on the long-term care of older people', *British Journal of Social Work*, 36, 8: 1411–29.

Taylor, B.J., Dempster, M. and Donnelly, M. (2003) 'Hidden gems: systematically searching electronic databases for research publications for social work and social care', *British Journal of Social Work*, 33: 423–39.

Taylor, B.J., Dempster, M. and Donnelly, M. (2007) 'Grading gems: appraising the quality of research for social work and social care', *British Journal of Social Work*, 37, 2: 335–54.

Taylor, B.J. and Devine, T. (2005) *Assessing Needs and Planning Care in Social Work*. Aldershot: Ashgate (Gower).

Taylor, B.J. and Donnelly, M. (2006a) 'Professional perspectives on decision making about the long-term care of older people', *British Journal of Social Work*, 36, 5: 807–26.

Taylor, B.J. and Donnelly, M. (2006b) 'Risks to home care workers: professional perspectives', *Health, Risk & Society*, 8, 3: 239–56.

Taylor, B.J., Wylie, E., Dempster, M. and Donnelly, M. (2006) *An Evaluation of the AgeInfo Database*. London: SCIE.

Taylor, B.J., Wylie, E., Dempster, M. and Donnelly, M. (2007) 'Systematically retrieving research: a case study evaluating seven databases', *Research on Social Work Practice*, 17, 6: 697–706.

Taylor I. (1996) 'Facilitating reflective learning', in N. Gould and I. Taylor (eds), (2002) *Reflective Learning for Social Work*, Aldershot: Ashgate Publishing Ltd.

Taylor, F.W. (1947) *Scientific Management*. London: Harper & Row.

Tew, J. (2005a) 'Core Themes of Social Perspective', in J. Tew (ed.), *Social Perspectives in Mental Health: Developing Models to Understand and Work with Mental Distress*. London: Jessica Kingsley. pp. 13–31.

Tew, J. (2005b) 'Power Relations, Social Order and Mental Distress', in Tew, J. (ed.), *Social Perspectives in Mental Health: Developing Models to Understand and Work with Mental Distress*. London: Jessica Kingsley. pp. 71–89.

Tew, J. and Anderson, J. (2004) 'The Mental Health Dimension in the New Social Work Degree: Starting a Debate', *Social Work Education*, 23, 2: 231–40.

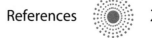

Thomas, C. (1999) *Female Forms: Experiencing and Understanding Disability.* Buckingham: Open University Press.

Thomas, C. (2003) 'Defining a Theoretical Agenda for Disability Studies'. Paper for the Disability Studies: Theory, Policy and Practice conference at Lancaster University. http://www.disabilitystudies.net (accessed 26/08/2008).

Thomas, C. (2007) *Sociologies of Disability and Illness: Contested Ideas in Disability Studies and Medical Sociology.* Basingstoke: Palgrave Macmillan.

Thomas, J.L.J. (2007) 'Legal Wales: Some Reflections on Our Future Tasks'. Lecture delivered in Cardiff, 19 January.

Thompson, N. (2000) *Understanding Social Work: Preparing for Practice.* Basingstoke: Palgrave.

Thompson, N. (2002) 'Social movements, social justice and social work', *British Journal of Social Work*, 32: 711–22.

Thompson, N. (2006) *Promoting Workplace Learning.* Bristol: The Policy Press.

Thompson, N. and Thompson, S. (2001) 'Empowering older people: beyond the care model', *British Journal of Social Work*, 1, 1: 61–76.

Thomson, M. (1998) *The Problem of Mental Deficiency: Eugenics, Democracy, and Social Policy in Britain c. 1870–1959.* Oxford: Clarendon Press.

Thorpe, S. (2004) 'To have and to hold', *Care & Health*, October: 87.

Tibbs, M. (2001) *Social Work and Dementia.* London: Jessica Kingsley.

Topss/Skills for Care (2002) *The National Occupational Standards for Social Work.* Leeds: Topss UK Partnerships. http://www.topssengland.net (accessed 12/04/2007).

Topss UK Partnership (2002) 'International Definition of Social Work' (International Association of Schools of Social Work, International Federation of Social Workers) in *National Occupational Standards for Social Work.* Leeds: Topss UK Partnership.

Torkington, C. (2007a) *Competence within PQ*, informal communication.

Torkington, C. (2007b) *Experiential learning*, informal communication.

Turner, B. (2000) 'Supervision and mentoring in child and family social work: the role of the first-line manager in the implementation of the post-qualifying framework', *Social Work Education*, 19, 3: 231–40.

UPIAS (Union of Physically Impaired Against Segregation) (1976) *Fundamental Principles of Disability.* London: UPIAS. www.leeds.ac.uk/disability-studies/archiveuk/index.html (accessed 16/10/2007).

Usher, R., Briant, I. and Johnson, R. (1997) *Adult Education and the Postmodern Challenge.* London: Routledge.

Van Maastricht, S. (1998) 'Work, Opportunity and Culture: (In)competence in Greece and Wales', in R. Jenkins (ed.), *Questions of Competence: Culture, Classification and Intellectual Disability.* Cambridge: Cambridge University Press. pp. 125–52.

Van Zwanenberg, Z. (2003) *Leadership and Management Development in Social Work Services: Report of a Research Study Undertaken by the Scottish Leadership Foundation on Behalf of the Scottish Executive.* Alloa: The Scottish Leadership Foundation.

Vernon, A. (1998) 'Multiple Oppression and the Disabled People's Movement', in T. Shakespeare (ed.), *The Disability Reader: Social Sciences Perspectives.* London: Cassell. pp. 201–10.

Vygotsky, L.S. (1978) *Mind in Society.* Cambridge, MA: Harvard University Press.

WAG (2000) *Circular NADWC 36/00.* Cardiff: WAG.

WAG (2003) *The Strategy for Older People in Wales.* Cardiff: WAG.

WAG (2005) *Designed for Life: Creating World-class Health and Social Care for Wales in the 21st Century.* Cardiff: WAG.

WAG (2006) *National Service Framework (NSF) for Older People.* Cardiff: WAG.

Walmsley, J. and Welshman, J. (2006) 'Introduction', in J. Welshman and J. Walmsley (eds), *Community Care in Perspective: Care, Control and Citizenship.* Basingstoke: Palgrave Macmillan. pp. 1–13.

Walton, P. (1999) 'Social work and mental health: refocusing the training agenda for ASWs', *Social Work Education*, 18, 4: 375–88.

Walton, P. (2000) 'Reforming the Mental Health Act 1983: an approved social worker perspective', *The Journal of Social Welfare & Family Law*, 22: 401–14.

Walton, R.E. (1985) 'From control to commitment in the workplace', *Harvard Business Review*, 63, 2: 76–84.

Ward, C. (2001) *Family Matters: Counting Families In*. London: Department of Health.

Ward, L. (2002) 'Whose right to choose? The "new" genetics, prenatal testing and people with learning difficulties', *Critical Public Health*, 12, 2: 187–200.

Warren, J. (2007) *Service User and Carer Participation in Social Work*. Exeter: Learning Matters.

Webb, S. (2002) 'Evidence-based practice and decision analysis in social work: an implementation model', *Journal of Social Work*, 2, 1: 45–63.

Webb, S.A. (2001) 'Some considerations on the validity of evidence-based practice in social work', *British Journal of Social Work*, 31: 57–79.

Weber, M. (1957) *The Theory of Social and Economic Organisation*. Chicago: Free Press.

Weijer, C., Shapiro, S.H., Glass, K.C. and Enkin, M.W. (2000) 'Clinical equipoise and not the uncertainty principle is the moral underpinning of the randomised controlled trial', *British Medical Journal*, 321: 756–8.

Welsh Assembly Government (WAG)/Llywodraeth Cynulliad Cymru (2002) *Unified and Fair System for Assessing and Managing Care/Creu System Deg ac Unedig i Asesu a Rheoli Gofal*. Cardiff: WAG.

Welsh Assembly Government (WAG)/Llywodraeth Cynulliad Cymru (2006) *National Service Framework for Older People*. Cardiff: WAG.

Welsh Assembly Government (WAG)/Llywodraeth Cynulliad Cymru (2007) *Fulfilled Lives, Supportive Communities*. February. Cardiff: WAG.

Welsh Assembly Government (2007) Gwenda Thomas, Deputy Minister For Social Services. *Legislative Statement on the Proposed Domiciliary Care Legislation Competence Order WAG* http://wales.gov.uk/caec/cabinetstatements/2007/word/27.11.07_Domiciliary Care L1.rtf?lang=en. Website accessed 15/04/08.

Welsh Consumer Council/Cyngor Defnyddwyr Cymru (2000) *Welsh in the Health Service*. Cardiff: Welsh Consumer Council.

White, S. and Featherstone, B. (2005) 'Communicating misunderstandings: multi-agency work as social practice', *Child and Family Social Work*, 10: 207–16.

Williams, J. (2007) 'The Older People's Commissioner: Human Rights and Older People'. Paper delivered at Swansea University, 16 February. Available as OPAN download.

Williams, P. (2006) *Social Work with People with Learning Difficulties*. Exeter: Learning Matters.

Williams, R. and Fulford, K.W.M. (2007) 'Evidence-based and values-based policy, management and practice in child and adolescent mental health services', *Clinical Child Psychology and Psychiatry*, 12, 2: 223–42.

Wilson, J. (2000a) *The Illustrated Mum* (a fictional book aimed at children aged 8–12, about two sisters who have a mum with manic depression). London: Corgi Yearling.

Wilson, J. (2000b) '"Learning difficulties", "Disability" and "special needs": some problems of partisan conceptualisation', *Disability & Society*, 15, 5: 817–24.

Wolfensberger, W. (1972) *The Principle of Normalization in Human Services*. Toronto: National Institute on Mental Retardation.

Wolfensberger, W. (1975) *The Origin and Nature of Our Institutional Models*. Syracuse, NY: Human Policy Press.

Wolfensberger, W. (1983) 'Social role valorization: a proposed new term for the principle of normalization', *Mental Retardation*, 21, 6: 234–9.

Wolfensberger, W. (2000) 'A brief overview of social role valorization', *Mental Retardation*, 38, 2: 105–23.

Young, H., Grundy, E. and Kalogirou, S. (2005) 'Who Cares? Geographic variation in unpaid care giving in England and Wales', *Population Trends*, 120 (Summer): 23–34.

Zwarenstein, M., Reeves, S., Barr, H., Hammick, M., Koppel, I. and Atkins, J. (2005) 'Interprofessional education: effects on professional practice and health care outcomes (Review)', *The Cochrane Library*, Issue 3. http://www.thecochranelibrary.com (accessed 08/06/2007).

Index

21st Century Social Work Review 168, 178

Abuse 26, 30, 31, 56, 57, 62, 66, 72, 91, 99, 100, 117, 118cf, 139

Abuse is Bad 118

Academic levels 13, 203, 204

Accountability, 23, 26, 33, 125, 153, 155, 175, 176, 179, 193

Accreditation of prior experiential learning (APEL) 12, 212

Accreditation of prior learning (APL) 212

Adult learning process model 155–156

Adult services 36, 37, 39, 95cf, 189

Adult social care 2, 82, 118, 119, 122, 131, 153, 194

Adults with Incapacity (Scotland) Act 2000 110, 119

Advocacy 2, 30, 37, 38, 41, 45, 48, 72, 103, 104, 107, 109–110, 116, 144

Ageing 77, 79
  feminisation of, 85
  mask of ageing 85

Ageism 84

Agreement(s) 205
  written 43

Aim and structure 3

Approach(es)
  analytical 17
  anti-intellectual 128
  assertive outreach 157
  capacity building 45
  cognitive behavioural 72
  collaborative 141
  collective 119
  collectivised 42
  competence 54
  CPD 73
  critical reflective 27, 154
  four-tier 9
  generic 120
  holistic 52, 129, 130, 186
  individual model 104

Approach(es) *cont.*
  joined up 140
  leadership 179
  liberation 45
  medical 92
  National Occupational Standards 38
  partnership 38
  person-centred 42
  preventive 44
  professional 209
  research 73
  systematic 159, 195
  teaching, learning and assessment 20
  technological 26
  theoretical 8, 51, 85
  user centred 39, 41, 45
  Welsh 82
  welfare 96

Approved Mental Health Professional (AMHP) 66, 71, 74, 75, 272

Approved Social Worker (ASW) 64, 66, 67, 70, 71, 73, 74, 75, 212

Argyris 19, 174, 191

Arnstein's ladder of participation 40

Assessment(s) 1, 7, 9, 10, 11, 12, 15, 16, 17, 20, 25, 26, 29, 34, 36, 38, 39, 42, 43, 53, 54, 56, 66, 67, 70, 71, 72, 73, 77, 78, 80, 81, 82, 83, 85, 100, 114, 115, 119, 138, 139, 140, 141, 143, 144, 145, 158, 162, 163, 164, 165, 166, 167, 168, 169, 170, 171, 180, 183, 185, 195, 196, 198, 207, 208, 212

Assessments, joint 137, 152

Assessor(s) 2, 76, 80, 85, 97, 161, 162cf, 165, 167, 169, 171, 185, 214

Asylum seekers 2, 24, 25, 39, 43, 47, 54

Attitude(s) 30, 31, 32, 35, 56, 86, 100, 102, 106, 112, 140, 145, 182, 191, 208

Attitudinal
  barriers 42, 89, 96, 106
  change 41, 182
  environments 91
  processes 42

Automaticity 208
Assessed year in employment (AYE) 12, 14, 23, 212

BA in Curative Education (Scotland) 131
BA in Pedagogy 127
Banks, S. 22, 26, 29, 33, 51, 52
Barnett, R. 208, 209, 210
Barr, H. 145, 208
Barrier(s) 36, 42, 43, 46, 74, 89, 91, 93, 95,
    96, 100, 106, 107, 116, 129, 136, 141,
    146, 163, 170, 204cf, 206
Basic ph 54, 58
BASW 92, 125, 158, 161, 222
    code of ethics 31, 32, 93
Baumann 135
Baumer 128
Beacon status 194, 196
Behaviour(s) 8, 16, 22, 30, 31, 32, 57, 69, 71,
    72, 81, 90, 95, 105, 106, 140, 150, 152,
    158, 174, 175, 179, 183, 208
Benner 17, 18, 19, 159, 208
Beresford 9, 41, 42, 43, 44, 45, 71, 74,
    75, 115, 128
Bichard 50
Biggs 85
Blewett et al. 9, 20, 119, 144
Boundary/ies 9, 23, 43, 49, 65, 76, 91, 96, 104, 105,
    109, 119, 126, 129, 133, 135, 136, 138, 140,
    144, 168, 177, 180
Bournewood gap 109
Bursaries 156, 200

Calder 154
    and Hackett 149
Campbell Collaboration 148, 151
Capability 5, 8, 17, 18, 19, 20, 21, 25, 27, 31,
    37cf, 44, 148, 154, 162, 171, 175, 203,
    209, 210, 213
Capacity 17, 24, 42, 44, 84, 109, 110, 114,
    119, 136, 144, 189, 190, 192
    building 44–5
    research 155–6
Care
    hegemony of 26
    management 29, 39, 78, 84, 88, 108, 189, 195
    manager 93, 135
    sector 79, 201
    standards legislation 22
    substitute 57
Care Council for Wales (CCW) 10, 11, 76, 166, 222
Care Councils 3, 22, 94, 131, 163, 200

Care Matters 57, 207
Career
    ladder 16, 187, 203, 205, 225
    pathways 23, 163, 167, 168, 171
    development 3, 11, 15, 16, 74, 169, 187
Carers 82–83
    and evidence-based practice 149
    balancing needs, demands 71
    benefits to 208
    consultation with 2, 3, 48, 142, 158
    champion 39
    involvement of 32, 168, 189, 208
    knowledge 19
    of children and young people, see Chapter 4 49–62
    outcomes for 177
    partnerships with 8, 21, 153, see also Chapter 3 34–46
    perceptions of risk 118
    pressures on 82
    reconciling priorities 83, 112
    relationships with 31, 143–4, 162
    requirements 174
    responsibilities, accountabilities towards 22, 23
    young carers 59
Carers NI 39
Carpenter 63, 65, 66, 139, 207, 208, 210
Celtic tradition 77
Central Council for Education and Training in Social
    Work (CCETSW) 163, 164, 168, 169, 212
Centre for Reviews and Dissemination 151, 212
Centre for the Advancement of Inter-Professional
    Education (CAIPE) 145, 212
Challenge(s) 22, 24, 33, 39, 51, 54, 58, 62, 70,
    76, 77, 84, 92, 116, 120, 125, 129, 133,
    135, 136cf, 140, 142, 143, 146, 150, 154,
    155, 156, 158, 170, 171, 174, 177, 178,
    179, 182, 183, 184, 185, 189, 190, 193, 210
    ethical 30, 150
    for practice 14
Change(s) 8, 14, 19, 34, 35, 36, 40, 41cf, 44, 45, 50, 51,
    57, 65, 72, 73, 81, 82, 91, 92cf, 94, 95, 97, 99, 109,
    118, 119, 125, 129, 130, 134, 140, 150, 165cf, 166,
    167, 168cf, 173, 174, 175, 176, 177, 178, 179, 180,
    181, 182, 183, 184, 185, 189, 190, 191, 192,
    193, 194, 195, 197, 198, 200, 207, 208
Change Consultancy and Training West
    Midlands 201
Changing Lives 9, 168, 174, 179, 183, 184, 185
Charges
    for domiciliary care 28
Chartered Institute of Personnel and Development
    200, 212

Chief Inspector for Wales, Annual Report 39, 82, 83, 85
Child and Adolescent Mental Health Services (CAMHS) 140, 212
Childcare Act 2006 52, 130
Childcare Strategy, 2004 Ten Year 52
Child protection 55cf, 56, 118, 125, 150, 151, 153, 174, 185, 193
  Cleveland 139
  see also Safeguarding
Childhood 54, 61, 101
Children (Leaving Care) Acts 54
Children Act 1948 34
  1989 53, 54
  2004 39, 50
Children and Adoption Acts 2002, 2006 57
Children and families 3, 23, 51, 123, 124, 130, 139, 144, 158, 181, 195, 200
Children and young people 2, 10, 39, 52, 124, 125, 128, 152, 194, 196, 206, 207
Children and Young Person Bill 2007 194, 196, 206, 207
Children
  disabled 55, 89, 99, 118, 121
  looked after 123
Children's commissioners 39, 50
Children's services 2, 24, 39, 40, 48, 50, 55, 57, 122, 125, 131, 136, 140, 142, 144, 147, 151, 153, 170, 200
Children's workforce strategy 194
Choice(s) 2, 3, 10, 13, 31, 32, 36, 41, 42, 43, 45, 67, 78, 81, 82, 93, 109, 113, 114, 116, 117, 118, 149, 155, 195, 204
Citizen 40, 42, 44, 102, 105, 109, 175
  advocates 110
  participation 40
Citizenship 8, 44, 95, 96, 99, 101
Cleaver et al. 150
Clements 82, 121, 190
  and Thompson 77, 78, 87
Cleveland Report 139
Climbíe, Victoria 50, 125
Cochrane Collaboration 151
Code(s) of Practice 11, 22, 33, 87, 144, 166, 209
Common Assessment Framework (CAF) 138, 141, 212
Common sense 49, 141
Communication 24, 25, 26, 32, 35, 79, 101, 113, 115–116cf, 139, 143, 153, 176, 192, 197
Communities 38, 52, 66, 67, 71, 79, 93, 105, 107, 108, 109, 112, 187
  Black and Minority Ethnic 106, 116, 117, 120
  building 44

Community Care 11, 164, 193
Community care 29, 37, 78, 81, 83, 87, 99, 100, 108, 196
Community Care Assessments 77
Community Care Assessments, Wales 85
Community Care (Delayed Discharge) Act 2003 78
Community Care (Direct Payments Act) 1996 82
Community Care and the Law 77, 87
Community Care Assessment Directions 77, 85
Community Mental Health Teams 65
Competence(s) 1, 5, 7, 8, 9, 11, 12, 14, 15, 16–17, 18, 19, 21, 47, 54cf, 123, 126, 158, 159, 162, 163, 164cf, 171, 176, 178, 192, 195, 203, 209, 210, 212
Compliance 71, 96
Confidentiality 23, 26, 37, 38, 43, 60, 172
Conflict(s) 24, 25–26, 28, 43, 45, 52, 64, 66, 118, 136–138, 139, 140, 141, 159, 169 *see also* Values conflicts
Consolidation 1, 5, 9, 14, 23cf, 24, 25, 27, 28, 30, 31, 33, 37cf
Context(s) 1, 3, 8, 9, 11, 14, 16, 18, 19, 20, 27, 29, 31, 36, 47, 48, 51, 53, 60, 61, 62, 63, 66, 70, 71, 72, 73, 74, 76, 77, 78, 80cf, 82, 84, 87, 89, 94, 99, 104, 109, 119, 131, 134, 140, 149, 150, 155, 159, 173, 175, 176, 179, 180, 181, 182, 184, 185, 191, 193, 205, 210
Continuing Professional Development (CPD) 1cf, 3, 7, 9, 11, 13–14, 15, 16, 23, 27, 28, 29, 73, 74, 129, 130, 134, 148, 155, 165, 170cf, 199, 204, 205, 206, 212
Convergence 128cf
Cooper 145
Correlation studies 152
Council for Social Care Inspection (CSCI) 21, 35, 36, 194, 212
Councils, sector skills 194
Cowden and Singh 22, 36, 40cf, 41, 45cf
Credit(s)
  academic 10, 11, 12, 14, 179
  professional 9, 10, 163
Criteria 38, 100, 154, 196
  eligibility 51, 52cf, 54, 55, 78, 83cf, 87
Critical Appraisal Skills Programme (CASP) 158, 212
Criticality 3, 187, 203, 208cf, 209, 210, 211
Children's Workforce Development Council (CWDC) 10, 126, 130, 161, 190, 194, 212

Decision-making *see* Social work decision(s)/ decision-making
Deficit 80, 104, 211
Definition of
  competence 192, 212
  leadership 174cf

Definition of *cont.*
  PQ 15–16
  learning disability 104–105, 110
  practice education 162
  social model of disability 89, 97–98
  social pedagogues/pedagogy 122–123
  social work 8cf, 45–46, 91, 93, 125
Dementia 84cf, 90, 133, 152
Department for Children, Schools, and Families
    57, 207, 213
Department of Health (DH) 9, 16, 31, 39, 44, 54, 66,
    67, 68, 69, 75, 76, 77, 78, 82, 94, 97,
    104, 108, 109, 110, 114, 116, 117, 118,
    119, 120, 121, 150, 152, 156, 159, 165,
    168, 190, 200, 206, 207, 213
Department of Health and Social Security (DHSS) 32,
    54, 159, 213
Dependence 44
Derbyshire Centre for Independent Living 213
Descriptors, level 20, 171
Designed for Life 39, 79
Detention in hospital, legal 72, 75, 109
Dewey 19, 155
DGov 157, 213
Dialogue 26, 49, 50, 125
  critical 41cf
Diesterweg 128
Difference(s) 17, 30, 32, 46, 51, 58, 63, 65, 68,
    77, 78, 79, 98, 99, 105, 100, 122, 123, 124, 127,
    131, 136, 137cf, 138, 139cf, 140, 142, 143, 145,
    146, 171, 176, 185, 207
Diploma in Social Work (DipSW) 163, 164, 178, 204, 213
Direct Payments 42cf, 82cf, 93, 96, 99, 101, 108,
    114–115, 119, 190 *see also* Individual budgets
Disability discrimination 90
Disability Discrimination (NI) Order 94
Disability Discrimination Act 1995 90, 213
  definition, 90
Disability 24, 48cf, 53, 86, 89cf, 90, 91, 97, 98, 99, 100
  studies 92, 95cf, 98cf, 99, 100, 119
Disabled people 44, 89–90, 91, 92, 93, 94, 95, 96, 97,
    99, 100, 101, 102, 106, 109, 119, 120. 120
Discrimination 30, 51, 66, 67, 68, 70, 80, 90, 94, 95,
    109, 112cf
Divergence 128
Dreyfus 17, 18, 19
Dual qualification 108

Early Years Professional (EYP) 126, 130cf, 213
Economics and Social Research Council (ESRC)
    13, 156, 210, 213

Effective Social Work with Older People 77
Efficiency 140, 141cf, 174, 176
Eligibility 29, 56, 138
  criteria 51, 52cf, 54, 55, 78, 83cf,
Employer(s) 1, 9, 10, 11, 12, 14, 15, 16, 21, 22, 23, 28,
    29, 38, 51, 74, 99, 112, 128, 129, 141, 142, 158,
    162, 163, 165, 167, 170, 171, 175, 187, 189, 190,
    191, 193, 194cf, 199, 200, 201, 203, 204, 205,
    206, 208, 210
Employment perspectives 189–202
Enabling Others 157, 161, 162cf, 166, 167, 170, 172
England 2, 7, 8, 9, 10cf, 13, 14, 15, 16, 20, 22, 23,
    34, 36, 39, 47, 48, 50, 63, 64, 66, 67, 68, 70, 73,
    74, 75, 77, 78, 81, 82, 83, 94, 110, 118, 122, 125,
    127, 129, 130, 131, 136, 144, 145, 164, 165, 166cf,
    171, 190, 194, 196, 200, 204, 205, 207
Entitlement 99, 141
Environment(s) 8, 19, 20, 28, 32, 50, 69, 91, 93, 94, 95,
    136, 137, 139, 144, 152, 158, 170, 176, 177, 180,
    182, 183, 193, 195, 197, 198,
Equality in Action 94
Eraut 17–18, 19, 44, 146, 155, 209
Erikson 58
Essential Shared Capabilities, mental health (ESC) 68, 213
European Convention on Human Rights 75
European social work models 1, 2, 47, 48, 122–132
Every Child Matters 50, 121, 125. 142
Evidence 3, 16, 28, 37, 57, 62, 65, 66, 71, 73, 74cf, 75,
    76, 83, 87, 91, 133, 140, 142cf, 148, 149, 151, 152,
    155, 157cf, 159, 162, 163, 164, 167, 180, 181, 183,
    196, 197, 198–199, 208, 210
  Based Practice (EBP) 11, 57, 74, 148, 149cf, 180, 182,
    191, 195, 196, 213
  Best 23, 27, 80, 151, 153, 159, 196
  Informed Practice 57, 148, 168
  Research 112, 118, 154
Evidence for Policy and Practice Information and
    Coordinating Centre (EPPI) 151, 213
Exclusion 67, 95
  circle of 140
  social 44, 67, 69, 71, 95, 105, 150
Experience(s) 1, 18, 19, 20, 23, 25, 26, 27, 28, 30, 31,
    32, 33, 35, 36, 41, 44, 48, 51, 59–60, 66, 67, 68,
    70, 71, 72, 74, 76, 79, 85, 95, 97, 99, 103, 106,
    107, 112, 135, 139cf, 141, 144, 145, 146, 148, 149,
    152, 155–156, 158, 163, 169, 170, 171, 177, 178,
    183, 185, 191, 193, 195, 206
Expertise 1, 5, 8, 11, 16, 17, 18, 20, 24, 25, 26, 35, 36,
    37, 38cf, 42, 44, 75, 80, 84, 95, 110, 133, 143, 146,
    148, 154, 157, 159, 161, 171, 203, 207, 209, 210
Experts by experience 21, 35

Factors, facilitating 192, 197
Family Group Conferences 152, 153
Family support worker 135
Fayol 174
Fellowes-Smith 150
Fellowships 156
Finkelstein 91, 98, 99, 101, 102
Fitness for purpose 14, 15, 165
Followership 175
Fook 2, 20, 21, 24, 27, 28, 45, 50, 125
Ford 208, 209, 210
Foundation degrees 129
Fragmentation 9, 11, 108, 133, 135
Freire 45
Frost et al. 140, 142, 143, 144, 147
Fullfilled Lives, Supportive Communities 9, 39, 79
Fundamental Principles of Disability 92, 97

Garmbrill 57, 149, 159
Garthwaite 9
Gaspar 126
Genericism 135
Gillick 54
Good practice 26, 31, 51, 139, 142, 153, 164,
    166, 167, 170, 193
examples 67, 200
Gough and Stanley 55
Group, control 150, 154
Group, experimental 150, 154
General Social Care Council (GSCC) 9, 10, 13, 16, 20,
    22, 23, 31, 34, 35, 36, 94, 95, 116, 119, 125, 133,
    144, 161, 162, 163, 166, 167, 168, 171, 190, 213

Hackney Reclaim Social Work Initiative 207
Harbin and Murphy 150
Hartley and Allison 175
Health and social care 2, 29, 39, 79, 140, 148, 151, 205, 206
Heifetz 175
Hierarchy 19, 40, 74, 127, 143, 175, 193
Higgins and Pinkerton 159
Holman 93, 94
Human Rights Act 30
Hunt, Paul 97

Identity 58, 61, 91, 99, 105
    cultural 11
    ethical 27
    professional 3, 22, 27, 30, 66, 100, 136, 143, 189
Iles and Sutherland 192, 197
Impairment(s) 40, 82, 89, 90–91, 95, 96, 98cf, 100cf,
    106, 107, 109, 110, 119, 120

In Control 103, 109, 114, 115
In Safe Hands 76, 118
Independence 42, 43, 66, 71, 80, 83, 114, 151
Independence, Wellbeing and Choice 94, 97
Independent broker 114, 115
Individual budgets 42cf, 82, 108, 114, 190 *see also*
    Direct Payments
Individualisation 42
Influence(s) 10, 23, 31, 36, 71, 74, 135, 138, 174, 175
Institutionalisation 104
    policies 108
Institution(s) 95, 105, 108, 109, 145
    academic 80
Inter-professional
    education (IPE) 145cf, 146, 213
    groups 157
    practice 66, 142cf, 143
    service delivery 133
    working 139, 147
Inter-agency
    assessment 140
    structures 8
    working 139
Intervention(s) 19, 25, 45, 50, 53, 54, 56, 58, 60, 61, 64,
    65, 66, 67, 70, 71, 72, 73, 74, 83, 84, 113, 119,
    120, 126, 130, 140, 141cf, 142, 144, 146, 149cf,
    150, 152, 151, 152, 153, 154, 174, 176, 208
Involvement 5, 32, 34, 35, 36, 38, 40, 41, 42, 44, 46, 48,
    58–59, 92, 96, 103, 109cf, 113, 116, 120, 146, 152,
    169, 181, 192, 197, 198cf,
Issue(s)
    access 1, 42
    contemporary 40
    contested 21, 23, 26
    critical 152
    cultural 37, 79
    equality 42
    ethical 33
    evaluation 145
    identity 58
    in evidence-based practice 149–152
    legal 36, 47, 54, 80
    organisational *see* Chapters 14 and 15 189–211
    participation 35cf, 40cf
    policy (Wales) 81cf
    policy and practice 37, 159
    power 33, 43
    PQ 3 *see* Chapter 15 203–211
    practice 2, 20, 37, 60, 159, 210
    priority 79
    problematic 137, 185

Issue(s) *cont.*
  protection 55
  real world 3
  recruitment and retention 14, 189, 191, 197,
    201, 206
  status 136
  theoretical 101
  workforce 9, 190
  workforce planning 194

Jernberg 58
Joint working 136, 140, 142, 143, 147, 151
Joint University Council Social Work Education
  Committee (JUCSWEC) 156, 161, 213

Keeping Children Happy 112
Kemshall and Pritchard 154
Knowledge 1, 3, 8cf, 10, 15, 16, 17, 18, 19cf, 20, 22, 23,
  24, 25, 27, 30, 31, 32, 35, 37, 40, 42, 45, 47, 52,
  54, 57, 58, 60, 65, 66, 67, 68, 69, 70, 71, 72, 74,
  75, 84, 94, 113, 114, 117, 129, 130, 131, 133, 134,
  134, 135, 136, 140, 141, 143, 144, 145, 146, 148,
  149, 151, 152, 155, 156, 157cf, 158, 159, 161, 168,
  169, 170, 171, 173, 174, 176, 177, 178, 183, 192,
  193, 196, 198, 200, 201, 205, 206, 207, 208, 209
Kolb 19, 27, 155, 156
Kornbeck 38, 122, 123, 131
Kotter 166, 186
Kraiger 208

Leadership 1, 9, 37, 38, 131, 134, 157, 162, 168, 170,
  187, 191, 192, 194, 195, 198, 199, 207, 209
Leadership and management 3, 10, 12, 23, 173–186, 133,
  134, 167, 169, 195, 206
Leading to Deliver 173, 174, 178, 179, 181
Learning
  difficulties 89, 90, 103, 104, 105, 106, 107, 108,
    109, 110, 112, 113, 114, 115, 116, 117,
    118, 119, 120, 126, 143
  disability/ies 2, 3, 41, 48, 83, 103–121, 139, 140, 158
  double loop 191cf, 197
  organisation(s) 3, 11, 19cf, 20, 39, 74, 161, 165,
    166, 167, 170cf, 171, 187, 189–202, 203,
    204, 206, 210
  organisational 19, 191, 192cf, 196
  reflective 175
  resource centre networks (LRCN) 194, 213
  single loop 191cf
  society 19, 191, 210
Legislation 12, 22–23, 29, 39cf, 54, 57, 66, 71, 78, 80,
  81, 87, 90, 96, 104, 109, 195, 210

Leiba 142, 147
  and Weinstein 143
Lewis 20, 144
Licence to practise 125, 129
Life-story work 58
Line manager(s) 14, 20, 37, 43, 161, 169–170, 171,
  172, 180, 203
Listening 35, 39, 115, 116, 126, 177
Local Government Act 2000 (WAG Circular) 78
Local Involvement Networks (LINks) 44
Lumsden 48, 59, 122, 123, 125, 130
Lymbery 8, 83, 84, 86, 88, 136, 137, 143, 143, 144

Macdonald 159
Management 23, 127, 134, 150, 153, 157, 162, 163, 166,
  167, 168, 173, 174, 175–176, 177, 178, 179, 180,
  181, 185, 192, 194, 195, 196, 198, 199, 205, 207
  of risk 37, 118, 154
  see also Leadership and management
Maria Colwell 52
Maslow 174
Mayer and Timms 35
Mayo 174
McGregor 174
Medical model 64, 74, 136, 138cf
Mencap 105, 114
Mental Capacity Act 66, 109, 110cf, 119, 121
Mental health 2, 3, 10, 11, 23, 30, 36, 43, 45, 47, 54, 59,
  63–75, 90, 92, 109, 124, 126, 130, 139, 140, 150cf,
  151, 153, 157, 158, 207
Mental Health Act
  1983 66, 109
  2007 66, 74
Mental Health and Social Exclusion 67
Mental Health Officer 64, 213
Mentor/mentoring 2, 23, 24, 25cf, 155, 162cf, 164,
  165cf, 166, 167, 168, 169cf, 170, 171, 172, 181,
  192, 207
Messages from Research 150
Middle managers 134, 173, 179
Miller and Gwynne 36
Milner 152
Mitchell and Glendinning 118
  Skills acquisition(s) 17, 208
Morale 14, 107, 189, 203
Morris 40, 45, 99, 100, 105, 106, 112
Motivation(s) 10, 28, 31, 134, 163, 174, 176, 177, 178,
  193, 197, 200, 205, 208
Multi-professional practice 3, 12, 51, 52cf, 66, 125, 133,
  136–147, 190 *see also* Inter-professional practice
Mutuality 94, 131

Narrative(s) 20, 27, 28, 58cf, 60, 61, 71, 164
National Assistance Act 1948 89
National Employers Skills Survey 190
National Institute for Mental Health England (NIMHE) 63, 68, 69, 214
National Occupational Standards for Social Work (NOS SW) 23, 31, 38, 214
  Statement of Expectations 116
National Organisation of Practice Teachers (NOPT) 161, 162, 165, 214
National Service Framework (NSF) Mental Health 67, 83, 214
National Vocational Qualification (NVQ) 163, 194, 214
  see also Vocational qualification
Natorp 128
Need(s) 8, 11, 12, 14, 25, 26, 29, 37, 38, 41, 44, 52, 53, 54, 56, 59, 60, 61, 66, 67, 68, 70, 71, 72, 74, 75, 79, 80, 81, 82, 83, 84, 85, 89, 91, 92, 97, 98, 101, 104, 106, 112, 113, 114, 116, 117, 118, 119, 120, 124, 125, 126, 129, 130, 135, 136, 138, 139, 140, 141, 142, 143, 144, 145, 146, 146, 148, 149, 151, 152, 153, 165, 167, 170, 172, 175, 176, 177, 178, 179, 180, 181, 192, 194, 195, 196, 197, 204, 205, 210
Nelson et al. 92
Network(s)/networking 10, 11, 19, 34, 43cf, 67, 74, 142, 157, 166, 167, 180, 183, 192, 194, 196, 198
Nevis et al. 192, 197
New Social Movements 36
Newly Qualified Social Worker (NQSW) 20, 24, 25, 26, 30, 32, 167
NHS Agenda for Change 205
NHS and Community Care Act 78, 81, 214
NHS Trust(s) 2, 64
No Secrets 76, 118
Normalisation 105cf, 106, 118
Northampton, University of 51, 54
Northern Ireland (NI) 7, 9, 10, 11–12, 13, 14, 16, 20, 22, 23, 34, 39, 50, 54, 64, 77, 94, 110, 118, 131, 133, 151, 153, 156, 157, 158, 166, 200, 204, 205, 206, 212, 213, 214
Northern Ireland Post-Qualifying Education and Training Partnership (NIPQETP) 11, 16, 34, 133, 157, 214
Northern Ireland Social Care Council (NISCC) 11, 13, 34, 39, 125, 166, 206, 214
Northway 118

Older people 2, 3, 37, 38, 89, 124, 136, 143, 144, 152
  and social work 47, 76–88
Older People (Wales) Act 2006 80
Oliver 36, 40, 45, 89, 91, 92, 95, 96, 97, 98, 104, 106, 119, 120

Options for Excellence 9, 39, 168, 190, 200
Organisation(s) 2cf, 7, 9, 10, 11, 14cf, 19, 25, 26,27, 28, 29, 30, 31, 32, 35, 37, 38, 39, 40, 41, 44, 46, 47, 48, 49, 55, 56, 63, 64, 75, 80, 82, 86, 97, 98, 104, 108, 135, 137, 138cf, 141, 143, 146, 151, 153, 154, 155, 158, 159, 161, 169, 173, 174, 175, 177, 180, 181, 183, 184, 185 202cf
  learning 11, 19cf, 20, 39, 74, 165, 166, 167, 170cf, 189–202, 203, 206, 210
  user-led 38, 42, 43, 44cf.
Our Health, Our Care, Our Say 39, 94, 120
Outcome(s) 12, 20, 21, 36, 38, 41, 45, 46, 50, 52, 54, 57, 61, 74, 85, 141, 142, 145, 149, 150, 152, 153, 158, 173, 177, 178, 180, 181, 183, 185, 190, 195, 199, 203, 204, 206, 207–208, 210
Outreach, Assertive 157, 180

Partnership(s) 7, 8, 9, 11, 12, 16, 21, 34–46, 50, 51, 58–59, 65, 68, 69, 71, 86, 92, 93, 95, 101, 141, 152, 153, 168, 169, 173, 179, 180, 181, 184, 185, 189, 196, 197, 198, 200, 207
  with users and carers 5, 8, 34–46, 71
Parton 125
  and O'Byrne 20, 24, 27, 41
Pay 9, 114, 190, 194, 194, 195cf, 196, 201, 205
  and Workforce Strategy Survey 200
Payne 31, 57, 85, 133
Pedagogy of the oppressed 40
Pedlar et al. 191
People, devalued 106
People who use services 2, 5, 8, 12, 21, 32, 34–47, 69, 91, 143, 149, 159, 162, 207, 210 *see also* Service users
Performance
  indicators 51
  outcomes 152
Person-centred
  approaches 42, 87
  planning (PCP) 138, 142, 214
Petrie et al. 124, 129, 132
PhD 156, 157
Phillips et al. 77, 79, 83, 84, 85, 86,
Piaget 62
Placement(s) 25, 61, 78, 108, 111, 162, 163, 164, 165, 194
Policy/ies 3, 9, 11, 19, 22, 23, 24, 25, 26, 32, 35, 37, 39cf, 42, 44, 45, 47, 48, 49, 50, 51, 55, 57, 58, 59, 61, 63cf, 64, 67, 69, 77, 79cf, 80, 81–82, 87, 90, 92, 94, 96, 103, 104, 105cf, 108, 109, 118cf, 119, 129, 137cf, 138, 140, 148, 151, 157, 158, 159, 172, 185, 189, 192, 194, 196, 197, 206, 209, 210
Portability 14, 203, 214

Portfolio(s) 9, 11, 27cf, 28cf, 80, 130, 155
Post-qualifying social work (PQ)
    as flagship for reform 7, 20–21, 210
    award(s) 1, 7, 12, 13, 14, 36, 49, 155, 161, 163, 167,
        169, 170, 171, 203, 204, 206, 209
    candidate(s) 2, 9, 15, 36, 38, 46, 49, 51cf, 52,
        53, 54, 55, 56, 57, 59, 62, 76, 77, 78, 80, 89,
        96, 100, 144, 162, 163, 166, 169, 171, 172,
        190, 204, 214
    Consortium/ia 9, 10, 11, 13, 14, 80
    issues 3, 203–211
    learning 3, 12, 15, 27, 43, 79, 122, 191,
        204, 205, 206, 209, 210
    opportunities 29, 206cf
    portfolio route(s) 80
    practice 2, 5–21, 22–33, 34, 38, 45, 85, 125,
        136, 146, 153, 154, 162, 168, 205, 210
    requirements(s) 14, 48. 89, 94cf, 157, 207
    stakeholders 12, 34, 42, 166, 177, 198, 210
Post-qualifying social work (PQ) frameworks 5, 7, 8, 9,
    10, 12–13, 14, 15, 16, 19, 20, 21, 23, 24, 34, 38, 63,
    73, 122, 125, 129, 130. 136, 146, 169, 171, 172, 190,
    191, 200, 203, 204, 204, 205, 206, 207, 210
    England 10
    Northern Ireland 12–13, 14
    Scotland 11
    Wales 10–11
Post Registration Training and Learning (PRTL)
    1, 3, 13, 165, 203, 214
Postle 46
Postle and Beresford 44, 45
Postle et al. 190
Power 2, 5, 8, 22, 23, 26, 29–32, 33, 35, 38, 39,
    40–41, 43, 45, 57, 71, 75, 78, 93, 110, 137, 147,
    153, 175
PQ1 9, 214
Practice
    anti-discriminatory 11, 61, 66
    anti-oppressive 57, 124, 144, 169
    Assessment Panel(s) 164, 214
    assessor 162, 165, 171
    'best' 23, 27, 80, 151, 153, 159,
    complexity/ies 25cf
    conflicts 24, 25cf, 28, 43, 45, 52, 64, 66, 87, 118,
        137cf, 138, 139, 140, 159
    consolidation 30
    constructive 20cf
    creative and innovative 140, 141cf
    critical 19, 41, 210
    critical appraisal of 47, 49, 148
    critical reflective 3, 5, 19, 27, 133, 148, 154–155, 187,
        203, 210

Practice cont.
    education 10, 12, 23, 133, 161–172
    emancipatory 2, 45
    ethical 24, 58
    evidence informed 35, 57, 148, 158, 168
    governmental control of 22, 23
    inter-professional 66, 142, 143
    intervention 208
    learning opportunity 41, 162, 165, 166, 167, 171
    mentor assessor 162, 214
    multi-professional 3, 12, 51, 52cf, 66, 125,
        133, 135–147, 190
    observation 16, 19, 20, 43, 76, 150, 155, 156,
        163, 164, 170, 172, 175, 208
    portfolio 164
    preventive and supportive 44, 52cf, 65, 83
    reconstruction of 27, 41
    reflective 3, 5, 18–19, 133, 148–160, 162, 210
    sharing experiences of 60
    social work 11, 29, 33, 36, 44, 47, 48, 64, 65, 75, 81,
        84, 94, 95, 100, 104, 116, 119, 129, 133, 144,
        154, 159, 168, 187, 194, 207
    supervisor 162, 169
    teacher(s) 161, 162, 163, 164cf, 165, 167, 172
    Teaching Award (PTA) 13, 163, 164, 165, 166, 167, 171
Primary Care Graduate Mental Health Workers
    (PCGMHW) 65, 214
Problem-solving 8, 20, 154, 176, 191, 192, 210
Professional
    boundaries 23, 91, 96, 126, 129, 144, 168
    doctorate(s) 13, 157, 203, 206cf, 207
    identity/ies 3, 22, 27, 30, 31, 32, 66, 100, 136, 189
Professionalism 39, 45, 89, 92, 101, 146, 147, 168
Professions
    allied to medicine 91
    allied to the community 91
Protection 39, 55cf, 56, 70, 76, 90, 108, 112, 113,
    117–118, 119, 125, 139, 151, 153, 174, 185, 193
Protection of Children (Scotland) Act 2003 50
Protection of Children and Vulnerable Adults (NI) 50
Protocol(s), information sharing 142
Patient and Public Initiative Programme (PPIP) 44
Public sector 175, 176, 177, 185, 190, 195
Purchaser/provider split(s) 99
Private, voluntary and independent (PVI)
    organisations 125, 214

Qualification(s) 1, 11, 12, 13, 15, 16, 20, 23, 28, 30, 34,
    65, 66, 80, 84, 85, 108, 125, 129cf, 131, 162, 163,
    164, 166, 167, 168, 187, 196, 197, 199, 204
Quality Assurance Agency for Higher Education
    (QAA) 8, 20, 214

Randomised Controlled Trial(s) (RCT) 214

Recovery
Guiding Statement on 68
promoting 68cf, 69

Recruitment and retention 3, 10, 14, 29, 187, 189cf, 190, 191, 194cf, 195, 196, 197, 199–200, 201, 203, 204, 206

Reeve 99

Reflection
critical 20, 21, 25, 26, 27, 31, 33, 35, 52, 60, 61, 74, 76, 89, 125, 133, 142, 148, 154, 155, 158, 159cf, 193, 202, 203, 210
in action 8, 155, 208
on action 155

Refugees 2, 54

Regulation of Care (Scotland) Act 2001 22, 190

Regulation of social work and social care 23, 26, 33, 39, 87, 128, 176

Relationship(s) 1, 2cf, 5, 8, 19, 26, 29, 30, 31, 34, 42, 43, 47, 66, 69, 70, 71, 72cf, 75, 82, 94, 96, 98, 99, 100, 108, 111, 116, 120, 125, 128, 130, 131, 135, 136, 142, 143, 144, 146, 147, 150, 152, 164, 169, 171, 172, 175, 177, 180, 181, 182, 192, 208

Research 2, 3, 11, 19, 48, 49, 55, 57, 59, 60, 62, 64, 65, 73, 74, 79, 80, 87, 95, 100, 103, 104, 109, 112, 118, 119, 120, 127, 129, 133, 139, 140, 142, 143, 168, 173, 194, 195, 196, 203, 205, 206, 207, 210
strategy for social work 156

Research and Development Office for Health and Social Services, NI 156

Resources 10, 20, 25, 27, 29, 38, 44, 51, 52cf, 55, 56, 59, 64, 65, 82, 83, 86, 91, 93, 101, 103, 104, 108, 115, 118, 119, 138, 141, 142, 150, 151, 153, 159, 166, 167, 178, 179, 182, 190, 192, 194, 198, 199, 203, 204, 206, 208, 210
finite 51, 52cf, 55
human 10, 167, 206

Respect 26, 27, 29, 38, 42, 52, 64, 66, 67, 68, 73, 99, 100, 117, 142, 143, 144, 145, 185

Responsible Clinician 74, 207

Review(s) 7, 8–9, 10, 17, 19, 20, 39cf, 69–70, 80, 82, 85, 100, 118, 142, 151, 152, 153, 156, 158, 159, 162, 168cf, 174, 176, 178, 190, 186, 199, 207

Right(s) 8, 31, 32, 35, 36, 40, 41, 46, 52, 62, 65, 66, 84, 95, 96, 105, 109, 114, 136, 144, 164, 172

Risk(s) 29, 37, 42, 43, 44, 52, 55, 56, 56, 57, 64, 65, 68, 69, 70, 72, 73, 83, 86, 107, 113, 117–118, 120, 149, 153, 154, 158, 159, 193, 198

Risk management 37, 69, 118, 154, 193

Robert Gordon University 173, 179, 184, 215

Roche and Rankin 193

Roles(s) 7, 8–9, 10, 11, 13, 14, 15, 17, 20, 28, 29, 34, 36, 38, 42, 43cf, 45, 47, 48, 49,50, 51cf, 52, 54, 56, 61, 62, 64–65, 66, 67, 68, 69cf, 70, 71, 72, 73, 74, 75, 76, 77, 77, 89, 90, 91cf, 92, 97, 98, 99, 100, 101, 103, 105, 106cf, 108, 109, 110, 114, 115, 116, 117, 118, 119, 120, 122, 123, 124, 125, 127, 128, 129, 130, 131, 135, 137, 142, 143, 144, 147, 158, 161, 162, 163, 164, 165, 166, 167, 168, 169cf, 170, 171, 172, 173, 174, 175, 176, 189cf, 190, 195, 197, 198, 205, 207

Rumsey 169

Safeguarding 9, 55cf, 118, 125, 130, 137, 139, 153
see also Child protection

Sapey 48, 89, 91, 93, 95, 96, 97, 99, 100, 101, 119, 120

Schein 191, 192

Schmidt 174

Schon 18, 19cf, 24, 26, 122, 133, 146, 154, 155cf, 191, 208, 209, 210

Scotland 7, 8, 9, 11cf, 13–14, 15, 16, 20, 22, 23, 34, 38, 39, 50, 64, 68, 77, 94, 110, 119, 131, 166cf, 173, 174, 178, 179, 183, 184, 190, 191, 200, 205

Scottish
Executive 9, 14, 39, 50, 69, 70, 77, 168, 173, 174, 176, 178, 180, 181, 184, 185, 189, 190, 215
Government 185, 200, 215
Leadership Foundation 173, 177, 185
Social Services Council (SSSC) 11, 16, 34, 125, 133, 166, 179, 190, 215

Self 209
advocacy 41, 48, 104, 107, 109, 110, 116
analysis 3
appraisal 3, 47
articulated needs 92
assessment 114, 115, 180
belief in 208
confidence 32
controlled rehabilitation 91
definition 89, 91, 99
destructive 71
determination 27, 29, 31, 42
development 167
diagnose 191
directed learning 181
directed support 109, 114, 115, 119
efficacy 208
employed 2, 32, 187
esteem 15, 32, 58, 65, 71, 107
fulfilment 80
funded 127
generated 27
government 94
harming behaviour 90

Self *cont.*
  help 44, 65
  image 29
  knowledge 31
  manage 23, 191
  perceptions 35
  personal 31, 209
  professional 31, 167, 209
  reflection 209
  regulating 86
  reliance 99
  researching 20
  sufficient 99
  use of 27
Senge 19, 89, 165, 191, 192
Service user(s)
  and ethical challenges 30, 150
  attitudes to 131
  contact with 29, 30, 100, 108, 125
  involvement 32, 40, 109cf, 116
    as fetish 36, 40, 45
  guidelines 35
  needs 25, 26, 104, 136, 140
  participation 34–35, 36, 61
  roles 34, 43
  views of 32, 152
  see also People who use services
Service users and carers 21
  and evidence-based practice 149, 152
  and PQ 42–43
  as consumers 39, 40, 42, 82
  consultation with 2cf, 151
  contributions to PQ 166
  critical dialogue with 41cf
  expertise 42, 44. 110, 146
  legislation 39, 66
  needs 71, 72. 79
  participation 33, 34, 35–45
  partnerships 43, 35cf
  relationships with 144, 164
  responsibilities to 22, 42
  standards for participation with 38cf, 116cf
  theoretical perspectives 8, 40cf
Services
  charges for 78
  family placement schemes 108
  user centred 39, 68, 142, 146
  user led 141
Shakespeare and Watson 40
Shaping Our Lives 36, 42
Single Assessment Process 78, 114

Six Part Story and BASIC ph method 54
Six strategic documents, Wales 79
Skills for Care 10, 15, 36, 38, 42, 43, 45, 116, 161,
    170, 194, 200, 215
Smith R. 133
  et al. 146
Social Care Institute for Excellence (SCIE) 19, 23,
    32, 35, 36, 58, 108, 109, 112, 114, 115,
    121, 151, 156, 190, 207, 215
Social Exclusion Unit 67, 150
Social justice 2, 8, 30, 46, 51, 92
Social model of disability 3, 40, 43, 45, 48,
    89–102, 106
  and GSCC 94–95
  and learning disability 103–121
  critical engagement with 95, 97cf, 98
  criticisms of 106–107
  definition 98, 106
  in practice 45, 95cf
  perspective 43, 89, 91, 95
Social pedagogues 122–132
  as a role 122, 124
  as holistic practice 123
  as inspiration 129
  Belgium 126
  definition 122–123, 124
  Denmark 126–127
  Germany 127–128
  Great Britain 129–130
Social professions 123
Social role valorisation 105–6
Social work
  ambivalence 63, 100, 143, 146,
  and empowerment 8, 28, 45, 48, 65, 70, 72, 91,
    93, 152, 175, 176
  art of 20, 155
  as a profession 21, 49, 51, 123, 125, 155, 158, 159, 162
  complexity of task 70, 84, 85, 135, 139
  constructive 20
  consultant 157, 168, 203, 205, 207cf
  decision(s)/decision-making 2, 13, 17, 18, 19, 29, 32,
    35, 38, 39, 40, 41, 55, 57, 64, 66, 67, 75, 93,
    110, 116, 136, 137, 138, 141, 148, 149, 151,
    152, 153–154, 155, 158, 159, 162, 164, 165,
    180, 182, 184, 192, 197, 198, 205, 210
  definition 7, 8cf, 15, 45, 46, 91, 93, 94, 125
  educators and researchers 3, 19, 109, 203,
    205–206, 210
  effectiveness 42, 99, 149–150, 152, 153, 154
  helpful aspects 58, 96, 111–112, 162
  image 193cf

Social work *cont.*
  intervention(s) 19, 25, 45, 50, 53, 54, 56, 58, 60, 61, 64, 65, 66, 67, 70, 71, 72, 73, 74, 83, 84, 113, 119, 120, 126, 130, 140, 141, 142, 144, 146, 149, 150, 151, 152, 153, 154, 174, 176, 208
  paradigm 122
  processes 149
  professional diversity 65, 127, 131, 204
  professional status 50, 94, 126, 136, 143
  registered profession/registration 1, 5, 13, 22, 23, 28, 29, 39, 74, 165, 179, 190, 203
  relational nature of 144
  relevance 12, 34, 67, 107
  to people with learning difficulties 107
  research capacity 155–156
  roles and tasks 8–9, 17, 20, 29, 109, 110, 144, 168
  support 13, 25, 30, 37, 42, 44, 45, 50, 51, 52–53, 54, 55, 63, 64, 67, 68, 69, 71, 79, 82, 84, 85, 92, 99, 101, 108, 109, 110, 111, 112, 114, 115, 116, 117, 119, 120, 149, 156, 159, 161, 162, 163, 165, 169, 170, 172, 178, 180, 183, 185, 192, 197, 199, 205, 207, 210
  three qualities 144
  unhelpful 112cf, 141
  value base 100, 144
  Welsh context 11, 76, 80, 87
Social work practices 207
Social workers
  dissatisfaction of 63, 66, 195
  lack of clear role and purpose 52
  specialist with learning disability 108–9
  views about 15, 16, 17, 65, 74,
Social Work with Older People 77
Socio-cultural animators 124
Sozialarbeit 124, 128
Sozialpädagogik 128
Social Services Inspectorate (SSI) Annual Report 190
  Wales 39, 82, 83
Stevenson 84
Stogdill 174
Strategic learning and research (StLaR) 206
Support, Time and Recovery (STR) 64–65, 215
Strategy for Older People in Wales 79, 86
Stress 189, 195
  in mental health practice 63–64, 71
  management 179, 181
Subordination theory 128
Supervision 17, 23, 25–26, 30, 37, 63–64, 80, 155, 162, 163, 169, 170, 176, 193–4, 195, 197, 199, 207
  policies 9
  records 28

SureStart 42, 52
System, two tiered 115

Tasks, administrative 125
Taylor, B. J. 149, 152, 154, 158
Taylor, I. 154
Taylor, F. W. 174
Taylor Clarke Partnership 173, 183, 184, 185
Teaching, connected 50
Technological approaches 26
Tennenbaum 174
Testimony, expert 74
Theme(s)
  emergent 175cf
  key 56
  priority 98
  prominent 177
  recurrent 136, 139
  underlying 190
Theraplay 58, 61
Thomas, C. 91, 96, 98–100, 102, 104, 106
Thompson, N. 86, 92cf, 125. 140, 169, 170
Torkington 16, 19, 41, 42
Trait theorists 174
Transport 68, 78, 86, 106, 113–4

Unaccompanied asylum seeking minors 24, 25, 39, 53
Unified Assessment Framework 83
Union of physically impaired against segregation (UPIAS) 92, 97, 98, 215
United Nations Convention of the Rights of the Child 39
United Nation Principles for Older People 80
Usher et al. 18, 155

Vacancy levels 190
Values 1–2, 3, 5cf, 22–33, 35, 94, 139, 144
  agency 26
  and critical reflection 155
  and Essential Shared Capabilities 68
  and ethics 3, 5,
  and holistic working 145cf
  and human development 126
  and inter-professional education 145, 146
  and relationships 1–2
  and social model 48, 94, 96
  conflicts 26, 28, 45, 177
  dilemmas 3, 5,
  for practice 2, 155
  mental health 47, 66
  negotiation of 31, 43
  of learning organisations 201

Values *cont.*
  personal 31
  professional 22, 26, 30
  questioning of 190, 191, 209
  shared 131, 131
  social work 22–33, 61,68, 69, 145, 146, 177
  societal 105cf
  standards 3, 8, 10, 11, 12cf, 22, 38
Valuing People Support Team 114
Valuing People White Paper 104, 108, 116, 119
Voices in Practice 158
Vulnerable adults, protection of 23, 29, 118, 119
Vygotsky 58, 62

Wales
  ageing population 77cf
  mental health 66cf, 70–71, 74–75
  PQ framework 10–11, 13, 34, 191
  practice education 166
  social services policy and legislation issues 39,
      76–82, 119, 200
  social work reports 9
  social workers from other countries
      working in 11
  view of competence 16
  consolidation 23
Weber, M. 174
Websites
  Department of Health 78
  EasyInfo 115
  General Social Care Council 9, 166
  National Organisation of Practice Teachers 165
  Social Care Institute for Excellence 121
  Scottish Parliament 78
  Welsh Assembly Government 78

Welfare, three different approaches 96
Welsh
  Assembly Government (WAG) 9, 39, 78, 79, 82, 84,
      85, 94, 215
  dimension 77, 80
  evidence 76
  experience 76
  language 79–80
  Local Government Association 200
  speakers 79
Welsh in the Health Service 79
Welsh Language Act 1993 80
What Works? 149
White and Featherstone 139, 140
Wolfensburger 105, 106, 108
Workforce
  children's 2, 130, 194, 205
  data 200–201
  development 9, 10, 11, 13, 23, 39, 84, 117,
      125, 168, 194, 196, 200, 205, 206
  across UK 190–191
  dissatisfaction 66
  issues 9, 190
  mental health 63, 69
  motivation 10
  multi-professional 129, 136, 158
  planning 9–10, 14cf, 171, 194, 195, 203, 204, 208
  strategies 3, 162, 168, 190
Working
  collaborative 136, 140, 142, 146, 180
  joined up 142
  multi-disciplinary 65, 66

Youth crime 140, 142
Youth Matters 52

The Qualitative Research Kit

Edited by Uwe Flick

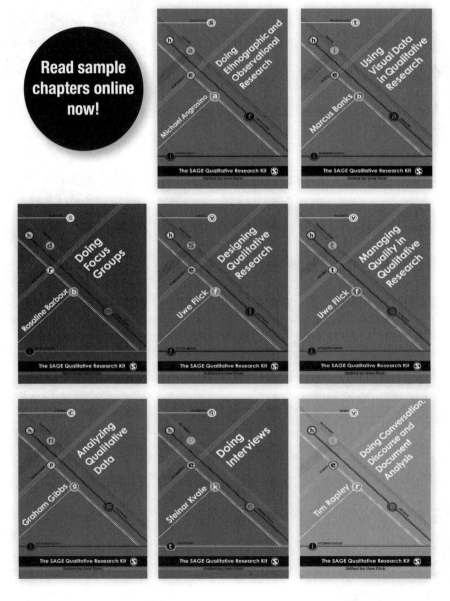

Read sample chapters online now!

Doing Ethnographic and Observational Research — Michael Angrosino — The SAGE Qualitative Research Kit — Edited by Uwe Flick

Using Visual Data in Qualitative Research — Marcus Banks — The SAGE Qualitative Research Kit — Edited by Uwe Flick

Doing Focus Groups — Rosaline Barbour — The SAGE Qualitative Research Kit — Edited by Uwe Flick

Designing Qualitative Research — Uwe Flick — The SAGE Qualitative Research Kit — Edited by Uwe Flick

Managing Quality in Qualitative Research — Uwe Flick — The SAGE Qualitative Research Kit — Edited by Uwe Flick

Analyzing Qualitative Data — Graham Gibbs — The SAGE Qualitative Research Kit — Edited by Uwe Flick

Doing Interviews — Steinar Kvale — The SAGE Qualitative Research Kit — Edited by Uwe Flick

Doing Conversation, Discourse and Document Analysis — Tim Rapley — The SAGE Qualitative Research Kit — Edited by Uwe Flick

www.sagepub.co.uk